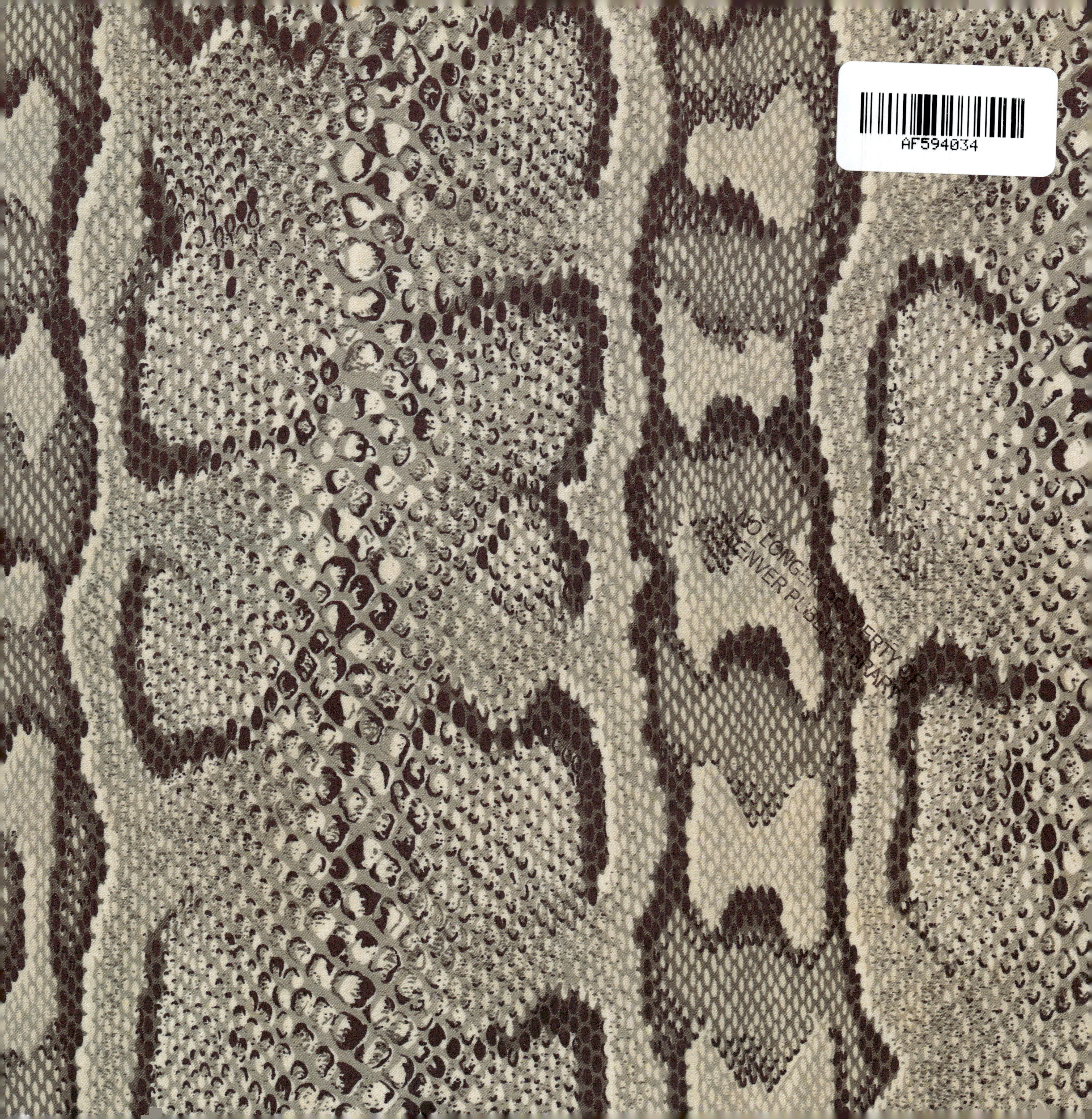

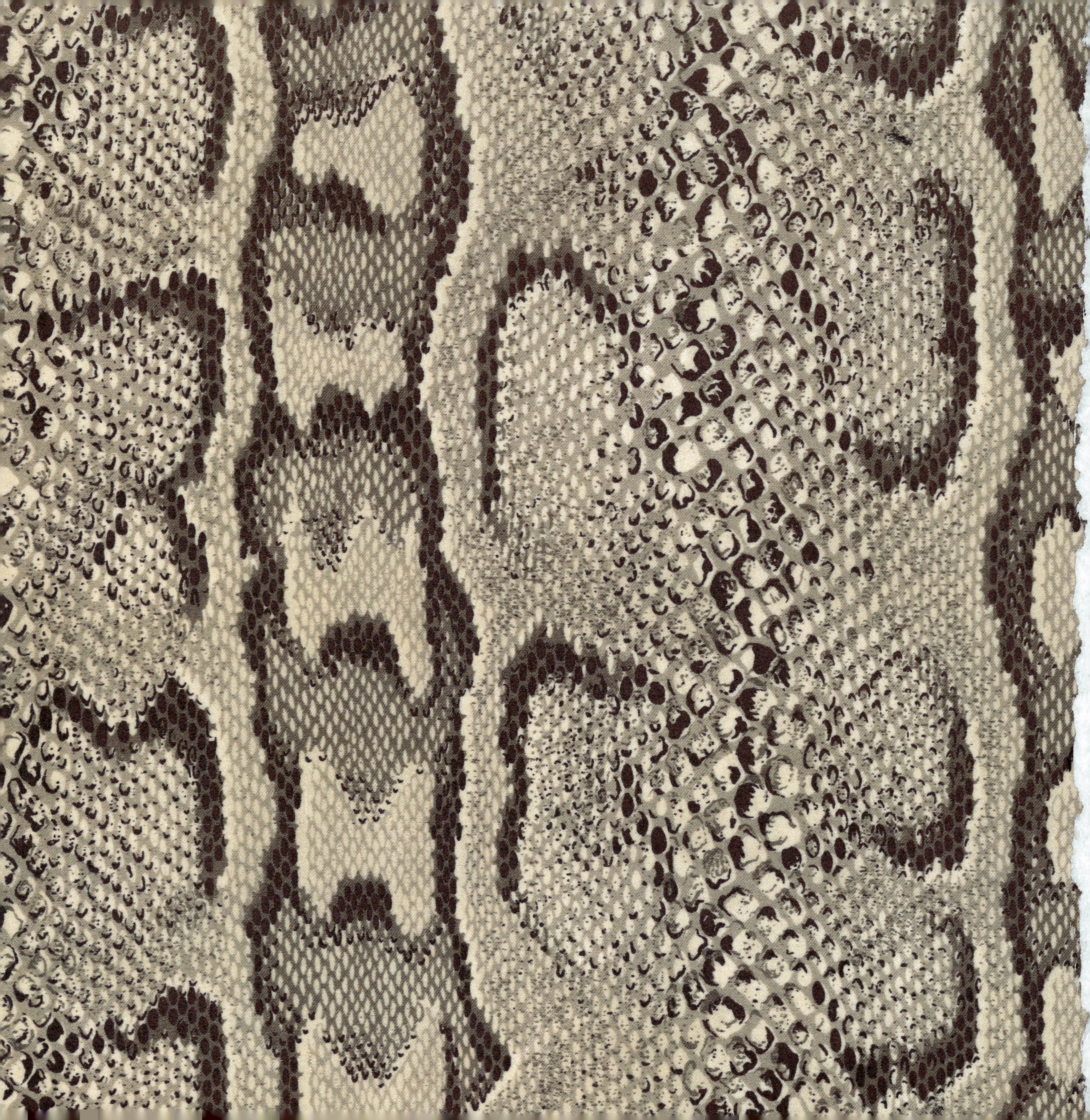

# JEAN MUIR: BEYOND FASHION

SINTY STEMP

FOREWORD BY FELICITY GREEN

ISBN 10: 1-85149-521-5
ISBN 13: 978-1-85149-521-4



British Library Cataloguing-in-Publication Data
A catalogue record for this book is available from the British Library

Publication designed and typeset by
John and Orna Designs, London

Printed in Spain
for the Antique Collectors' Club Ltd., Woodbridge, Suffolk

Antique Collectors' Club

# JEAN MUIR: BEYOND FASHION

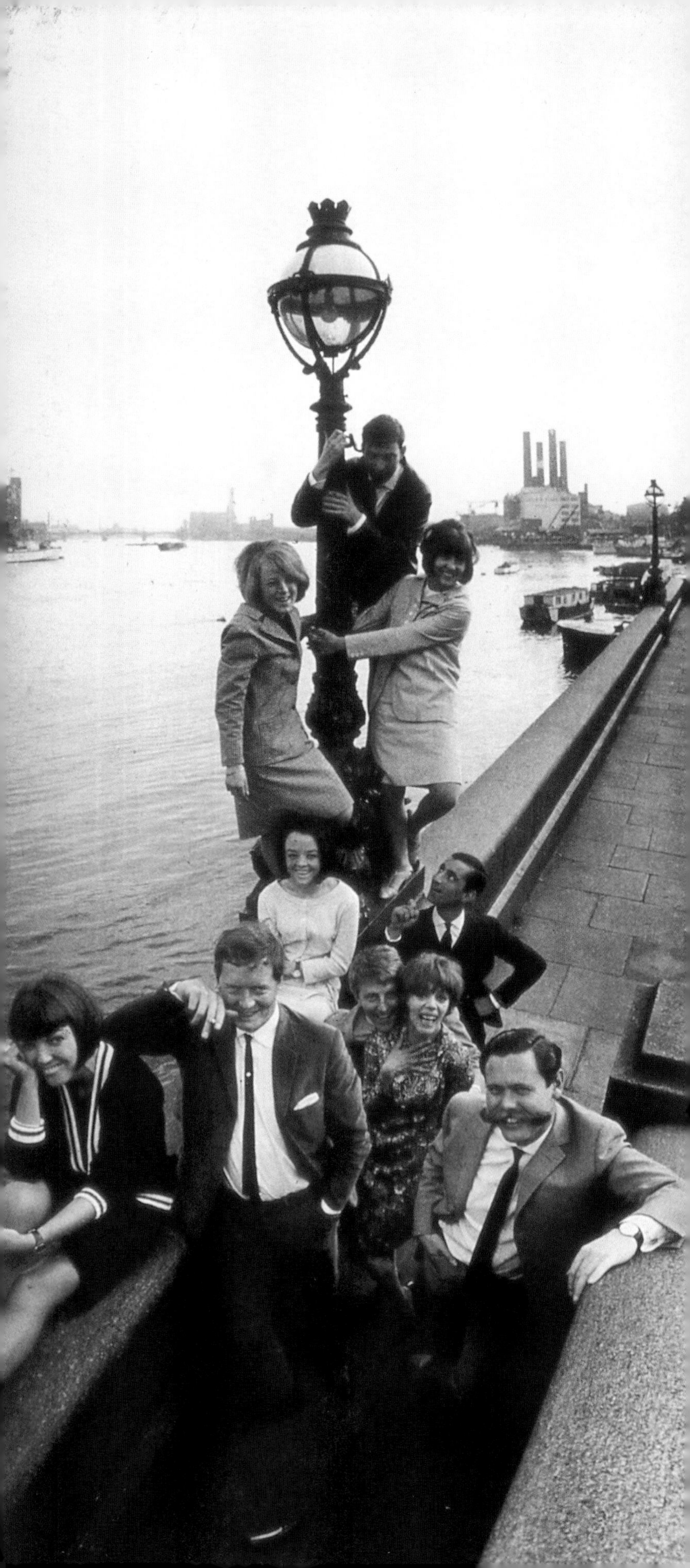

# FOREWORD

FELICITY GREEN

How it all began – up a lamppost in London in the sixties as pictured for Life magazine by Norman Parkinson. First row from left to right: Mary Quant and her husband Alexander Plunkett Greene, moustachioed Kenneth Sweet. Behind, Jean Muir of Jane and Jane, Gerald McCann, Kiki Byrne, David Sassoon. Hanging on the lamppost Sally Tuffin, Marion Foale, and milliner James Wedge. Photograph & © The Norman Parkinson Archive.

"The things most dear to me are art and craft and design and the upholding of standards and quality, maintaining them and setting new ones"

JEAN MUIR

**JEAN MUIR**, for me, has been a constant star in that famous sixties fashion firmament ever since she first burst on to the scene in 1962. When London started to swing, Jean Muir was part of a talented team of designers and photographers who established this country as the epicentre of that extraordinary style revolution. As ephemeral fads and fantasies came and went, Jean Muir never for one moment lost her distinctive way and from the start remained her own woman. Her originality on the one hand, plus her commitment to excellence, made her an international star and she has taken her place in fashion history alongside such fashion legends and luminaries as Chanel, Fortuny and Vionnet.

Jean Muir died in 1995 and this year, the company she and her husband Harry Leuckert started back in those wild and wonderful days, celebrates its fortieth anniversary. Today, Jean Muir clothes and accessories continue to sell around the world and the Jean Muir shop in London's Conduit Street flourishes under the aegis of the team Miss Muir created, inspired and led over the years.

This book will tell you the story of an icon whose message has been constant – and magical – ever since. Constant because she had a vision of perfection, knew how to achieve it and by doing so how to make every woman look her best. Why magical? Because when you put on a Jean Muir something extraordinary happens. Whoever you are, wherever you go, suddenly you not only LOOK your best – you FEEL your best. You feel taller, slimmer, more elegant, more confident and every one of us lucky enough to have owned a Jean Muir can confirm this.

What we cannot do is totally explain it. It is a combination of so many things, a technique so precise in its application that Jean Muir described it as being as much about engineering as dressmaking. It's about the minimalism that dramatically combines the simple with the sensual and in doing so created the Jean Muir signature: a dress that has little or no interruptions on its way down and around the body creates pure sensuality. A Jean Muir little black dress, devoid of decoration, often high at the neck and decorous in length will be more sexy than any over exposure of flesh.

This book will also tell you about my friend Miss Muir the fashion icon who declared she was not about fashion at all. She was about style and what a difference that makes... fashions come and go – style goes on forever. Certainly she herself was as stylish as they come – in her look, her language, the way she moved in her chosen surroundings; her stunning all-white flat opposite the Albert Hall was a typically stylish lifestyle statement. Tiny, perky and full of fun, the inimitable Miss Muir could at times be as formidable as a six footer, calling on her Scottish background for the required degree of pugnacity. Her vision was clear and demanding and certainly she demanded perfection, not only from herself but from all those around her, who in time benefited from this schooling in the art of perfection.

Jean Muir fully justifies her place among the international fashion luminaries while, closer to home, those of us who wore and continue to wear our 'Jean Muirs' can guarantee a compliment or two when we, and it, appear in public.

**FELICITY GREEN**

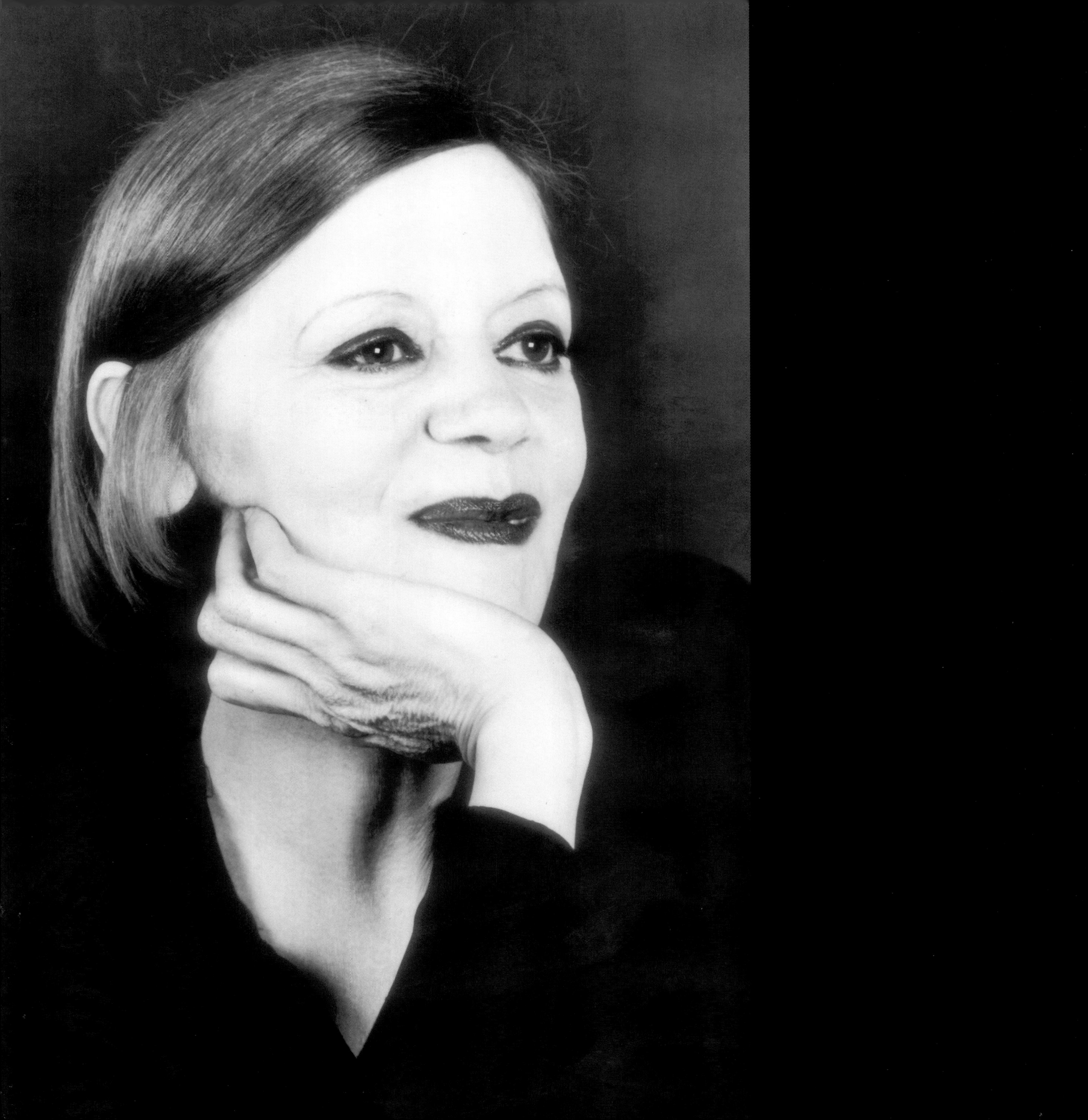

# INTRODUCTION

"Tain't what you do, it's the way that you do it, that's what gets results"

SY OLIVER/TRUMMY YOUNG

"It ain't what you wear, it's the way that you wear it..."

JEAN MUIR

**JEAN MUIR**, doyenne of British fashion, always properly addressed as *Miss Muir* and hailed as 'the greatest dressmaker in the world' is an iconic figure in the world of fashion design. A true original, she was a visionary who unwittingly carved out a niche for herself as one of the great figures of contemporary design. She is in a line with Vionnet, Madame Grès, and Chanel. Jean Muir redefined the way women dressed, meticulously crafting clothes with an intrinsic femininity and timelessness to create her own concept of prêt-a-porter couture.

Muir started her career in the way she meant to carry on. Although a product of her time, her clothes were not dictated by this; secure in her own style, Jean Muir stood outside and independent of fashion. Pursuing her vision, with an overriding preoccupation with craft, she was interested in clothes as an extension and enhancement of a woman's personality. When London began to swing, she was already making clothes that were always, and still are, more about the wearer than the label – clothes that, by defying seasonal fads and the vagaries of passing taste, transcend fashion itself.

Forever associated with the little black dress, when she showed in Paris in the early seventies, the French accorded her the supreme accolade, '*la nouvelle reine de la robe*' – the new queen of the dress. Dismissive of the word fashion, she described her approach to design as "evolutionary not revolutionary" and her approach as "engineering in cloth". The actress and cultural icon, Joanna Lumley, one of Miss Muir's first house models declared, "*every* woman should have a Jean Muir in her wardrobe." Revered and admired throughout her career, Muir came to prominence in the sixties, and was the only British designer from that seminal time who would consistently remain at the cutting edge of international fashion for over thirty years.

Jean Muir's clothes withstand time; they are refined, understated, stringent, yet feminine, and above all, liquescent on the body. Her style has to do with integrity, technique, quality and individuality. A true master of her craft, the complex construction of her clothes becomes artless simplicity and flattery on the body. While Jean Muir worked with a range of materials, it was her work in matte jersey – a fabric that she practically made her own – and particularly her jersey dresses, that would make her legendary.

Jean Muir set up her company in 1966, showing her first collection in October of that year. Choosing sensuous supple suedes, leathers, tweeds,

**PAGE 8** Jean Muir by Gemma Levine. © Jean Muir Ltd.

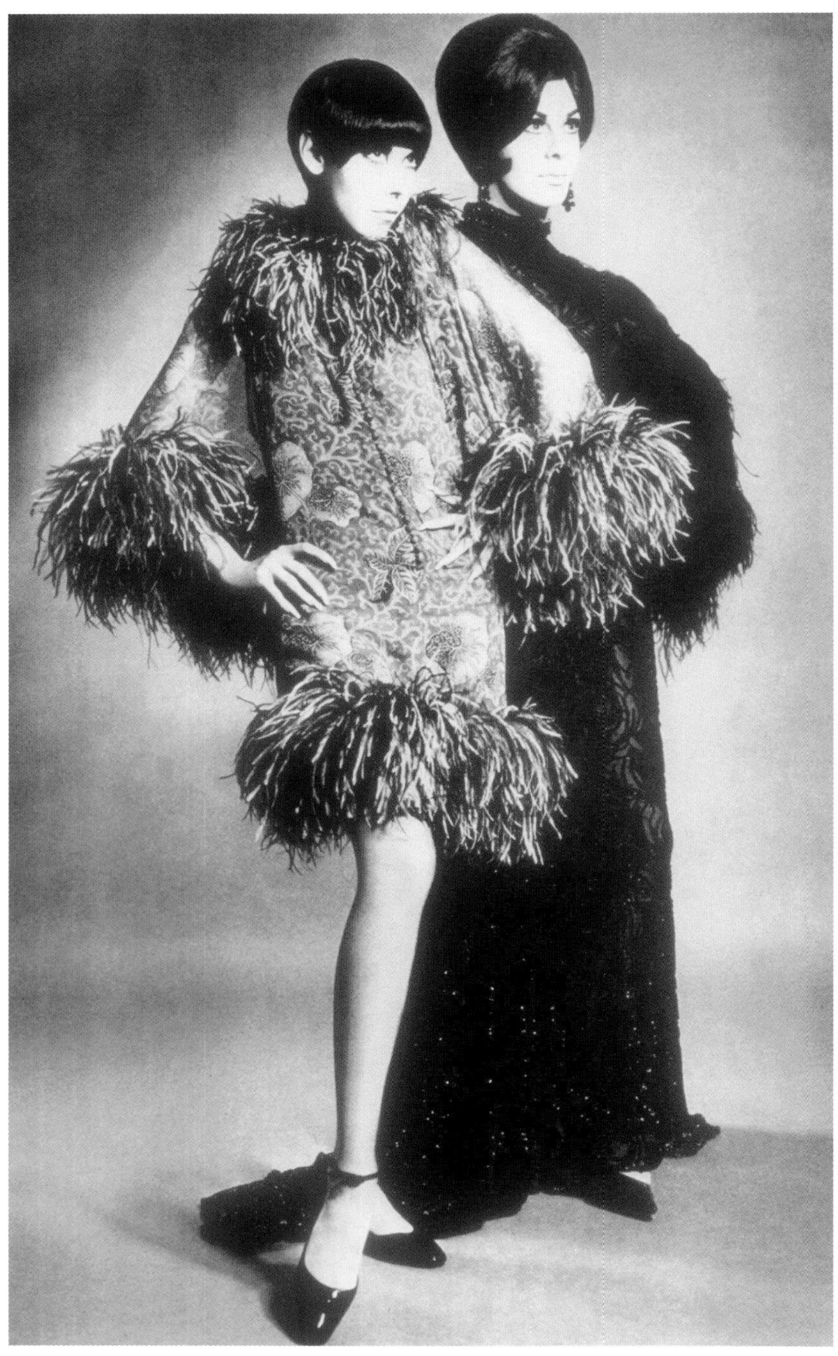

silks and chiffons, and later matte jersey, her uncompromising vision and perfectionism established a new softer 'womanly' contour, one that had an innate fluidity and femininity that was to define her distinctive style of 'couture ready-to-wear', and the Jean Muir look.

Though she was keen to dispense with the restrictive and rigid construction associated with the Paris couture, Muir was determined to uphold and utilise the skills and standards associated with couture workmanship by employing specialist craftsmen and women in the manufacture of her clothes. A passionate crusader and stickler for high standards, a need and respect for technical skills defined Jean Muir's work. As a consummate, if self-taught, technician, the design process for her was a wonderful, three-dimensional synthesis of hand, mind and eye – an intellectual and physical exercise addressing the problems posed by the discipline of designing for the human body, which moves and comes in different shapes and sizes.

"Craft in its true sense is totally necessary", she insisted, "not only from the aesthetic point of view, but also because in economically difficult times, the products which have an innate feeling of craft and quality are the ones that suffer least. So craft is a means of survival." She regularly commissioned craftspeople to produce exclusive pieces for her collections, including buttons, buckles, belts, hats, and jewellery, as well as special decorative fabric finishes. She believed passionately in the renaissance of the artist-craftsman, viewing it as the most significant and exciting movement in late twentieth century design.

As the American writer, Paula Dietz puts it, "Intellectually, Jean Muir was a descendant of the Arts and Crafts movement that was the nineteenth century's antidote to industrialization. But with her contemporary sensibility, she embraced the new technology of dressmaking and raised it to an art. Hers was not the rarefied world of couture but the more lively world of ready-to-wear complemented by handcrafted accessories."

She was a complete all-rounder: as adept at prints at she was at plains, as skilled with colour as she was with navy and black, as successful in knitwear and skins as in wool, silk, and her trademark matte jersey. Fashion commentator Lucia van der Post, writing in the *Financial Times* in 1991 acknowledged the subtlety and originality of the Jean Muir look,

**ABOVE** Renowned for restraint and minimalism, Jean Muir also loved the exotic and the unusual. Here, American Peggy Moffitt, one of the first international top models, wears a Jane and Jane by Jean Muir multicoloured paisley chiffon dress with transparent sleeves falling into a cape bordered with ostrich feathers. Behind her is the cabaret star and female impersonator, Danny La Rue, a favourite of Jean Muir. *Queen* magazine, 17 August 1966. Photograph & © William Claxton/courtesy www.demontphoto.com

"Miss Muir's clothes seem simultaneously classic and radical, familiar yet new – they are highly fashionable and yet have nothing to do with fashion."

Often cited as a quintessentially British designer – the writer, Drusilla Beyfus called her "the arbiter of English taste" – Jean Muir tapped into the British desire for individuality. A required look was an anathema to her, and she viewed clothes as unimportant in themselves, rather thinking of them as a foil to the wearer's personality. In Muir's case, whether it was the dictates of Paris couture or the hype of here-today-gone-tomorrow fads, she would have none of it. In her own collections skirt lengths were not the be-all-and-end-all; she frequently offered a variety, leaving the final decision up to the customer.

Whilst we may think of Muir as a very British designer she was in fact international – throughout her career she was one of the few British designers with a distinguished reputation on both sides of the Atlantic as well as in Europe. Fashion editor Suzy Menkes, commented, "in international fashion, Jean Muir is one of the rare people who really rate. A lot of people in England might be quite surprised to know that somebody who makes so little noise and brouhaha in her own country is actually tremendously renowned in Paris, the capital of fashion."

John Fairchild, the influential owner of America's style bible, *Women's Wear Daily*, observed: "When it comes to an unique style in fashion – Jean Muir can wave proudly – the Union Jack. Her style has an English grace and elegance. Her technique – the way her clothes move – is equal to the best of the Paris Haute Couture. Somehow a Jean Muir is like Jean Muir herself – a sparkling star in a big room."

Through a single-minded approach, Muir developed her own timeless style, rejecting the ephemeral trends–driven demands that characterise the fashion world. "I was never afraid of myself", she once revealed, "because I always knew I would do *something*." Her vision was focused and independent. Whether she was above fashion or defied it, she achieved the far more difficult task of never being out of fashion, or style. Chanel's maxim "fashion changes but style remains," seems made for Jean Muir.

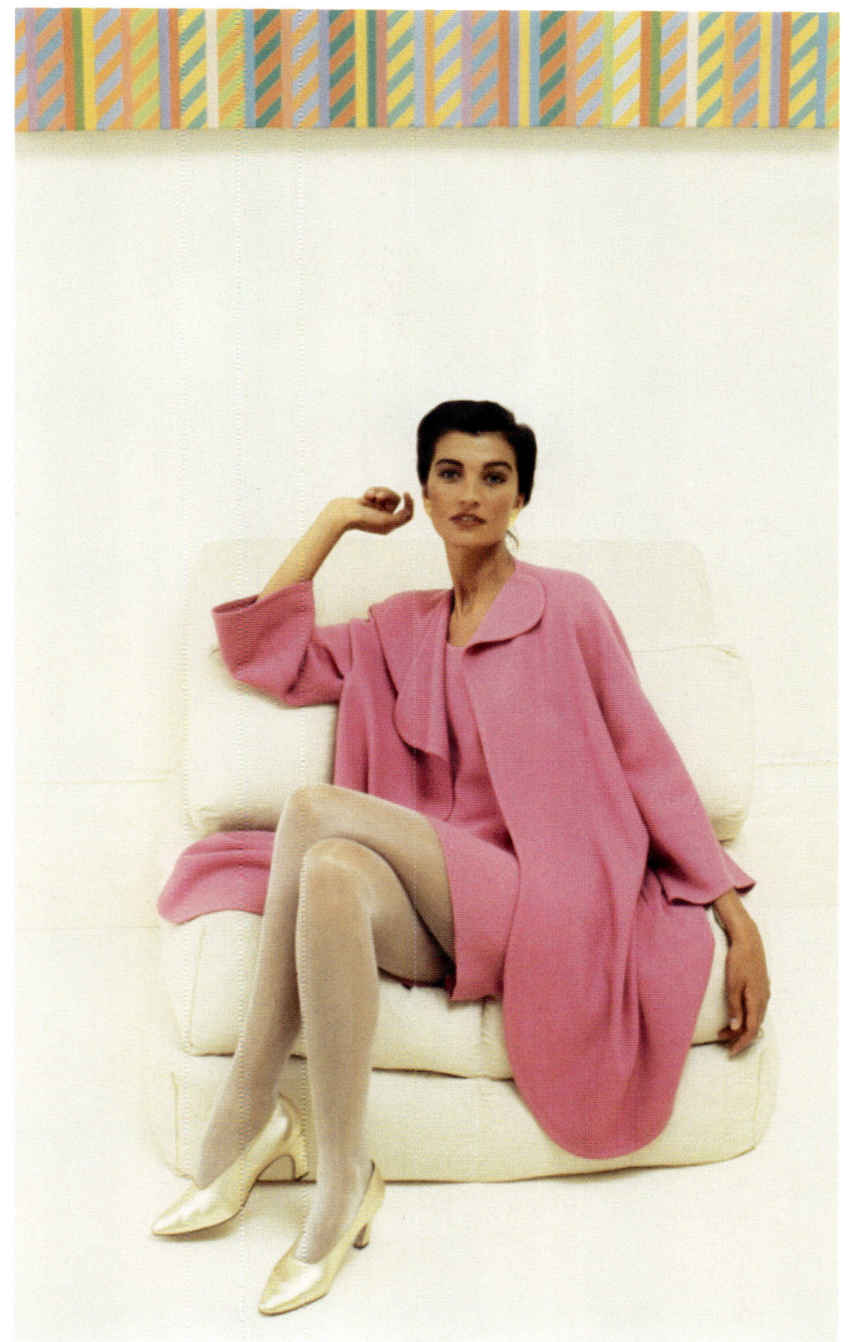

**ABOVE** Pink wool crepe coat with asymmetric curved lapels over matching sleeveless shift dress, Spring 1991. Above the model, Bridget Riley's painting *Broken Gaze*, 1986. Photograph: Michael Williams. © The Trustees of The National Museums of Scotland.

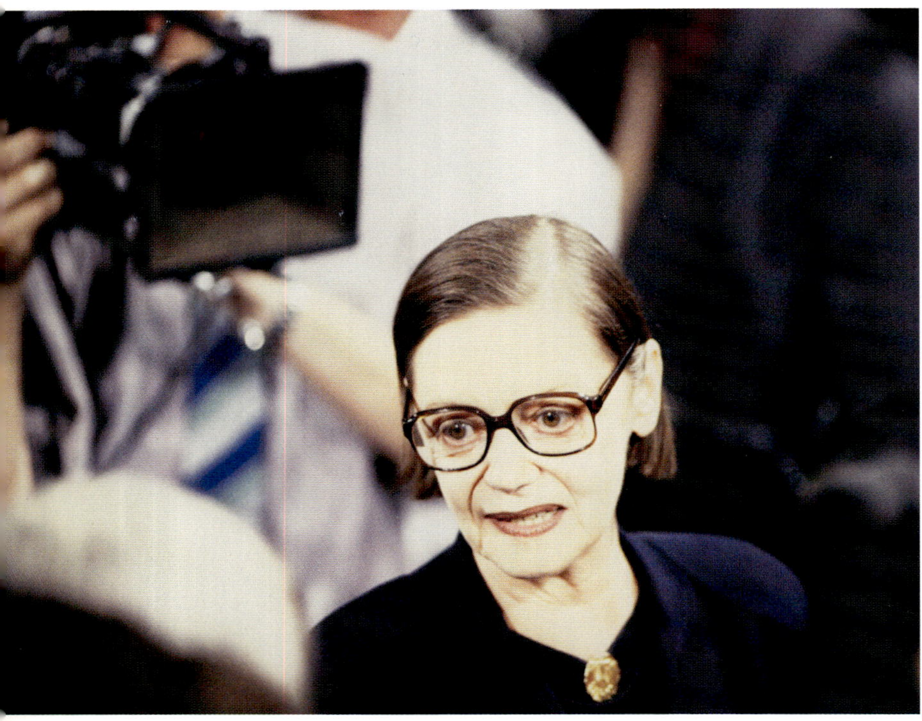

"There is a lovely quote by Oscar Wilde: 'What is fashion?' he asks – 'It is usually a form of such ugliness so intolerable we have to alter it every six months.' We are about to be unusual and prove that dotty Irishman very old fashioned."
**JEAN MUIR**

Though wary of trends nevertheless, throughout her career, unconsciously, she also set them. Nor was she blinkered. She embraced the arrival of Punk as "a wonderful divertissement", appreciating the time and creative energy that its followers put into individualising their appearance. "I love people who have the courage to express themselves," she said, "that's why I thnk that Punk is so exciting." As she pursued her own course, she was often ahead of her time. However, the pendulum of fashion coincided with her viewpoint, most notably in the late sixties, the seventies, and again in the nineties.

From the start, her clothes were regularly featured in *Vogue*, *Queen,* and *Harper's Bazaar*, championed by editors such as Ailsa Garland, Beatrix Miller, Jocelyn Stevens and in newsprint by fashion editors such as Prudence Glynn and Barbara Griggs. Editorials heralded Muir as the precursor of key new looks, new proportions, and new sensibilities in fashion. In 1975 a survey for a large American textile manufacturer reported that the two most copied designers in the world at that time were Jean Muir and Yves Saint Laurent.

At times, the very consistency of her collections, and the subtle nature of the seasonal refinements that she would present, seemed to confound certain elements of the press. Others were quick to recognise her innovative contribution. Amy Spindler, writing in the early nineties in *The New York Times*, hailed Muir as "one of London's most influential and modern minimalists", whilst Iain R Webb, writing on Jean Muir's twenty-fifth anniversary in 1991 for *Harper's & Queen,* named her as one of the current top ten influential designers in the world. Both quotes made in the fourth decade of her career showed her creative strength at that time was undiminished, despite the fact she was by then in her sixties.

Jean Muir was honoured throughout her career with a host of international awards, amongst them Dress of the Year three times. The French awarded her l'Hommage de la Mode by the Fédération Français du Prêt-à-Porter Feminin in 1985 and America saluted her with six awards for distinguished service in the field of fashion.

The significance and distinction of her achievements are also reflected in the industrial and academic titles that she held, including her appointment as a Royal Designer for Industry in 1972. Muir was a member of the Design Council, and a long-standing trustee of the Victoria & Albert Museum. These titles were followed by a CBE in 1984, and culminated

**ABOVE** Jean Muir backstage after the show, early '90s. Photograph & © Chris Moore.

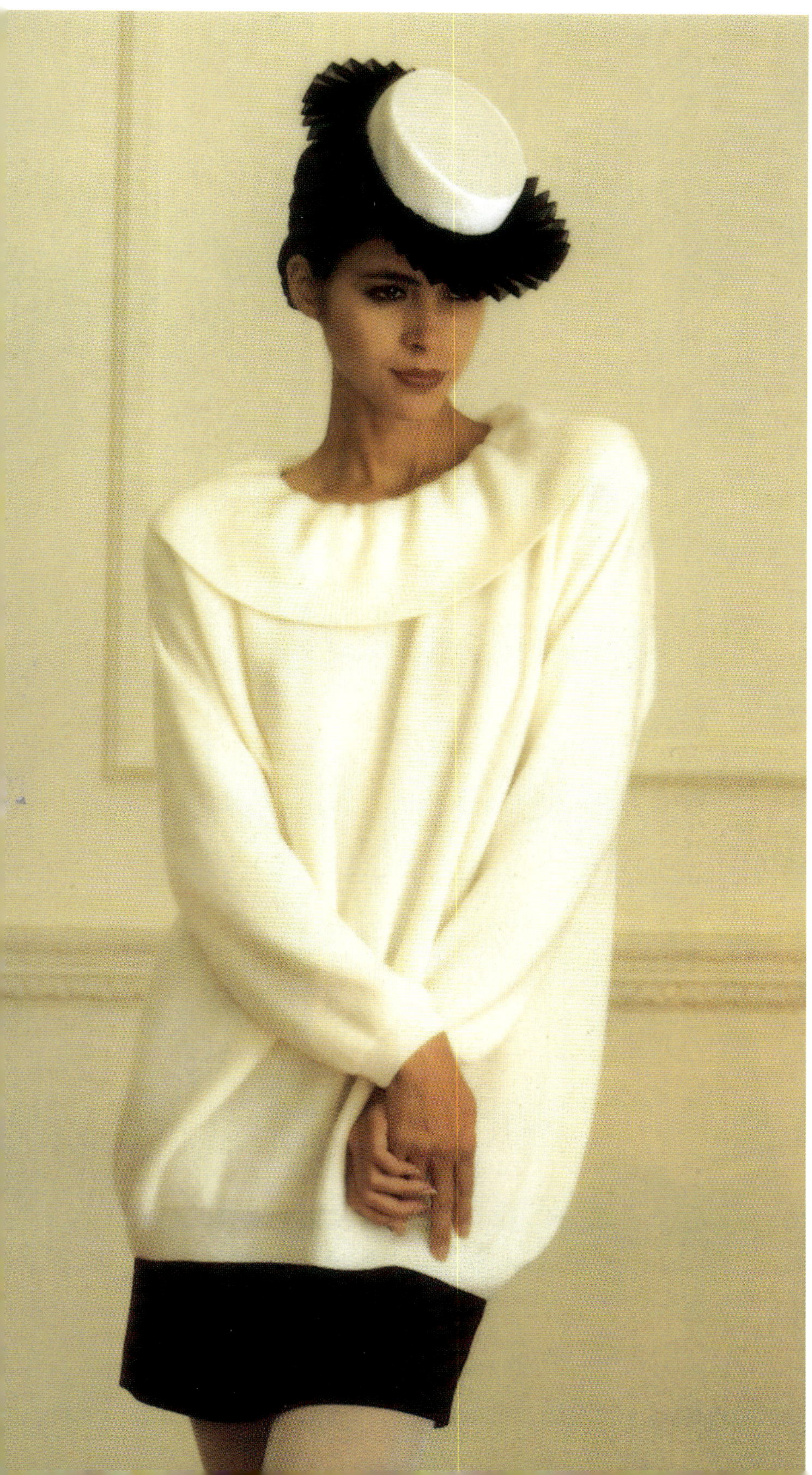

in her appointment as Master of the Faculty of Royal Designers for Industry in 1993, the same year that Channel 4 Television devoted a three-part documentary series to her, the first to be specifically dedicated to a British designer.

Jean Muir's achievements are all the more extraordinary given that she was self-taught. They are a tribute to her steely determination and self-reliance, which she proudly ascribed to her Scottish heritage. "My Calvinist blood gives me the ability to be ruthlessly objective with myself if need be, without fear or unnecessary sentiment." Her father was from Aberdeen and although she never lived in Scotland, she always felt herself first and foremost Scottish; "In a way you are born what you are. I always put it down to my Scots blood, I have always thought that's been my greatest strength in life." She added, "I'm a great believer in national characteristics. I'm the Celtic type, tiny and wiry. And I'm all the things the Scots are meant to be, tenacious, self-assured, independent and very strict...with some kind of Celtic wisdom. I always think that *something* stood me in good stead."

In a highly competitive industry and a career spanning four decades, before her untimely death in 1995, Jean Muir consistently retained her position at the top. Her period covered swinging London and Mary Quant's miniskirt, seventies bohemianism, Punk, the New Romantics, eighties excess and women as logo-brandishing shoulder-pad-clad power symbols, Grunge, and the deconstructivist minimalism of first the Japanese and then the European avant-garde. Throughout it all, she quietly continued to hone her minimalist vision, constantly refining her particular brand of couture ready-to-wear. She never diluted her identity or her work, and brooked no compromise in her quest for excellence. To this day her clothes and style remain aspirational, a formidable record of achievement.

Like all great designers, her creative curiosity and energy were the forces that kept her looking and moving forward, eager to explore the possibilities of the future. Nostalgia was not for her. In 1973 she made her views clear: "Nostalgia is a sickness. Fantasy is something to dream about, not to put on your back. Repeating clothes from yesterday is a denial of today."

As she put it: "I am irritated by indulgent looking back; there's so much to move on to. The past, present and future form one marvellous continuous movement and one can help shape it."

**LEFT** Timeless and quirky: white cashmere pierrot-collared tunic over slim black double matte jersey skirt. Tip-tilted hat in pleated organza and satin by Bridget Bailey for Jean Muir, Spring 1988. Photograph & © Neil Fenwick.

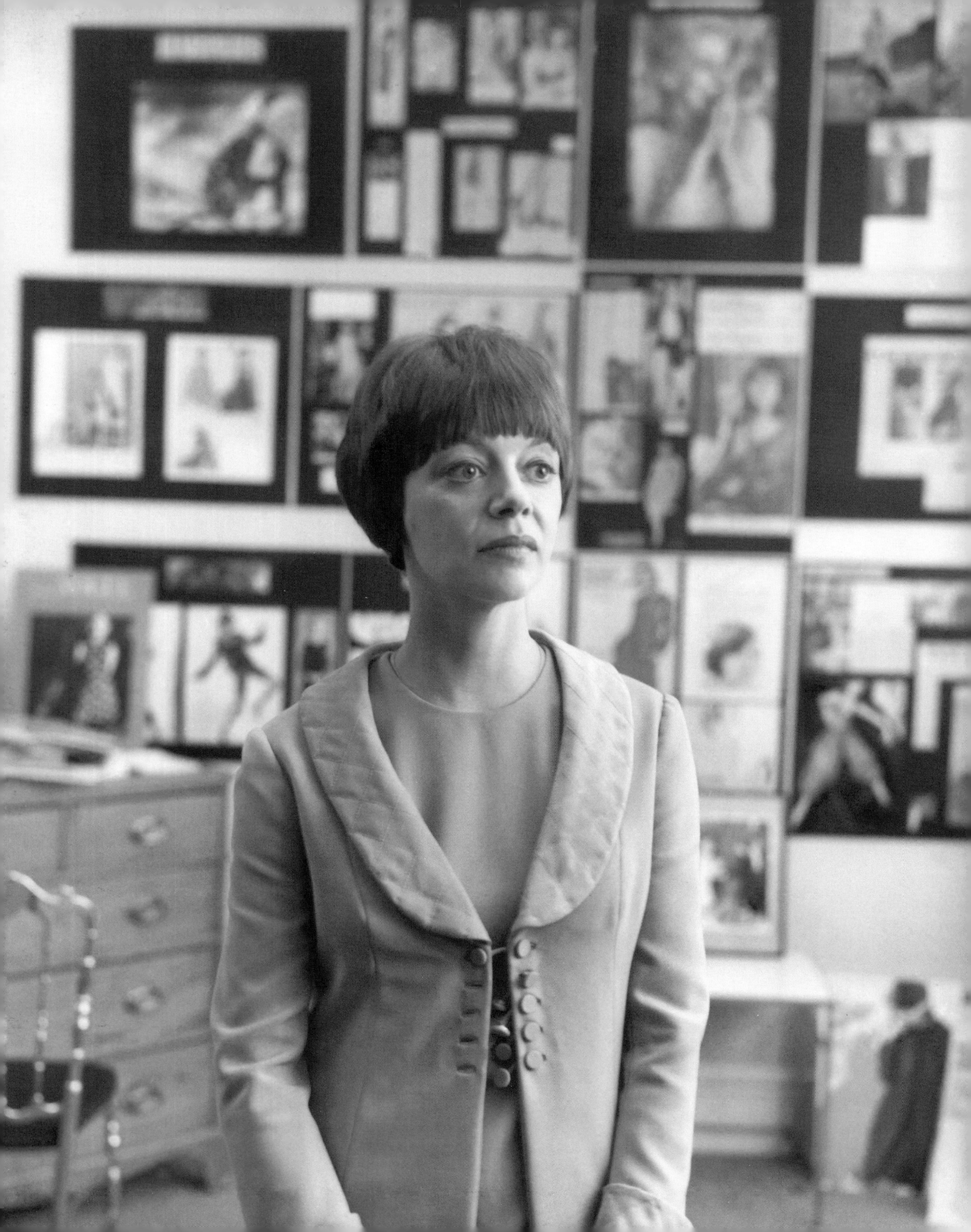

Chapter One

# BEGINNINGS

"I guess you could say I'm a dressmaker by accident"

JEAN MUIR

**MISS MUIR'S** entry into her trade has a sense of serendipity, of chance pointing out a logical progression, "I find it awfully difficult to pinpoint a moment in my life and say this is when my career started to take off. I didn't know what sort of career I wanted, so there was no sense in which I could plan it."

Born in London on 17 July 1928, Jean Elizabeth Muir attended Dame Alice Harper girls' school in Bedford. Here she came under the tuition of an art teacher who had a profound influence on the young Muir who could remember being able to draw, sew and embroider from an early age. Electing to take history of art as an extra class where pupils were encouraged to collect and study fine art postcards, Muir was enthused. "We had a wonderful art mistress at school who unconsciously had an enormous effect on me...I can remember from the age of ten knowing the great painters and their most famous works. I can't remember ever not knowing them and the thrill when you came face to face with the originals years later was almost too much!" Acknowledging the impact of these studies on her later work and her highly developed visual sensibility, she explained, "if you know a marvellous Velasquez or whatever ... there is a wonderful sense of proportion which unconsciously one is assimilating." It was this 'visual literacy' that Muir would take with her and advance throughout her career.

It would become something of a holy grail and she constantly sought to promote the importance of it throughout the nation's education system. Later, when she embarked on a personal campaign to improve educational standards, she would lament not only the lack of technical skills in the fashion students she came across, but also the lack of visual skills generally in current education, extolling the value of art appreciation as a means of introducing the importance of shape, proportion and colour to schoolchildren.

Jean Muir did not go to art school – something she viewed as an advantage – and instead learned to be a designer by absorbing and applying her practical experiences at each consecutive job. She left school at seventeen, with a moderate School Certificate and took a job first in a solicitor's office, and then one in Bedford's Electoral Registrar's department. Assisting at the local county council elections introduced her to the world of politics, a valuable background for her later quest to improve design education. Leaving Bedford and moving to London, she secured her first formative job, in 1950, at the London department store, Liberty & Co. where the only

**PAGE 16** Jean Muir, acclaimed by British and American press. Photograph by Baron Studios, April 1965. © National Portrait Gallery.

# "A Faun in the Fashion Forest is Jean Muir of Jane and Jane"

**THE SUNDAY TIMES, SEPTEMBER 1965**

DAILY MIRROR, Friday, November 9, 1962 PAGE 15

# The Young Designers

✱ On the final day of London's fashion week, the Mirror focuses on the unfamiliar fashion names—the ones you'll soon be hearing a lot more about . .

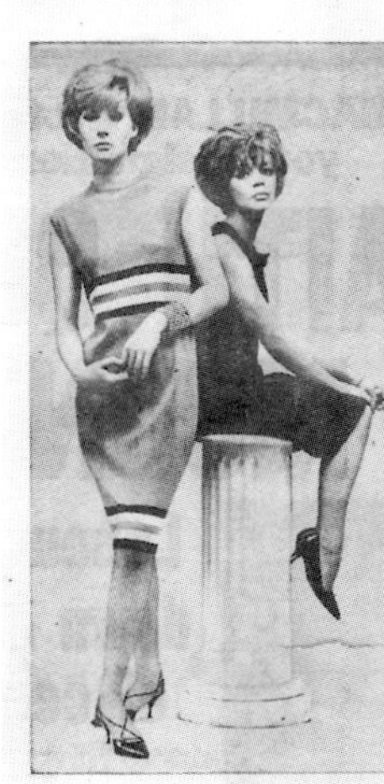

DESIGNER Jean Muir (right). Speciality: jersey and soft wool dresses. Has witty ideas, like making a black jersey dress with ruffled lace collar and cuffs or putting a baby lace skirt on a black jersey bodice. Seen here with model Leise Denix, in camel jersey dress banded in black and white.

*Dress by Jane & Jane, price 7 guineas.*

IT couldn't have happened at any other time but the present.

A couple of students, looking too young to be taken seriously, finish their fashion design training and set up in their own business.

All that separates them from disaster are a few lengths of fabric and their talent.

They struggle, it's true, but within a few months they are established as two of the new wave of young designers surging into the fashion world.

**The secret of their success? They are all on the same young and light-hearted wavelength as the young and light-hearted girls who buy their clothes. Let's call them "Kookie" clothes for want of a better word.**

## ADVENTUROUS

A shade too adventurous for the ordinary run-of-the-mill shop, they are the clothes that are more and more in demand by the zingy young departments many stores are opening up, and by the mushrooming boutiques that cater for girls who are looking for something young and chic.

**On the left meet JEAN MUIR. Age, 27. Label: Jane and Jane.**

**SET-UP:** A showroom, stockroom, workroom and office so new it's still being decorated. A factory in London makes her clothes.

**TRAINING:** Unorthodox. Started by sketching and selling in a London West End store, and graduated to designing for Jaeger.

Got the chance to design her own clothes with a large exporter. Her designs proved too distinctive for their more conservative customers, so they made her an offshoot with a label of her own. Her first range carrying this label is in the shops—including a chain of fashion shops—now.

**FASHION PHILOSOPHY:** A simple dress, the right hemline and a stunning pair of shoes make an unbeatable combination.

Meet **SALLY TUFFIN** and **MARION FOALE**, in the picture on the left below. Ages, Sally 24, Marion 23. Label: As their names.

## BARE

**SET-UP:** A huge bare room in a pleasant Kensington flat where they design and cut patterns. Three outworkers make their clothes.

**TRAINING:** Four years at the Walthamstow School of Art, three years at the Royal College of Art. Started their business without a bean. Now produce about three or four dozen dresses a week, selling to snob shops in Knightsbridge and Birmingham, and to a New York store.

**FASHION PHILOSOPHY:** A dress or suit isn't fashion—a look is.

On the right, meet **MOYRA O'DONNELL.** Age 25. Label: Mary Murray, Ltd.

**SET-UP:** A corner house in a suburban street in Harrow, Middlesex. In her workroom: Three machinists and one finisher. Outside workers on tap when required.

**TRAINING:** Four years at Harrow School of Art, three years at the Royal College of Art. Left fifteen months ago. Selling to an exclusive Mayfair shop, and to top Knightsbridge and Manchester stores.

**FASHION PHILOSOPHY:** "Keep it simple and let colour and fabric work for you."

**PEGGY BRIGGS**

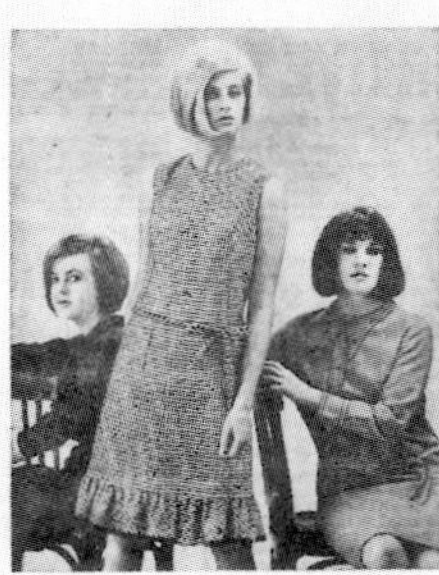

DESIGNERS Sally Tuffin (left) and Marion Foale (right). Speciality: casual clothes in good fabrics with the accent on fun, such as anchors emblazoned on the front of sleeveless tweed dresses. Seen here with model Jill Kennington in a sleeveless black and white check wool dress with lace trimmed flounce.

*Dress by Sally Tuffin and Marion Foale, price 9½ guineas.*

*Pictures by John French.*

DESIGNER Moyra O'Donnell (right). Speciality: casual tailored clothes in soft tweeds distinguished by their impeccable cut and finish; young and chic cocktail dresses. Seen here with model Ros Watkins in a coffee bean organza dress.

*Dress by Mary Murray Ltd., price 10½ guineas.*




**On the left meet JEAN MUIR. Age, 27. Label: Jane and Jane.**

**SET-UP:** A showroom, stockroom, workroom and office so new it's still being decorated. A factory in London makes her clothes.

**TRAINING:** Unorthodox. Started by sketching and selling in a London West End store, and graduated to designing for Jaeger.

Got the chance to design her own clothes with a large exporter. Her designs proved too distinctive for their more conservative customers, so they made her an offshoot with a label of her own. Her first range carrying this label is in the shops—including a chain of fashion shops—now.


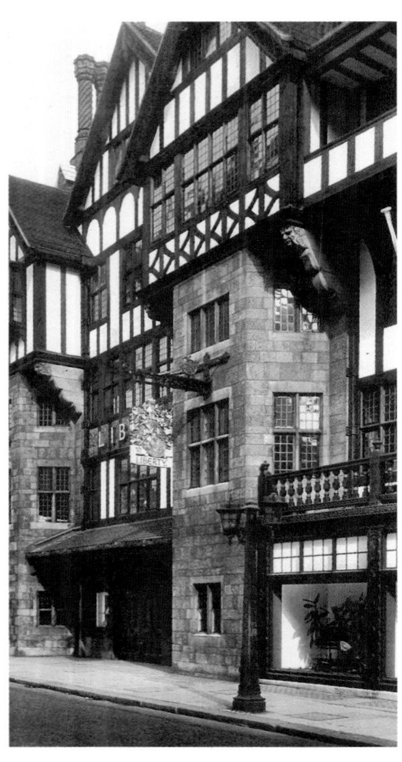

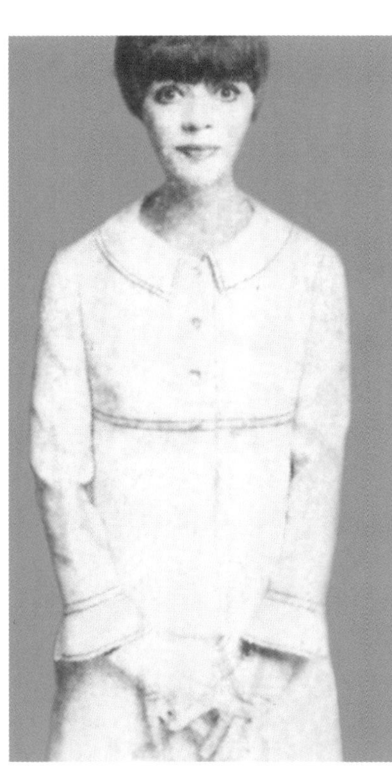

**LEFT** The Great Marlborough Street façade, Liberty & Co. circa 1950s where Jean Muir's fashion career began…in the stockroom. © Liberty Plc. **CENTRE** "A Faun in the Fashion Forest is Jean Muir of Jane and Jane" photographed for *The Sunday Times* in September 1965 before her departure to the States for a trip sponsored by Butterick Patterns. Pictured wearing her own design, a coat for Butterick Patterns priced at 4s. 6d. **ABOVE RIGHT** How the *Daily Mirror* introduced Miss Muir to their readers – an extract of the copy from 9 November 1962.

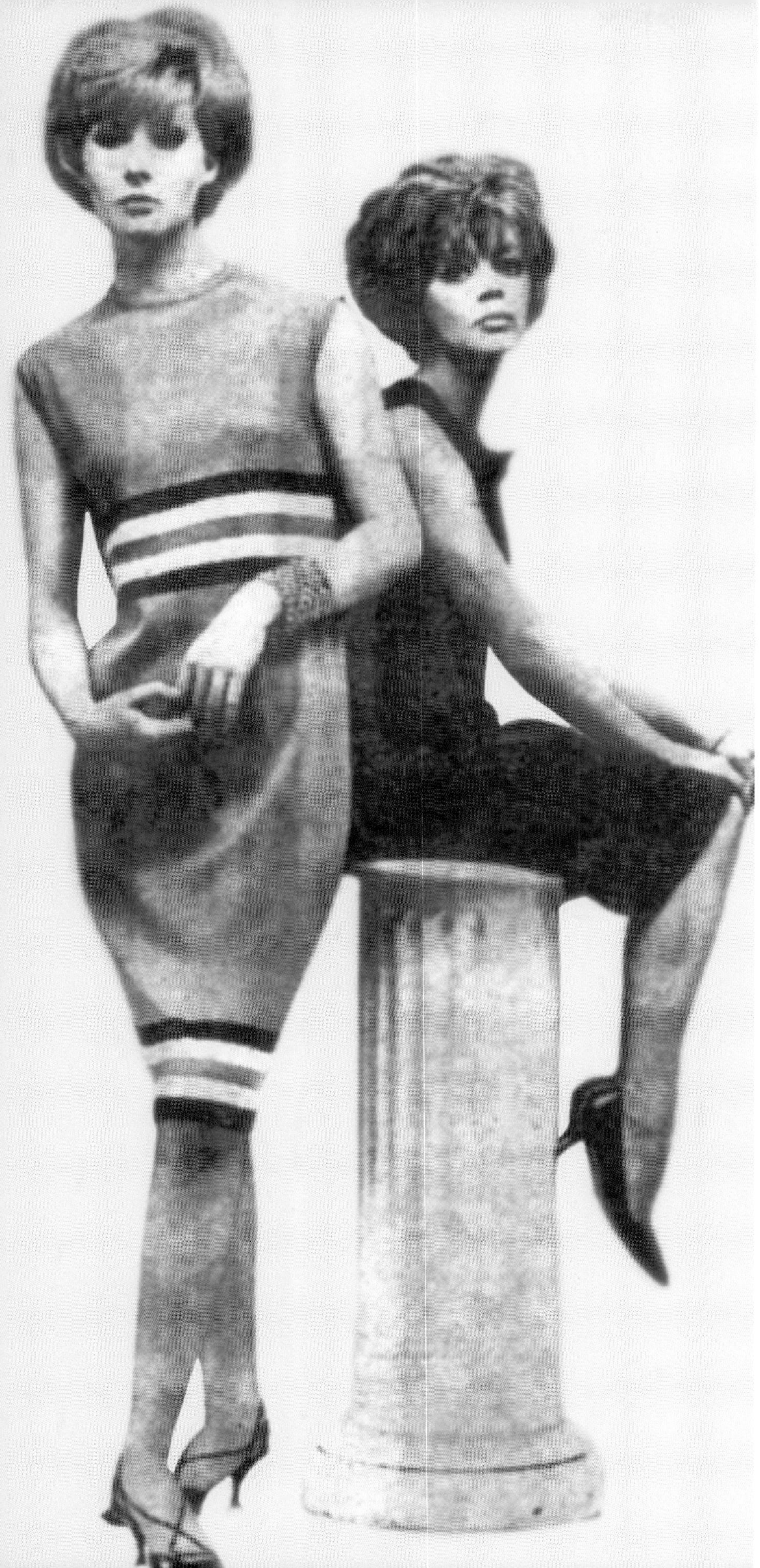

available vacancy was as a junior in the stockroom, which served the clothing departments.

For Muir, Liberty was a magical place, especially set in the continuing context of the post-war austerity of early fifties Britain; clothes rationing had only ceased the year before she arrived. She later described Liberty as her first spiritual home "I love the materials and I love the historical associations... it was just my place"; her time there would serve both as her apprenticeship and her epiphany.

It seems fitting that Miss Muir's introduction to commerce and her future métier should have taken place within such a richly aesthetic, yet practical environment, and one in which quality of workmanship and design were the basic criteria. At the same time that she was absorbing the pleasure of working in the beautiful building with all its special historical associations – the Pre-Raphaelites, the Aesthetic movement, William Morris – and the merchandise, often inspired by the Orient, rich in colour, shape and pattern, she was also assimilating stock control, mark-ups, buying and selling, and above all, looking at different styles.

From the stockroom she moved to the lingerie department, where she began to sell and sketch. The department sold made-to-measure Liberty silk dressing gowns, and she was required to produce and send sketches to customers. She was promoted to the new Young Liberty department, where the stock was a combination of modern, sophisticated styles from leading London fashion manufacturers and made-to-measure merchandise inspired by the latest Paris collections and produced in Liberty's own workrooms. Here she became involved in the store's fashion shows, which were noteworthy social events with famous guests drawn from artistic and literary milieux; she would remember this interesting mix when it came to her own shows.

During this time, as well as selling and sketching, the young Miss Muir was taking careful note of the fitters at work on made-to-measure outfits. This led to a wide knowledge of fabrics, shape and fit, as well as the relationship between a retail organisation and its wholesale suppliers. "At Liberty, I got used to selling clothes and to seeing a great many shapes getting into them ... I learnt the business from A to Z. Designing, manufacturing, export, what sells best in which parts of the country."

Concurrently, Jean Muir was making her own clothes, teaching herself to cut her own patterns, always saving up to buy the best-quality black wool from

**LEFT** The *Daily Mirror*, 9 November 1962, puts Jean Muir on a pedestal: one of the first accolades features Jane and Jane designs by Jean Muir whom they name as a key young designer.

Liberty that she could afford for her work clothes, whilst she made her 'Dior' party outfits from less expensive lining taffeta from Dickins & Jones. She tried pattern-cutting classes, but found she already knew more than they could teach her: "I always used to make my own clothes and there was no conscious thought that I would be a 'Dress Designer'. I just did it as a *force nécessaire*. Being so small I couldn't buy clothes so I made them. I bought a pattern and I didn't like it, so I started to change it. Then I taught myself to make my own patterns and I did it all really without thinking that I would end up as a designer." At the same time that she was working at Liberty, Muir attended evening classes in fashion illustration at St Martin's School of Art – interestingly, she thought this might be a possible profession – and worked as a model for the fashion classes to earn extra money.

Whilst working at Liberty, Muir met her husband-to-be, Harry Leuckert, then a student at RADA, at a Valentine's Day party. "We met when I was invited to this party by my friend and fellow student at RADA, Margaret Capstick. I had digs in Onslow Square, SW7 and she lived in St John's Wood, NW8. The bus fare in those days was about tuppence – and I didn't have tuppence so I declined the invitation. Valentine's Day arrived and I still wasn't going. I wasn't going in the morning. I wasn't going in the afternoon – and then the evening came and I said, 'Heck, I *am* going to that party'. And I walked all the way from Onslow Gardens to St John's Wood. When I got there the party was in full swing – and I saw Jean. And it was instant for both of us. Our partnership began and from then on we did everything together, we discussed everything, every decision was mutual." They married just over a year later in 1955. It was to be a fortuitous pairing; Harry Leuckert would become a successful actor, his earnings helping to establish Jean Muir Limited. He would later become Muir's business manager and co-director and was the perfect sounding board for the talented Muir. "We never had the urge for frequent holidays or to go nightclubbing" he recalls. "We valued our evenings together and would often spend time bouncing ideas off each other."

With six years of commercial experience behind her, Muir sought a fresh challenge and left Liberty. During a brief stint at Jacqmar, an introduction by the Danish milliner, Aage Thaarup led to her next move. In 1956, she joined Jaeger; another business rooted in tradition and whose style and reputation were based on quality. Here she met fellow designer, David Watts, who was to become her colleague and close friend for the rest of her life. "She and I joined at the same time and within Jaeger we were known as "the children". We had to come up with designs for the whole range and the two of us covered the Paris collections, buying toiles which we would reinterpret for Jaeger. We went to Balenciaga, Dior, Chanel, and Balmain. Jean always had a very independent spirit and I recall that even then, in the late fifties, she had a preference for something different, a feeling that things were moving away from Paris – if you're a designer you feel things like that…sniffing the prevailing air…"

It was at Jaeger that she first began to work with wool jersey and knitwear. Working within the confines of particular industrial machinery she met the

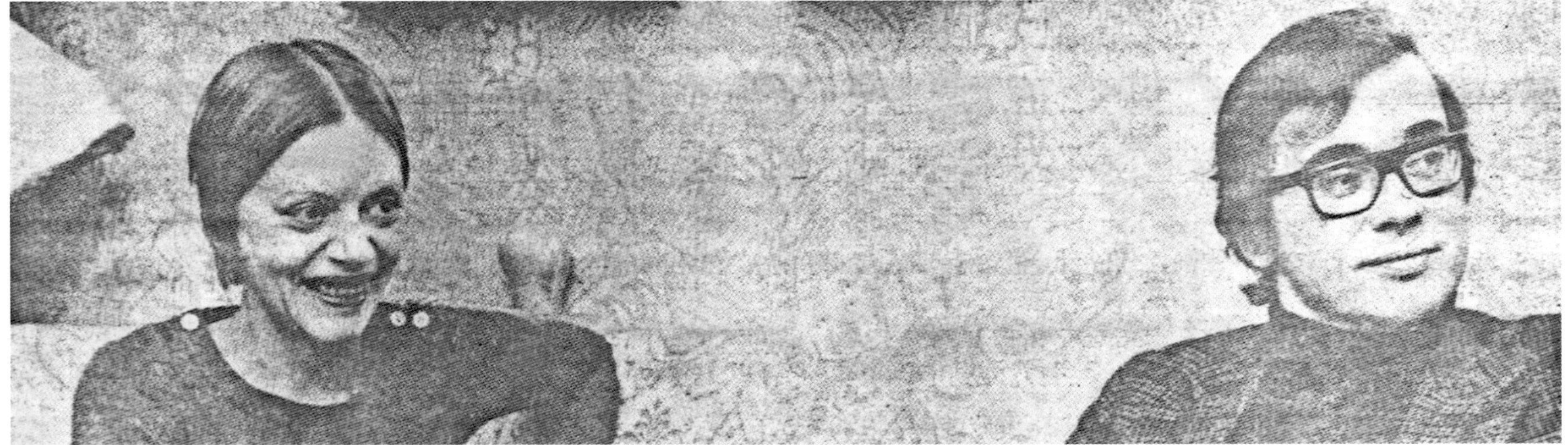

**ABOVE** Partners in life, partners in business: Jean Muir and her husband Harry Leuckert photographed at their Pont Street flat for American fashion trade bible *Women's Wear Daily*, June 1972. At this time Jean Muir was already an international star, fêted in Paris as well as on both sides of the Atlantic, sought after by the press as the figurehead of British fashion.

"I realised that I had a far better idea of what suited people than they had themselves. Or at any rate, I thought I had, so that started me off. The accent, as far as I could see, should be on youthful simplicity..."
**JEAN MUIR**

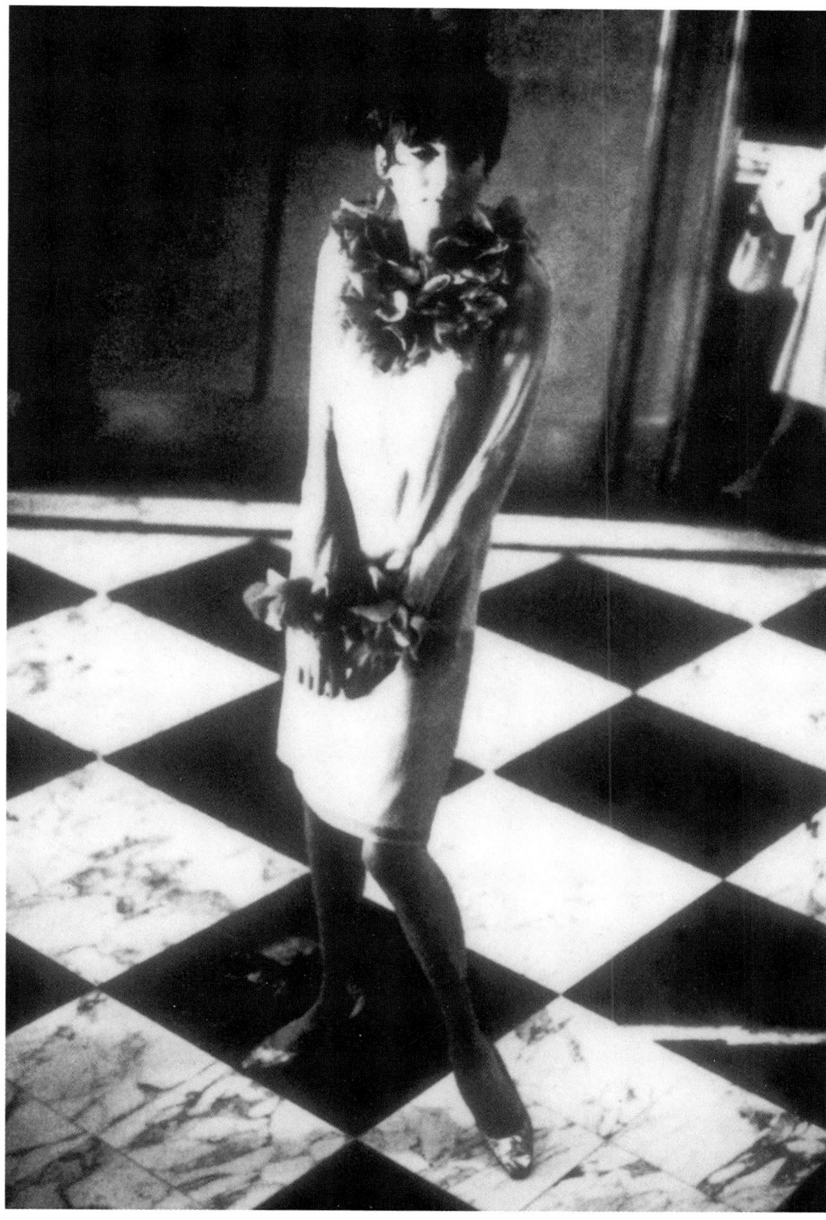

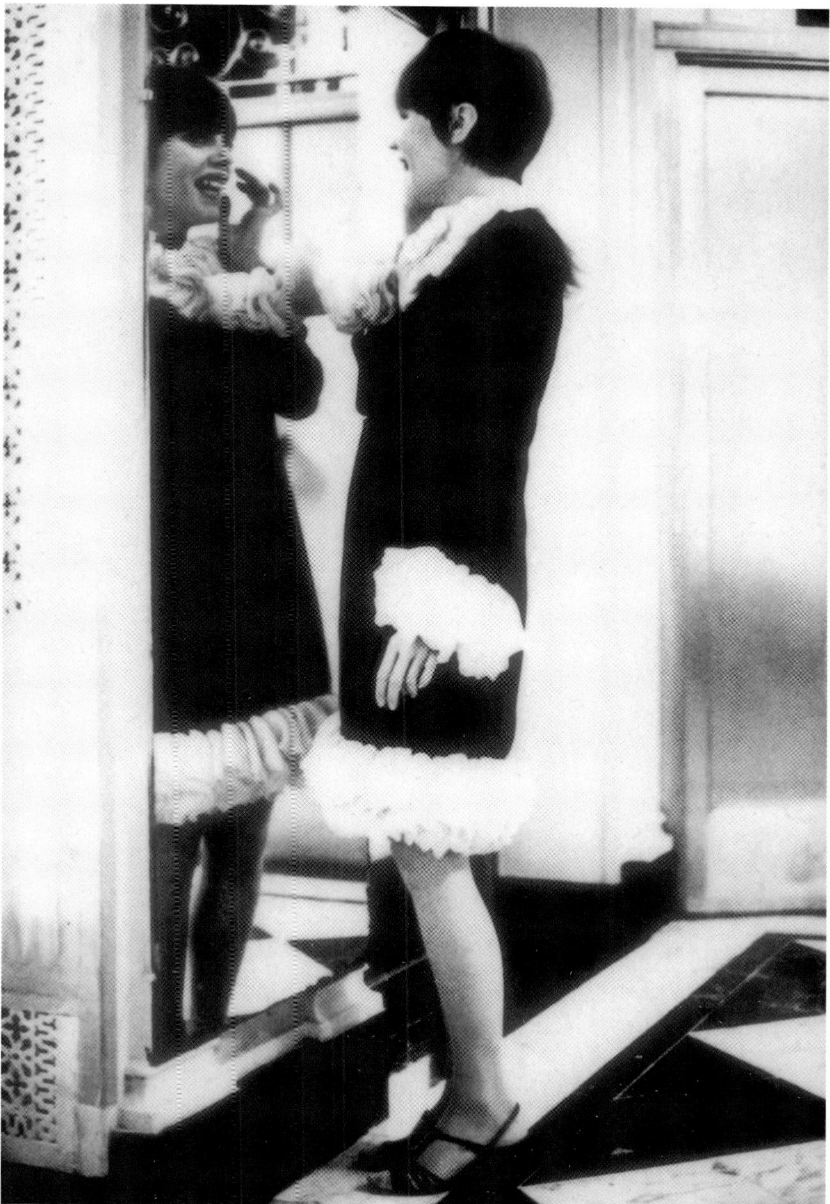

**ABOVE** A pair of early Jane and Jane dresses, demure yet flirty, dramatised with a froth of ruffles. **RIGHT** Jean Muir wears one of her own designs.

challenge to produce "a really beautiful shape". David Watts recalls, "Fairly early on Jean developed a real feeling for knitwear and she became the main person designing this part of Jaeger's collections. She was also responsible for a small capsule collection, 'The Boutique', a more expensive line of principally dressy, smart formal daywear through to cocktail. There were little suits and dresses with designer-y details which you would not have found on the normal Jaeger stock." This was the time that she came up with the idea and name of 'Young Jaeger' – a forerunner of the youth movement that was to play such a large part on the international fashion scene.

In 1962, feeling it was time to move on, she left Jaeger. She was immediately approached by David Barnes, a mass-market jersey dress manufacturer, to design a collection for him. Known as Mr Dynamite because of his energy and shrewd business acumen, he was the first to export to Russia, even as early as those days. Miss Muir declined the offer. Recognising Muir's talent he offered to fund and set up a company for her so that she could design her own collection. So in 1962 she produced her first independent collection under the Jane and Jane label, working out of premises at 19 Great Portland Street in London. Although Muir did not own the label, its design and direction were under her complete control. Later it was bought by the Susan Small Group, who were bought by Courtaulds.

It was here that her intuitive sense of what was right for her dramatically came to the fore, as did her name in fashion circles. In January 1964 British *Vogue* hailed Jean Muir as "one of the new young names that are giving the Sixties an accent all their own." In recognition of her work Muir was awarded Dress of the Year in 1964, chosen by members of the Fashion Writer's Association. In 1965 she received the Ambassador Award for Achievement, "For applying the highest professional standards to British ready-to-wear which has made her an absolute authority among young fashion designers." This was followed by the *Harper's Bazaar* Trophy the same year, "Our reason for the 1965 choice is simple – Jean Muir is a perfectionist, her contribution to the British fashion scene is considerable."

It was at Jane and Jane that Jean Muir began to make clothes with a couture look and feel – beautifully shaped and crafted with a modern adventurous outline and cut, in luxurious fabrics. At this time she coined the phrase 'Wholesale Couture' – before then, says Harry Leuckert, there was Couture or wholesale but nothing in between. This created a whole new movement, leading to such innovations as the YSL Rive Gauche line. Unlike couture, Muir's clothes eliminated any unnecessary 'structure', cutting down on the lining and superfluous seaming to facilitate flow and movement on the body. Her unique way of tailoring shapes with softly rounded lines made them essentially feminine. Her impact – applying couture quality to ready-to-wear – was described by Prudence Glynn, in *The Times* as 'bistro couture'.

In her *Evening Standard* column on 26 July 1965, the journalist Barbara Griggs acknowledged the important impact of the Jane and Jane label and Jean Muir's influence on the high street. Under the headline 'On the eve of the Paris shows I report on a London collection as much to the point – The big news now is London right off the peg' she highlighted the collection and Muir's power to influence fashion in no less a way than the Paris couture. "Will you, dear reader, be buying yourself a nice little Jane and Jane this Autumn – prices from 12 guineas upwards? You might well be. And if you don't you might well be investing in a cheaper COPY. For Jean Muir, like all talented and original designers, gets paid over and over the unenviable compliment of being copied over and over. She is, to be precise, an influence on what gets sold off the peg over here in a way that only Paris used to be." Among the first to introduce short, short skirts at this time, Jean Muir's look for Jane and Jane was featured in US *Harper's Bazaar* headlined 'Who's for Tennis?'

Not only the press but also buyers were beating a path to this emerging star. The retailer, Lucienne Phillips, a chic Frenchwoman working as a buyer at Harrods, remembers her first glimpse of the Jane and Jane look. "I was choosing evening wear for the departmental show and I glanced, quite by chance, into the fitting room at a single grey flannel shift, sleeveless and softly round-necked, a few mother of pearl buttons down the middle. It was under a cellophane bag on a wire hanger, beckoning me. I asked Angela, a top model of the time where she had got it. 'In Great Portland Street' she said, 'there's a girl called Jean Muir working under the label 'Jane and Jane' – go there; you'd love it!' I found pure ready-to-wear at its best."

Just as fate called Miss Muir into the fashion business, so fate did the same for Mr Leuckert and it all started with a phone call from New York. A V.I.C. (Very Important Customer), Mrs Berenice Whiteman who owned the

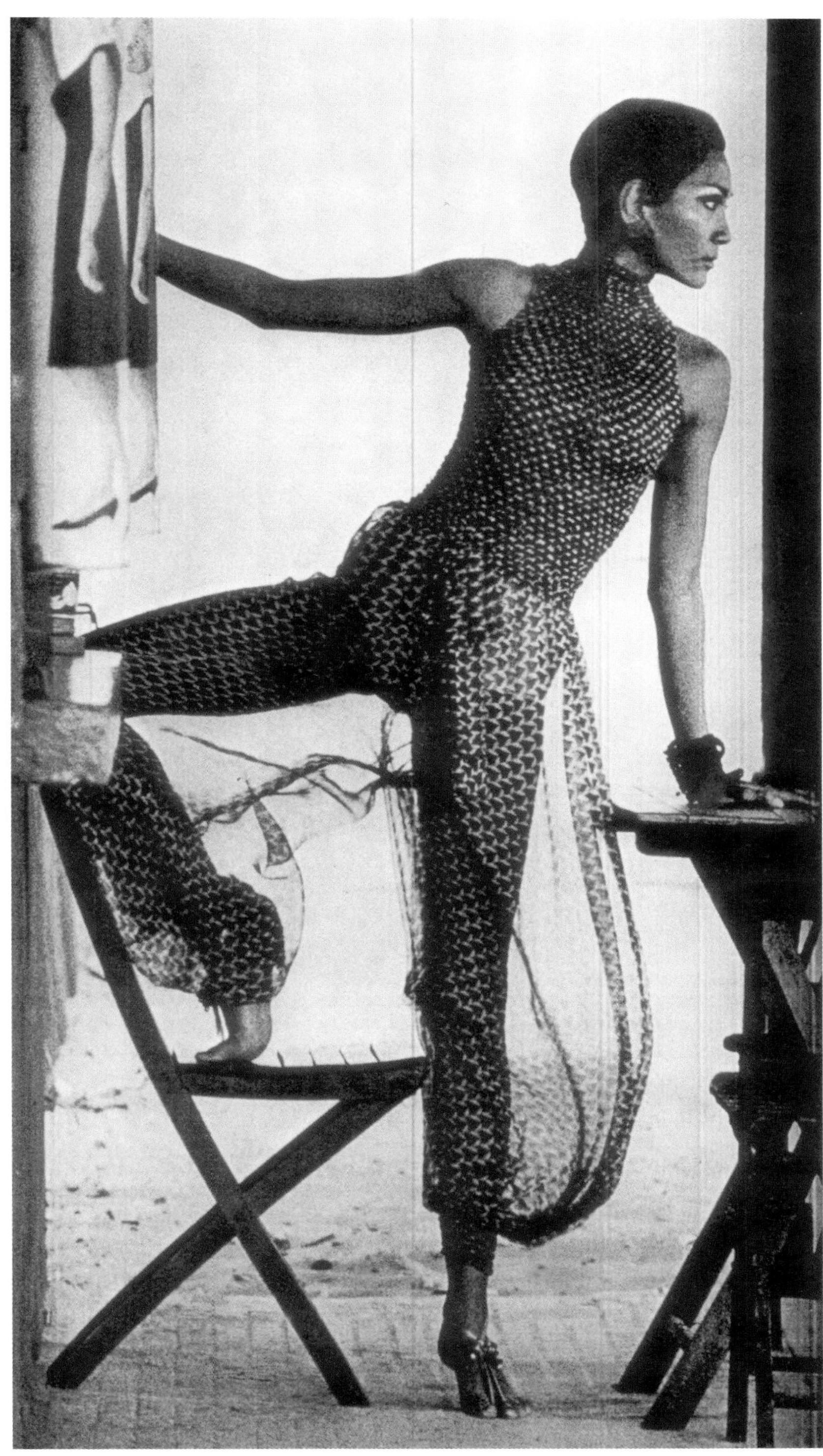

influential Chic boutique in London's Hampstead, was coming in to see the collection. Miss Muir was in New York – could Mr Leuckert personally look after Mrs Whiteman and see that everything was in good order. "I went in" says Mr Leuckert, "and I never came out again." Harry's rôle was key. "We came into the business with our different talents. I was able to deal with the purely business side so that Jean was completely free to devote herself to her work without any distractions. But we made every important decision together – we were very close and we never once had a serious argument, and it worked like a dream."

In 1966, Jean Muir set up independently, under her own name with Harry as her co-director. From their Bruton Street showroom she pioneered a distinctive purity of line and a sophisticated minimalist approach, which outlasted the dictates of seasons for so many decades. Her style was the antidote to ephemeral frivolity and over-embellished design, and was a reaction not just against the restrictive stiffness and formality of the couture that had been the defining source of fashion for so long, but also a reaction against the throwaway excesses of the swinging sixties.

Joanna Lumley, who had become one of Miss Muir's house models at Jane and Jane in 1964 – "I didn't go to university. I went to work for Jean Muir instead" – eloquently noted: "The eyes of the world looked at Britain and saw a mass of new, young, fizzing talents, many of whom spluttered out after a brief spell centre stage, and a very few whose names would remain to be carved in marble. Quite separate, yet leading it all was Jean Muir. She seemed even then, to be beyond fashion. She didn't follow trends or share anxieties about hemlines: she was, at the same instant, at the forefront and yet not of her time, like Fortuny."

Jean Muir was, of course, 'of her time' yet in another sense she was not, as she herself explained. "Although it seemed to the outside world that I was very much part of the clothes explosion in London, my view was that of an onlooker, who, by accident of time, coincided with a certain moment. One sensed the need for change through experienced eyes and had an evolutionary not revolutionary approach… my path had already started and I continued to go up that path and about my work. I remember one very conscious decision at this time. I knew there was danger in becoming involved in the seasonal ins and outs of trends. This was not at all what I wanted. I would make my own style of clothes for better or worse."

**ABOVE** Dramatically different and ahead of her time: Jean Muir's Jane and Jane chiffon harem pants and shirred top in Liberty of London silk print. *Queen* magazine, June 1966.

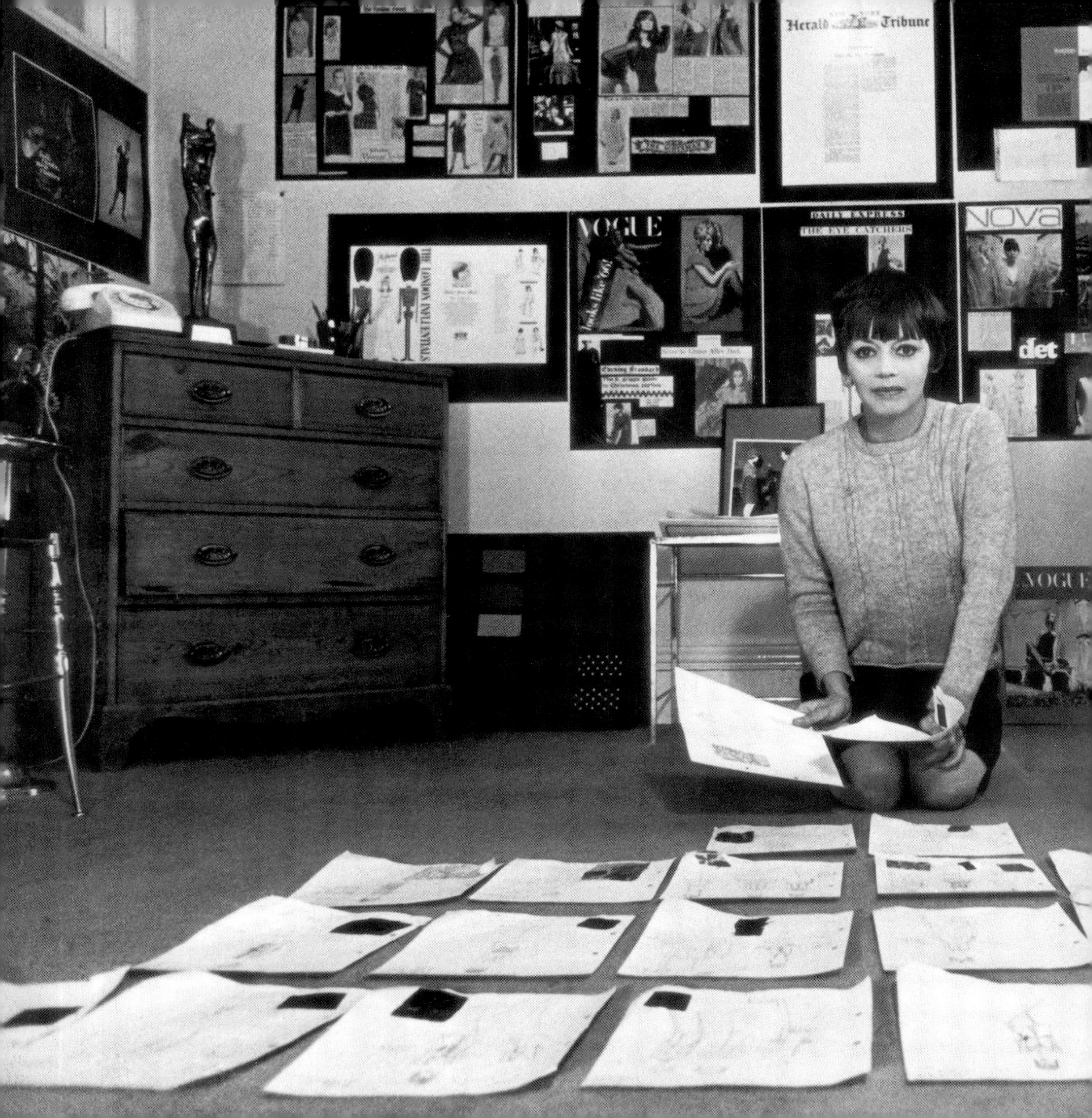

Herald Tribune
VOGUE
THE LONDON INFLUENTIALS
DAILY EXPRESS
THE EYE CATCHERS
NOVA
Evening Standard
det
VOGUE

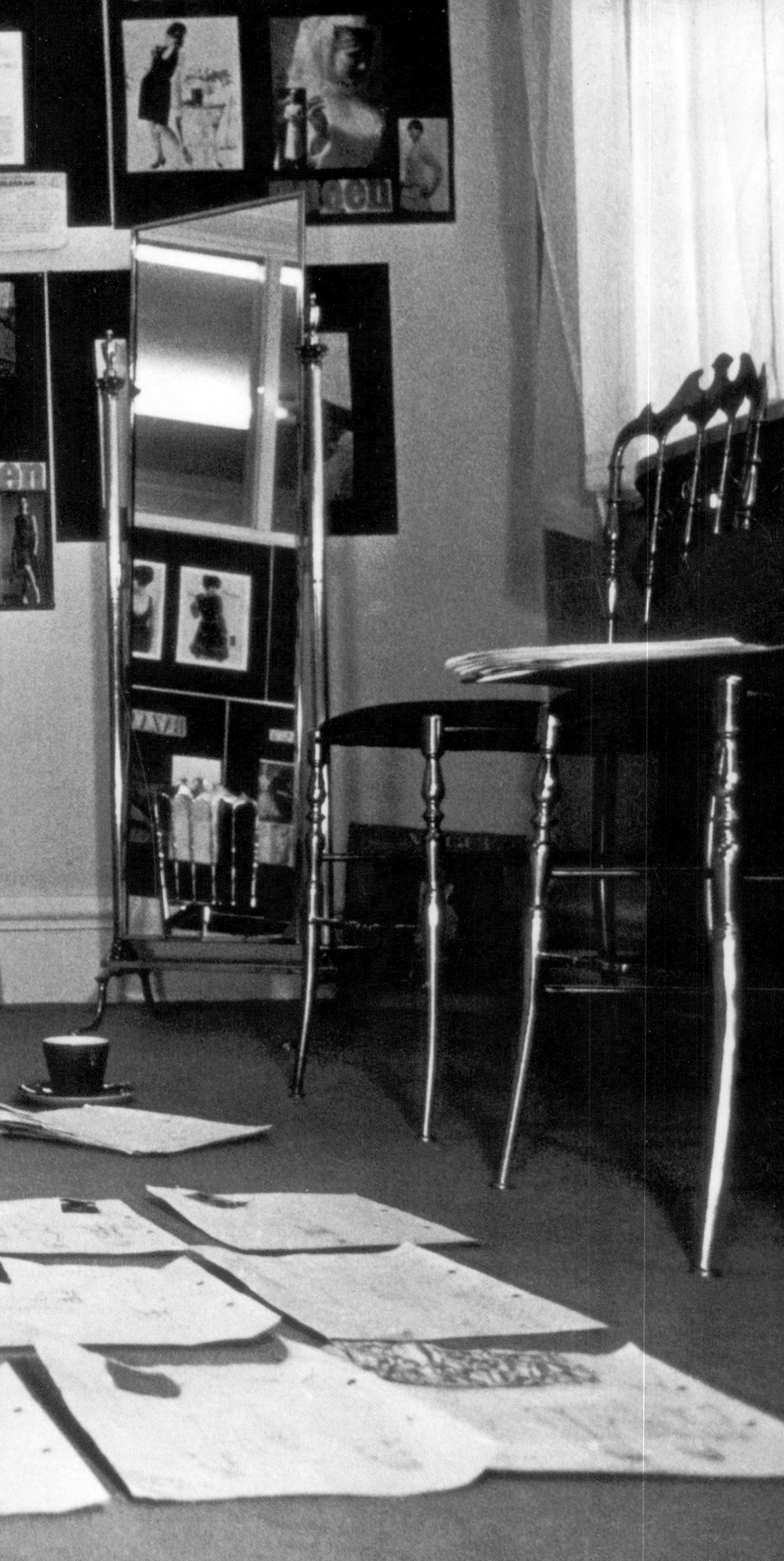

Chapter Two

# THE MUIR DECADES
# SIXTIES
# SEVENTIES
# EIGHTIES
# NINETIES

“Ideas have to make sense in their own time – on the other hand I have always felt that even in clothes, through shape and workmanship and a total comprehension of the material – one can produce a lasting quality that overrides the transient, superficial areas of fashion”

JEAN MUIR

**JEAN MUIR'S** career coincided with the rise of a new style of fashion photography and, in British *Vogue* in particular, her work was charted in the sixties and seventies by David Bailey, the pre-eminent photographer of the time. Throughout her career her designs were featured on more than twenty British *Vogue* covers, and were photographed by a host of notable talents, amongst others: Henry Clarke, Bob Richardson, Ronald Traeger, Horvat, Norman Parkinson, Jean Loup Sieff, David Montgomery, Clive Arrowsmith, David Bailey, Terence Donovan, Helmut Newton, Deborah Turbeville, Michael Roberts, Barry Lategan, Patrick Demarchelier, Arthur Elgort, Neil Kirk, Peter Lindbergh, Mario Testino and Snowdon.

The change in photographic style was dramatic: until the sixties, fashion pictures were beautifully and brilliantly lit and almost always the model's face was so re-touched that reality played little part in the images that leading photographers presented on the pages of the international fashion magazines. Every imperfection disappeared and every waist was rendered ever more waspish. And then London began to swing and the new young photographers swung with it. The beautiful static studio picture was blown away in the blast of the new photo-realism. The generation of young photographers, most of whom had learned their trade in the studios of the previous masters took over the fashion scene. Photographers, in the language of the youth generation began telling it like it was.

Outdoors in natural light became the favourite location, whether in the city streets, on building sites or in the heart of the country and the model girls now had to MOVE. They had to run, to leap, to dance and their clothes had to move with them and the over-constructed, stiff styles were no longer right. Fashion like fashion photography entered a new era and it was the era when Jean Muir launched her brilliant career. Her designs with their grace and mobility were perfect for the new generation of wearers.

An editorial in the February 1972 issue of *Harper's & Queen* led with the assertion that: "Jean Muir's signature is as clearcut, as firm, as Chanel's braided tweed suits, Saint Laurent's safari jackets, Courrège's geometrically precise dresses. Long hailed in this country as our foremost designer, she took the French by storm when she showed at the Prêt-à-Porter collections in Paris for the first time last Autumn..."

**PAGE 26** Jean Muir at work in the late sixties: on the floor, sketches and swatches lined up for the new collection. Behind her the walls are covered with her press cuttings.

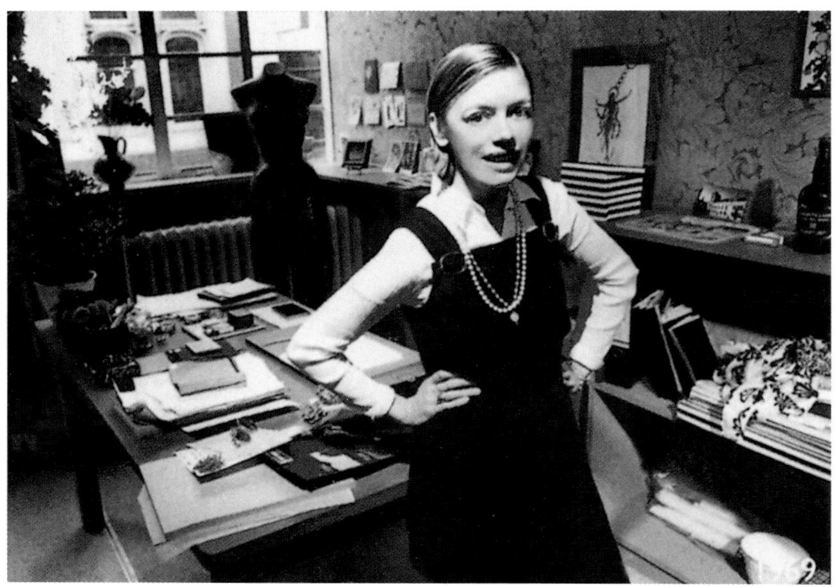

## SIXTIES: ARRIVAL

The sixties saw a new phenomenon: the culture of youth took over the world, and its fashion centre was London. Fashion was no longer derivative. The previously formal became informal – fresh, exciting and exhilarating. Couture no longer reigned supreme as the pyramid of influence was completely turned upside down. Fashion no longer filtered down from the top, it burst out from street level. Prevailing shapes were geometric, hard-edged and angular, in thicker fabrics, influenced by Op Art, Pop Art, and space travel. Clothes were essentially of the moment, geared towards a new type of consumer, hungry for constant change – and cheap and cheerful ready-to-wear burgeoned.

The built-in obsolescence of many of these clothes was part of the general appeal, but not for Muir. Her method was to use the best quality fabrics and properly craft them in such a way that they were the original true investment dressing. These clothes were simply too good just to be discarded after one fashion season. Muir was very clear about the silhouette and style she wanted for her clothes. "The stiff space-y things of the sixties seemed to me a very jolting and sharp look," she said, "I couldn't see how they followed on in the great big pattern of things. Everybody was kidded into thinking this was the modern trend, whereas I believe people want clothes which have much more ease and that's proved itself now. I hate all this going back business but I am sure the average woman looked more graceful during the thirties, simply because the fabrics were crepey and drapey and the shapes fluid."

Clothes with the emphasis on good cut, youthful styling and a fluid form were her version of the sixties, first at Jane and Jane and then, from 1966, under her own label. Joanna Lumley, her house model recalled: "In her tiny [Jane and Jane] showroom, buyers and press would see me in dresses fastened with swirls of buttons, Liberty chiffon harem pants, cobwebby knits, twill coats and woollen smocks… and rushed to place their orders. Weeks later the clothes would appear in the pages of *Vogue, Queen* and *Harper's Bazaar,* on model icons such as Jean Shrimpton and Grace Coddington, looking utterly sumptuous."

David Watts, her friend from Jaeger, remembers the exciting atmosphere of her first Bruton Street show in October 1966. "It was an evening show, salon-style, 6.00pm start. There was no music, just the model girls with the audience packed into the two rooms seated on the little gold chairs. After

**ABOVE** Jean Muir in her office, 1969. Photograph & © Peter Rand. **OPPOSITE** Faye Dunaway, photographed in *Vogue*, May 1968, fresh from her 'Bonnie and Clyde' success. Jean Muir dress in white spotted voile topped with a tiny Magyar-inspired braided bolero in black linen, the pintucked shoulders and bodice breaking out into a softly-pleated skirt and bell sleeves. A similar dress was chosen as Dress of the Year in 1968. Photograph: Jerry Schatzberg/Vogue. © The Condé Nast Publications Ltd.

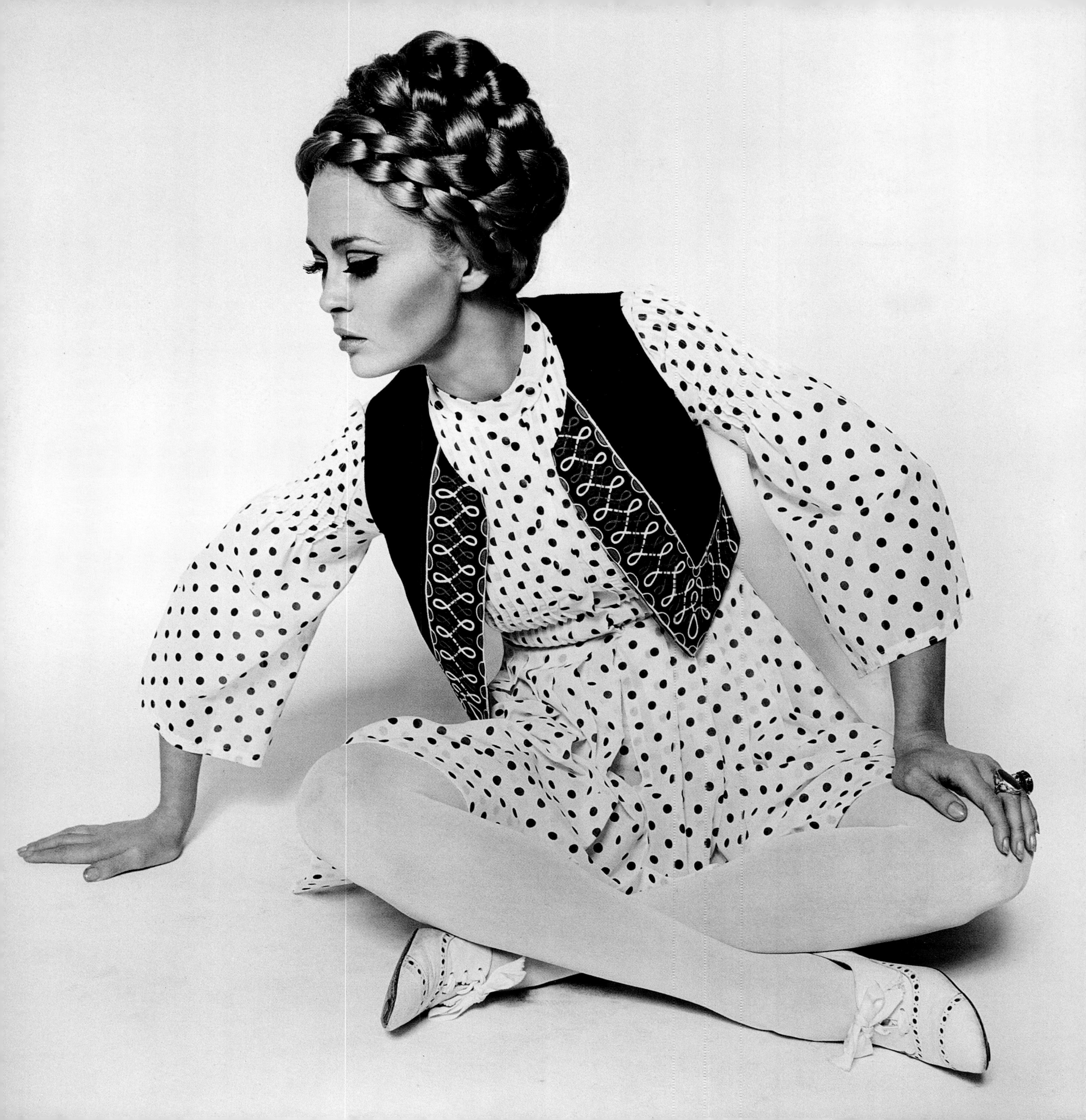

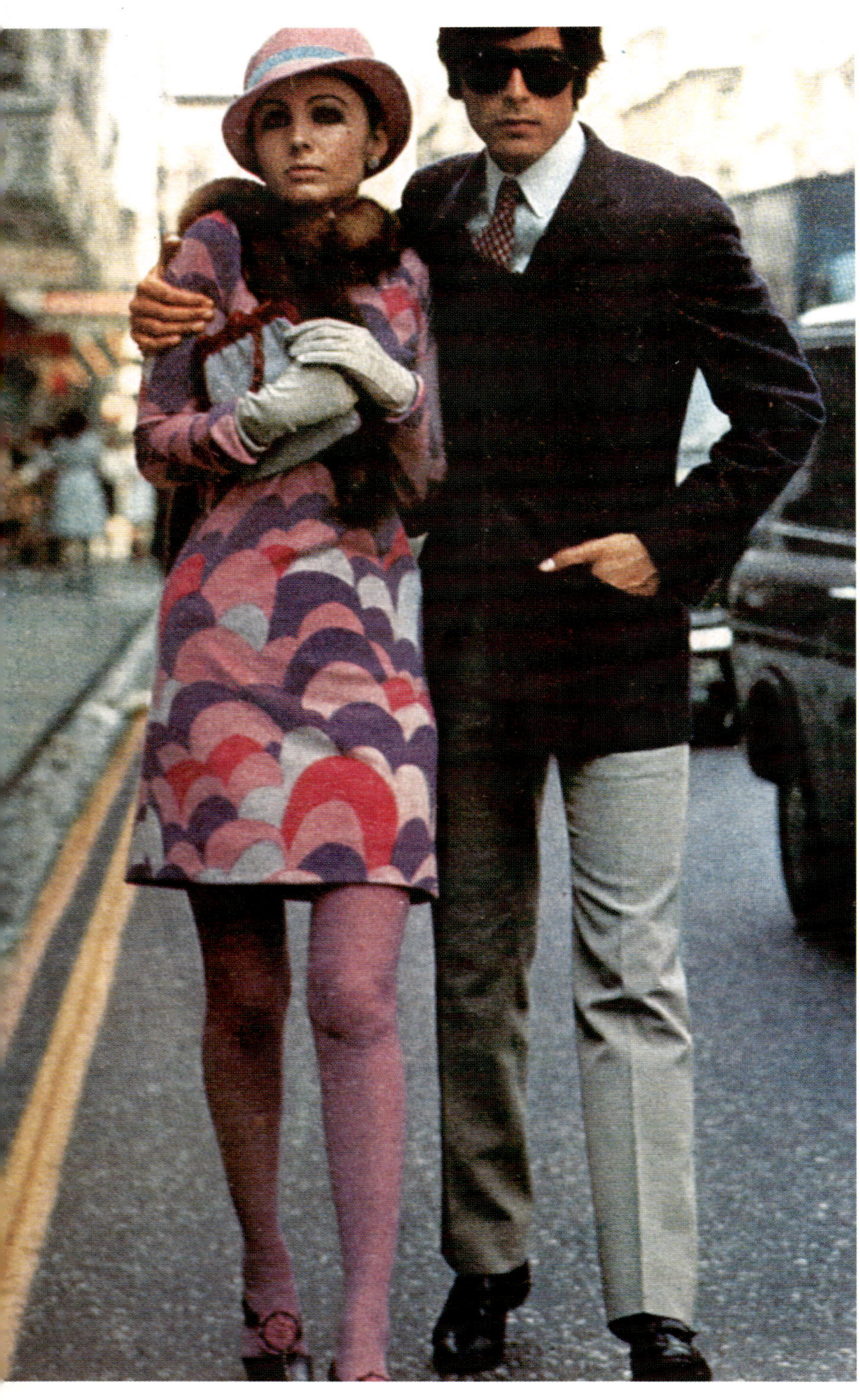

the show a select few, ten or twelve of us, went on to dinner at the Penthouse at the Dorchester – the famous Oliver Messel suite. There was myself and Harry, Geraldine Stutz of the New York store Henri Bendel – she really helped put Jean Muir on the map in America – and another of Jean's great friends, the actress Coral Browne. It was a wonderful show and a marvellous evening. In fact it was a wonderful time to be in the fashion business in London and Jean Muir was a star."

The deconstructed couture approach was quite different as journalist Suzy Menkes remembers: "Jean Muir was not in sync with the sixties and the swinging London scene, but she was doing something else. She was taking the idea of the pieces of fashion which had broken down and re-modelling them in a very fluid, gentle way which really made its mark in the sixties and seventies."

Jean Muir's view of the decade was coloured by her perception of its negative impact. "In my opinion the swinging sixties did enormous damage to the fashion industry and the design industry as a whole. Everything seemed too easy, too instant; you put a sign on your door, got your name in the paper and that was that. Few people were given any chance to develop or learn. You didn't have to learn your trade and consequently very little was soundly based. Real skill and craftsmanship began to die then in Britain and it has never truly revived."

Nevertheless, the sixties was the decade that brought Jean Muir to prominence, and her innovative style and handwriting can be traced in the fashion offerings of such influential glossy magazines as *Vogue* and *Queen*. Her designs were voted Dress of the Year twice in this decade – once in 1964 at Jane and Jane, and again in 1968 at Jean Muir. As the decade drew to a close a new sense of style and proportion was coming to the fore, spearheaded by Muir. From about 1967 the silhouette changed, to longer, softer lines, in lighter weight fabrics.

**ABOVE** Signs of the times: Jane and Jane minidress in swirl-printed angora, *Vogue,* September 1966. Photograph: Bob Richardson/Vogue. © The Condé Nast Publications Ltd.
**OPPOSITE** "New short evenings – midnight tinsel woven with chiffon, it fastens with one million looped buttons", Dress £85 15s., matching turban 25s. *Vogue*, September 1969. Photograph: David Bailey/Vogue. © The Condé Nast Publications Ltd.

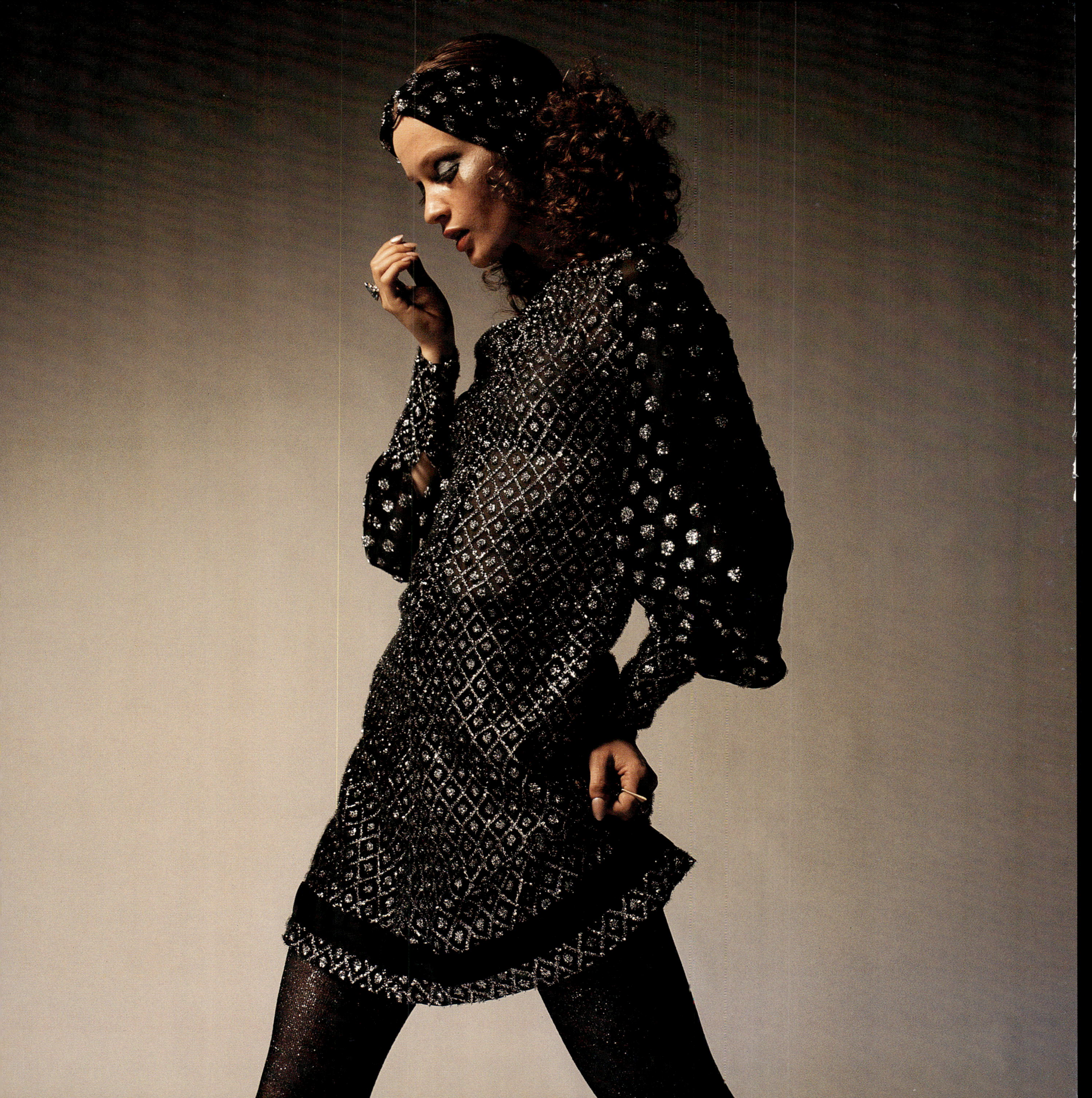

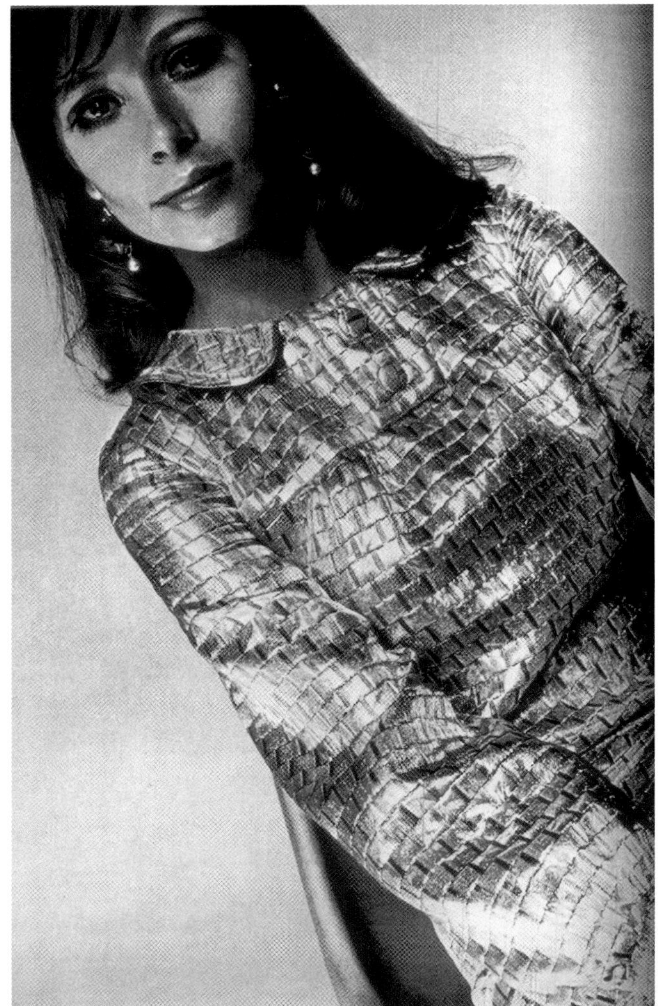

**ABOVE LEFT** Jane and Jane sprigged cotton voile shirred from neck to waist, outlines the contours of the body. *Queen* magazine, April 1966. Photograph & © Marc Hispard. **ABOVE RIGHT** Silver brocade dress, Jane and Jane for Butterick Patterns, *Queen* magazine, September 1966. **OPPOSITE** "The New Exotics. Marvellous dressing up for out-and-out escapist evenings", *Vogue*, July 1967. Hollywood actress, Yvette Mimieux in emerald green Petrouchka pantaloon dress. Photograph: David Montgomery/Vogue. © The Condé Nast Publications Ltd.

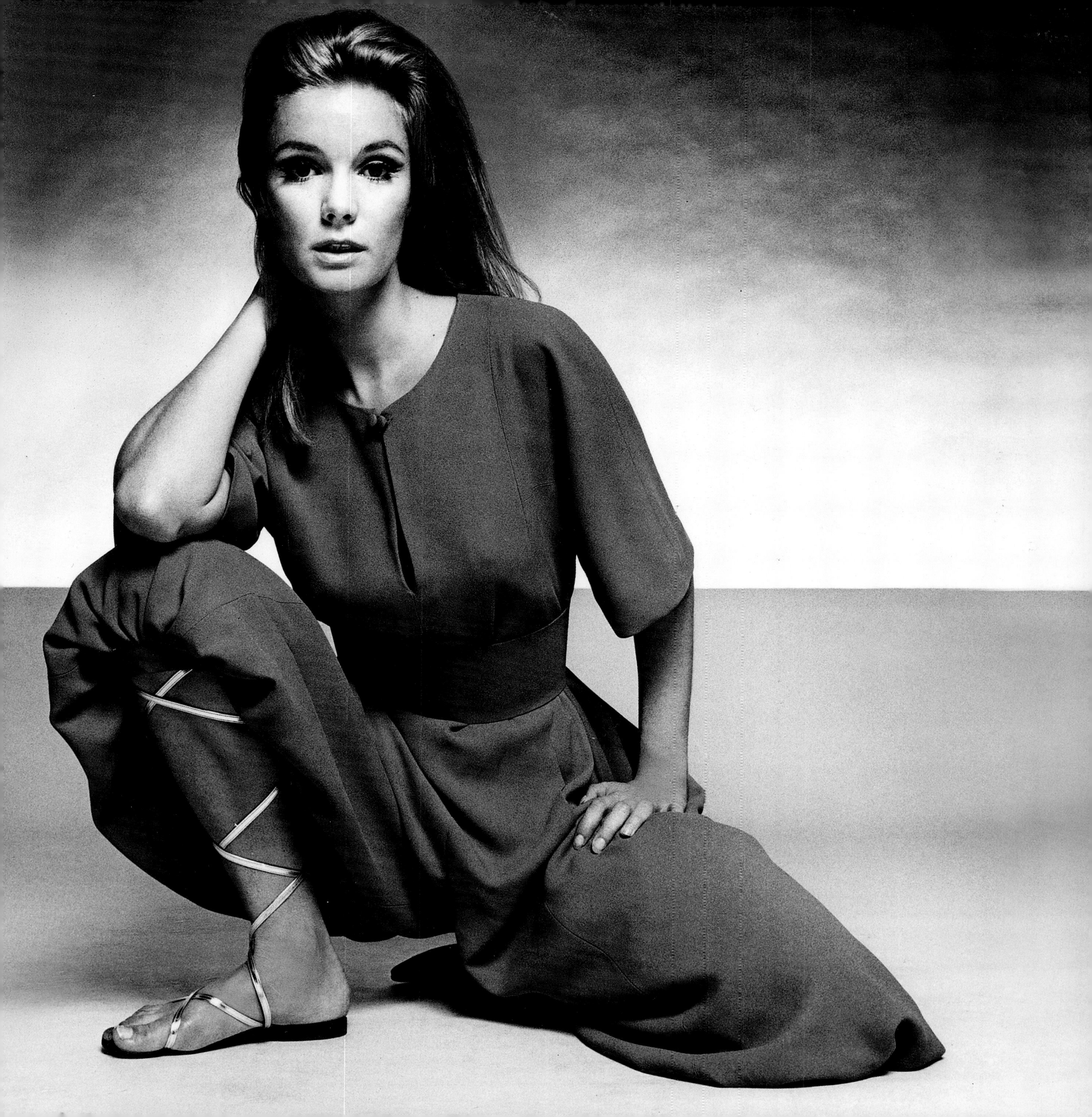

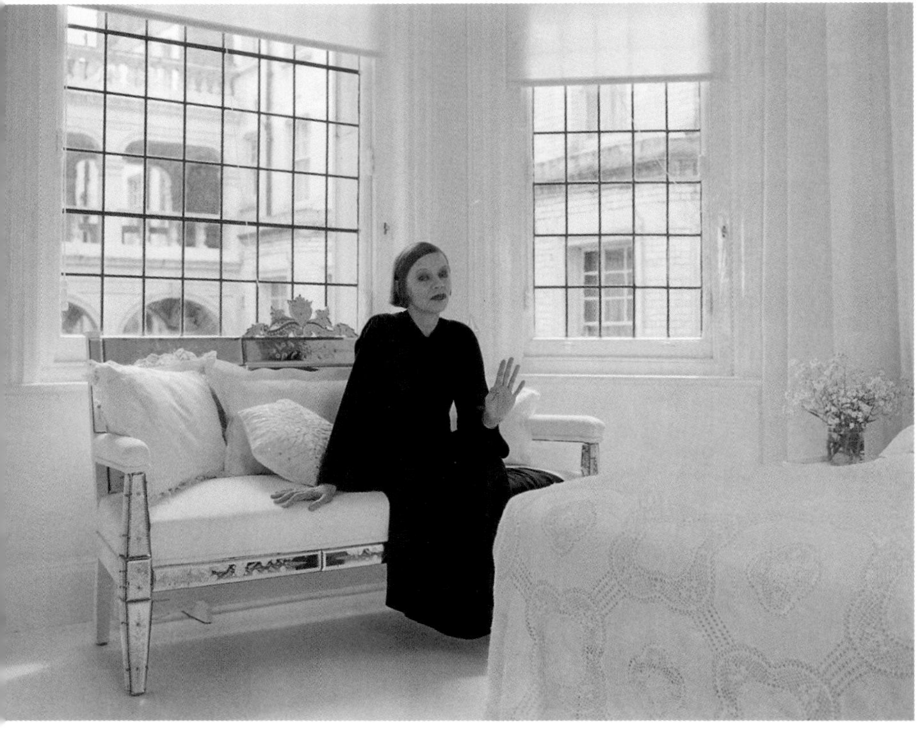

## SEVENTIES: TRIUMPH

While in general the seventies in Britain marked a period of economic decline, for Miss Muir it was hugely successful. Her clothes appealed to a wide variety of women – politicians, diplomats' wives, actresses, businesswomen, writers, journalists and housewives. They all wanted to wear the seductive jersey dresses, the luxe suedes and leathers, the light wools and tweeds – whether they were able to afford her prices or not, Muir's were the clothes they wanted.

Increasing numbers of women were asserting themselves in the workplace, and, like Miss Muir, they travelled frequently. They needed clothes that were practical and hard working, but also stylish and individual. Miss Muir advocated a practical, versatile wardrobe, one that could be relied upon for different occasions and added to each season. A Muir enthusiast, the author Lady Antonia Fraser noted "A number of women who have to define themselves in public by their appearance... turn to Jean Muir's clothes with ecstasy and relief."

The decade began for Muir with the accolade of the Churchman's Award as Designer of the Year, and her appointment in 1972 as a Royal Designer for Industry. It would end in 1979 with Dress of the Year, for the third time, a unique honour at that period. She appeared on American style guru Eleanor Lambert's Best Dressed list in 1972, 1974, and 1978. In October 1971 she was invited to show at the Paris prêt-à-porter collections by Didier Grumbach, owner of the French manufacturer C. Mendès, which produced Yves Saint Laurent's Rive Gauche line, amongst others, at the second of his Createurs & Industriels shows. The event was a phenomenal success.

Miss Muir also went further afield, to Bombay (now Mumbai), where she made a special Indian collection with its own label, a brown background with the Jean Muir logo in bronze. Made from hand-loomed printed silks or fine printed cotton, there were cool Summer dresses, and dressing gowns made in contrasting panels of different prints, in colours such as emerald green and egg yolk yellow, with red, or bronze and soft black. The model, Marie Helvin was photographed on the cover of British *Vogue,* May 1974, wearing "Jean Muir's scarf of a dress...marine blue and daisies, orange and paisley Indian silk ties at the nape."

In the seventies, fashion came round to Muir's way of thinking, with the emphasis on longer, leaner, fluid lines, midi or maxi lengths, and trousers.

**ABOVE** Jean Muir at home in her all-white flat in Albert Court, London. Photograph & © Mayotte Magnus. **OPPOSITE** A quartet of Jean Muir dresses modelled in the mid-seventies by Joanna Lumley: [clockwise from top left] floral print on silk; leaf print on silk georgette – reprised and re-coloured for the 40th anniversary collection, Autumn 2006; two tunic dresses in abstract print on matte jersey. Hats and turbans by Graham Smith for Jean Muir. Photograph: Michael Barrett. © The Trustees of The National Museums of Scotland.

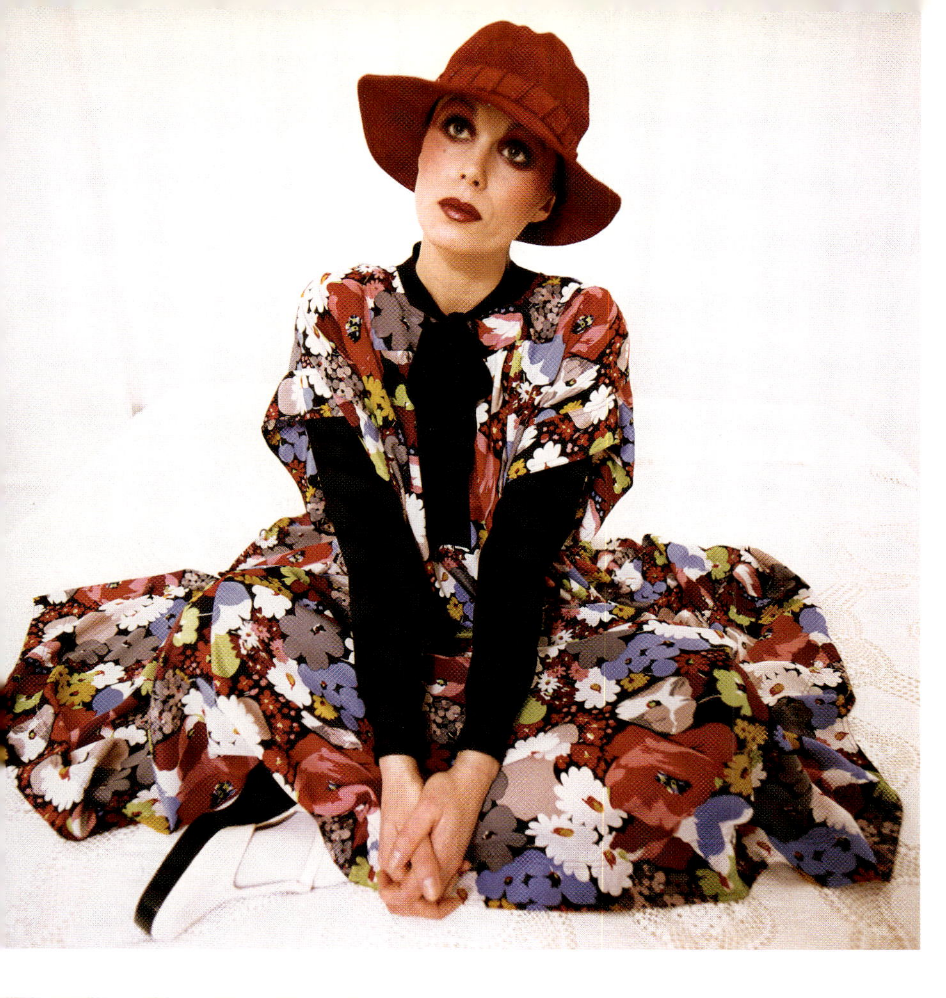
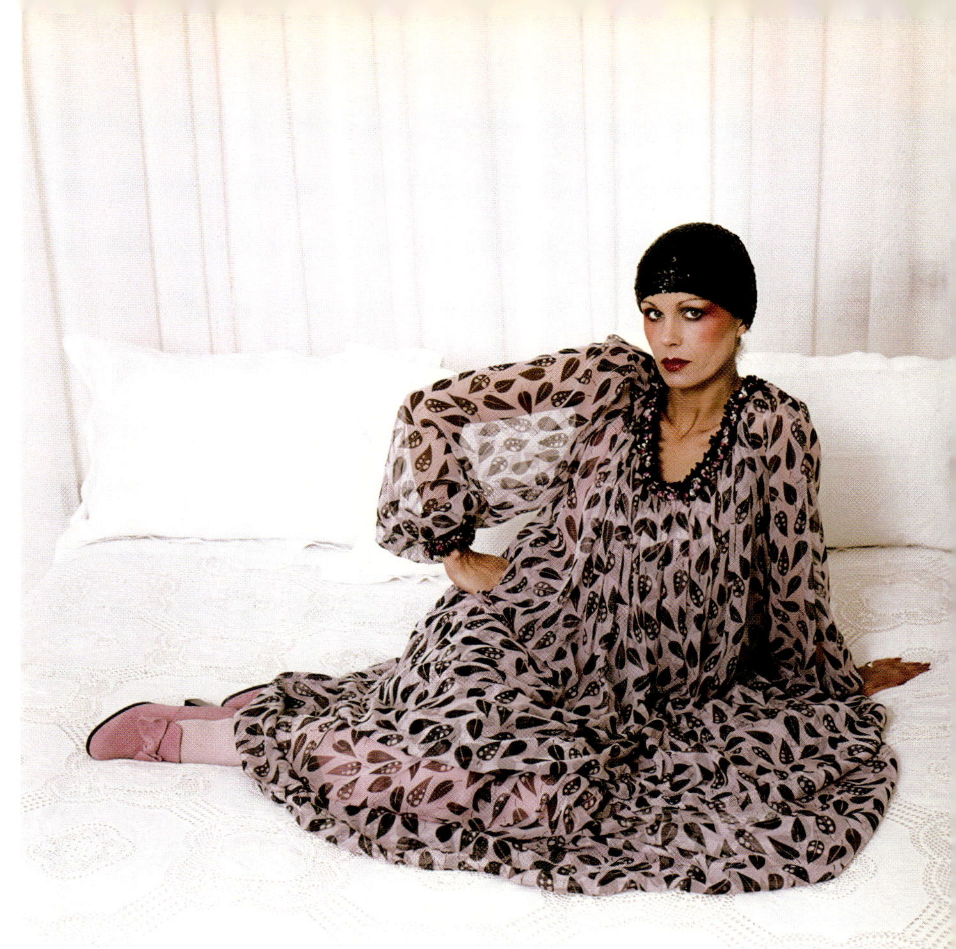
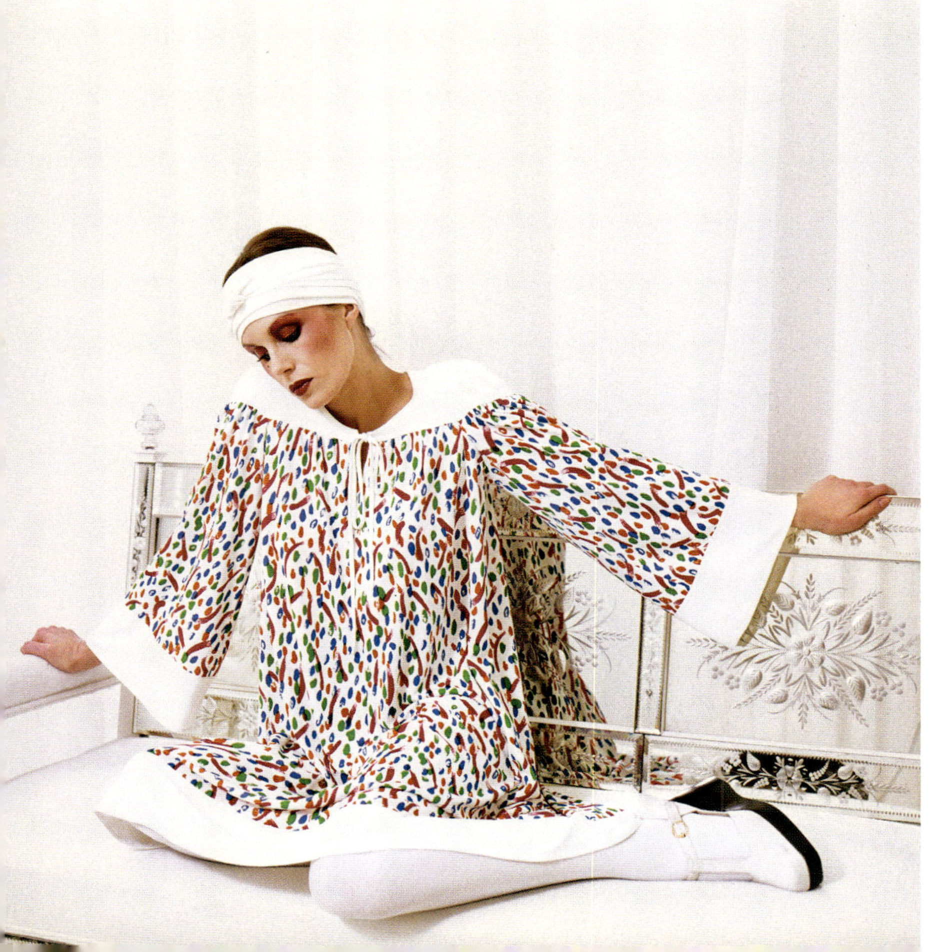
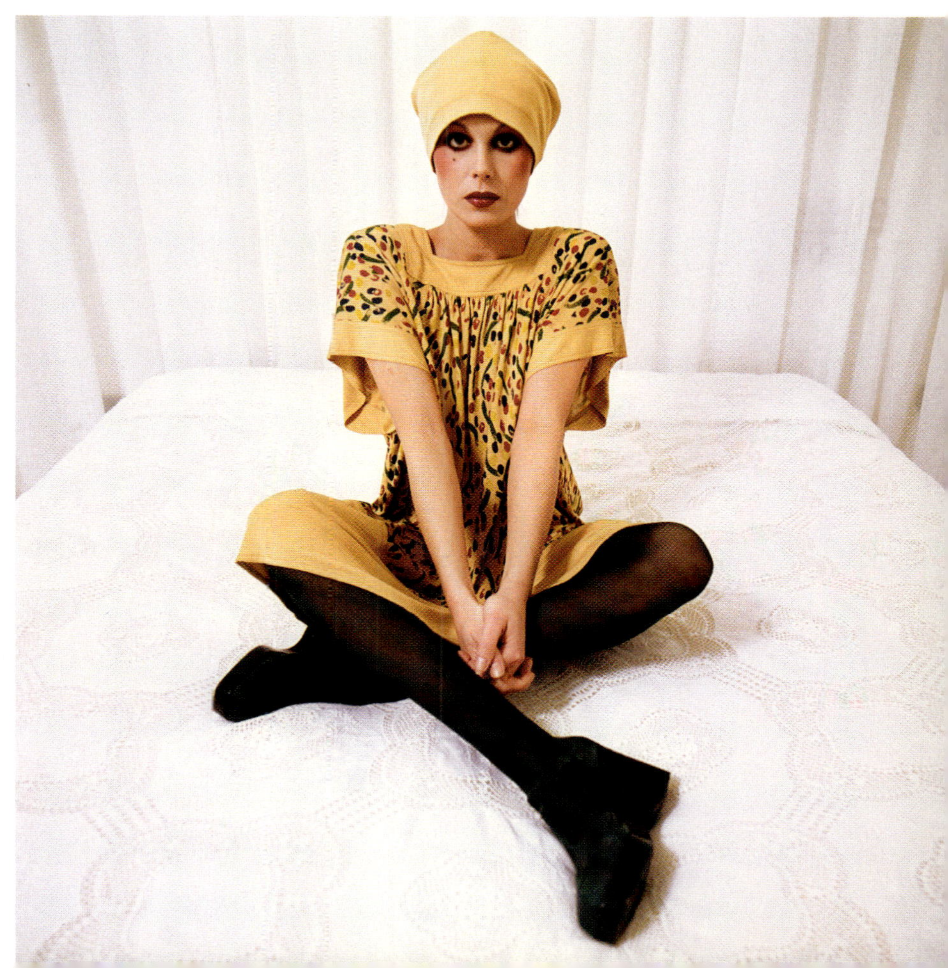

In October 1971, showing there for the first time, Jean Muir took Paris by storm. The international trendsetting magazines *ELLE* and *Marie Claire* devoted page after page to 'la nouvelle reine de la robe', as *ELLE* christened her. At the time, Miss Muir, thrilled at the accolade, described the gesture as "uncharacteristic Gallic generosity". For a time in the early seventies, some of her production for the French market was made in France by the manufacturer, Mendès. Her second show the following season took place in a much larger venue, a theatre packed with an audience of press and buyers. At the end of the show, Pierre Bergé, Yves Saint Laurent's business partner, dramatically stood up and shouted "Bravo!" sparking a standing ovation. Backstage at the end of the show one excited French journalist demanded to know "Where is zis Monsieur Jean Mweer?"

This wasn't the only time Miss Muir was thought to be Monsieur Muir. On another occasion she was to be presented with a French design award, which took the form of a sculpture by the artist Nikki de St Phalle, a curvy one for women and a manly one for men. Confusion broke out backstage – Miss Muir was to receive the male award. Urgent changes had to be made and a sculpture in the appropriate sex was hastily despatched across the Channel.

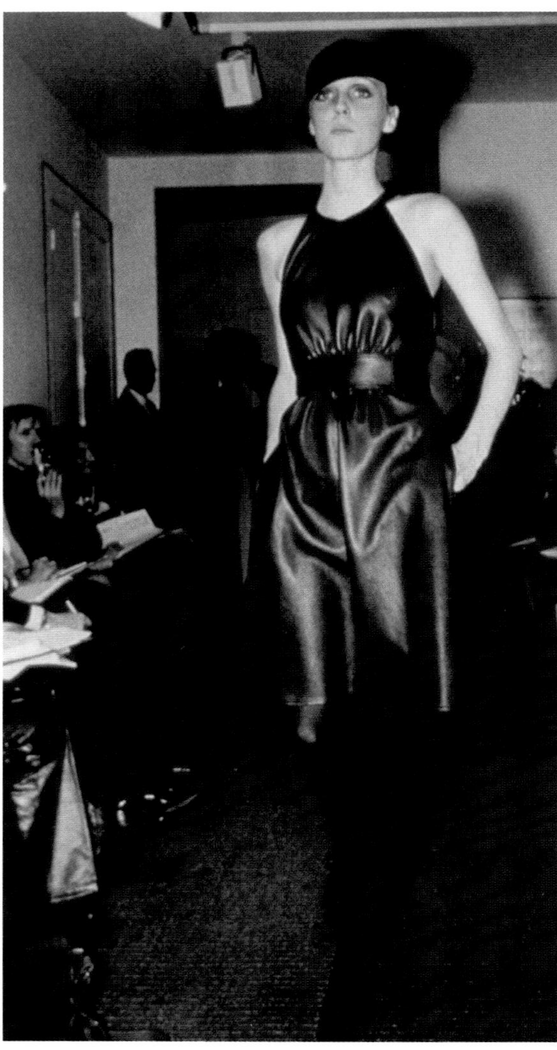

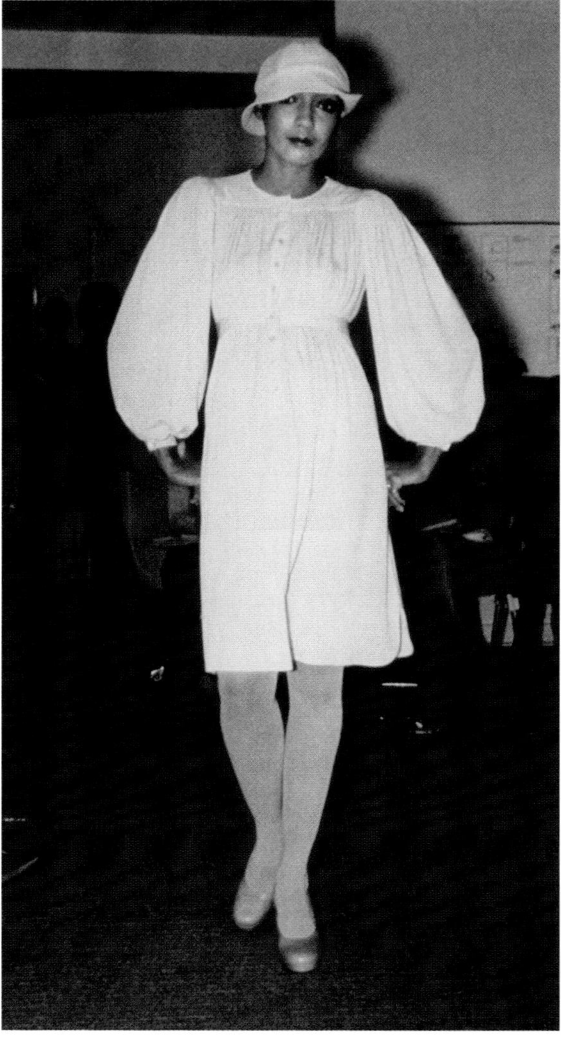

**ABOVE** Jean Muir shows in Paris, 1971: halter-neck dress in nappa leather [left], bell-sleeved dress in matte jersey [right], matching hats by Graham Smith for Jean Muir. **OPPOSITE** Narrow-shouldered cardigan in pearl grey angora jersey cut in a fine circle with skinny sleeves and ties. Matching wide-leg trousers and toning jersey shirt, *Vogue*, December 1976. Photograph: Jean-Claude Benôit/Vogue. © The Condé Nast Publications Ltd.

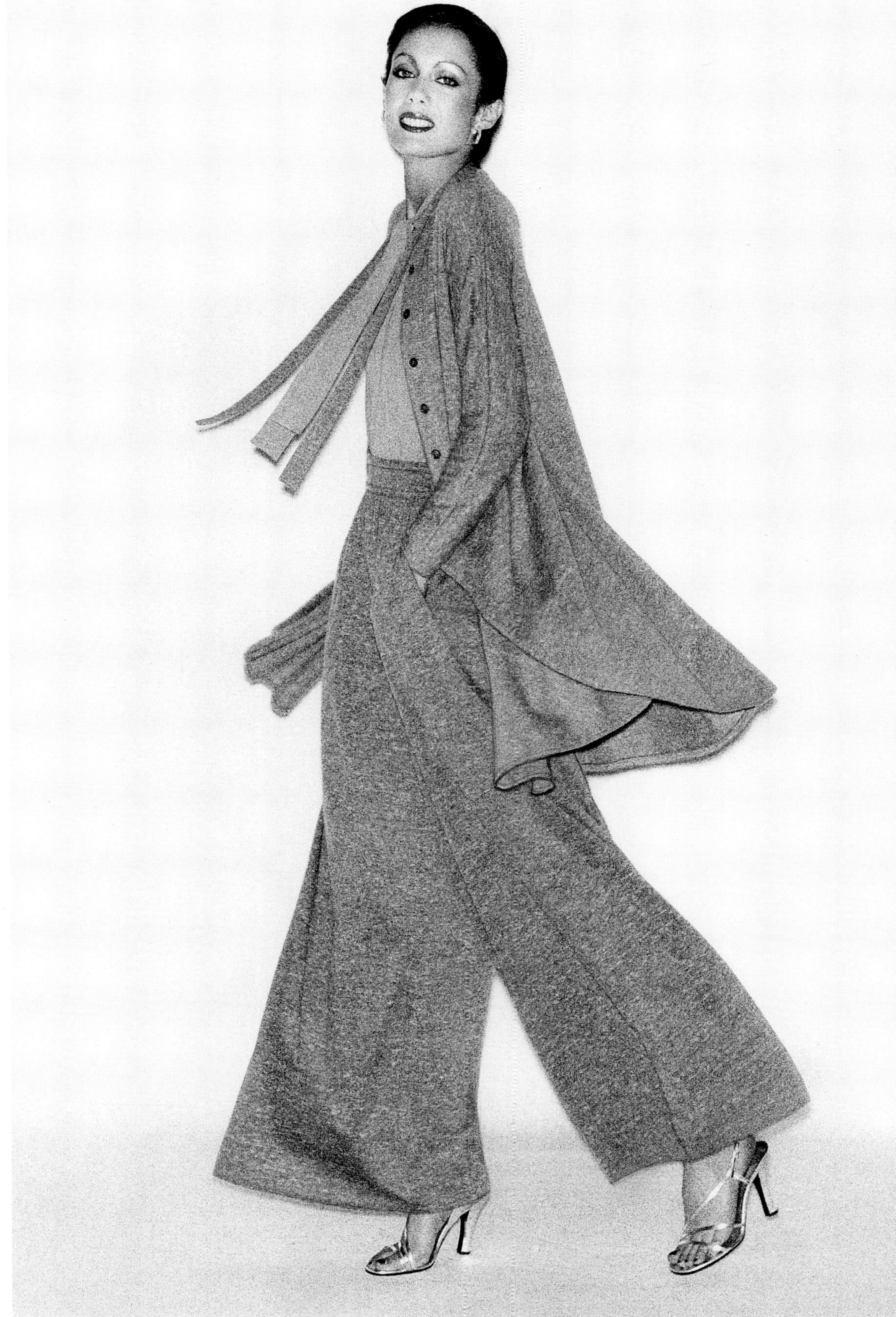

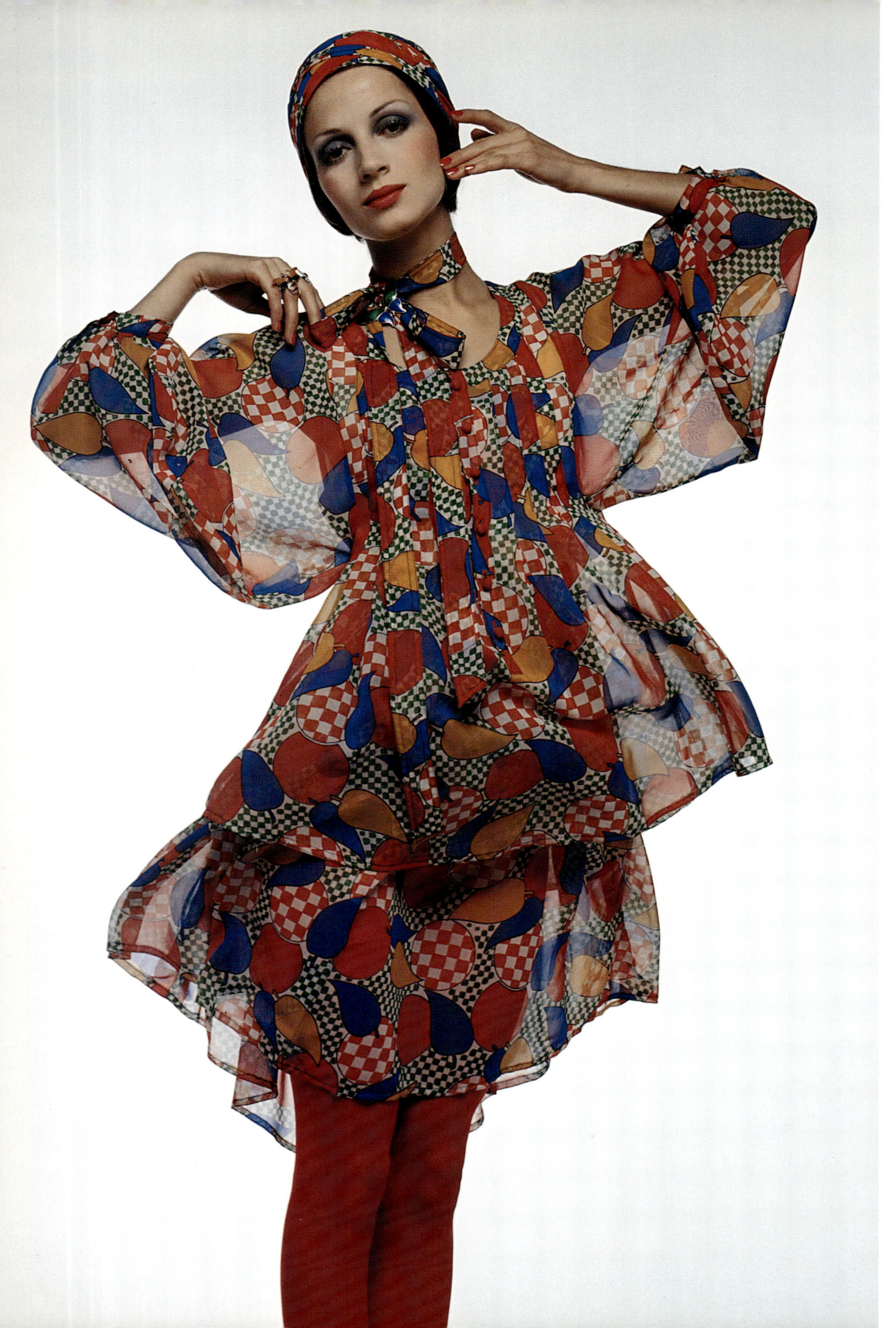

**LEFT** Balloon-sleeve smock tucked to the waist with dipping skirt in 'Apples and Pears' printed georgette, matching cap and tie. *Vogue*, April 1972. Photograph: Barry Lategan/Vogue. © The Condé Nast Publications Ltd. **OPPOSITE** Seventies glamour – a dress to dance in. Black jersey with flared skirt, black suede bolero with wide, short sleeves finished in silvered snakeskin. *Vogue*, August 1972. Photograph: Clive Arrowsmith/Vogue. © The Condé Nast Publications Ltd.

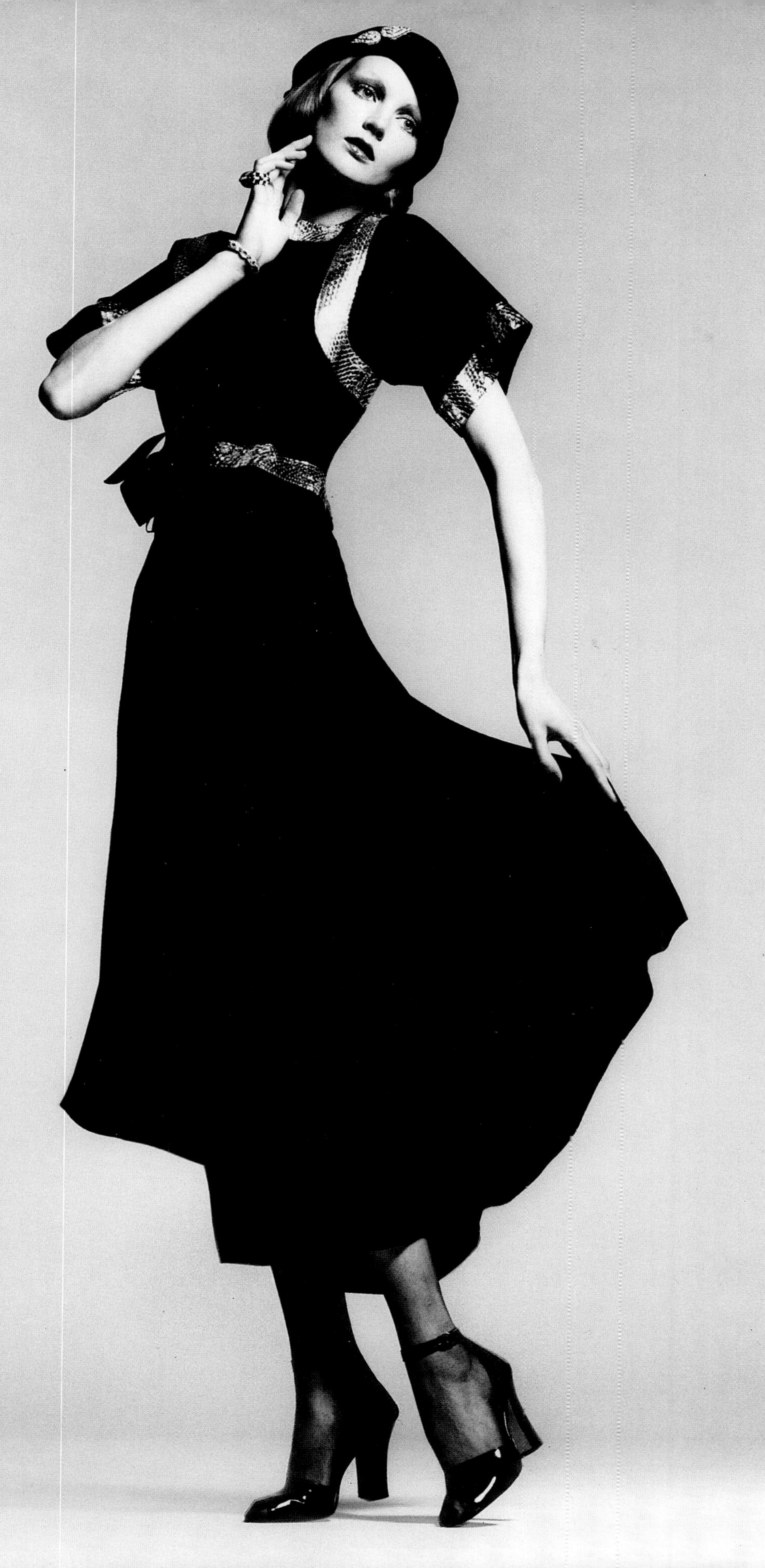

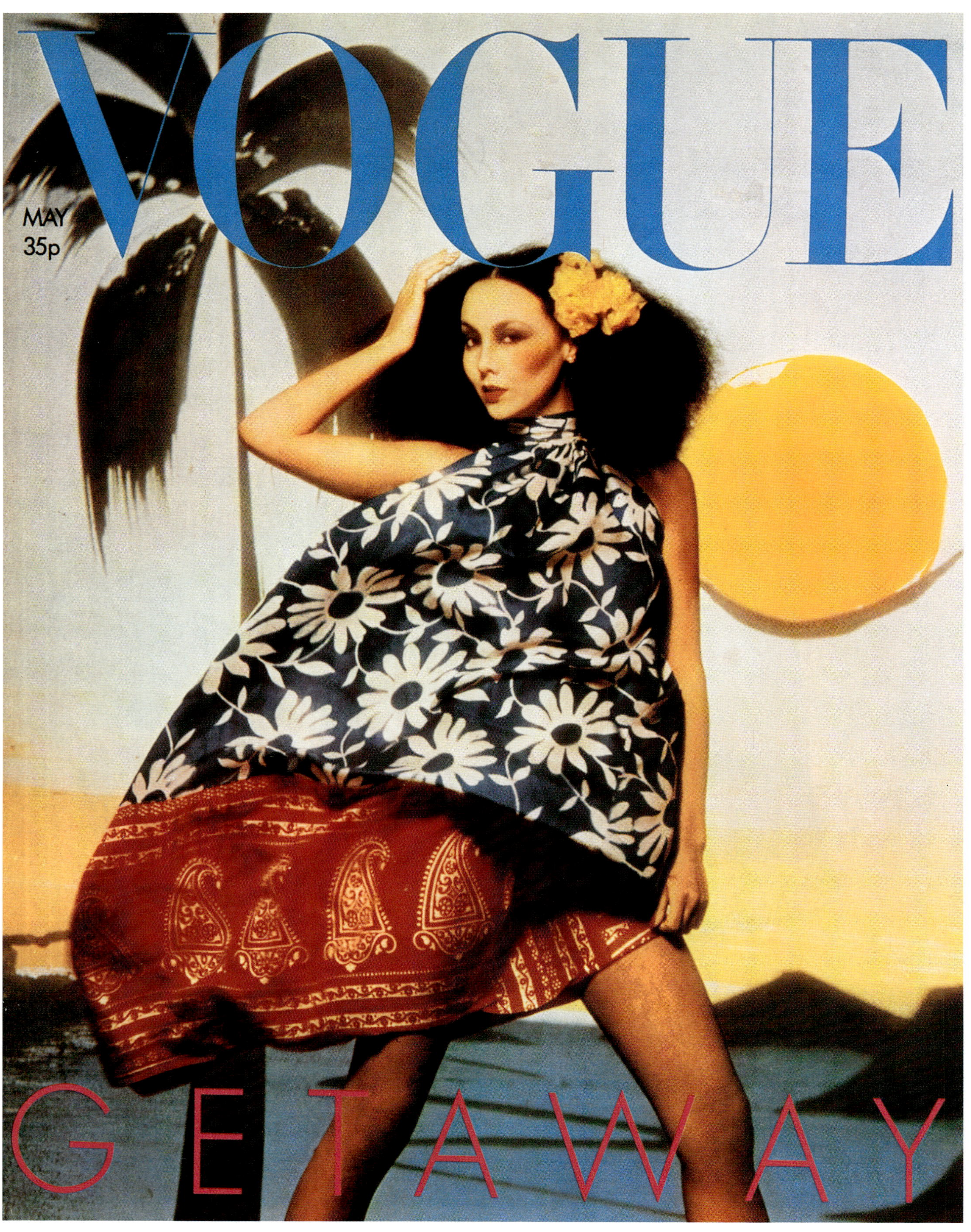
VOGUE
MAY
35p
GETAWAY

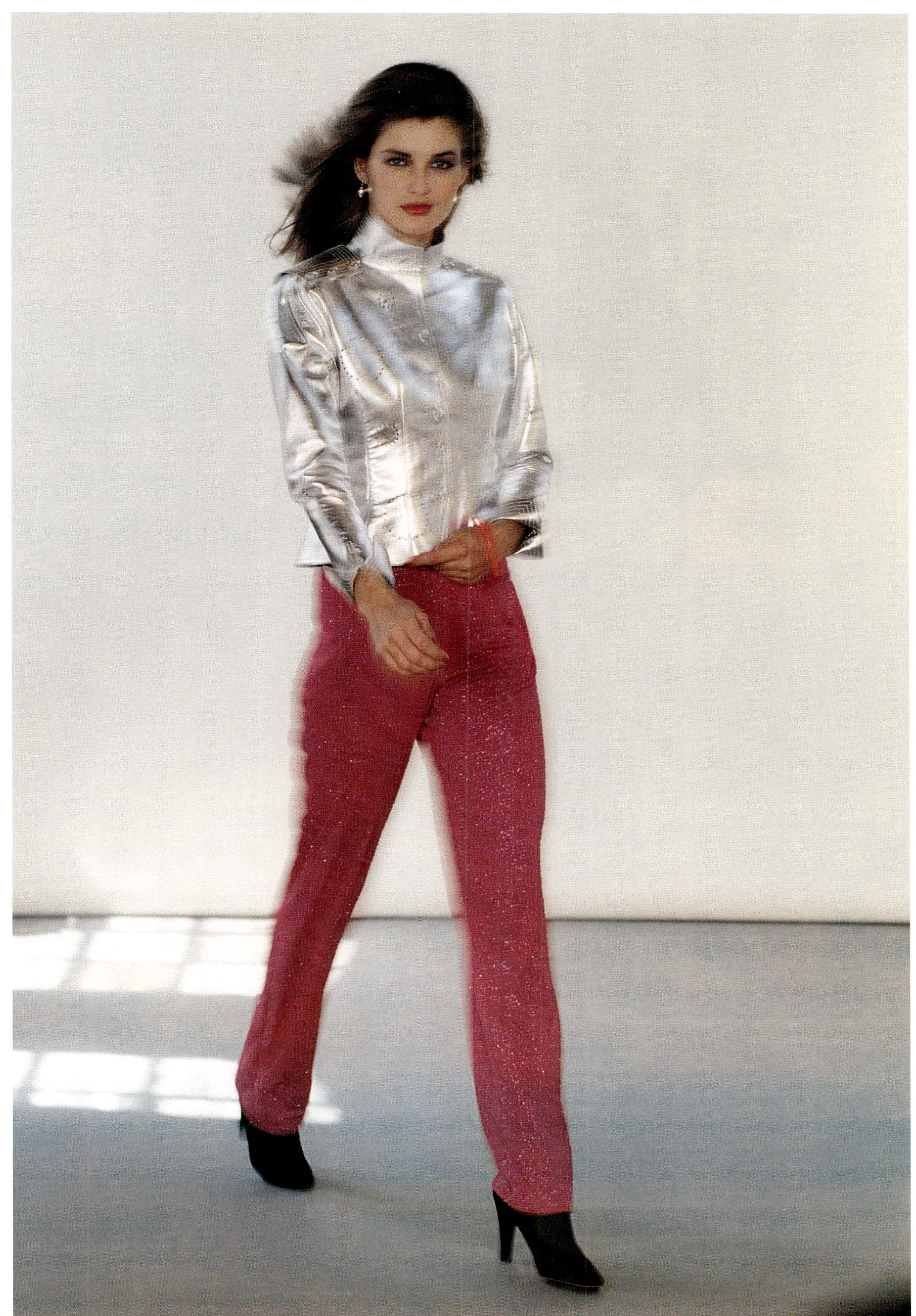

**OPPOSITE** Marie Helvin in "Jean Muir's scarf of a dress" with daisy and paisley designs in silk, photographed for the cover of *Vogue*, May 1974. Photograph: David Bailey/Vogue. © The Condé Nast Publications Ltd. **RIGHT** Jacket in punched silver leather with clear Perspex buttons, shocking pink glitter-flocked jersey trousers, featured on the cover and inside *Vogue*, September 1979. Photograph: Eric Boman/Vogue. © The Condé Nast Publications Ltd.

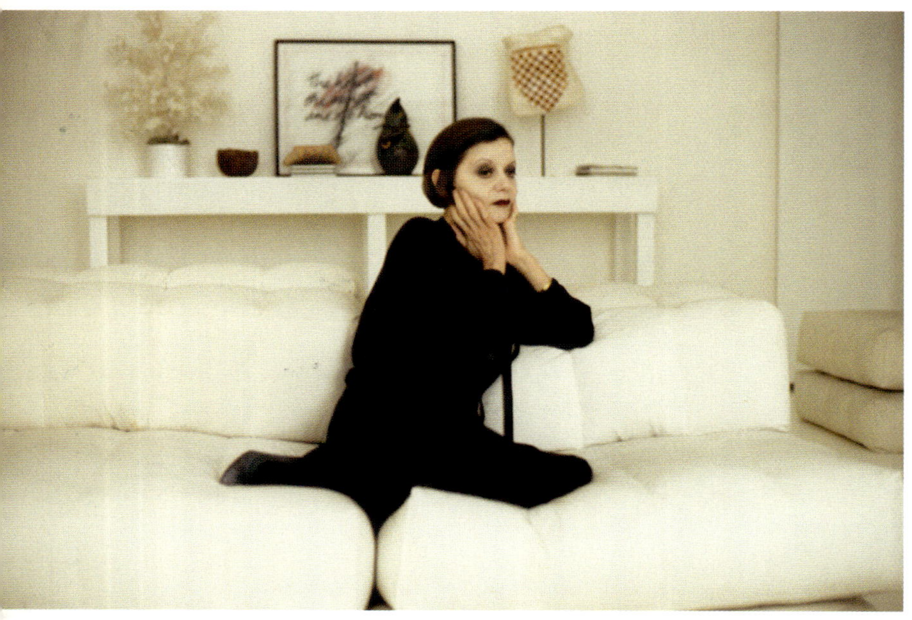

## EIGHTIES: CONSOLIDATION

In a turnaround from the seventies, the eighties were a period of boom, marked by conspicuous consumption: power and money represented glamour. The ostentation and excess were typified by the cult of the logo as status symbol, and by power dressing with exaggerated shoulder pads.

Despite the understated quality of her collections, Muir's upward trajectory continued with more and more awards and titles, including a CBE in 1984. Her collections in the latter part of the decade were influenced by the success of her 1988 Australian Bicentennial collection.

In May 1980 the Jean Muir exhibition opened at Lotherton Hall, Aberford, a satellite venue of the Leeds Art Galleries. This was the first exhibition in Britain to be devoted to the work of a living dress designer, an honour and an indication of Jean Muir's status and the respect in which she was held.

Initiated and curated by Peter Walton and Michael Sheppard, Keeper and Curator of Leeds City Art Galleries, it also had major input from Jean Muir. From the recreation of her workroom environment to the clothes and accessories themselves, it was a rich and educational experience that offered the visitor a highly visual glimpse of Jean Muir's work and her design philosophy. Selected artists' work adorned the walls: John Bratby's portrait of Jean Muir, Anthony Green's painting of 'Jean Muir Checking Buttons' and Patrick Procktor's portrait of the actress Jill Bennett wearing a Jean Muir jersey dress. These were complemented by photographer Shirley Beljon's portraits of Muir and images of personalities wearing her clothes. Lady Antonia Fraser, Bridget Riley, and Sir Roy Strong were among those who contributed essays to the special exhibition booklet, whilst Muir's own text was illustrated with drawings by the artist, David Gentleman.

Reviews were universally glowing. More than twenty thousand people visited the first venue in Leeds alone, and the exhibition reached a far wider audience when it subsequently opened in Birmingham, Belfast, Bath and Stoke-on-Trent. A feature in the *Arts Review* magazine in June 1981 described the exhibition: "This is a world apart – a world of superb craftsmanship.... Is this glamour, sex, haute couture, ready-to-wear? It is all of them and more!"

In the early part of the decade, Jean Muir introduced a number of specialist collections each with its own label. JM at Home, a collection of sumptuous

**ABOVE** More of Muir at home in navy jersey. Photograph & © David King. **OPPOSITE** Supermodel Naomi Campbell in sunflower yellow wool coat buttoned and buckled in scarlet Perspex, inspired by Muir's Australian collection. *Vogue*, January 1988. Photograph: Eddy Kohli/Vogue. © The Condé Nast Publications Ltd.

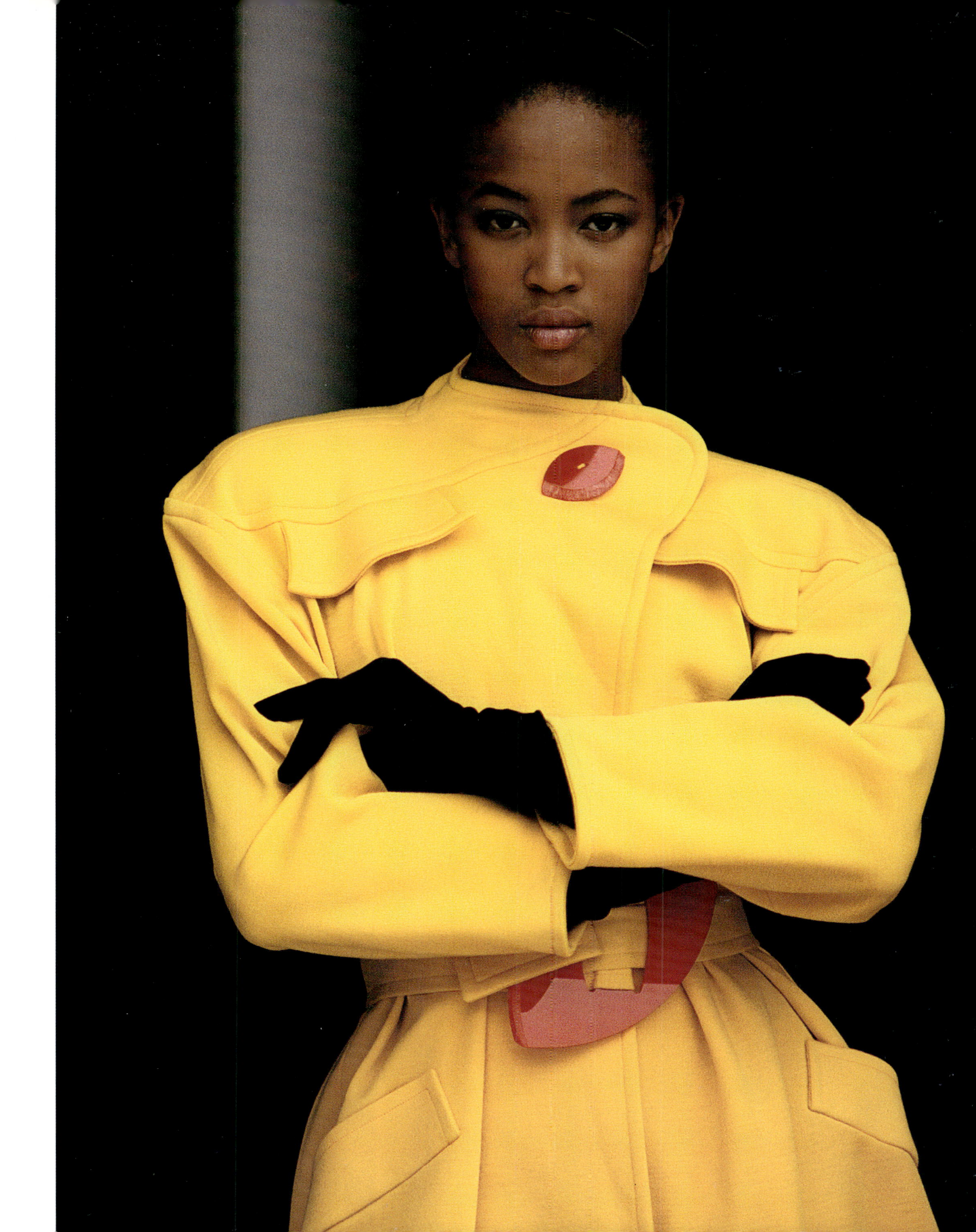

lounging robes, relaxed pyjama-style tops and trousers, and dressing gowns in silk satin, silk crêpe de Chine or cashmere, became the inspiration for JM for Men. This collection came into being when Harry Leuckert, half in fun, demanded to know, "When will *I* get something?!" The result – similarly luxurious cashmere knitwear, both plain and patterned intarsias, toning trousers in flannel, worsted and tweed, smoking jackets in brocade or moiré, and cashmere dressing gowns. Accessories included men's slippers, wallets in Macclesfield tie silk and sterling silver cufflinks.

Jean Muir was aware that the exclusive cachet and price point of her collection excluded many of her would-be customers. She was keen to embrace those who admired and aspired to her clothes but could not necessarily afford them. It was her interaction with visitors to the 1980 Jean Muir exhibition, many of whom brought their *Vogue* patterns to be autographed, that convinced her that there was an opportunity for diversification.

In Spring 1983, JM in Cotton was launched. Primarily made in white, navy, and black plain and pique cottons, it was consciously set at a lower price point than the Main line collection. Carrying on her egalitarian theme, JM in Wool followed for the Autumn.

JM in Cotton and JM in Wool were the precursors to the Jean Muir Studio Collection, launched in the mid-eighties. It was essentially designed by students contracted by Muir, who also oversaw all their work. These clothes had a different feel, outline, and price point to the Muir Main line, but according to Jean Muir, who disliked the term, it was not a lesser 'diffusion' line.

Though the shapes had a simpler construction, nevertheless, cut and original detail were all-important and good quality was still the overriding principle. Single wool crepe was used where the Main used double; lamb's-wool and merino yarns where the Main had cashmere; and Liberty viscose or wool prints where the Main had silk.

From the late eighties to the mid-nineties, Muir herself became more directly involved in the design of the Studio Collection, and as she did, it became increasingly popular. She simplified and re-interpreted previous shapes from her Main collection. Many of the Muir stockists also stocked the less expensive Studio Collection, offering their customers a more casual alternative.

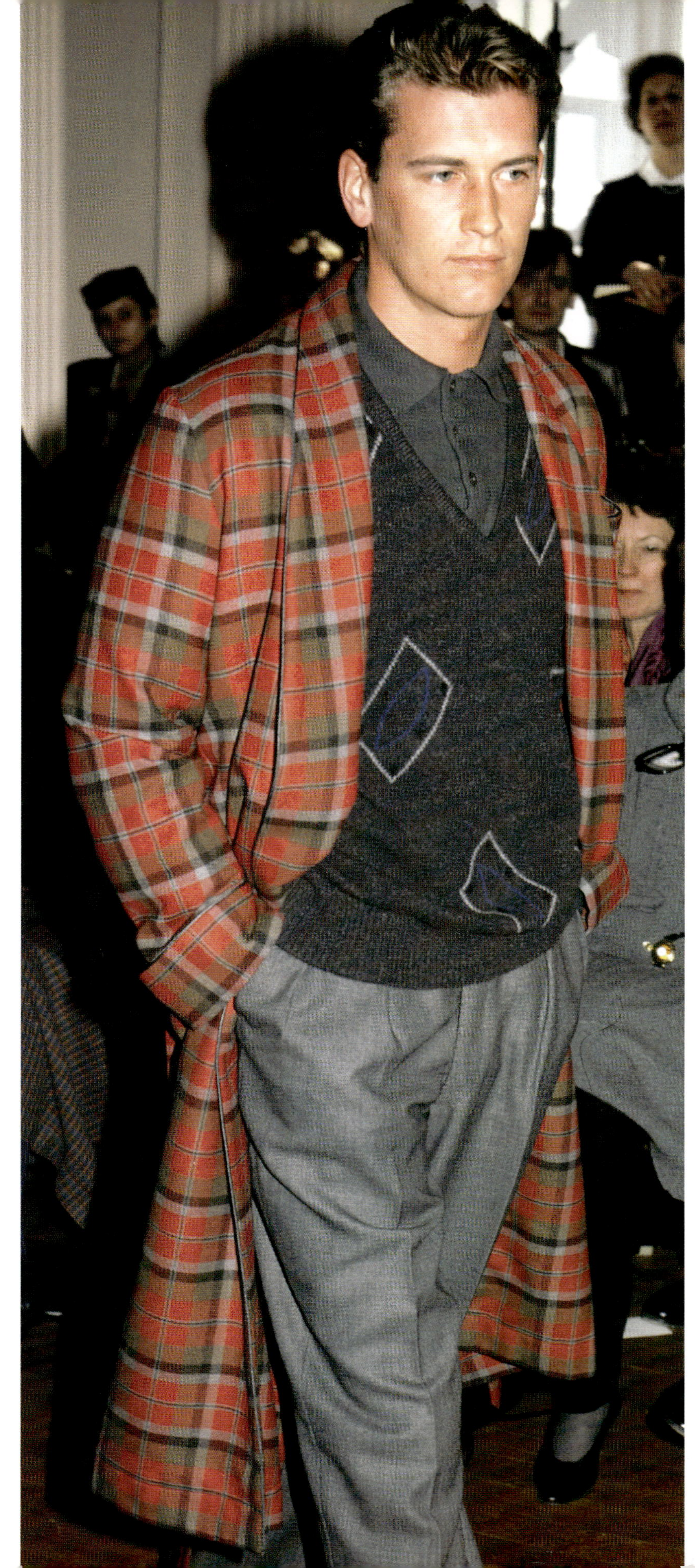

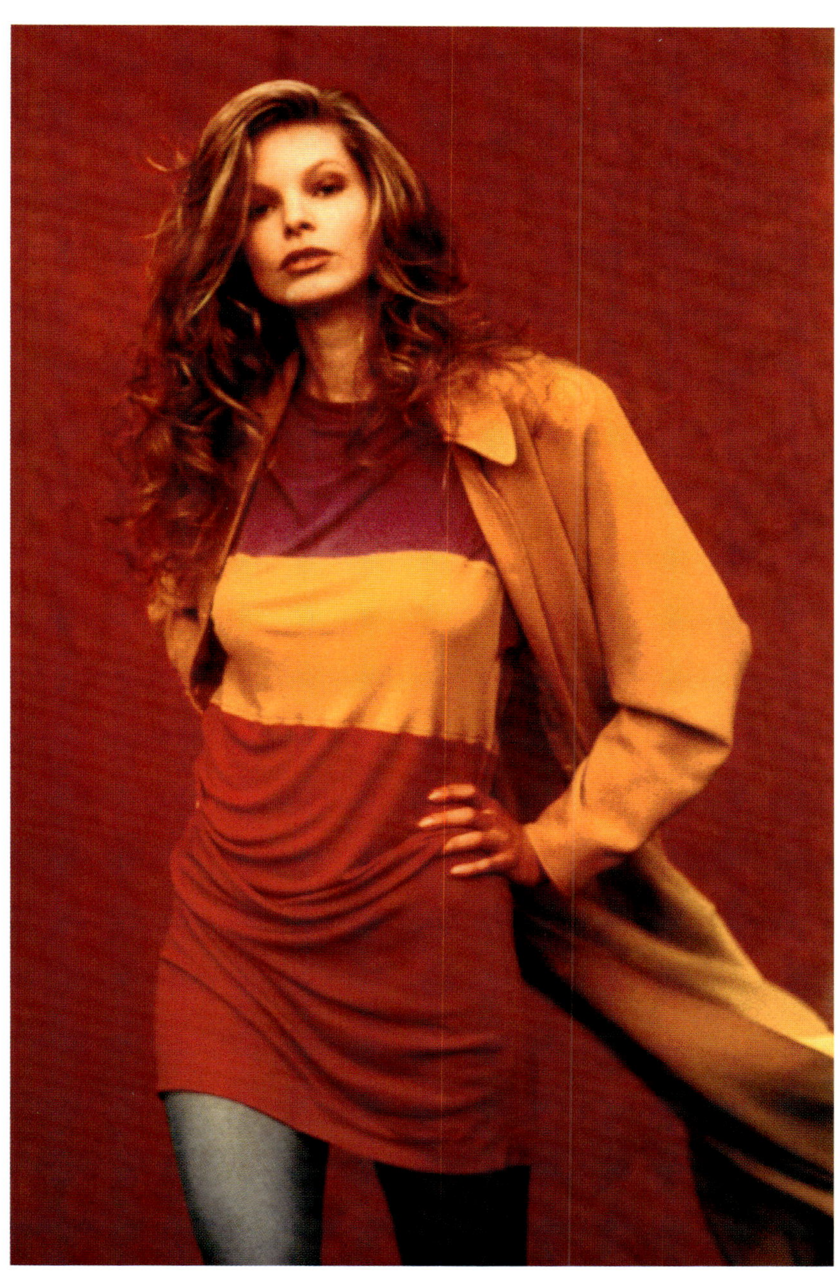

**OPPOSITE** JM for Men: layers of cashmere – plaid dressing gown, intarsia V-neck sweater, polo shirt, and trousers, Autumn 1985. Photograph & © Niall McInerney. **ABOVE LEFT** Tunic dress in colour-blocked jersey with unstructured coat in mustard suede. Spring 1989. **ABOVE RIGHT** "The new cool…the untrammelled perfection of light-catching ice-pale satin". Magnolia silk satin robe, Jean Muir at Home, *Vogue*, April 1984. Photograph: Lothar Schmid/Vogue. © The Condé Nast Publications Ltd.

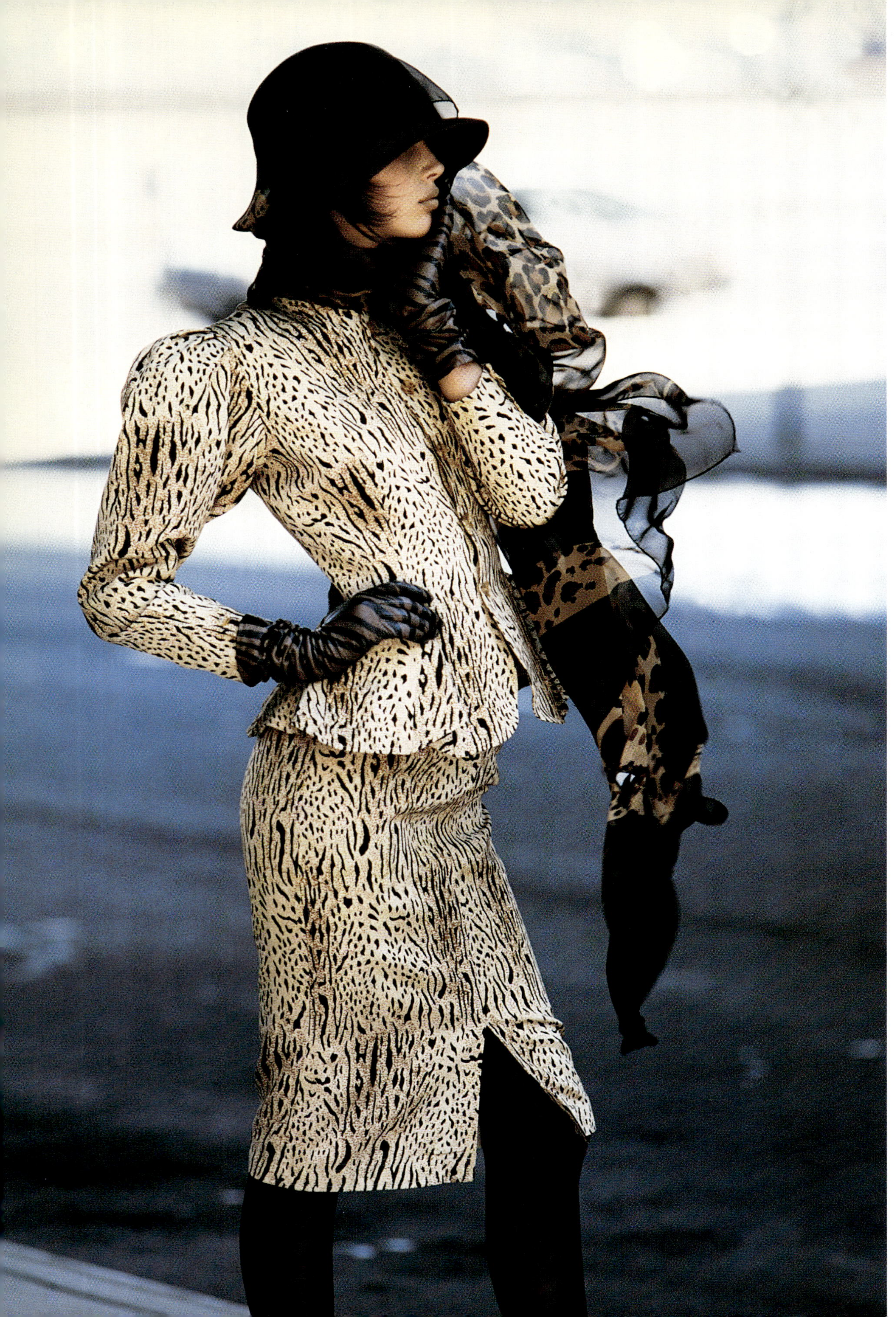

**LEFT** Supermodel, Christy Turlington, wears curvy peplum jacket with power shoulders to accentuate the waist, matching front-split skirt in leopard print silk faille. *Vogue*, September 1986. Photograph: Patrick Demarchelier/Vogue. © The Condé Nast Publications Ltd.

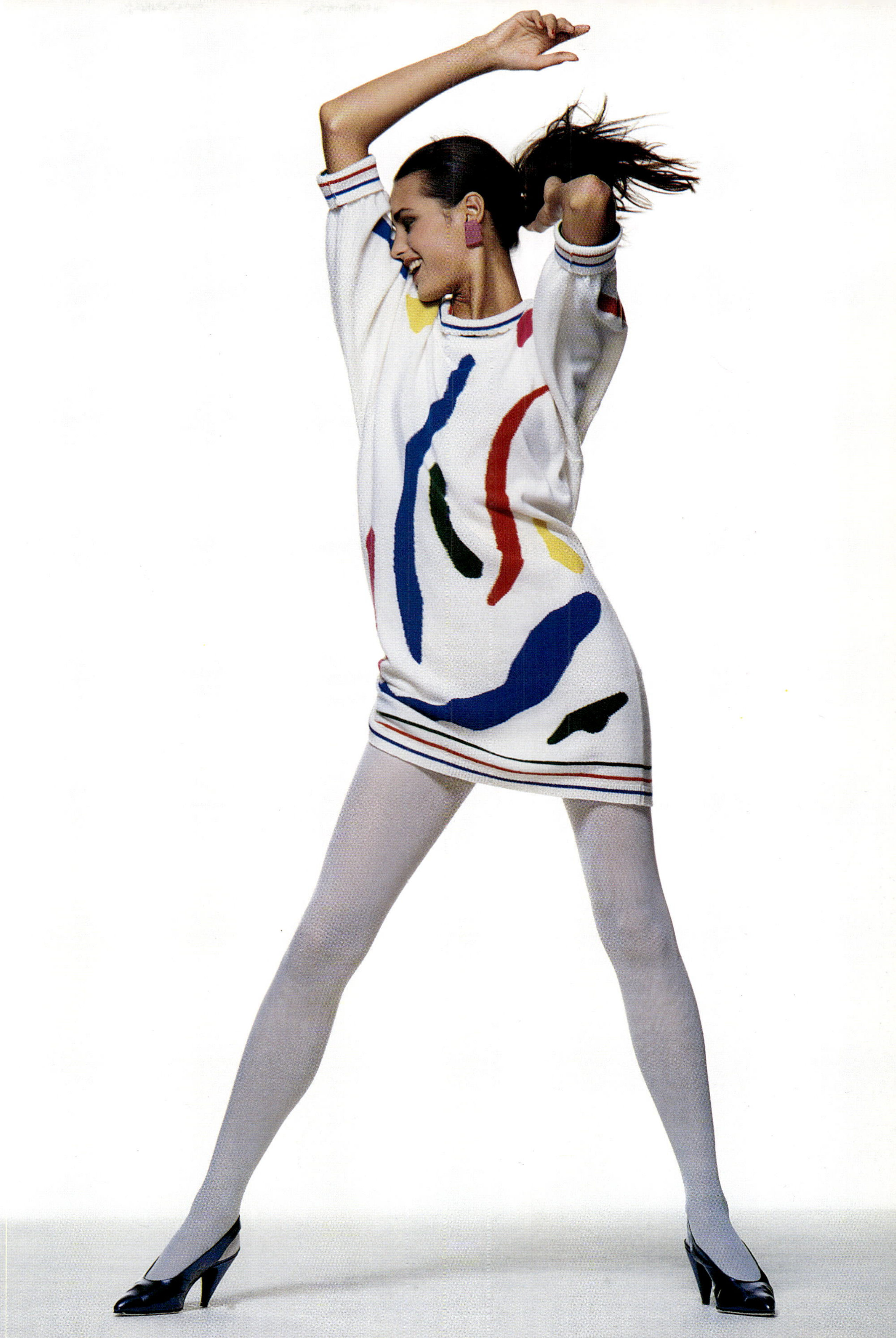

**RIGHT** Supermodel, Yasmin le Bon, wears white cashmere intarsia tunic with multicolour abstract design inspired by Muir's 1988 Australian collection, January 1989. Photograph: Robert Erdmann/Vogue. © The Condé Nast Publications Ltd.

# NINETIES: CELEBRATIONS & DIVERSIFICATIONS

The nineties saw a move away from the excess of the eighties to a new minimalism, which was very much in tune with Miss Muir's own philosophy. She began the decade by celebrating the twenty-fifth anniversary of her company in 1991, which was widely acknowledged in the international press. Fashion Editor Bernadine Morris writing on the occasion for *The New York Times* called Muir "The jewel in the crown of British fashion".

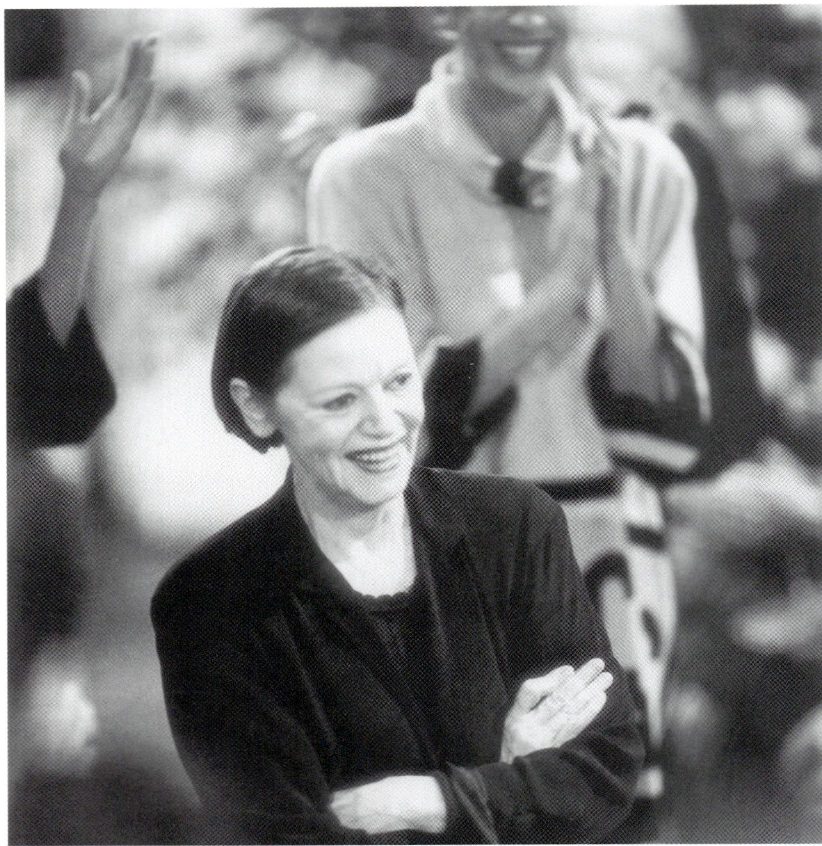

In Spring 1993 Jean Muir was the subject of a three-part Channel 4 documentary series, a unique portrayal of a designer at work. Tracing the design of her Spring collection, it revealed the varied artistic and creative processes involved, the level of craftsmanship, and the overriding discipline required in her search for perfection.

Also in 1993 Miss Muir was elected Master of the Faculty of Royal Designers for Industry, a highly prestigious title and position. In her inimitable style she immediately set about galvanising the Faculty with a series of "bridge-building" dinners at which engineers, product designers and graphic designers, would be seated next to bankers and politicians, artists and museum directors with the aim of raising the profile of the RDIs and the role of design itself. As an extension of her role she wrote her significant 'Manifesto for Real Design' article in *The Sunday Times* in 1994, and embarked on a lecture tour.

One of her great enthusiasms was for improving the standing of contemporary design in the North East. She played a large part in transforming Belsay Hall, Northumberland, into an important centre for

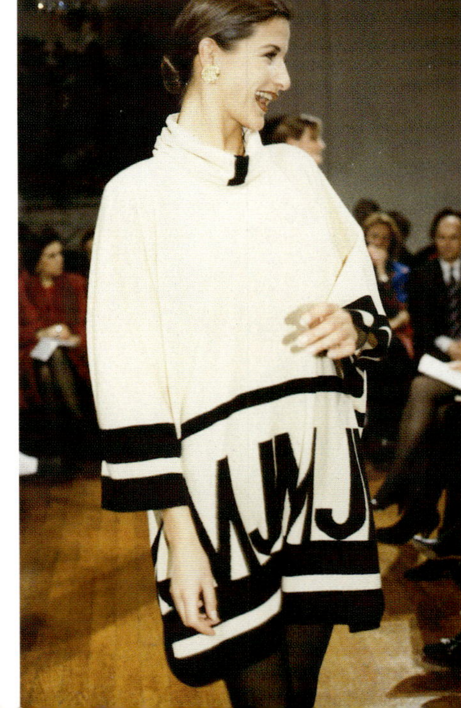

**ABOVE** Jean Muir receives a standing ovation in her Bruton Street showroom after her twenty-fifth anniversary show in 1991, the year Bergdorf Goodman in New York devoted its entire run of 5th Avenue windows to this collection. **OPPOSITE, TOP** Jean Muir's face sketch, which she used as a design motif on cashmere and jersey styles, as well as the invitation for her 25th anniversary show, Autumn 1991. ©Jean Muir Ltd. **RIGHT** Designs from the 25th anniversary collection incorporating stripes, swirls, Jean Muir's initials and the face sketch, Autumn 1991. Photographs & © Niall McInerney and Chris Moore.

contemporary design. The early nineteenth century neoclassical stone house, which she knew well, had fallen into disrepair. She lobbied English Heritage, until she had persuaded them to promote the building as a revitalised popular local and national resource, which it now is. The hugely successful 2004 Fashion at Belsay exhibition, a series of installations by selected British fashion designers, was in part a tribute to Muir's dedication to Belsay Hall. It showcased a trio of her early matte jersey dresses together with examples of her Australian Bicentennial collection in wool, many of which had been made nearby in the Borders area.

For her final collection, Autumn/Winter 1995, Miss Muir chose to showcase the clothes at an evening soiree at her Bruton Street showroom. The theme was black and red and the collection was recorded backstage by the international catwalk photographer Chris Moore.

As well as being thrilled to receive Honorary Degrees from various universities in the early nineties, the three things that gave Muir particular pleasure at this time were her company's twenty-fifth anniversary, the Channel 4 television series, and her role as Master of the Faculty of Royal Designers for Industry. Perhaps more than anything, however, it is her clothes that speak most eloquently for her legacy and will endure as a lasting testament to her achievements.

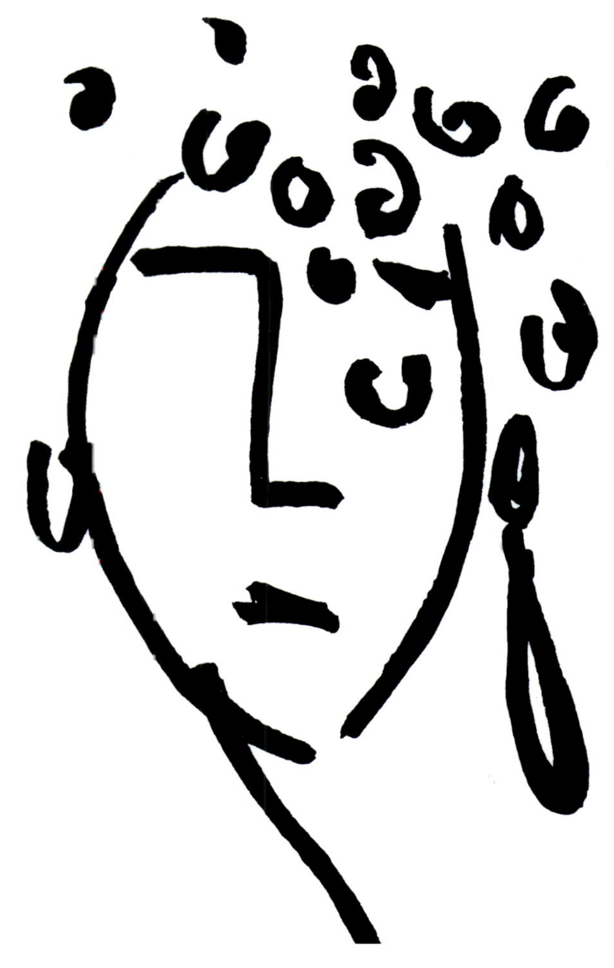

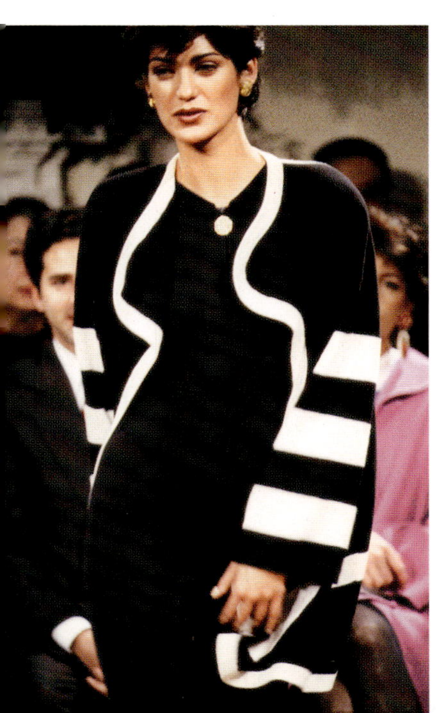

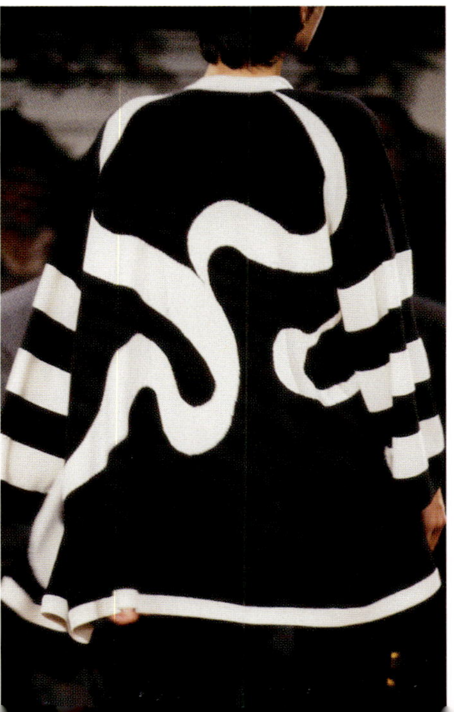

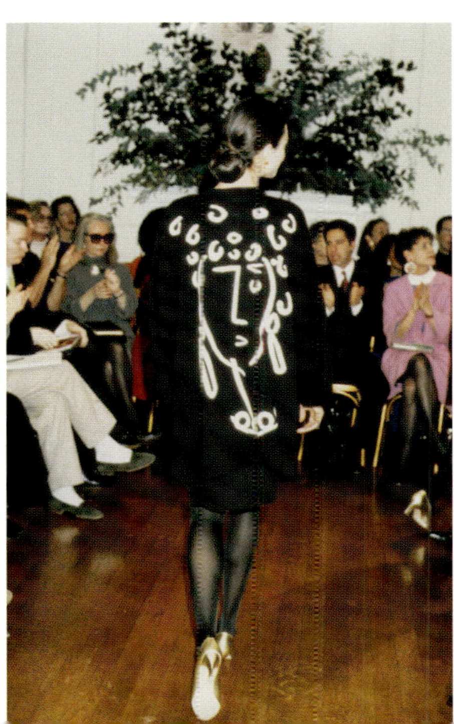

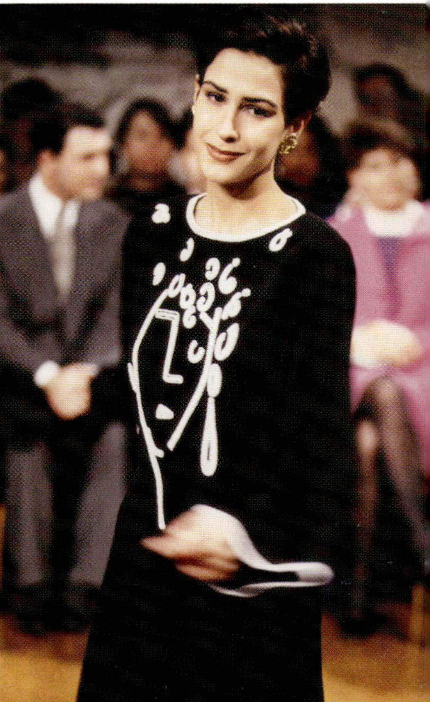

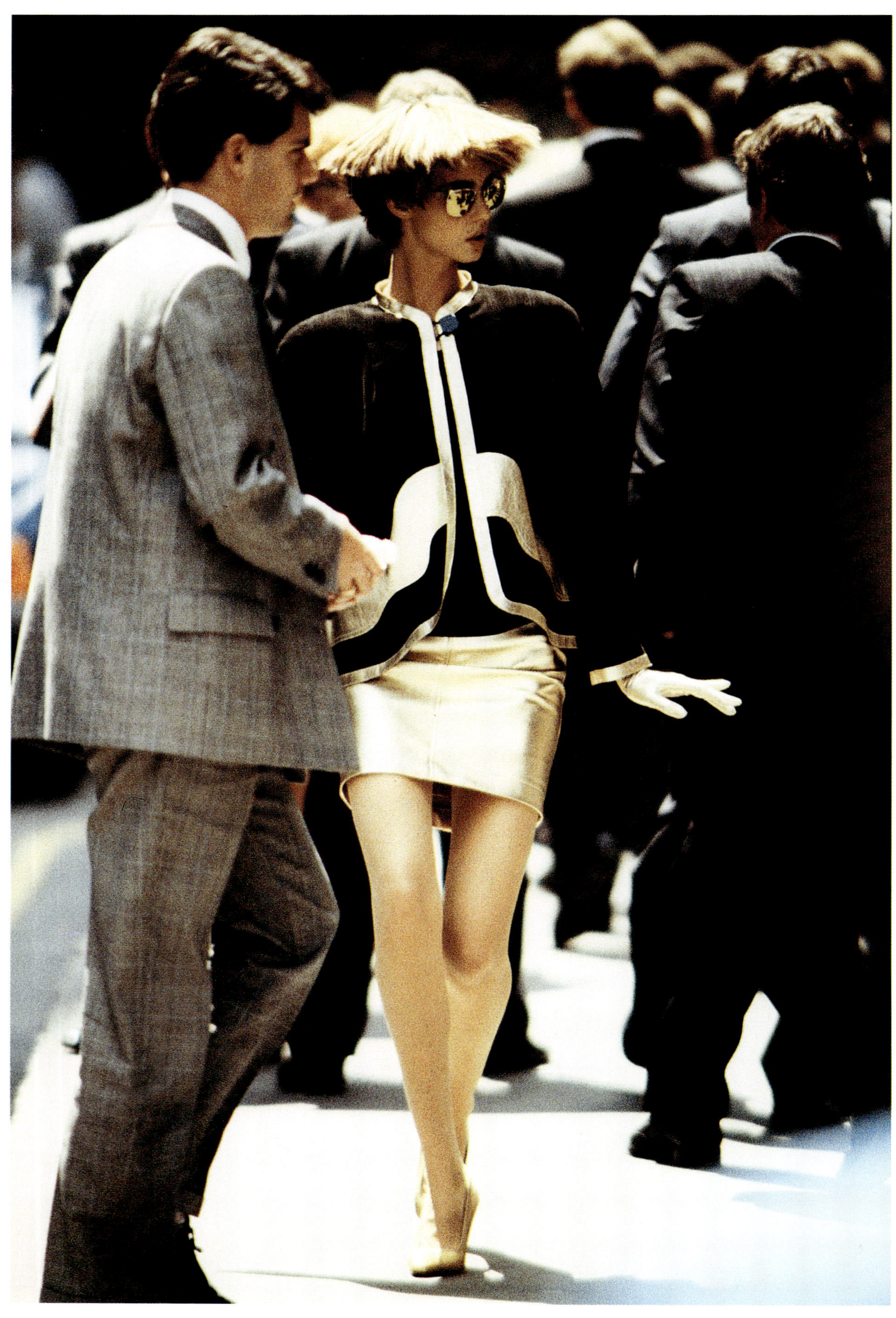

**LEFT** Maximum impact: black suede jacket with gold metallic leather trim, matching gold leather skirt, September 1990. Photograph: Eddy Kohli/Vogue. © The Condé Nast Publications Ltd.

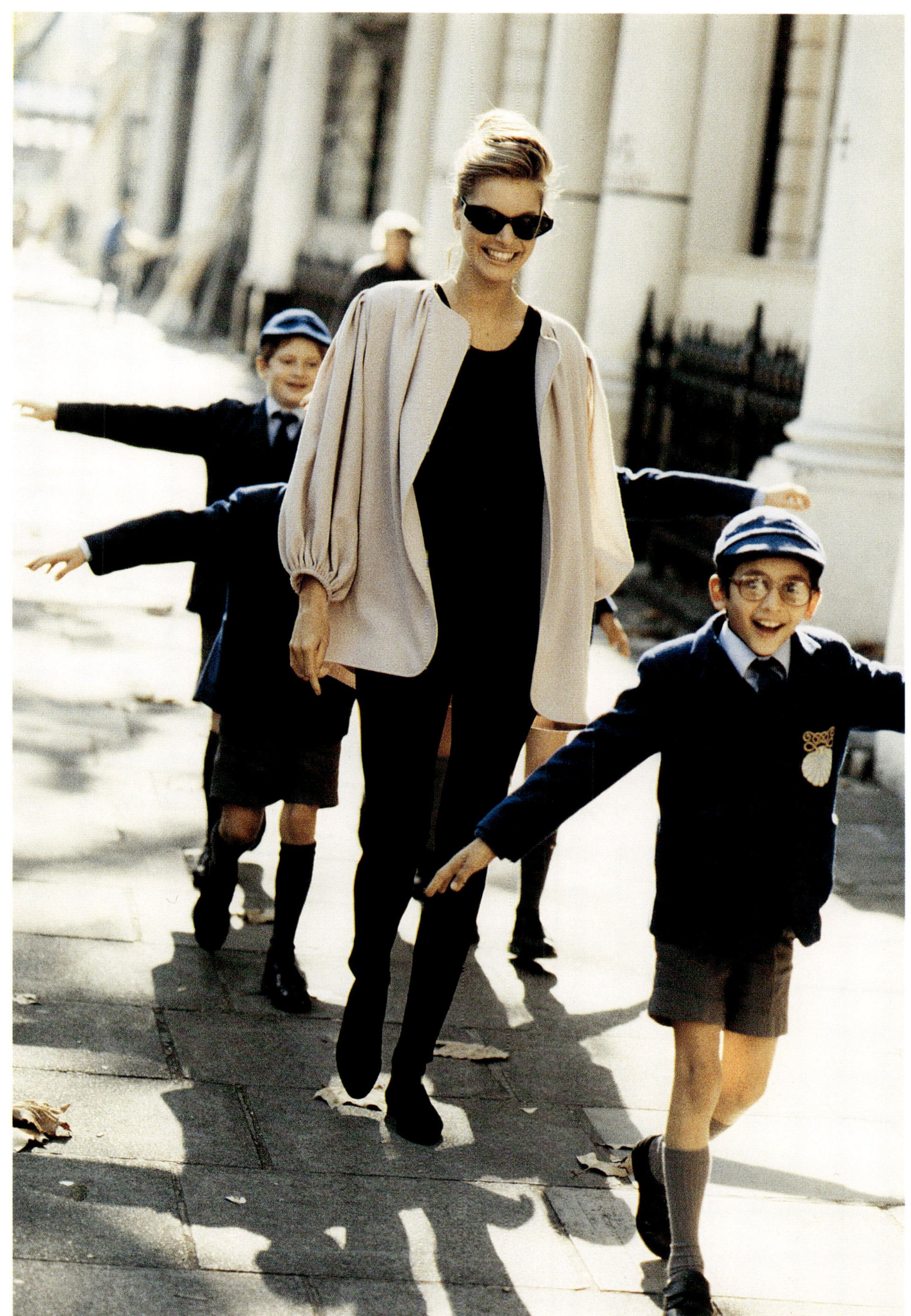

**RIGHT** "Relaxed urbanity", *Vogue*, January 1990, tea rose double wool crepe jacket over black jersey vest and leggings. Photograph: Neil Kirk/Vogue. © The Condé Nast Publications Ltd.

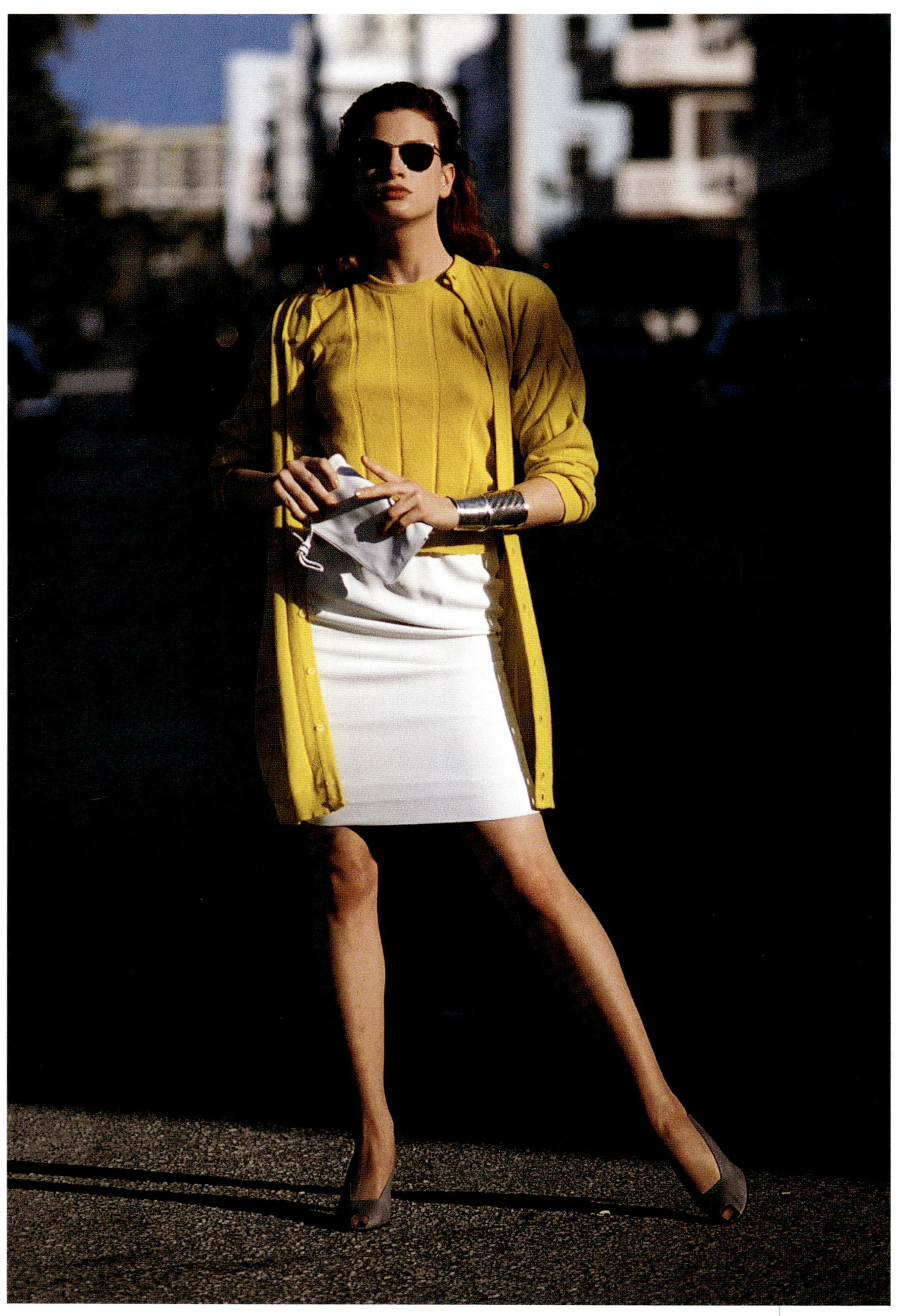

**LEFT** Kristen McMenamy in wide rib cashmere in zingy citron – one of Jean Muir's favourite knitwear colours – short-sleeve t-shirt sweater with long cardigan, skirt in white double matte jersey, Photograph: Neil Kirk/Vogue.

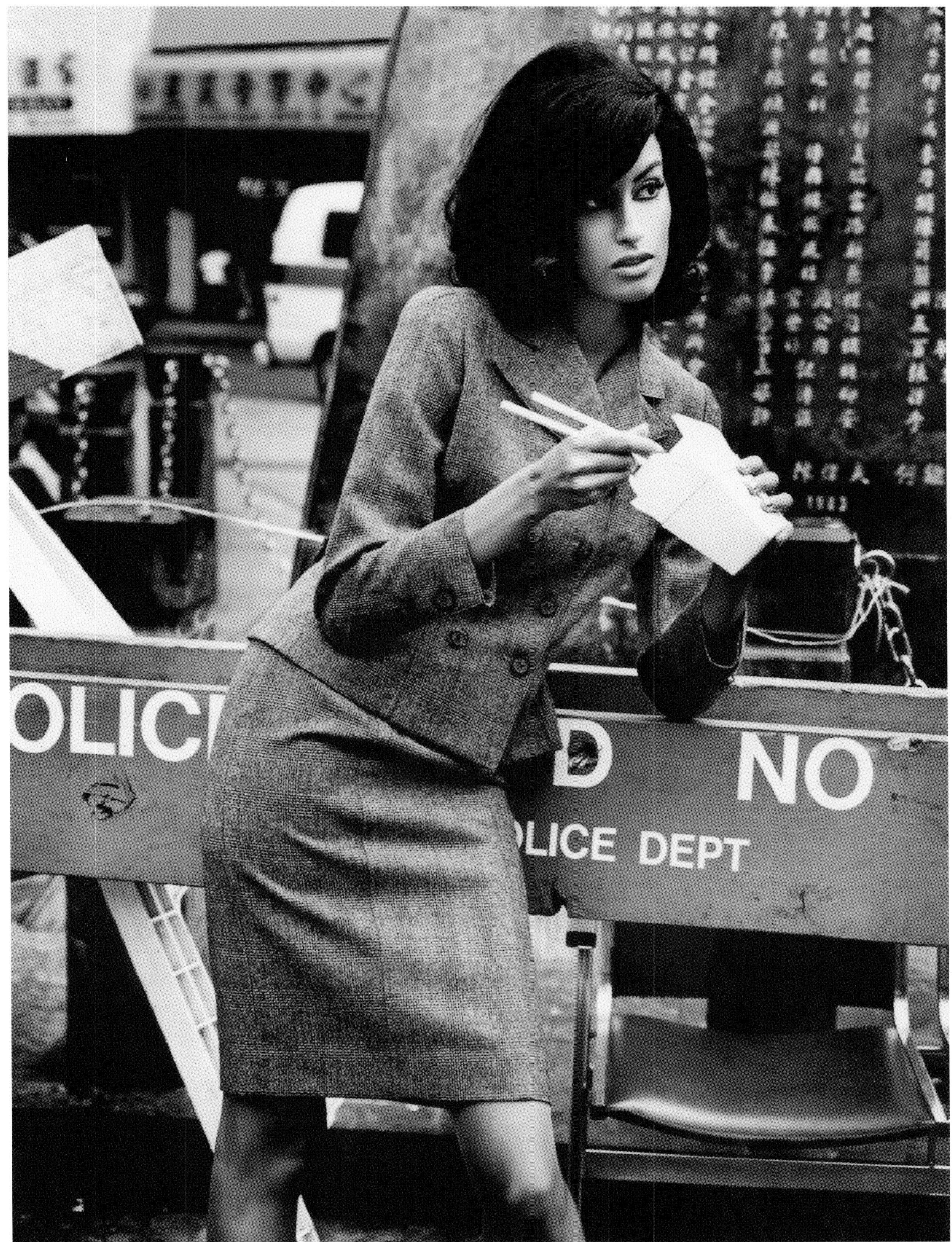


**RIGHT** Yasmeen Ghauri wears neat suit in grey check tweed. High lapels on a short double-breasted jacket, seamed tapered skirt, *Marie Claire*, November 1995.

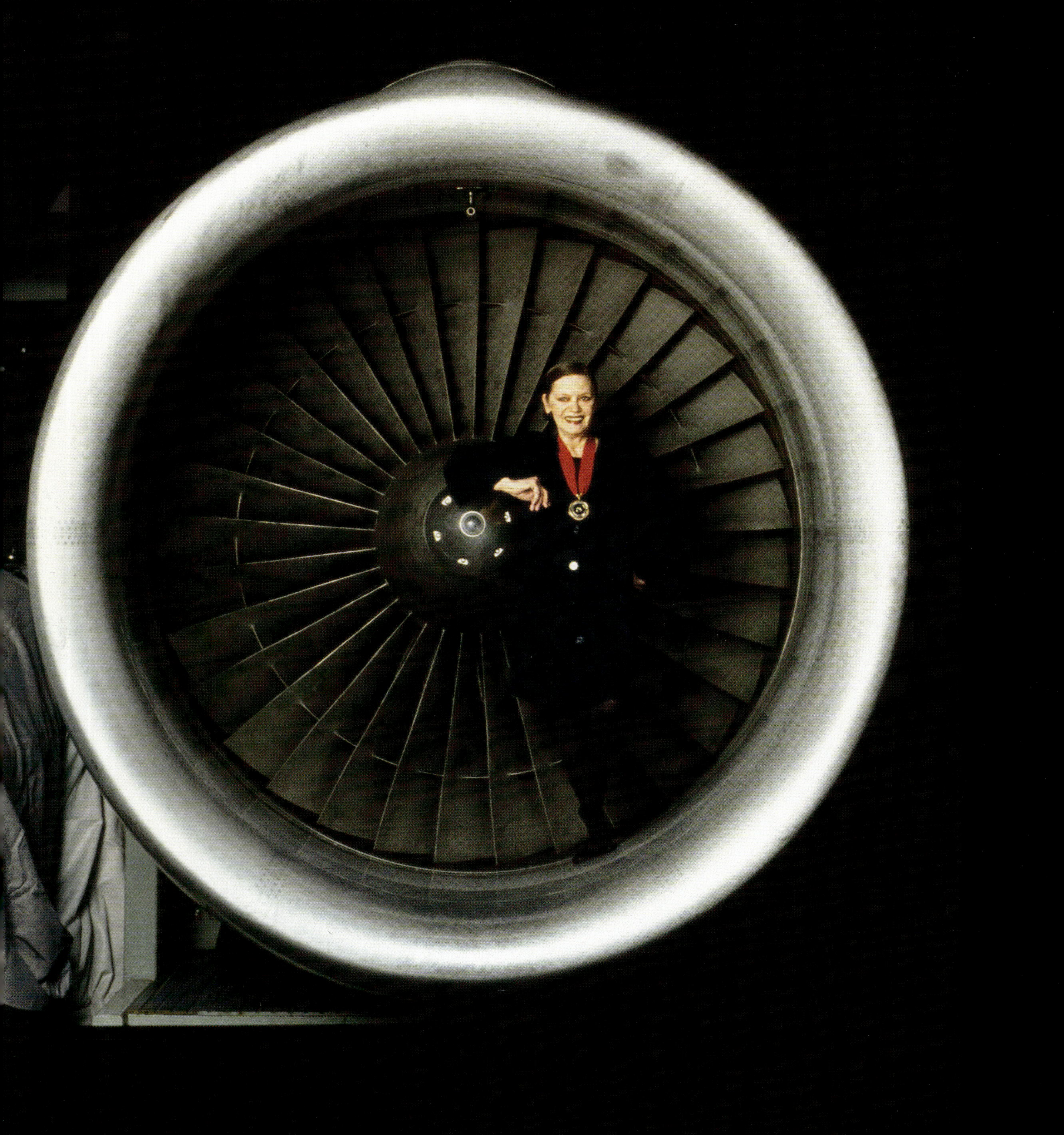

Chapter Three

# "FASHION IS NOT ART IT IS INDUSTRY"

JEAN MUIR

“Fashion is a very serious craft, and an important one”

JEAN MUIR

**JEAN MUIR'S** favourite quote was: "Proper attention to dress is a sign of self respect and respect for the order of things." To Jean Muir, dress is the way in which people present themselves, the way in which they register to others. Clothes are the result of an ever-changing desire and deep-seated instinct to decorate oneself. They reveal the individual image. As Muir liked to comment, with humour: "Clothes are the way people make pictures of themselves – that others have to look at!"

Clothes suit climate, environment, and lifestyle. Clothes also affect behaviour – the fact that one knows one's clothes feel right, makes a difference to one's attitude, one's confidence and how one behaves and how others in turn behave to you. As a woman designing for other women, she appreciated the importance of comfort and practicality. "I've always hated fashion hanging on a skirt length," she said. "It's a pity these things are put on fashion."

Whilst she enjoyed quoting the fact that its definition in the Greater Oxford Dictionary required a span of six closely packed columns, Miss Muir always insisted 'fashion' would have more relevance within her own industry in its first straightforward interpretation, as a verb – to fashion, to make, the art and process of making, implying craft and skill. "I don't like the word designer, it has been debased. And what is better than to be a *maker?* It takes generosity of soul to make something well and the act of making creates something in the soul. You see it in artists and in craftspeople."

She preferred the title dressmaker. "In dressmaking" she said, "the design has to be made to wear, to fit, to be comfortable, to last, to be attractive, to enhance, and most of all to work on a body. Fashion is a very serious craft and an important one."

Muir was mindful that the skills required to keep her industry alive needed to be given more kudos, be revitalised and rekindled in the national psyche. She always respected the home dressmaker, perhaps because at heart she was one herself, and was thrilled at the success of her *Butterick* and *Vogue* couture paper patterns.

At her Farringdon Road headquarters, where she had moved her workrooms and offices in 1985, she opened up the Aladdin's cave of her fabric hoard, setting up a small fabric shop, the Turquoise Room, named after its vivid interior, which became a mecca for home dressmakers and students in the know. Here she would give up for sale an ever-changing selection of her special fabrics – sampling pieces, and short left-over lengths

**PAGE 56** Jean Muir at the Science Museum with a Rolls Royce RB-211 fanjet, wearing the Master's Medal of the Faculty of Royal Designers for Industry for *The Sunday Times* to accompany her 'Manifesto for Design' article, 6 March 1994. Photograph & © Paul Massey.

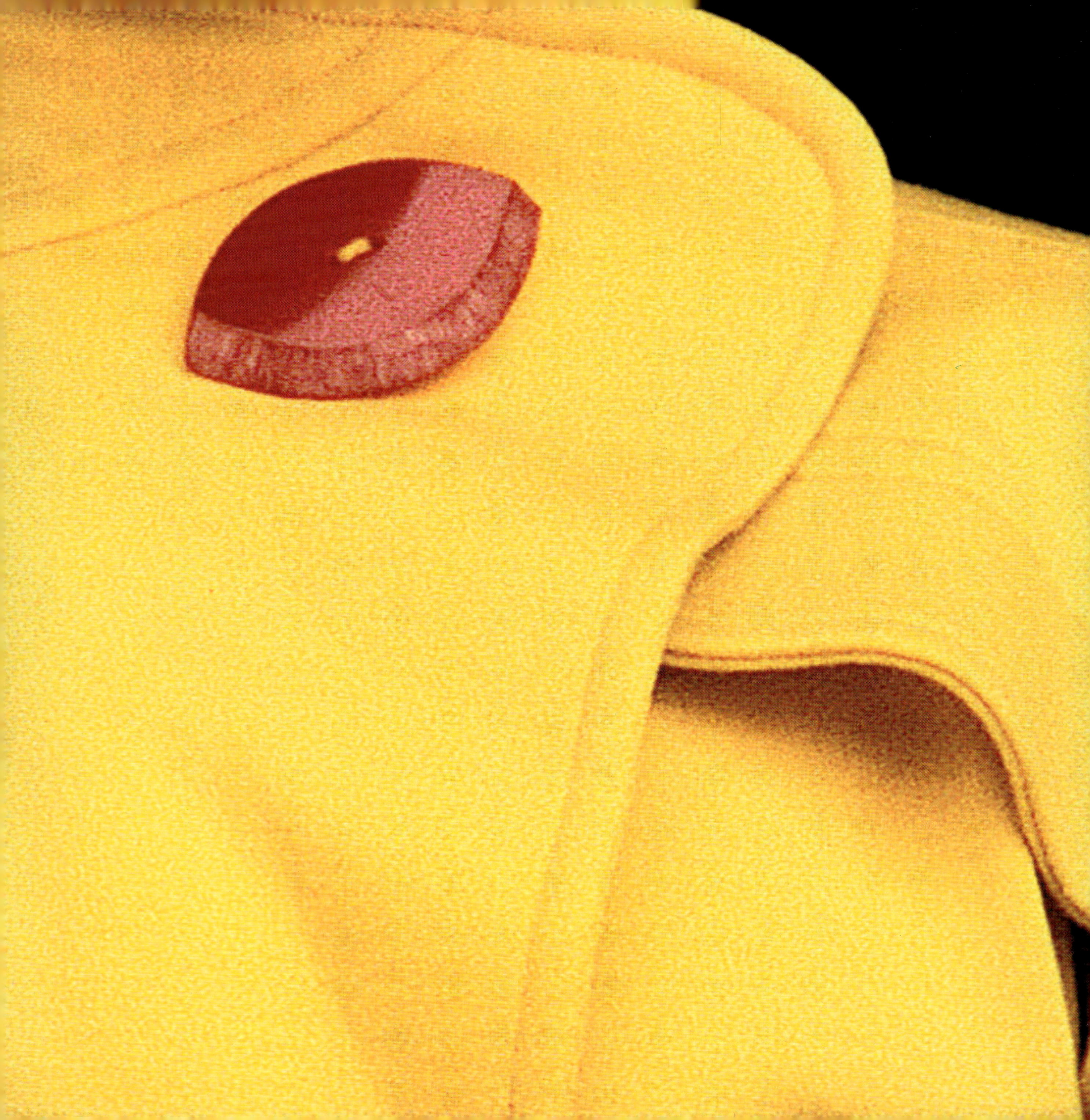

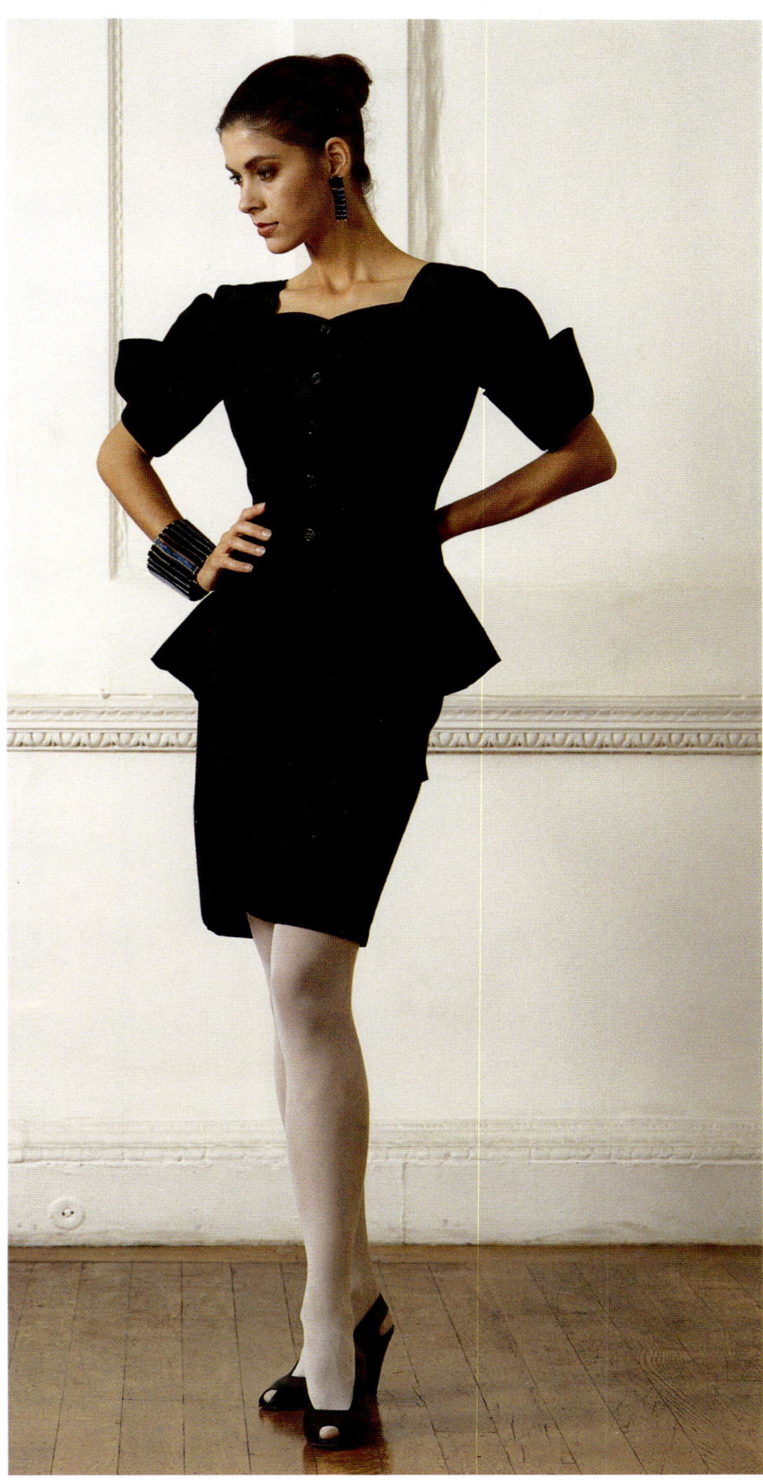

of exquisite silks and brocades, moiré, animal-printed angora, wools, tweeds, with an accompanying selection of buttons and trimmings. Miss Muir would sometimes make a detour from the private staircase that led to her fourth floor studio, much to the delight of her visitors. She was always unerringly courteous and interested – these were just as much her customers as the women who purchased her finished clothes in the shops.

Muir's was a down-to-earth, common sense approach, in which an intuitive sense of aesthetics, technical expertise, and commercial thought were totally integrated and balanced. As Muir herself explained, "I try never to compromise, either with something that is coldly commercial or overindulgent in flights of fancy."

She embraced commerce – "Commerciality is based upon excellence" – which she recognised was the basis of her business. "As far as making clothes is concerned, whilst one sees oneself as a craftsman, nonetheless, it's commerce. To a certain extent I always feel that the sort of aesthetic enjoyment that one gets is one's own private enjoyment in the doing of it, and if somebody recognises it, then that's lovely. But nonetheless, it's commerce. You're making clothes, manufacturing clothes. People have got to buy them, wear them. And that is what it is."

She described herself as an extremely pragmatic designer. "Progressively, making clothes for women in a modern world stems from a practical point of view – practical from a manufacturing viewpoint – practical from a wearing viewpoint – evolutionary not revolutionary." Her clothes prove the point – they are well made, they fit, they make sense to the wearer.

There was much she deplored about the '60s. "The two flimsy premises of the sixties – one that dress designing could be treated in fine art terms – the other, that the true craft of the trade was no longer necessary", and called for "a return to reality", insisting design education should be based on "more craft, less art." Muir memorably stated: "Fashion is not Art, it is Industry", a remark she qualified explaining that for her, "only when you really know your industry, really know your trade, can you then make it into what is your own kind of art, a very particular, personal thing." While she focused on the fine detail of her business, she also had a wider view – "making things is the basis of a healthy society." In 'My Manifesto for Design' an article she wrote for *The Sunday Times* in 1994, she argued: "the art of the designer is about making, therefore employment, therefore the success of the country and its future, therefore the quality of life."

**LEFT** An eye for detail: topstitching defines a curvaceous lapel on a sunflower-yellow wool coat. A scarlet hand-carved Perspex button by C&N for Jean Muir provides a vibrant contrast, January 1988. Photograph: Eddy Kohli/Vogue. © The Condé Nast Publications Ltd. **ABOVE** Hourglass black moiré suit with peplum jacket, topstitched cuffed sleeves and short pencil skirt, Spring 1988. Black Perspex buttons, earrings and wrist cuff by C&N for Jean Muir. Photograph & © Neil Fenwick.

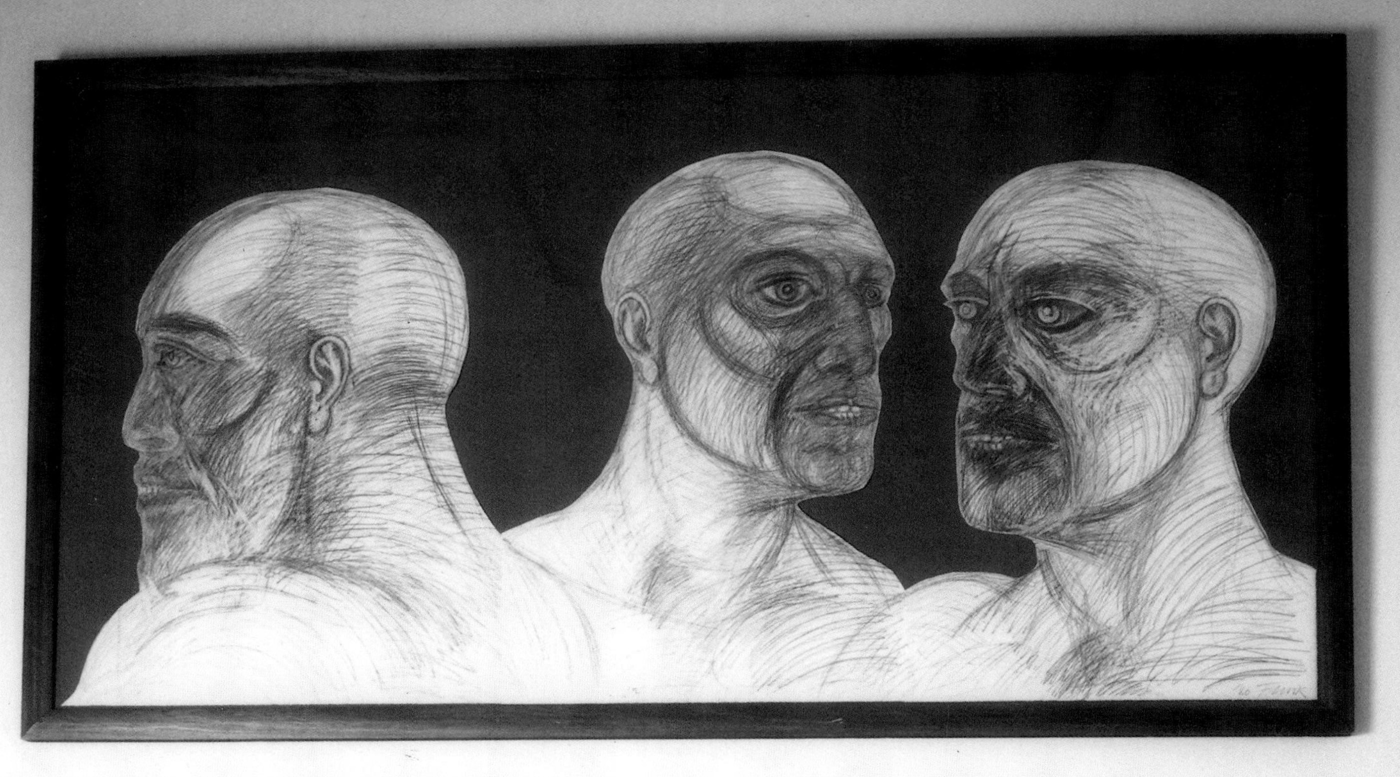
HANDBOOK OF
RUSSIAN LITERATURE

Chapter Four

# A COLLECTION TAKES SHAPE

"I haven't always wanted to be a designer. I remember thinking at one time that I might be a dancer"

JEAN MUIR

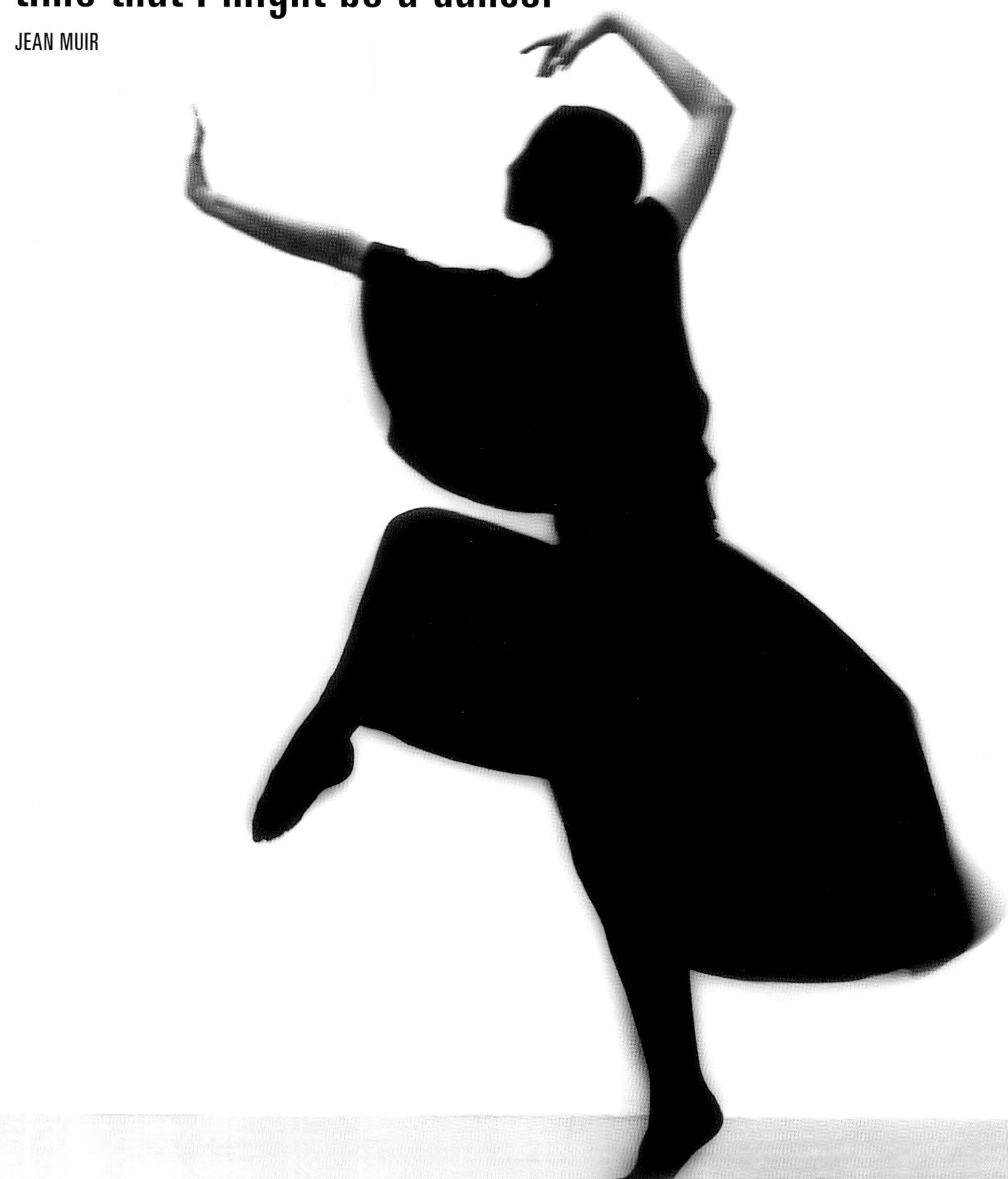

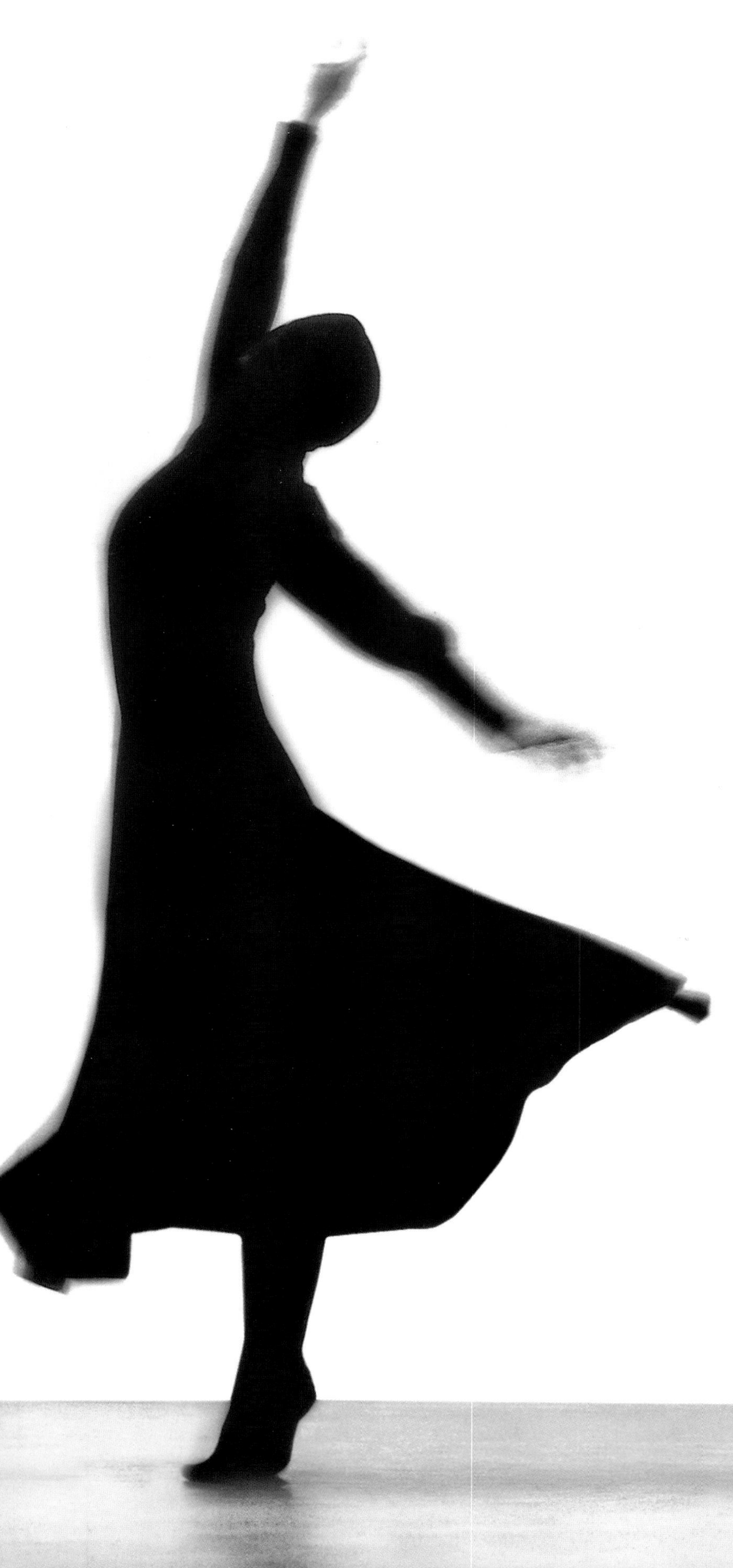

**THE MUIR** design process begins with the female body. "The first thing to remember when thinking of clothes" she said, "is that you are covering a body that already exists; that is the reason for the craft. Second, to remember that that body comes in different shapes and sizes, and thirdly, that it moves. So my particular style of dressmaking has developed through an adherence to the anatomy."

She attributed her signature purist shapes to the fact that being tiny herself, she always found excess cloth both uncomfortable and unnecessary – "hence my pared down shapes, depending on structure and colour."

Jean Muir loved to dance and appreciated dance of all kinds – from the pure form of classical ballet to the contemporary American choreography of Bob Fosse and Jerome Robbins. It gave her an innate awareness of the human body, its structure and gravity, and she translated this into her work – movement is an essential and inherent ingredient of her clothes.

"I haven't always wanted to be a designer," she said. "I remember thinking at one time that I might be a dancer. If that had happened, I'd probably have ended up as a choreographer because that's how I feel about my clothes – I sculpt them and choreograph them. I love and enjoy that sense of structure – what I call the geometry or mathematics of the anatomy – or in dressmaking terms – the balance and grain." This approach is similar to that of an artist or a sculptor, who must work out the axes of movement, working within a system of cubes and spheres. This underlying knowledge, and her skill with her materials, would produce the famous soft flowing lines and contour-skimming curves on the body.

It was her belief that in the curriculum of a design school life drawing classes should be compulsory for an understanding of the anatomy vis-à-vis the fit and balance and proportion of clothes, and that they should be given greater emphasis than classes in fashion illustration.

Jean Muir's particular approach to design, "her engineering in cloth" took as its muse not an individual or an idealised woman, but every woman, the female form itself. Muir made clothes that looked as good on a petite woman as on her statuesque counterpart.

In putting together a collection, the Muir concept was based on the concise formula: "Good ideas, accurate patterns, accurate production" and it was no coincidence that, as Master of the Faculty of Royal Designers for Industry, she felt most empathy with the engineers of the faculty. "I see myself as

**PAGE 62** "This is my favourite place to work", the picture over the bed is *Northumberland Triptych*, 1986, by her friend Elisabeth Frink. Photograph & © Rory Carnegie. **LEFT** Dancers emphasise the fluidity of Jean Muir's matte jersey. Photograph & © John Swannell.

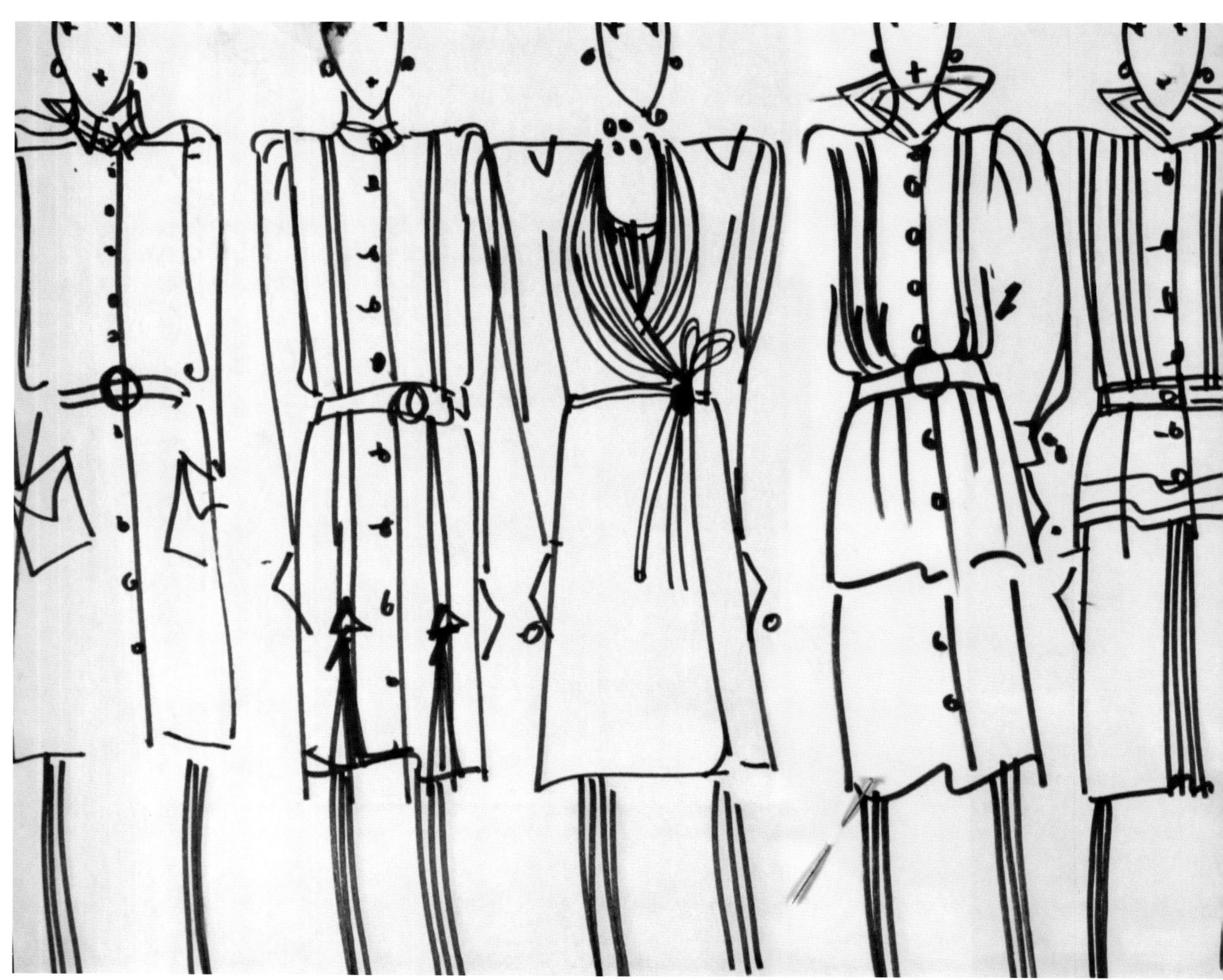

**ABOVE** Variations on a seasonal theme: the colours and fabrics have been chosen and the individual sketches are put together to make up the whole collection with its different styles and details. © The Trustees of The National Museums of Scotland. **FAR RIGHT** Thinking aloud on paper: Jean Muir's rough handwritten notes – a creative stream of consciousness for each collection. Line 6 includes one of her favourite words "nifty". © Jean Muir Ltd.

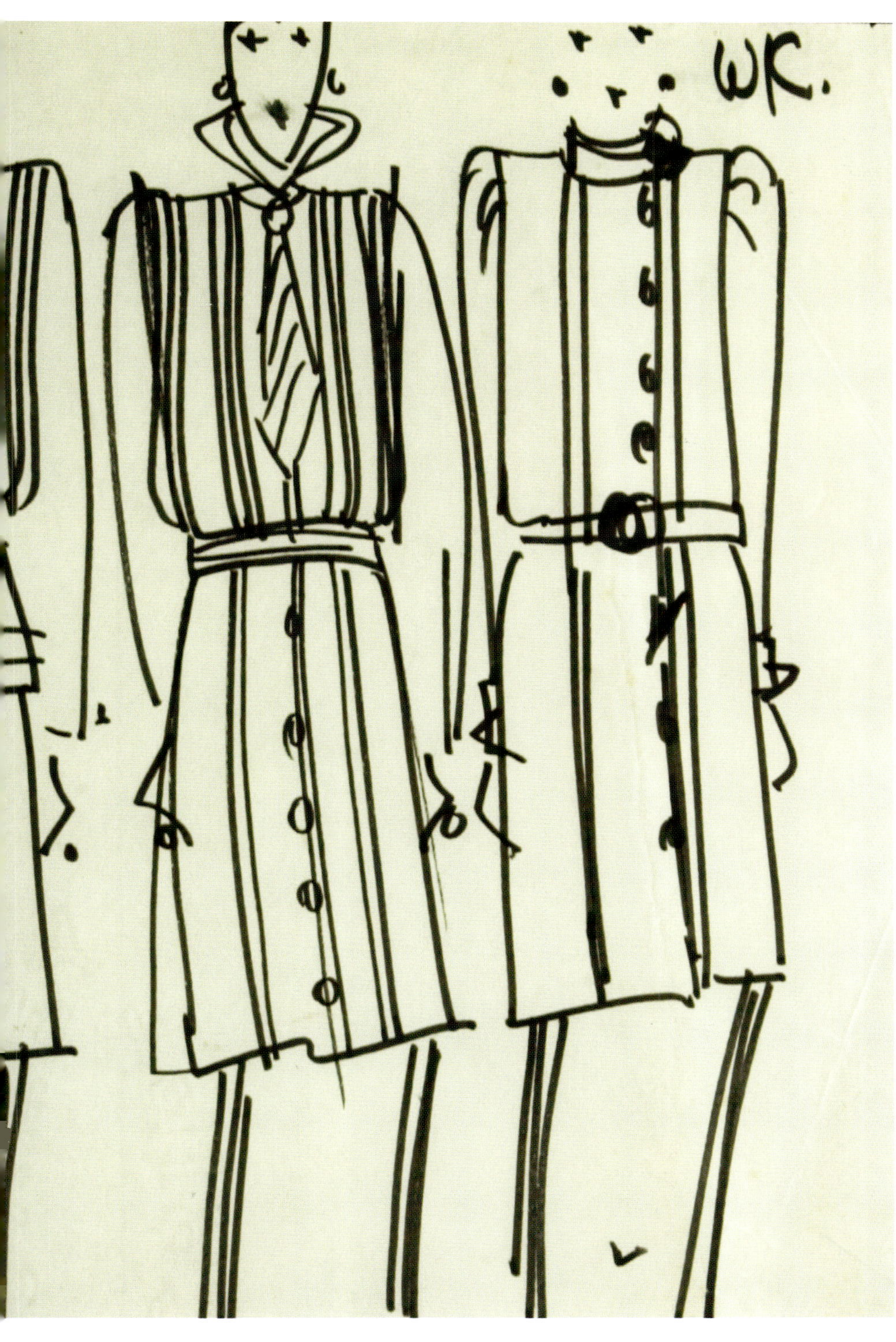


A Wonderful
Fine Pure Wool
Merino Jumper.
— A Very Very
Pretty Neck
Nifty With a Little
Straight Skirt —
Great in Black for
Evening —
— In Creamy white for
Everything.

And Very Useful.
In Milk Chocolate
Colour.
A tiny Scarf.
An Easy Longish
Length. *.

a technician. I approach my work in a very academic way – I reason it out. I've evolved a formula for myself, a system really like an algebraic formula." She derived great satisfaction from working out the mathematics or 'mechanics' of a collection – the blend of thought processes and technical skills that would ultimately turn her ideas into garments that would strike a chord with the many different women who would look forward to buying and wearing them. Fashion writer Lucia van der Post observed, "At the heart of the Jean Muir style there lies a skillful resolution of apparently irreconcilable paradoxes. While her style is based on this most disciplined, almost geometric attention to proportion, the end result is fluid and rich with intuitive flair."

Whilst the main elements: colour, shape, line and fabric define a collection, ideas are obviously the starting point. At the start of the process – "the best time to start a new collection is just when you've finished with the last one" – Miss Muir would set aside one or two weekends at her London flat, during which she would devote herself entirely to sketching, armed with reams of white A4 paper and her favoured black felt-tip pens, "I will go to bed with these and sit and draw and draw and draw – four or five hours at a time without stopping" – until she had the basis for the new collection.

As evidence of the evolutionary nature of her work, she would first look back over the sketchbooks of the previous two seasons. "I ask myself, where shall I push myself onto now? I don't know where I'm going until I actually sit down and draw."

As Harry Leuckert recalls, "She was never without her little notebook. She was constantly jotting down ideas, observations, sketches and descriptions of shapes and colours. Her mind never stopped working and she never stopped looking. Sketching in bed for a weekend was really just the finalisation of everything that she saw and absorbed and mulled over."

Muir clearly enjoyed the working through of shapes, exploring all the possibilities of an idea, but the ideas themselves were not her main concern. "What you see scribbled on a piece of paper is only the beginning... Once one's got the ideas, it's much more how you use those shapes that make them what they really are." Her preoccupation with technique was always there: "I was never superficially concerned with ideas, much more the cut and the craft – how something was made. I have always felt that ideas were two a penny, but what to do with those ideas, how to make them make sense in whatever sphere one is working is of the principal importance."

From the initial sketch, a toile is made – a prototype in white calico – in order to work out how to get right the shape and fit of the garment. As well as her own technicians, Muir worked with a Parisian toileist trained to the standards of the Haute Couture. Miss Muir would always try the toile on, comparing it to the original sketch, always checking but this time on the body, not in terms of a specific size, but using herself more as an 'animate' stand. In this way she could find out not only that she was getting the proportion she wanted, checking the sketch had been correctly interpreted, but also that the garment felt comfortable.

From the toile, flat patterns are made from card. This is a job of extreme precision – Miss Muir liked to say that in fashion "system and accuracy are as imperative as in any engineering process!" Every measurement has to be exact to the millimetre – every line has to flow throughout – the grain of the fabric must be totally in balance. This is the most important part of manufacturing because if the initial pattern is not correct, the sizes graded from it will not be correct. An accompanying technical sketch outlining all making and stitching details has to be exact and comprehensive for both the cutter and the machinist – every point to watch in making has to be listed to avoid inaccuracies. For Miss Muir it was "the blueprint on which manufacture sinks or swims."

Once the flat pattern has been perfected, a costing is made to determine the wholesale selling price of a garment. A pattern-check garment is then made – a first garment produced from the flat pattern, to ensure the manufacture and the accuracy of the pattern – which Miss Muir would personally approve: "I always fit the clothes because that way I can *feel* the garment." Once this is done the final technical stage is the grading. Again this requires absolute precision. Patterns are graded to a range of five sizes, from eight to sixteen, always remembering that the garment has to look exactly as the original prototype size ten, all the way through the sizes. Her garments could have as many as forty separate pattern pieces but the resulting shape would always be fluid on the body.

Finally she would line up all her samples, to see whether she had covered all the requirements of her store buyers and customers – all those who would buy her clothes.

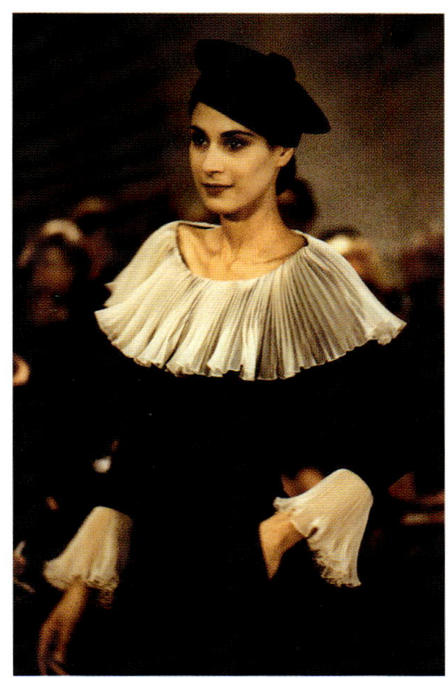

**FABRIC** Simultaneously she would be deciding which fabric to use for each shape – sometimes the same shape was made in two very different fabrics with diverse but equally successful results. She used butter-soft suedes and leather as though they were as light as silk or as pliable as wool. "I like to use a fabric that is supple and sympathetic" she explained, "but also with weight, a fabric that responds to a shape, that shape ultimately being based on the female anatomy. I never like materials that do things on their own, those that are too stiff, or too flimsy, and are therefore out of control."

Wool crepe and matte jersey would become the underlying bases for her collections, with matte jersey as the principal fabric. Often mistaken for silk, Muir's matte jersey was actually a finely knit construction in rayon. She had specific requirements and the French manufacturers provided her with a superior quality, woven to her specification, with a particular weight and a certain number of stitches to the inch.

She explained its special appeal: "I have always enjoyed working out a very geometric or architectural shape and then 'dropping' it into jersey, where it immediately relaxes – is supple and giving – is human and moveable. Also working in one fabric can give one the key to working in another – working in jersey gave me the clue, as it were, to working in suede – treating the skin as a soft, supple fabric."

Miss Muir actively sought out fabrics that would work for her in this way: fabrics that did not necessarily need to be lined, that reacted superbly to her way of making, and by extension, that would react sympathetically to a body. Whilst she would vary them, and add new finds, on the whole, rather than having to rely on new fabrics for innovation, Miss Muir preferred to work with a carefully selected group of what were, for her, proven fabrics, skins and yarns that responded to her way of making – principally, jersey, angora, wools, silks, suedes, leathers, cashmere – almost as a master craftsman works with the same traditional materials. Her skill and knowledge would always be moving them on, leading to a constant repertoire of invention and refinement. This would result in unusual combinations, such as fluid forms in suede and, conversely, severe shapes in jersey.

"I like to use a fabric that is supple and sympathetic"
**JEAN MUIR**

**ABOVE LEFT** A contrast of fabrics: finely pleated ivory chiffon softens the austerity of black matte jersey. Photograph & © Chris Moore.

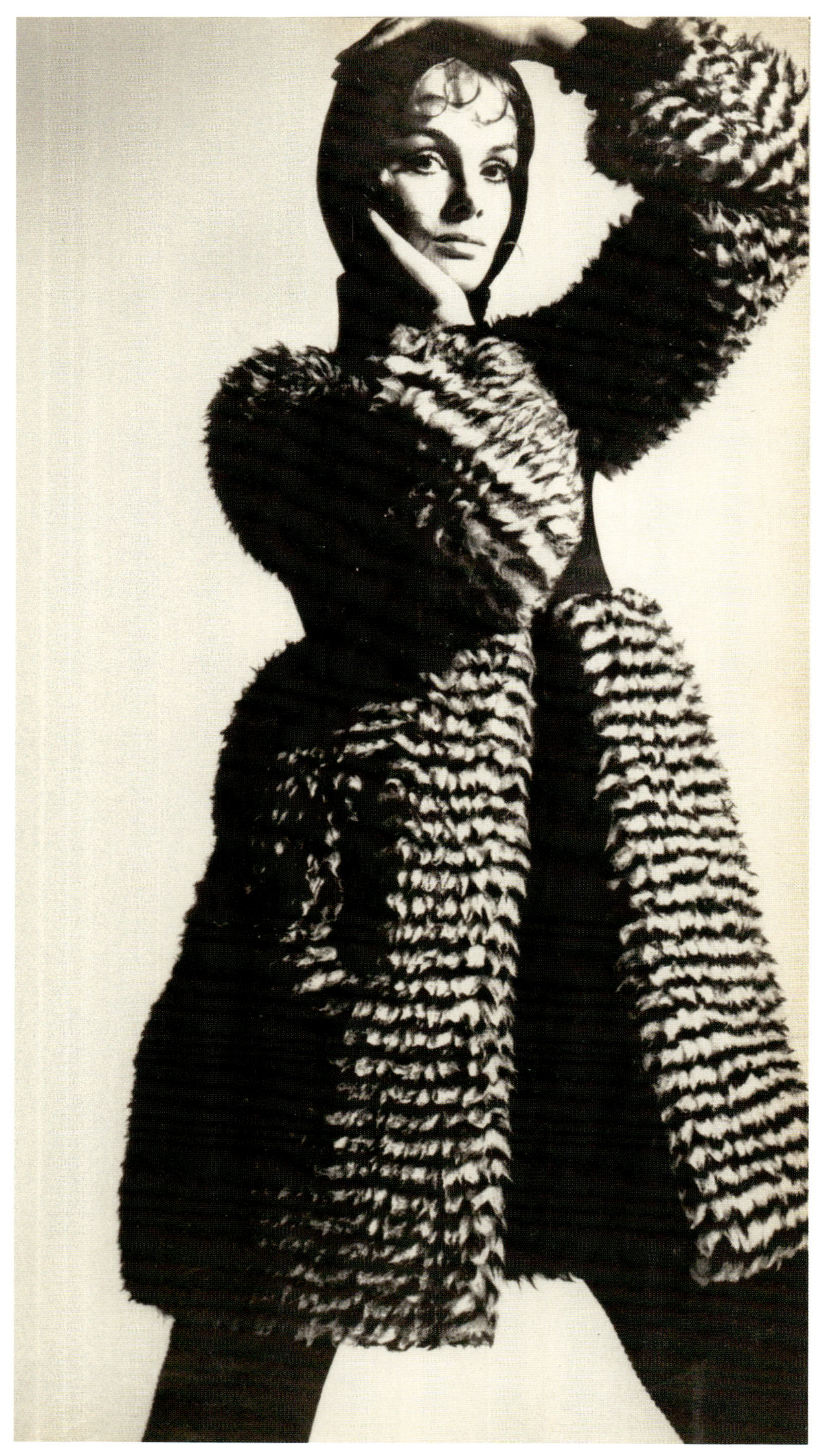

**LEFT** Black and white wool coat in "striped fur fabric gathered into panda bear arms and a bubble skirt. Stretchy black knitted bodice pulls them together and does up with glass buttons". *Vogue*, 15 September 1969. Photograph: David Bailey/Vogue. © The Condé Nast Publications Ltd.

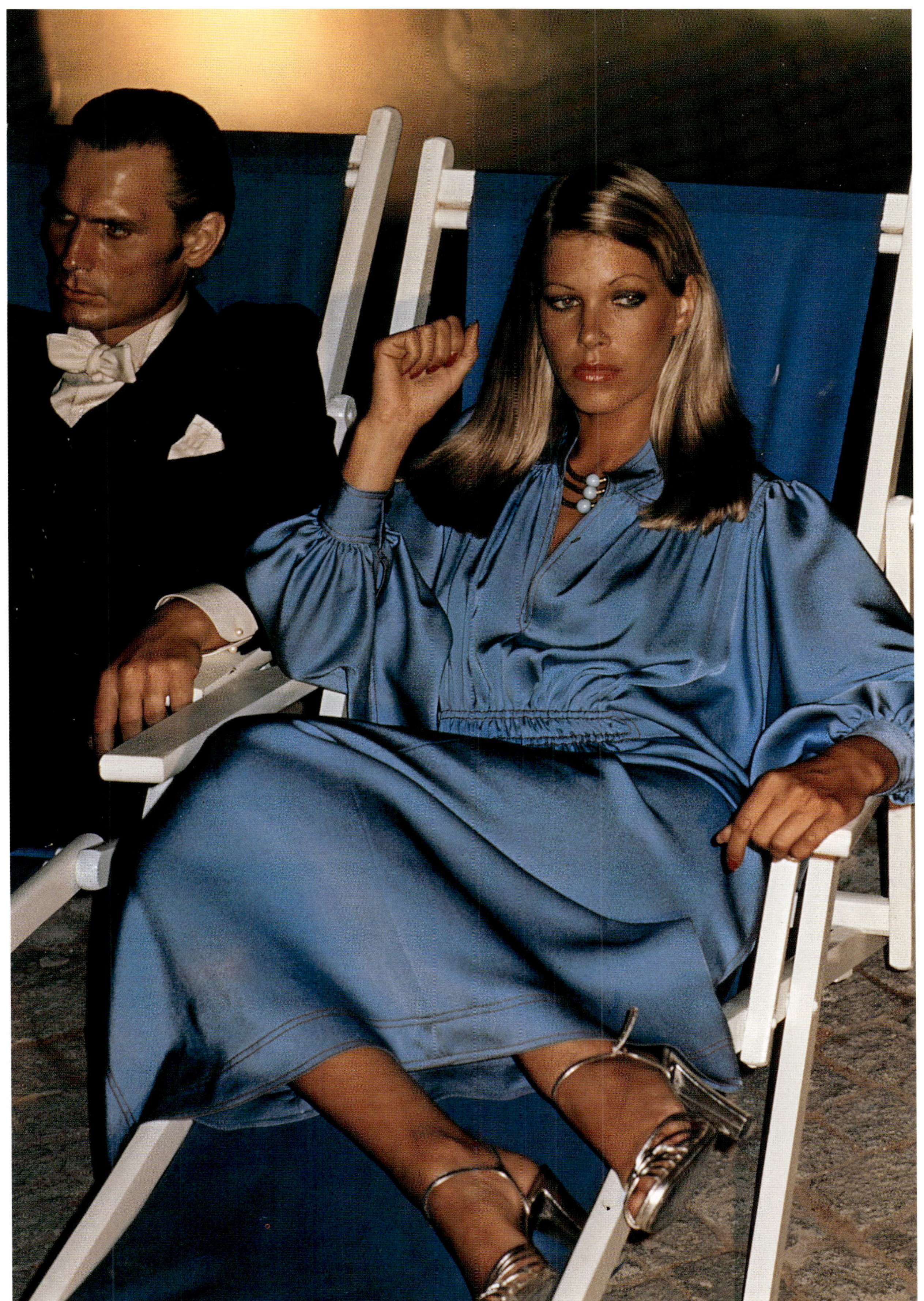

**RIGHT** Sensuous and slinky: "Sunny sky satin" dress, highlighted with scarlet contrast stitching at the shoulders, cuffs, waist and hem, *Vogue*, October 1973. Photograph: Helmut Newton. © The Helmut Newton Estate/Maconochie Photography.

**COLOUR** Just as the sketches and fabrics provide a launch pad of ideas, colour is also an important inspiration. Even before the initial sketches are done, Miss Muir would be deciding on her colours for the season. Unlike many designers who order their cloth in stock shades, Miss Muir's choice of cloth, skins and yarns was dyed to her own specification with complementary fabrics dyed to match each other. Cashmere and suedes would be coloured to link in with matte jersey to produce in one outfit a single rich colour fusion across a sumptuous blend of textures.

Just as Diana Vreeland, the legendary editor of American *Vogue,* opined that "Pink is the navy blue of India", so Jean Muir would claim a particular inky navy as her own colour. For Muir, navy became the new black: softer, less radical, more subtle. She elevated it to a higher level on the fashion radar making it altogether different from before. She explored its infinite range from marine through to virtually black, imbuing it with a seasonless elegance. Just as she later chose to wear navy blue for her personal wardrobe, it was a colour that appeared in the vast majority of her collections, season in, season out, selling phenomenally well to this day.

Muir became universally known for a subdued and restrained palette of principally black and navy, "I seem to have been lumbered with the myth that I only make in navy and black and that's simply not true at all." Muir in fact loved colour. Her palette could take in the most brilliant of shades from aquamarine to tangerine, fuchsia to Venetian red, from regal purple to royal blue, lime to citron. Journalist, Felicity Green suggests these jewel-toned colours were 'exclamation marks', foils to the more predominant darker tones.

The American fashion designer, Bill Blass highlighted Muir's colour sense: "She sees things in a totally pure light. When she does colour it is such a clear bright colour it's as if she has discovered 'yellow'. It seems as if she goes right to the core of a particular colour." Her choice of colour is vividly brought to life by Gai Pearl Marshall, Jean Muir's former PR and vendeuse, now UK PR for Missoni: "I remember the time when the supplier of her famous jersey came in to take her brief on the next season's colours. Cutting swatches she cut her finger by mistake and a drop of blood fell on a piece of paper. 'Ouch!' she exclaimed. '*That's* the colour I want!' and we all had to laugh."

Muir was never one for gimmicks yet her clothes could have a certain 'razzmatazz'. As Michael Roberts, photographer and stylist put it in *Tatler* magazine (March 1983): "Jean Muir has a great deal more in her make-up

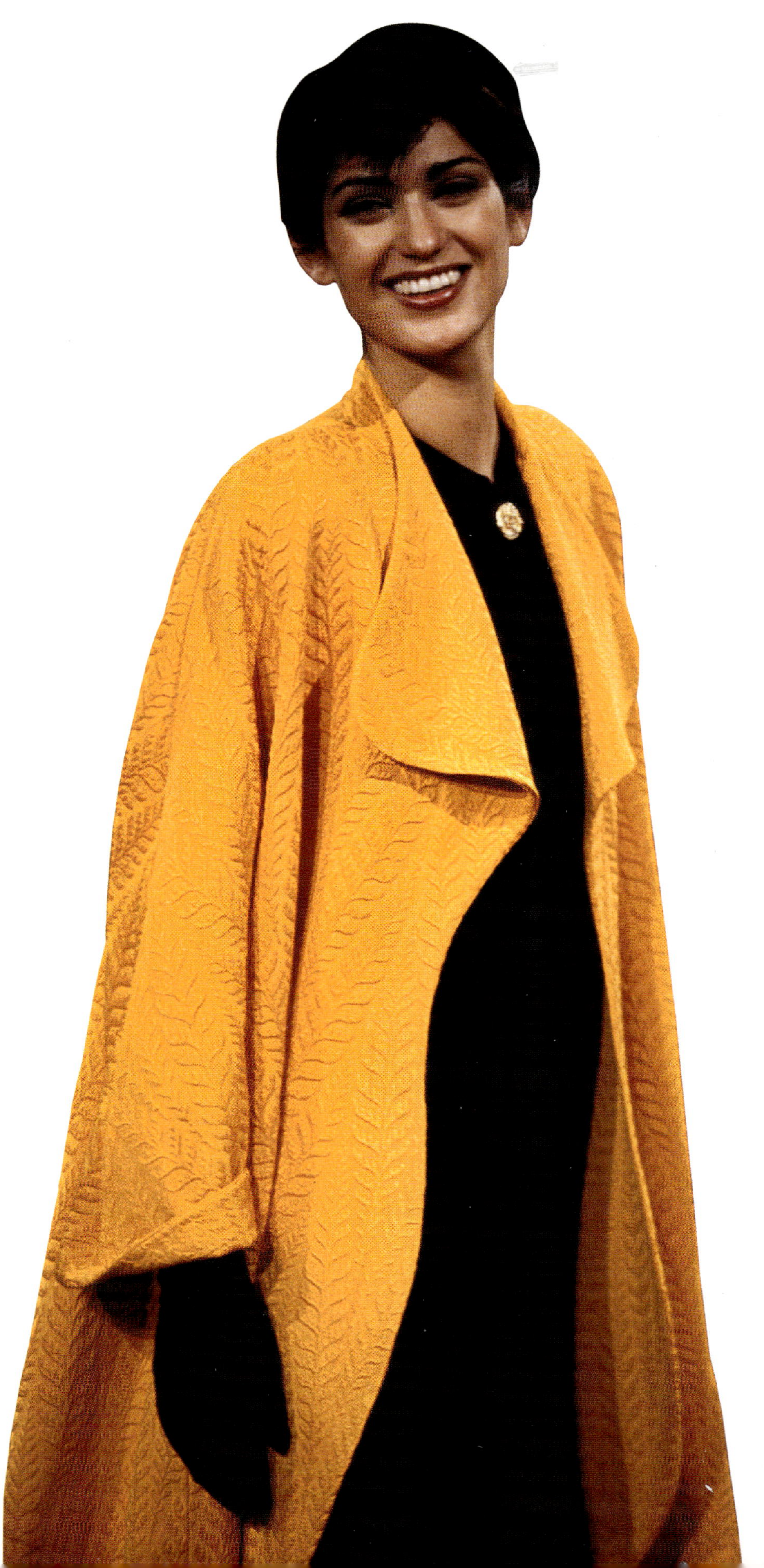

**RIGHT** Colour contrast: Sunshine-yellow swingback coat in leaf brocade with curving outline. Black jersey separates serve as a foil for the intense yellow of the coat, Autumn 1991. Photograph & © Niall McInerney.

than the navy blues, greys and blacks we tend to associate her with. Indeed, over the past few seasons, our premiere designer has made a positive point of including several vivid eye-popping designs in each new collection. Not that her palette ever runs to that cheap look of 'manufactured' colour: 'I'm totally affected by colour and bad colour makes me miserable,' she shudders. This season the colourful part of Ms Muir's collection is a positive Fauvist riot. Her suedes have taken on a jewel-like intensity and her staple jerseys are, in several cases, almost electric. However, her signature details and precision cut are still apparent beneath the razzmatazz of scarlet, fuchsia and clashing electric blue."

Miss Muir delighted in the colours of nature, and often found her colour inspiration in detail there. Her choice was governed by her eye and instinct. "I love natural colour," she said, "whether it be grey stone or a golden grey sky, the particular misted red of a hawthorn berry in Winter frost or the dark black-ish mauve of a tulip". Often her eye was caught in surprising places, as Harry Leuckert recalls. "On a trip to Brittany she spotted the ideal green – a piece of seaweed. I pointed out it would be dry and a totally different green by the time we got it home. She insisted, so I bought a bottle of lemonade, emptied it, filled it with seawater and the seaweed came home with us. Another time, in the Atlas Mountains, she spotted something on the road and asked the driver to stop. I got out and picked up a particular clod of earth and I saw it was a fantastic deep red – another colour for the collection!"

From these initial inspirations, a spectrum was built up – anything from intense, dark colours to soft chalky pastels. Colour reference, which could be in the form of silk threads, packets of spices, or crayon-coloured samples, was sent to a dyeing laboratory, which then produced a series of 'lab dyes' for approval. In the 1993 'Very Jean Muir' television series, she enjoyed recalling how the computer took several attempts before it could accurately reproduce swatches to match her hand-coloured samples to her satisfaction. From these the shades of the season were selected and sample lengths ordered. Miss Muir always held all the colours she was considering up to her face checking that they were a true and enhancing colour – "never forgetting that they have to go out into the world and suit somebody."

Muir consciously chose materials that take colour extremely successfully. Wool crepe is always the first to be dyed – "it's like my paint" – forming the core from which the other fabrics follow. Once the palette is complete, the decision is made as to which colour should be done in which fabric.

**RIGHT** Coat of many colours: A medley of scarlet, orange and pink cowskin suede, patchworked into a swagger jacket worn over skinny black jersey leggings, Autumn 1991. Photograph & © Chris Moore.

"I'm mad about good colour, simply mad about it! I think it's one of the most important things in one's life."
**JEAN MUIR**

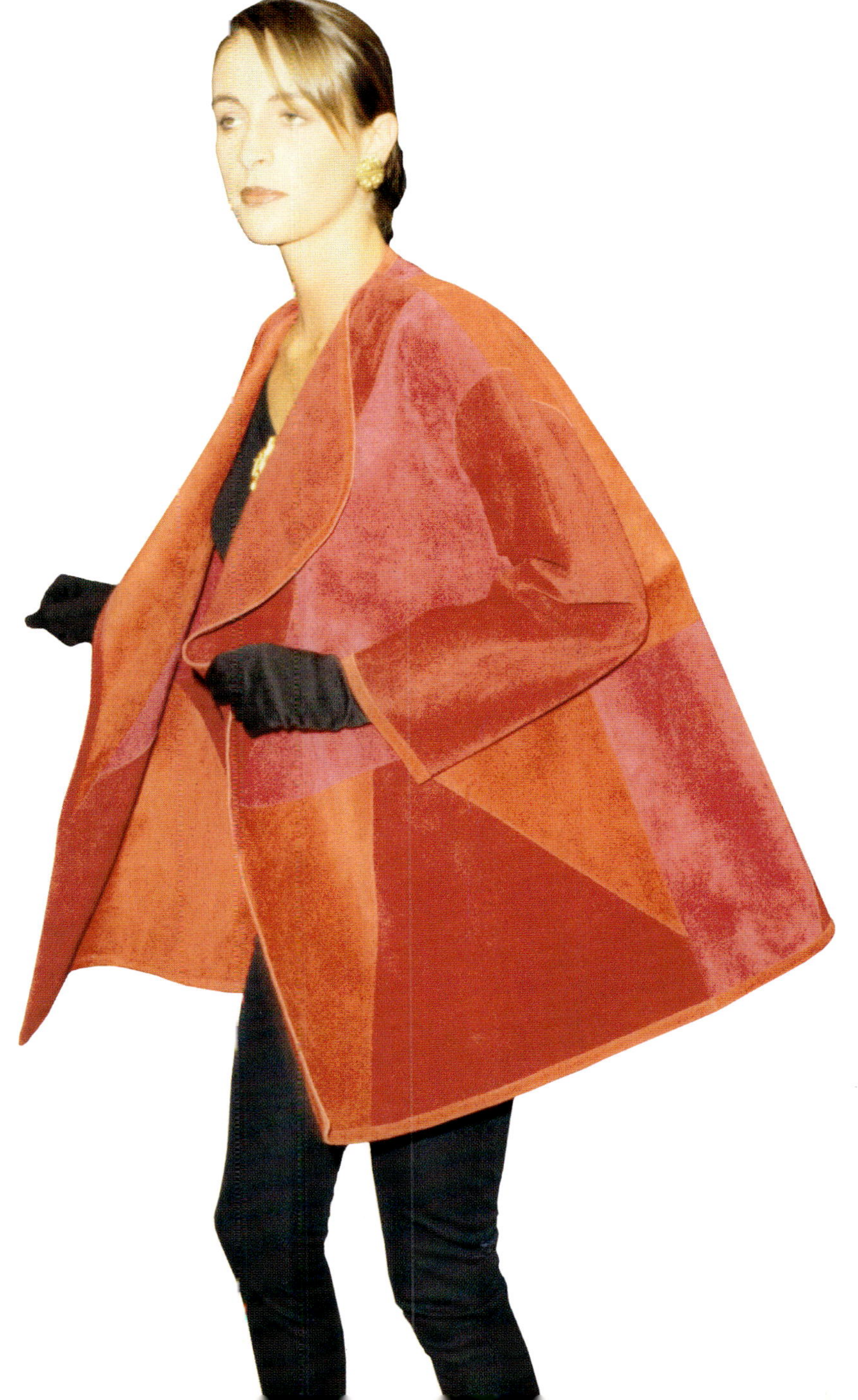

# BEST OF BRITISH: CLOTH SUPPLIERS

To know one's cloth – how it hangs, how it stitches, what it will and will not do – is obviously an essential part of the design and manufacture. The majority of Muir's materials, apart from her French matte jersey and certain silks, came from British suppliers: wools, tweeds, silks, leather, and Welsh lambskin suedes, with Miss Muir following her diktat to buy the best and buy British wherever possible.

The North East of England and the Borders area of Britain, from Yorkshire up to southern Scotland, held strong personal and professional ties for Muir. For her it was an inspirational landscape, "Oh, there's definitely something about the place, it's grand and it's straightforward and that is what the people are like… I think it's magnificent… it never lets you down. It's simply wonderful at any time of the year." Moreover, she was a great fan of the skills and expertise encapsulated in the area's textile and knitwear industries.

Muir preferred specialist companies who could work with her to achieve her exacting standards like Linton Tweeds of Carlisle, a traditionally-based weaving firm producing world-class cloth for international luxury labels. Muir used a variety of Linton's beautiful wools and tweeds.

She also used men's tweeds and worsteds from Hield, a Yorkshire company, but she looked at them with a fresh eye and subverted them, turning

"One must use materials with the respect they're due. It doesn't matter if it's knitted cashmere or a beautiful piece of woven British wool, you must treat them with respect."

**JEAN MUIR**

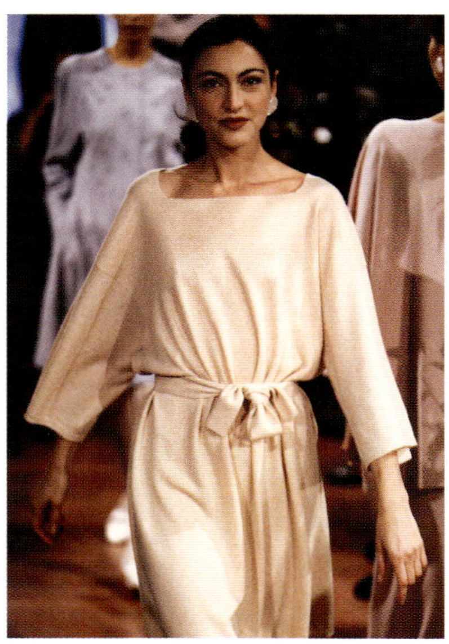

**ABOVE** Separates in double wool crepe with cashmere sweater. **RIGHT** Loosely belted cashmere dress. Both Spring 1993 collection, featured in the 'Very Jean Muir' Channel 4 television series.
**OPPOSITE** Muir's British wools: tunic sweater in pale grey cashmere [left]; jacket in tomato-red wool crepe with flaring sleeves and matching skirt [right], from the Autumn 1995 collection.
Photographs & © Chris Moore.

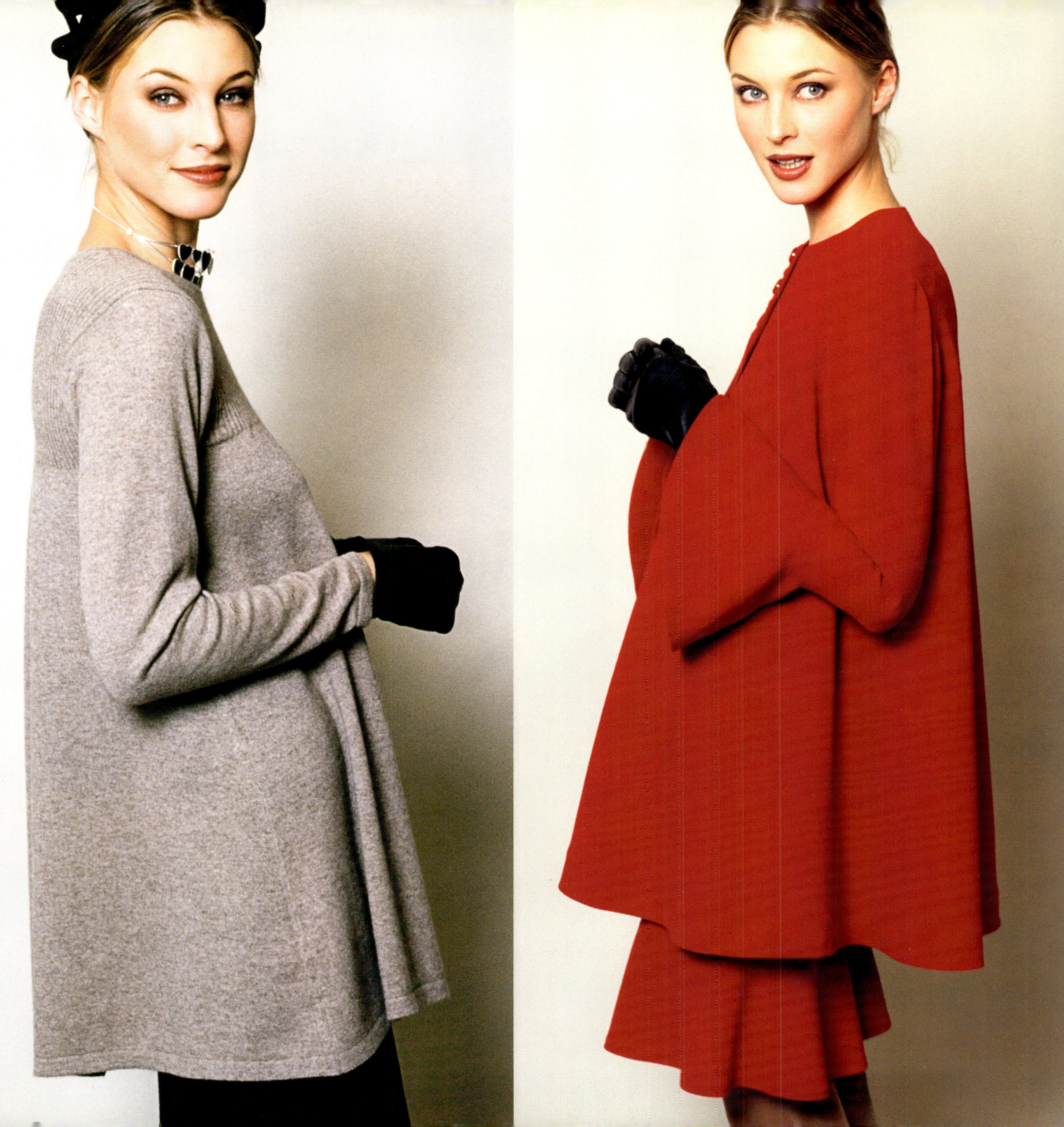

typically masculine, hard-wearing fabrics, such as charcoal-grey herringbone into softly-moulded, feminine shapes. The finished product was as far away from men's overcoats as it was possible to get, as the journalist, Cathy Horyn noted in *The Washington Post*, "Muir's clothes tend to float; even her herringbone tweeds, cut into fancy hacking jackets, look weightless." From the sixties Muir also used Harris Tweed, but in her hands it was cut and seamed to a refined softness; Princess Diana chose an outfit in this material for her honeymoon at Balmoral.

The same was true of her liking for Macclesfield silk in rich swirling paisley designs – usually used for men's ties – which she appropriated for curvaceously lapelled jackets, coats, and dresses. She also favoured tartans, pairing them with cashmere knits, which she coloured in the soft tones of the tartan, sometimes in stripes, or using intarsia in order to layer the woven patterns.

Similarly, Muir worked with a small number of specialist knitwear companies based in the Borders region. Scotland's unrivalled knitwear-producing heritage and worldwide reputation for excellence, not least of all for their cashmere, was something that Muir was happy to champion as one of her signature looks.

Using luxurious and pliable materials to produce garments with a feeling of lightness and ease, her favourite yarns were the finest qualities of merino, geelong lamb's wool, silk, and, above all, cashmere. Miss Muir worked particularly closely with one family company in the Borders, all highly-skilled craftspeople. Muir's knitwear reached its apotheosis in her intarsia pieces, taking knitwear to a new artistic level, which she likened to painting in cashmere, "I love those knits, they are like paintings. It's like drowning in colour!"

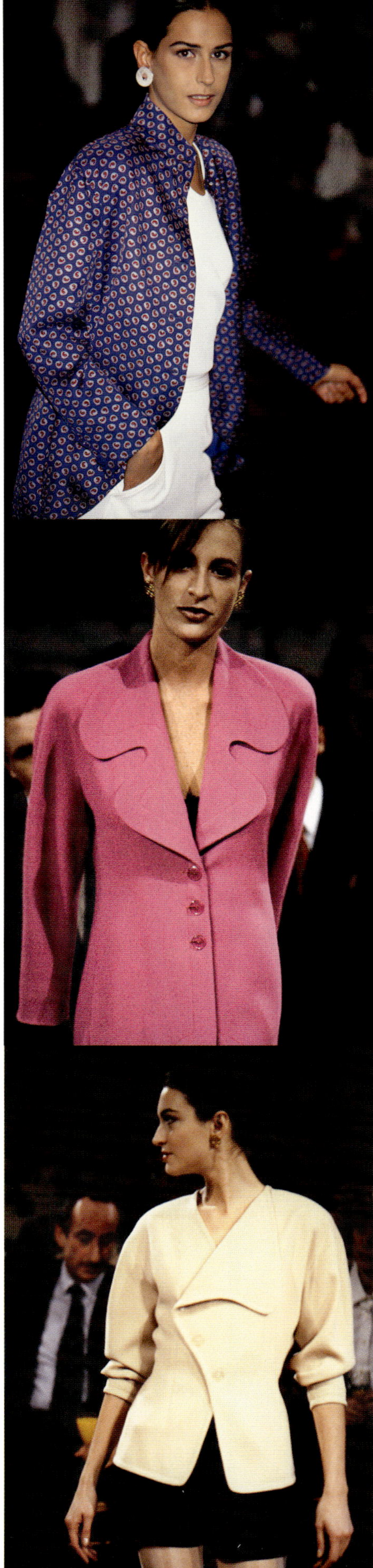

**TOP** Softly curved jacket in Macclesfield 'tie' silk. **CENTRE** Jacket in wool crepe with cutaway curved lapels. **RIGHT** Wrap-over jacket in double wool crepe worn informally over suede shorts, Spring and Autumn 1991. Photographs & © Chris Moore & Niall McInerney.

# BEST OF BRITISH: MANUFACTURERS

Not only did Muir champion British textile suppliers wherever possible, she supported British manufacturing throughout her career, insisting it was possible to produce clothes to the most exacting standards in this country. She began to address the issue in the seventies at a time when British manufacturing was declining fast, beset by recession. She maintained her campaign into the nineties when many British designers had moved their production abroad.

Muir had an almost religious zeal on the subject, feeling that it was not just a moral and ethical choice, but also a practical and cultural one. She stalwartly campaigned for a greater awareness of the importance of the clothing industry to the country's economy – at the time the fourth largest sector in the country. She emphasised the need for the requisite technical training in colleges to drive and feed that industry. Her ideal platform was the Downing Street design seminar chaired by Margaret Thatcher in the early eighties, where she made such an impression that she was immediately co-opted onto a number of advisory groups and committees.

She persuaded her fellow Scot, newspaper editor, Andrew Neil to publish her 'Manifesto for Real Design' in *The Sunday Times* in March 1994. In this she called for a renewed awareness of the advantages of being a skills-based manufacturing society, and a new appraisal of design comprehension in industry and the educational system.

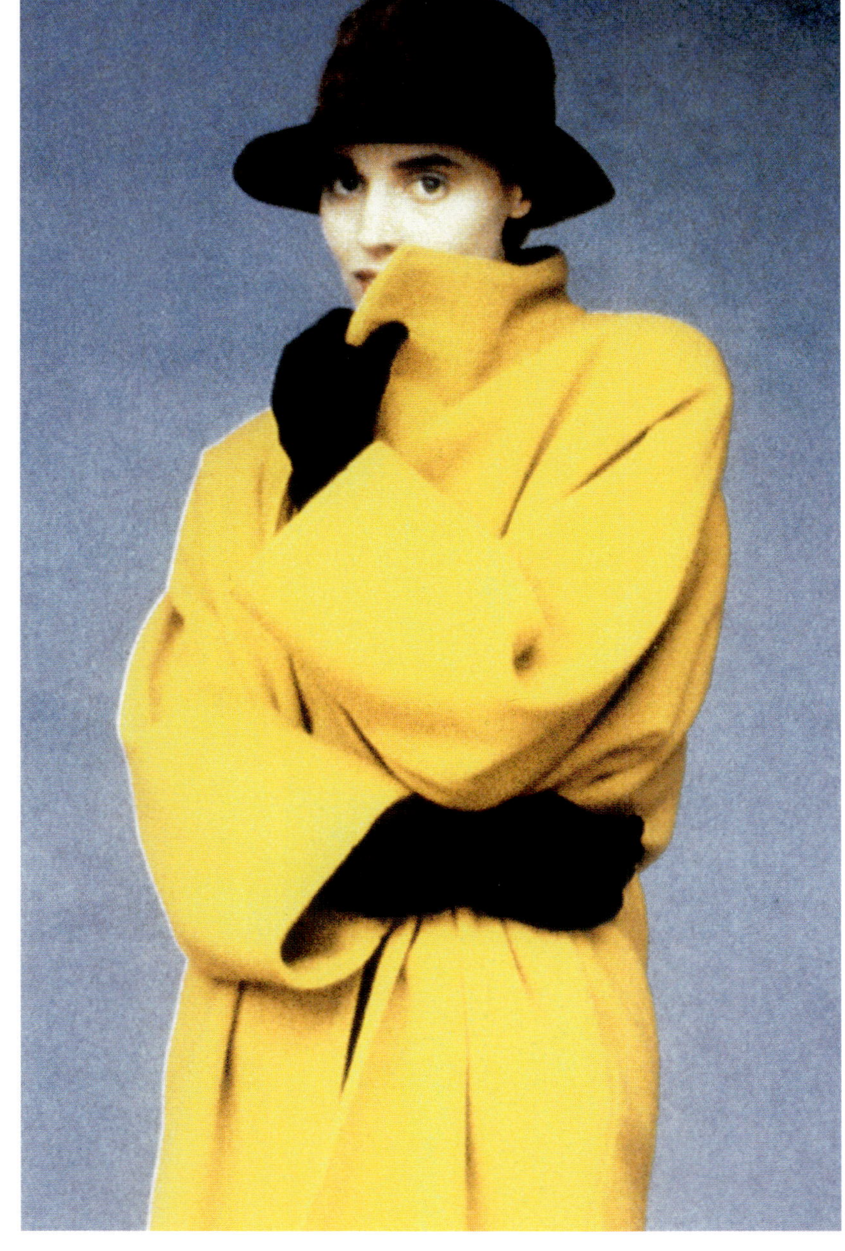

"As a nation, we are too often concerned with what rather than *how*."
**JEAN MUIR**

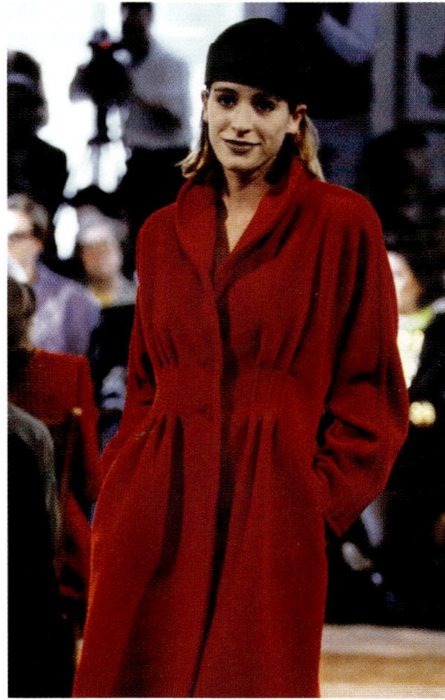

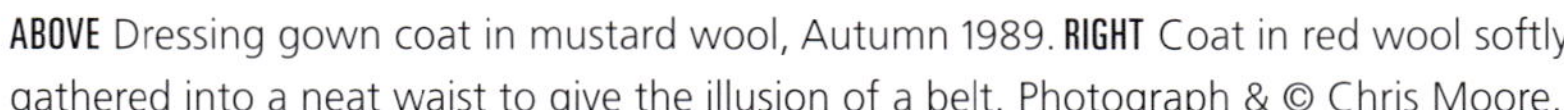

**ABOVE** Dressing gown coat in mustard wool, Autumn 1989. **RIGHT** Coat in red wool softly gathered into a neat waist to give the illusion of a belt. Photograph & © Chris Moore.

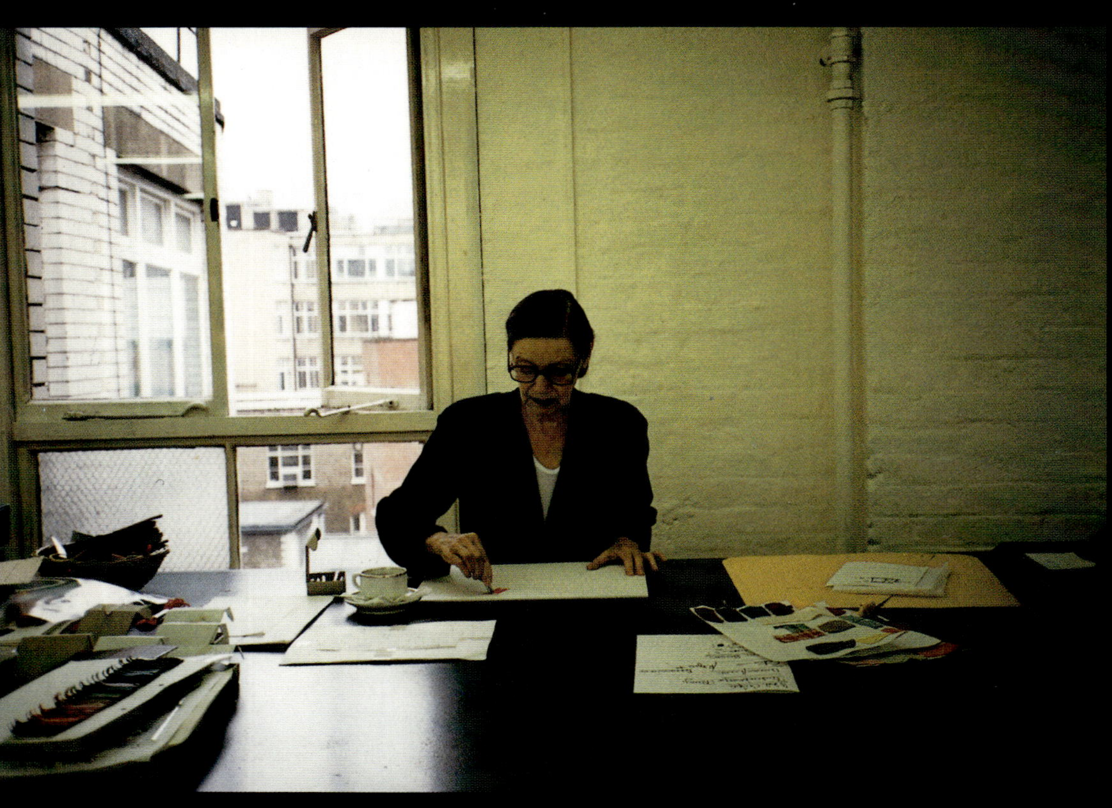

Chapter Five

# TECHNIQUES OF MAKING

Muir liked to live and work in a serene all-white environment. In her studio in London's Farringdon Road she created an atmosphere of immaculate order and space. Photograph & © Geoff Dunlop.

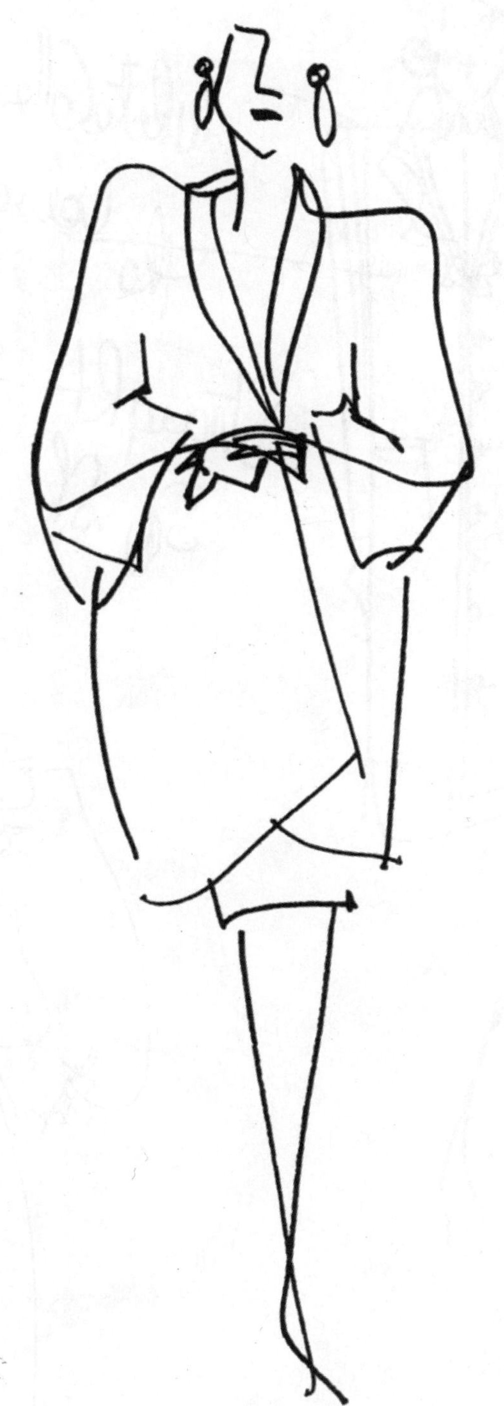

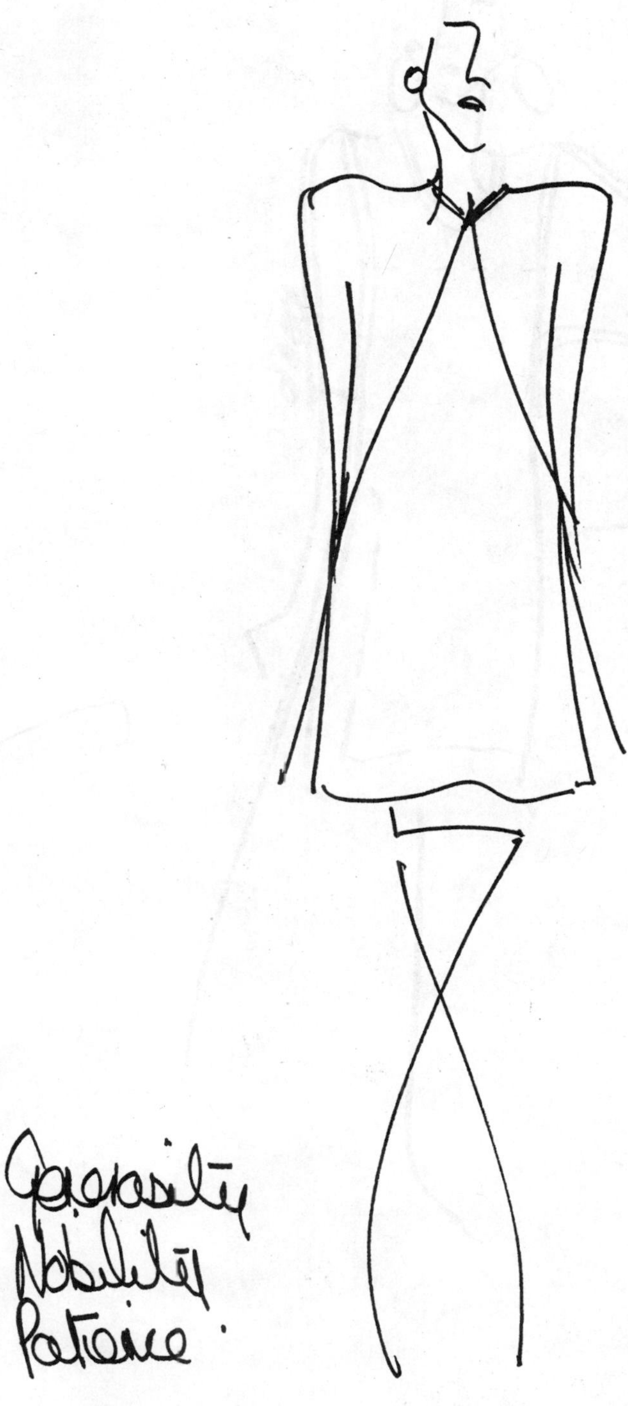
Generosity
Nobility
Patience

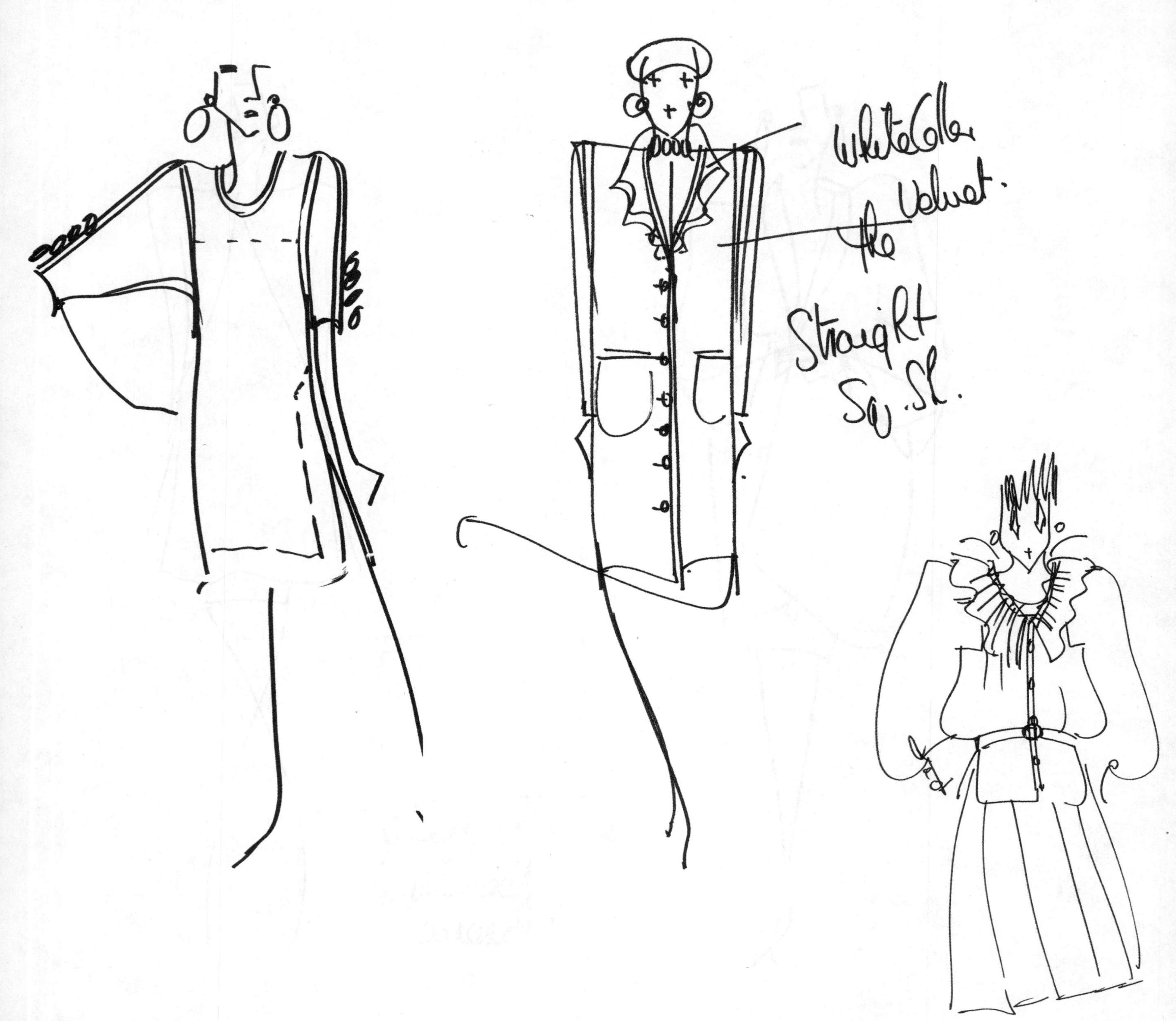
White Collar
the Velvet.
Straight
Sq. Sl.

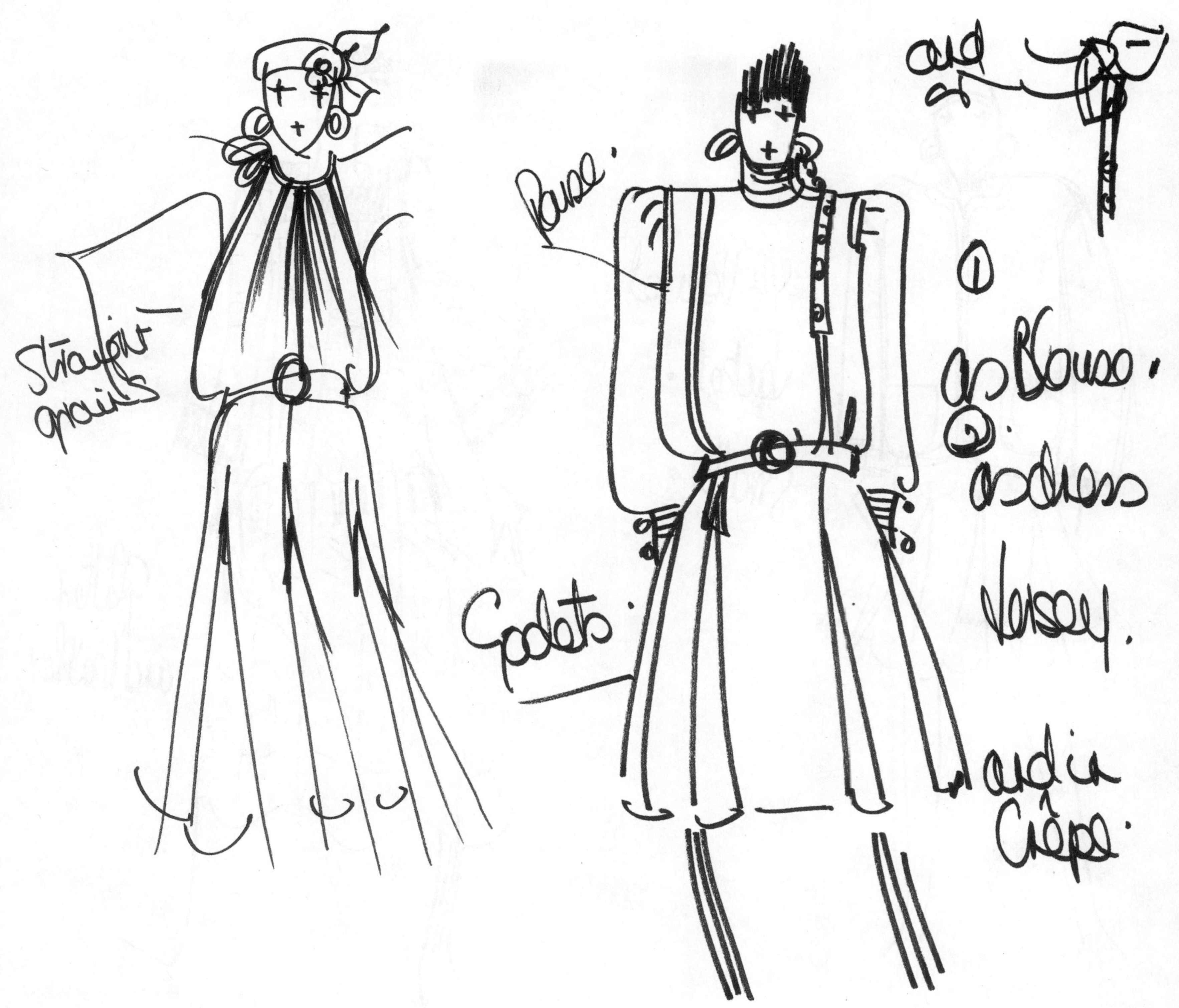
Straight grains
Blouse.
Godets.
①
as Blouse.
②
as dress
Jersey.
Crêpe.

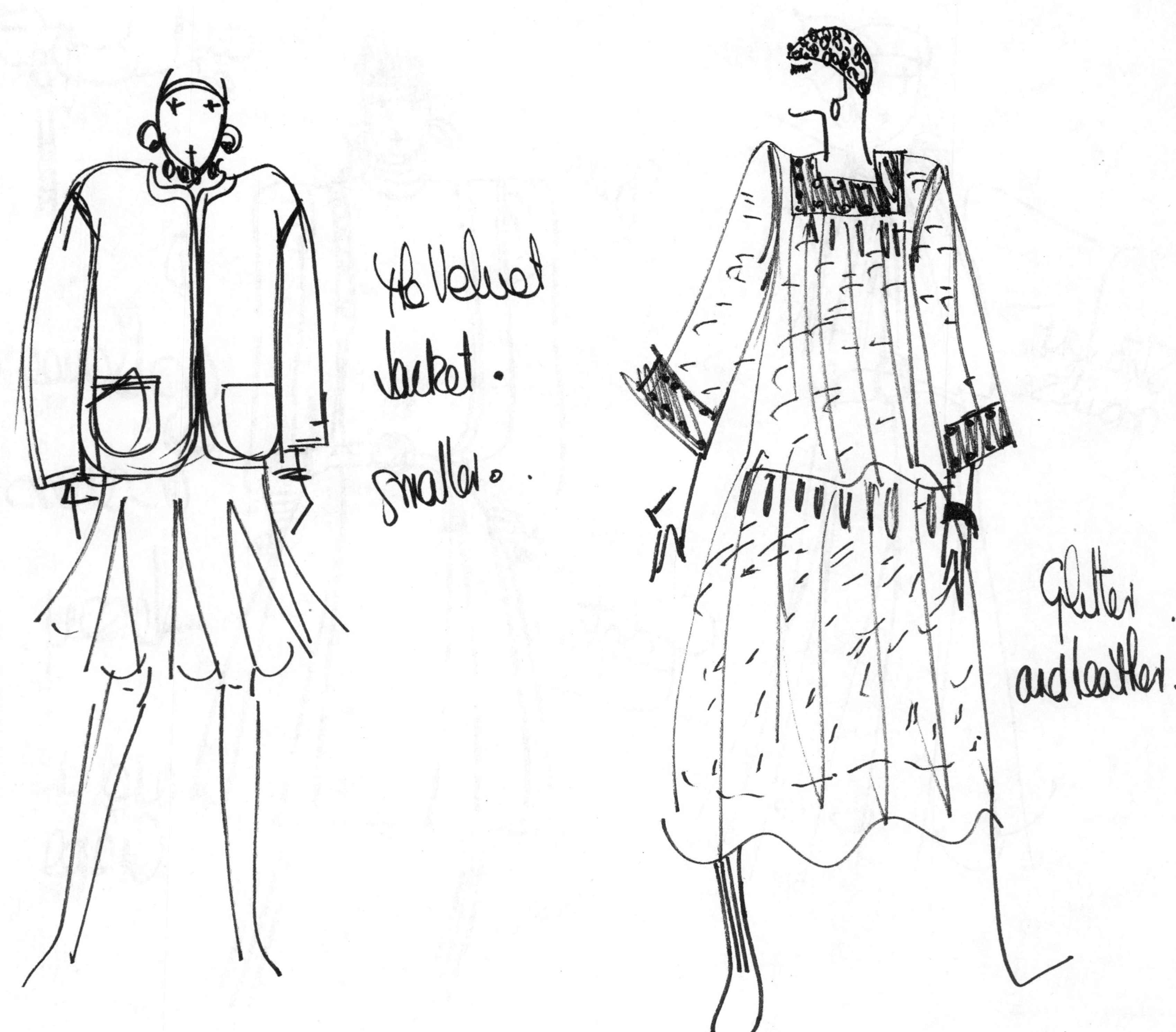
The Velvet
Jacket.
smaller.
Glitter.
and leather.

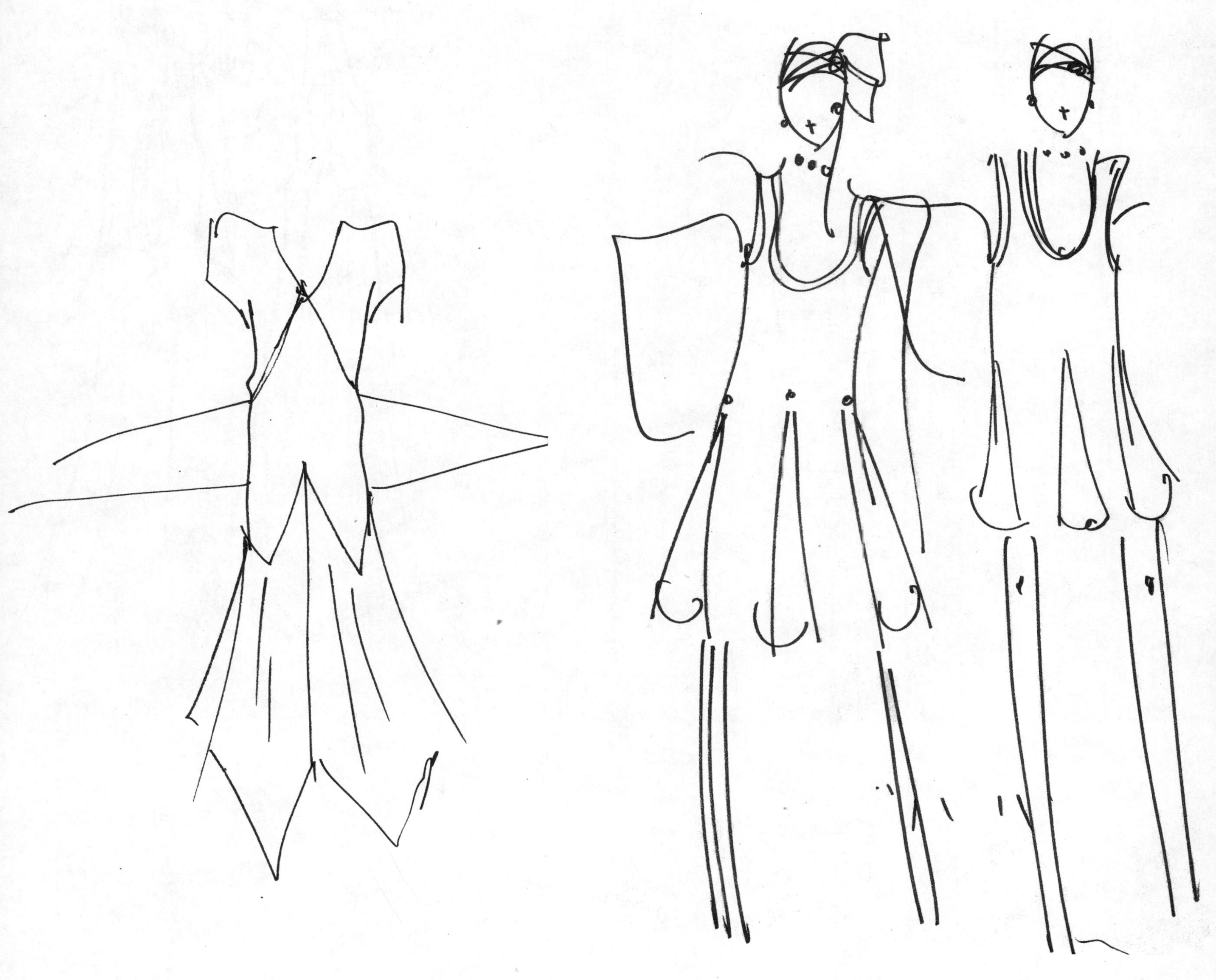

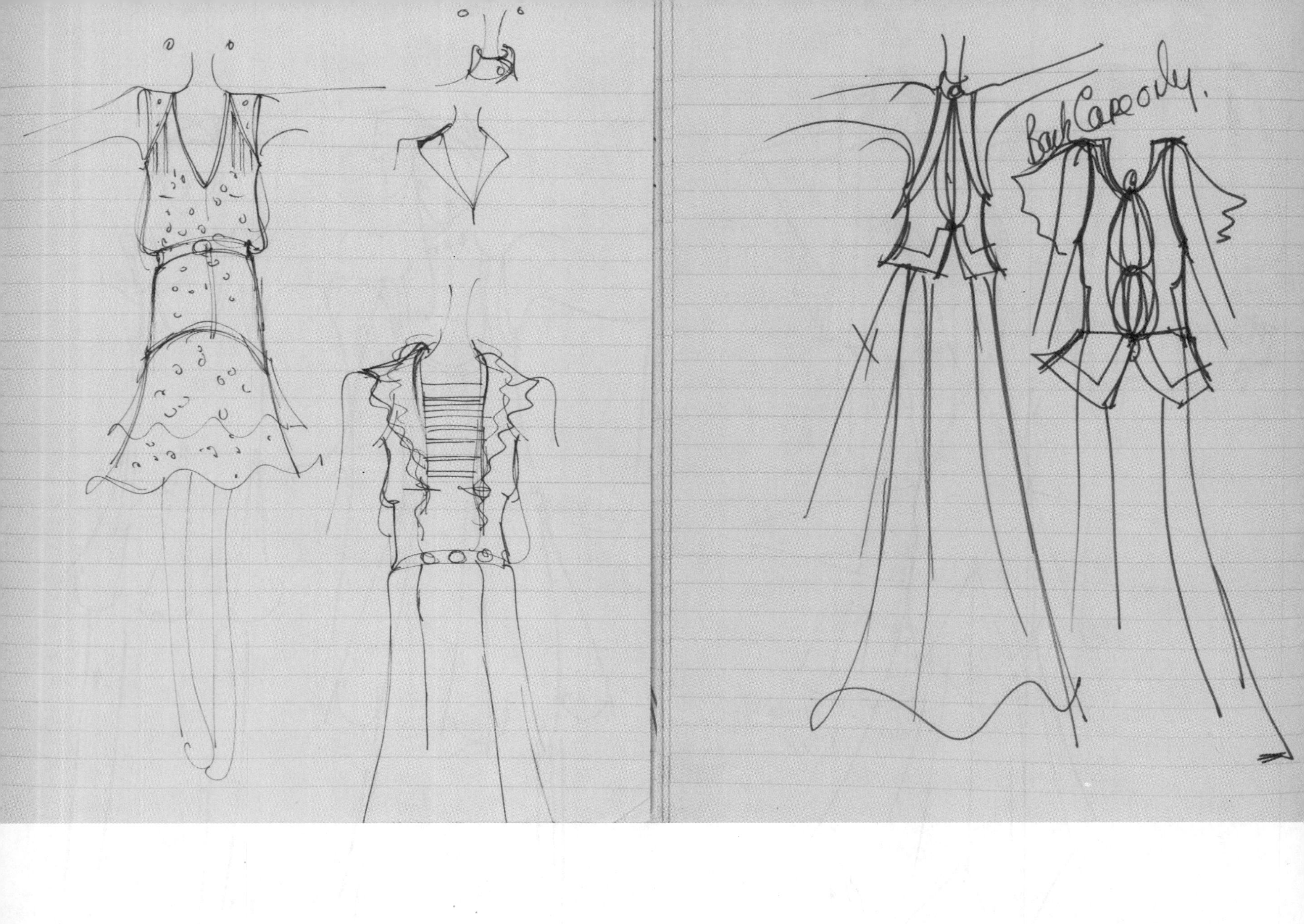
Back Cape only.

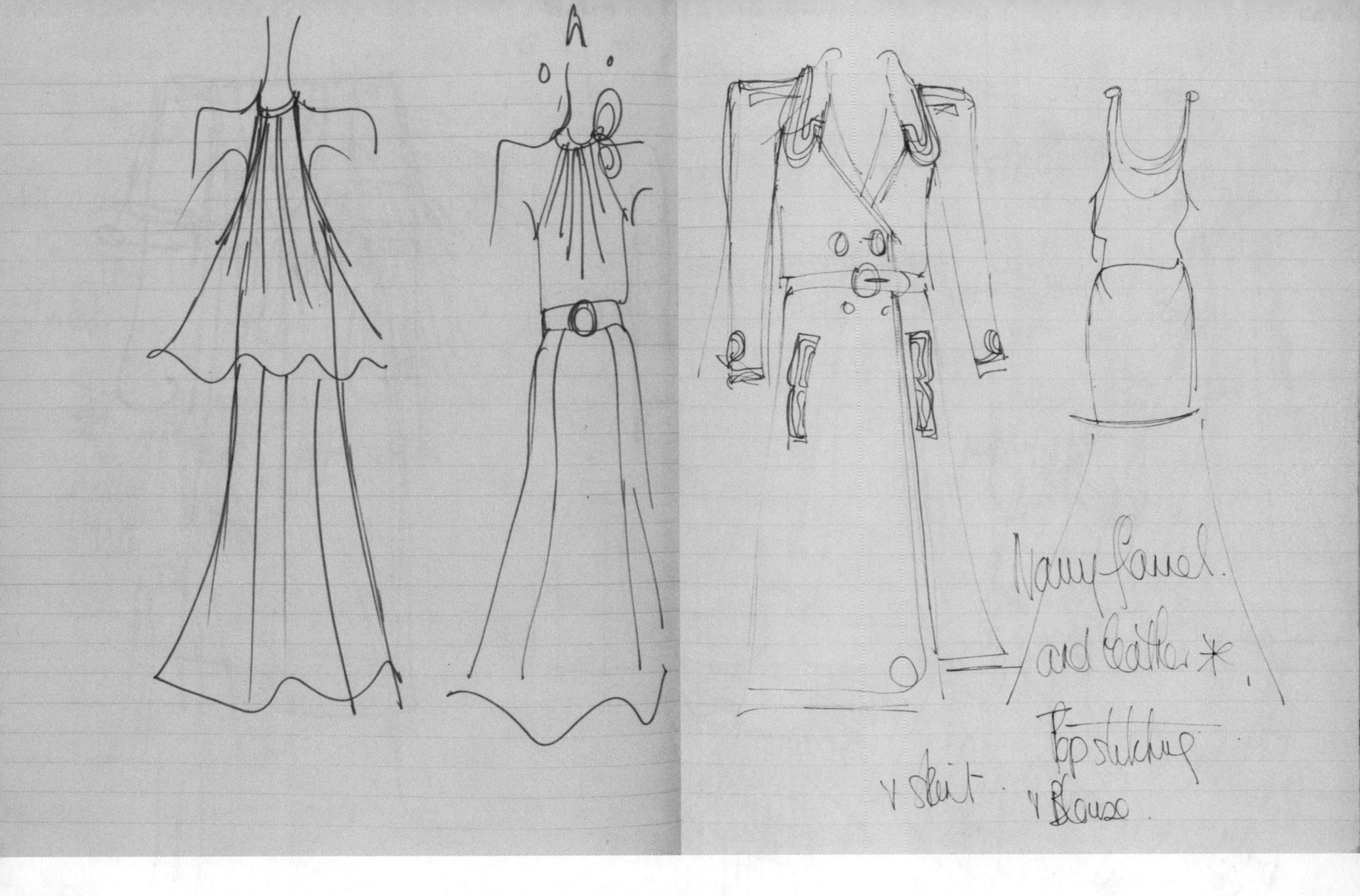
Navy flannel.
and leather *.
Top stitching
v Skirt.
v Blouse.

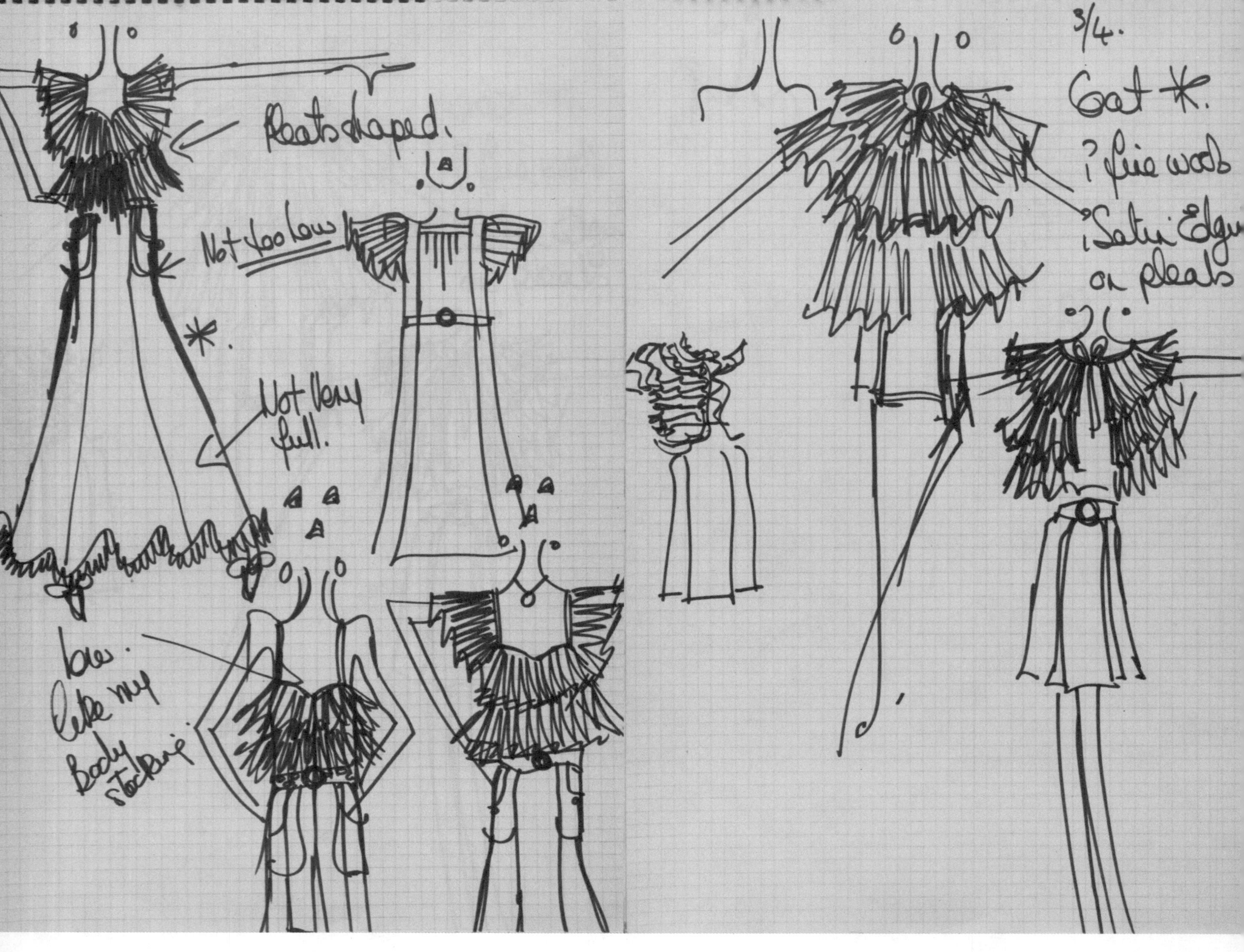

Pleats shaped.
Not too low
Not very full.
bows. Like my body stocking.
3/4.
Coat.
? fine wool
? Satin Edge on pleats

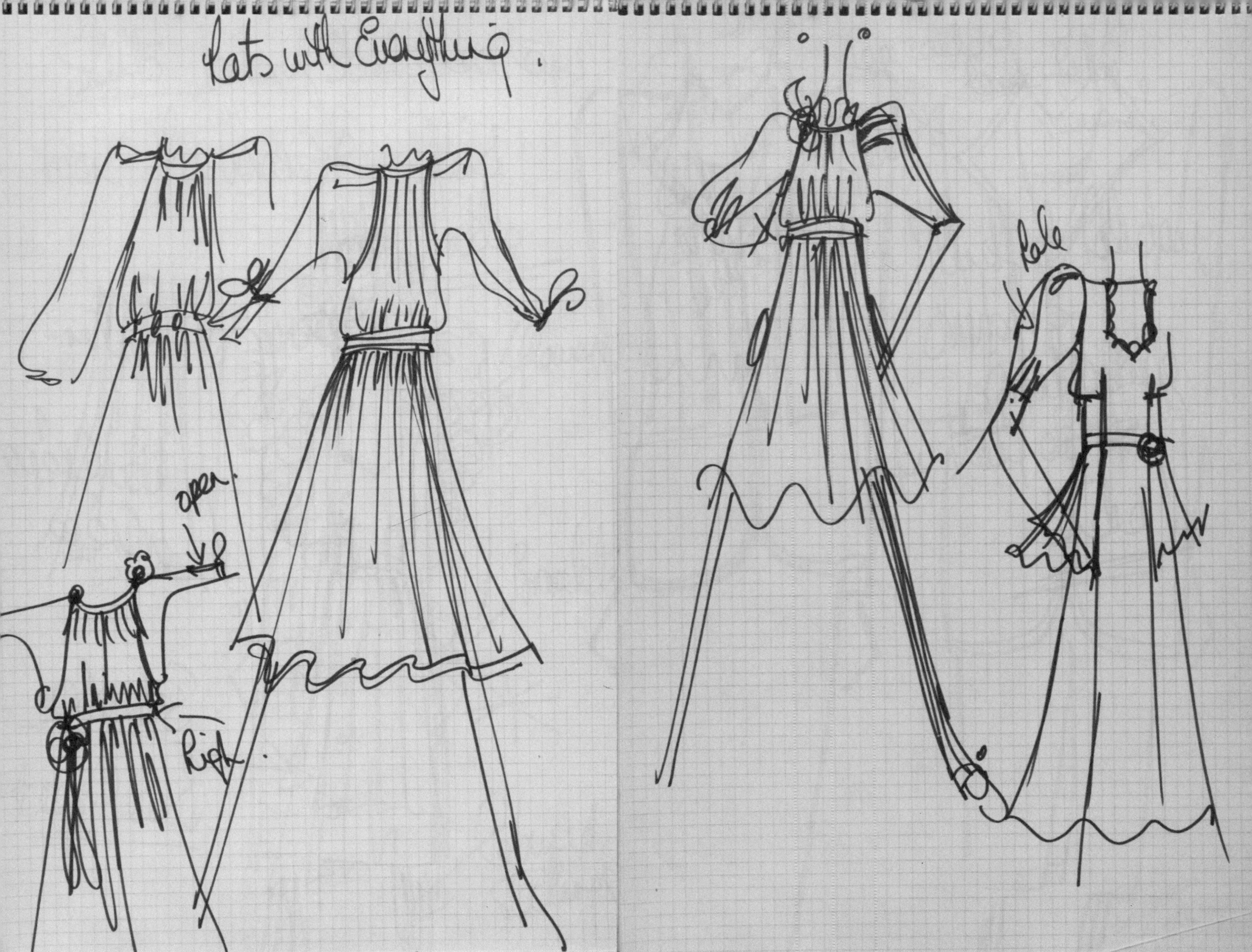
Hats with Everything.
open
Rich

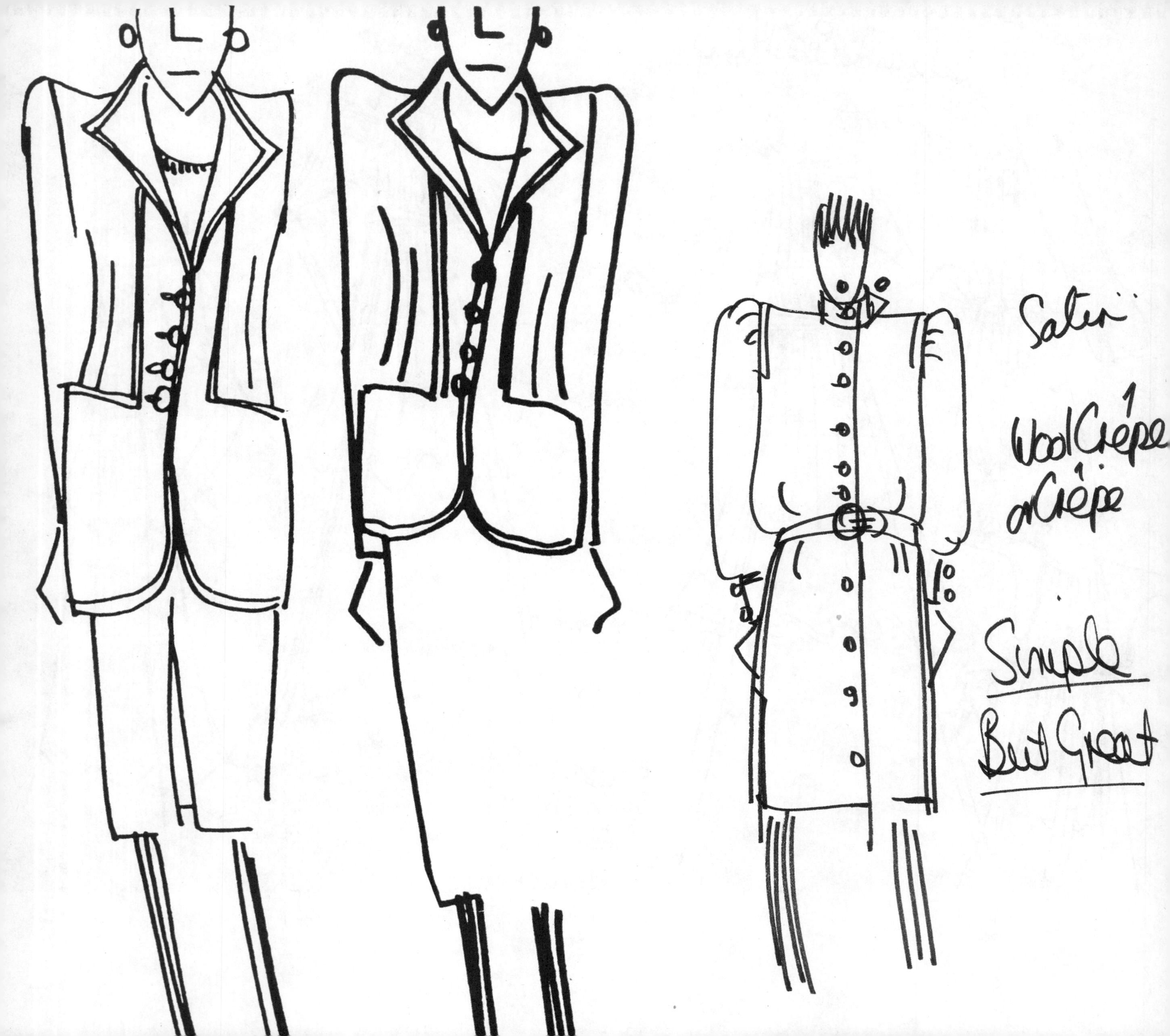

Satin
Wool Crêpe
or Crêpe
Simple
But Great

Wool Crêpe.

Jacket.

Get Skirt Right.

Ribbon Ruffle Top.

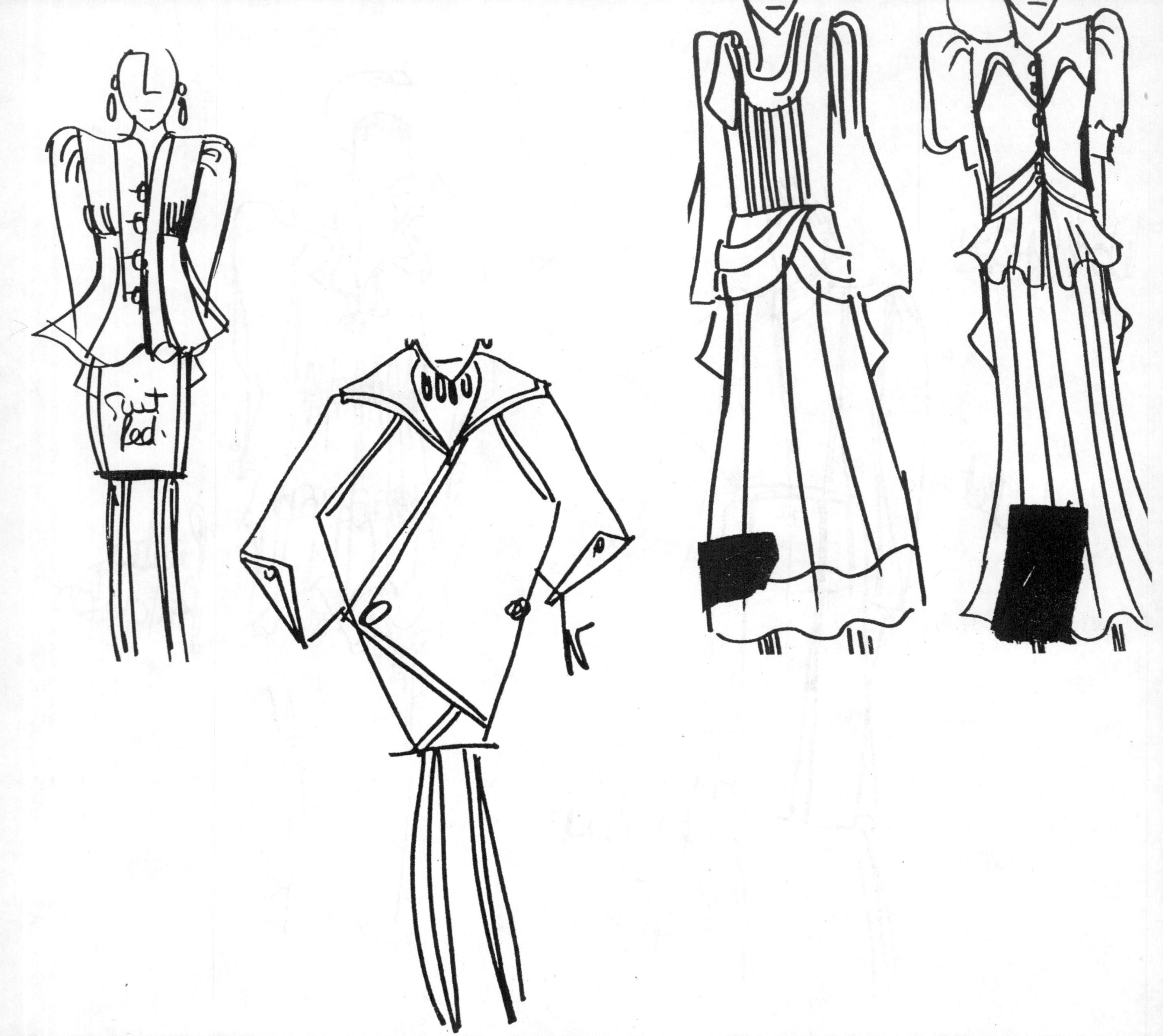
Suit
Red

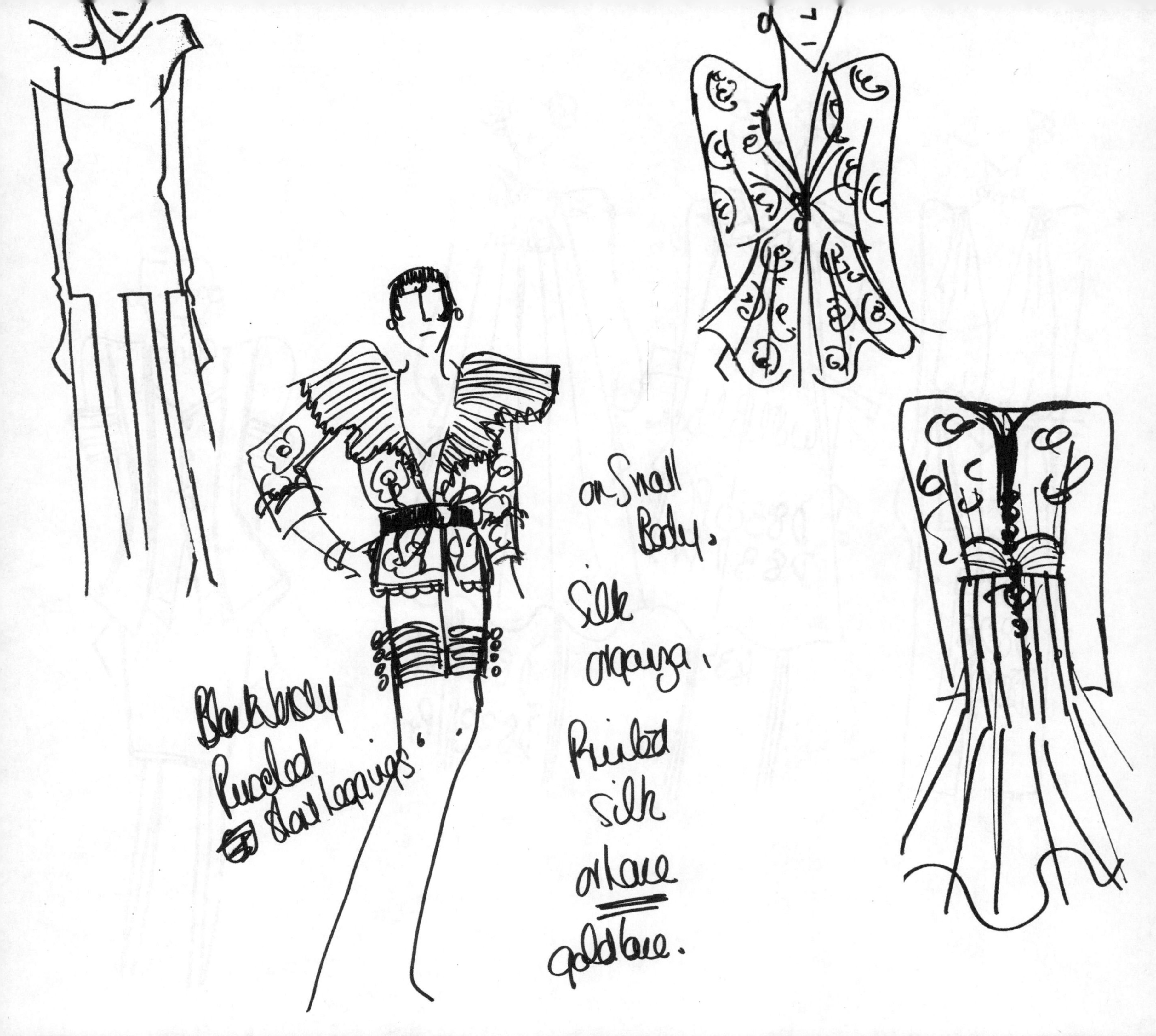
on Small Body.
Silk organza.
Printed silk
or lace
gold lace.
Black jersey
Ruched
short leggings

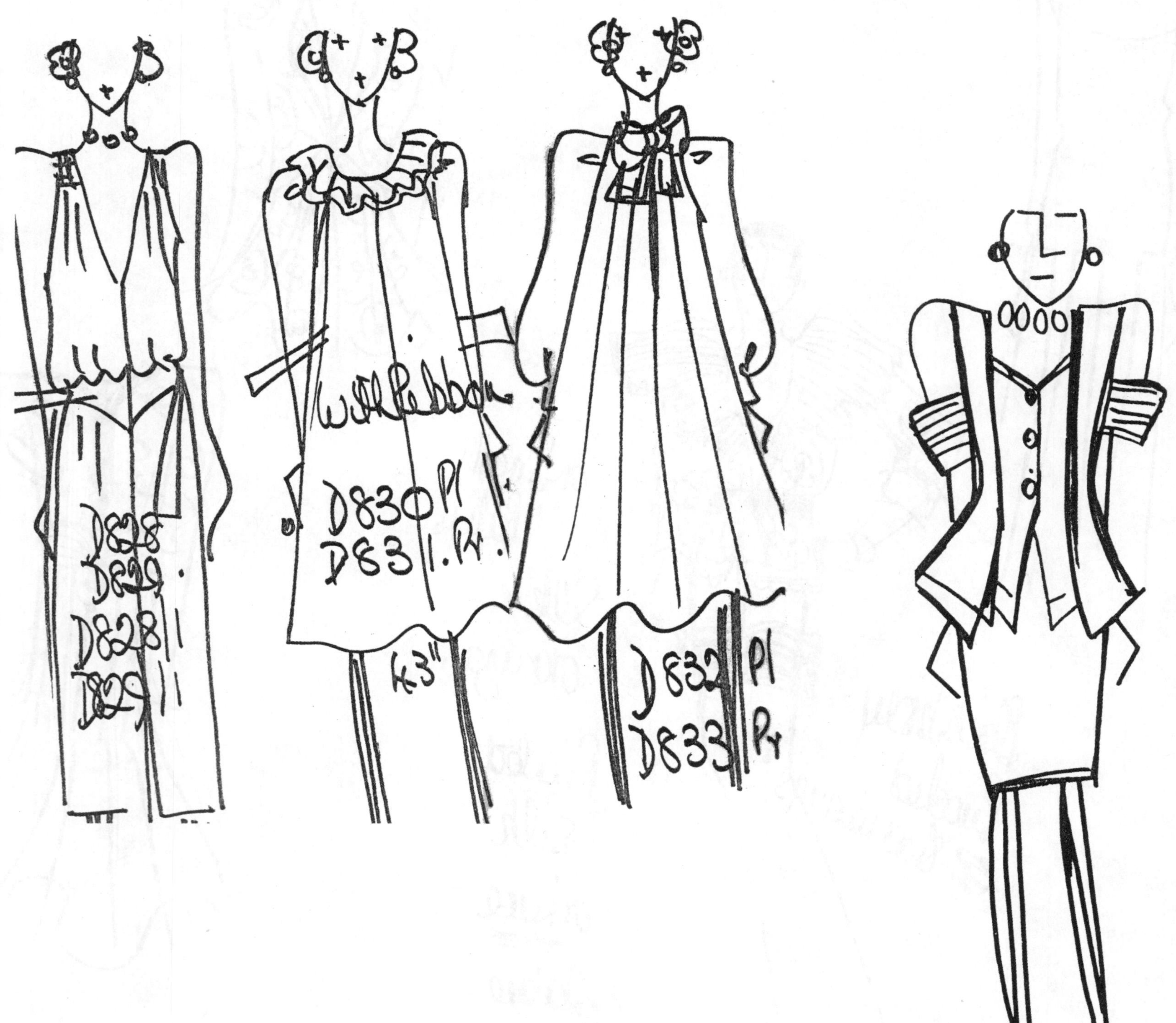

D828
D829
D828
D829
with Ribbon
D830 Pl
D831 Pr.
D832 Pl
D833 Pr

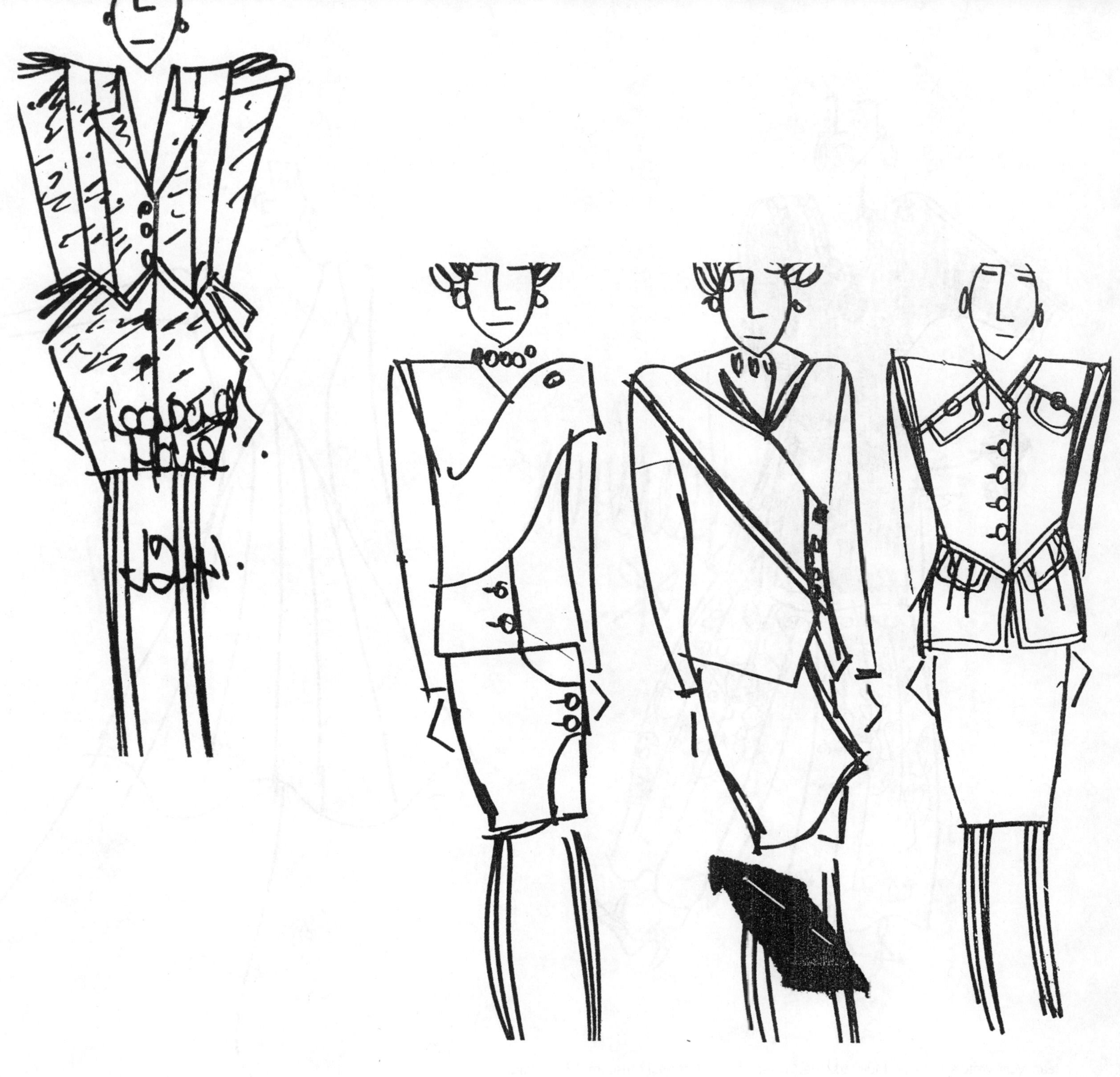

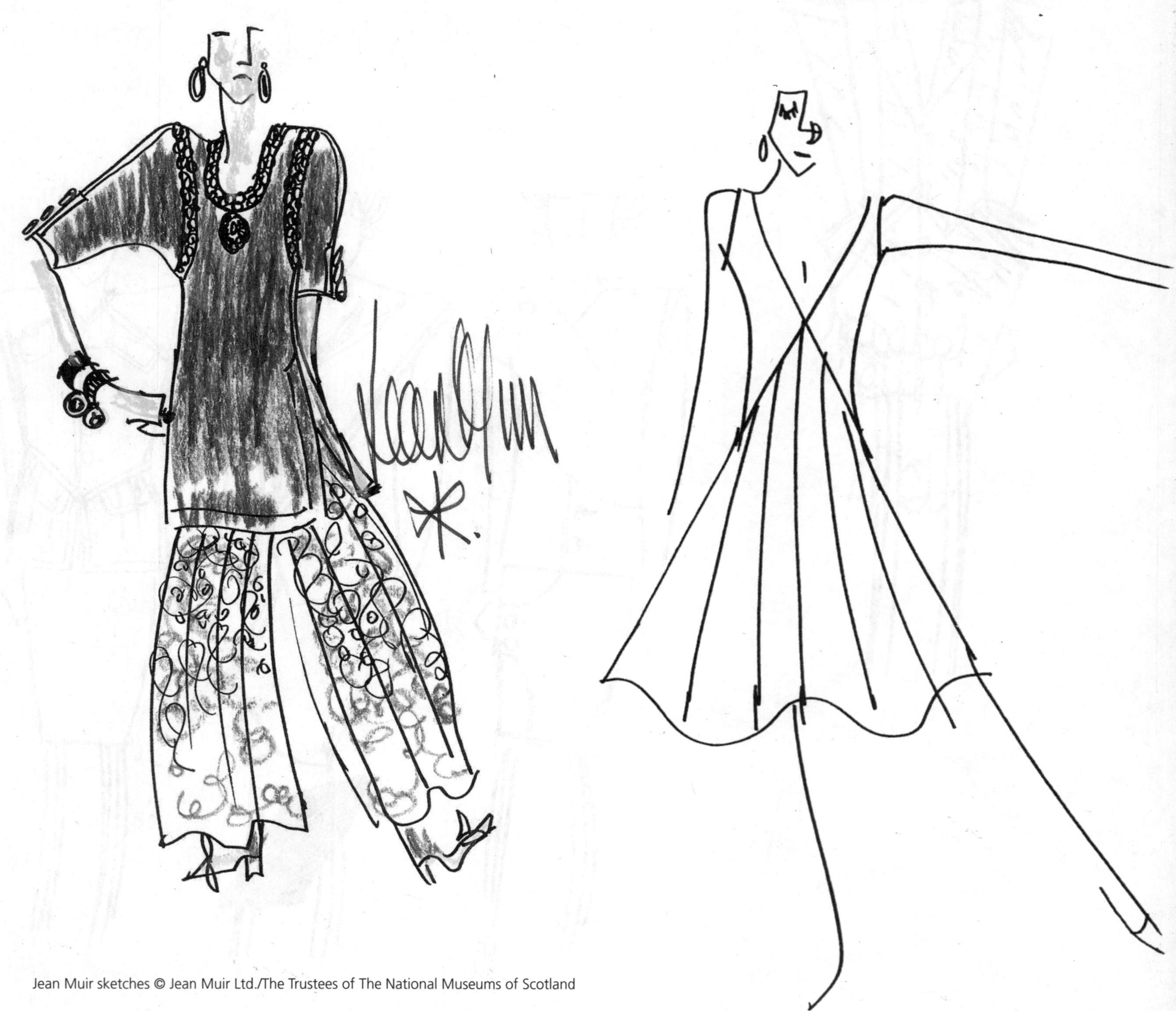

Jean Muir sketches © Jean Muir Ltd./The Trustees of The National Museums of Scotland

"Never has the power of individual skill and style been so important as an essential balance and enhancement – in a technological world the crafts are truly one of the great strengths of this country"

JEAN MUIR

**JEAN MUIR'S** clothes are characterised by an extensive use of highly-skilled and labour-intensive handwork and hand finishing, akin to those used – together with the hours involved – in couture. To own one of her garments is to own a piece of craftsmanship. Each one is a refined blend of multiple crafts. She sought out individual makers: embroiderers, leatherworkers, print designers, hand printers, textile designers, silversmiths, jewellers and milliners, directing and harnessing their skills to help realise and decorate her work. Her enthusiasm for this collaborative interaction was wholehearted: "It's always a great working relationship. I am such an enormous fan, both professionally and privately of the resurgence of the artist craftsman in this country…it has such variety in the way people are taking old skills and pushing them on in new forms, but always exquisitely well made and beautiful."

While much of her garment production was made by a hand-picked group of small-scale companies, and individual outworkers, many of whom still work for the company today, her own staff came from a variety of backgrounds. Shirley Free, a couture dressmaker, previously worked for the London couturier John Cavanagh; some like Fay Lee, an expert finisher, had traditional tailoring skills. Others came straight from school or college to be trained by Muir, who ran her workrooms along the lines of a Parisian couture house atelier. She presided at the helm, in charge of an ordered white space, "I do think a workroom which is dealing in technical work has to be impeccable and look beautifully organized and find one's staff respond to that sense of order."

Working for Miss Muir could be daunting and she didn't suffer fools gladly, if at all! Her perfectionist standards, ceaseless energy and application made her a formidable role model. Several journalists drew parallels between Miss Muir and the heroine of Muriel Spark's novel, *The Prime of Miss Jean Brodie*. Like Miss Brodie, Miss Muir was certainly the moulding, controlling, central force and of Scottish extraction. Not only did her staff need to comply in the normal professional sense, she also appraised potential candidates for the neatness of their presentation and handwriting, good grooming being a prerequisite. Commenting on individual skills, Miss Muir observed, "… the way the girls push the cloth through the sewing machine and they know what the cloth has got to do and when to hold it tighter or when to stretch it slightly. And it's innate in their fingers, and I think it is something we should appreciate infinitely more in this country – all these wonderful skills."

# MATTE JERSEY

Of all the fabrics Miss Muir worked with, matte jersey was the one with which she became most identified. Whereas Madeleine Vionnet perfected a bias cut, and Madame Grès perfected draping on the body, Jean Muir tailored it to perfection.

She made jersey not just a fabric for evening, but made it popular for daywear too. Her trademark detail, layers of neat machine topstitching, accentuated and emphasised the cut and shape. She introduced contrast-coloured stitching to further play on the lines of construction. Shoulders, which were softly rounded, would often have pleats or stitched down tucks for a better fit. Bodices were pintucked, softly pleated, or gathered from yokes. She also variously shirred shoulder lines, bodices, waists, sleeves, and cuffs on blouses and dresses.

Often mistaken for silk, the matte jersey Muir used was in fact a superior rayon jersey of a very fine knit construction and its particular matte quality made it an extremely sophisticated and flattering cloth. Jersey had previously been used to make men's longjohn underwear until Chanel revolutionised its use in the '20s with her relaxed, sporty looks for women. Since then it had languished until Muir recognised it as an ideal cloth to work with. It was made to her own specifications – she stipulated the fineness of the gauge (the number of stitches to the inch) – by companies such as Brochier and Racine.

The manner of construction of her matte jersey was very deliberate – she simply pinked the seams after stitching them to ensure a lightness of finish. "When I first started my business, the kind of dressmaking was still very much clothes that needed to be mounted, lined and bound, so consciously I eliminated the stiffness. I started to use jersey in about 1968; again, consciously, I was updating a kind of manufacturing, using a material that did not have to be neatened. Stitching on the hems would neaten the seams so the manufacturing became part of the design."

Though she was averse to overt ornamentation, Muir was drawn to sophisticated shimmer effects. In the eighties and nineties she developed her penchant for this using glitter-flocked matte jersey as well as sequin embroidery on her matte jersey pieces. In the eighties, Miss Muir also commissioned two craftswomen to decorate her garments with different forms of silk embroidery. Lucy Goffin's speciality was a fine tracery usually in feather stitch silk thread incorporating tiny beads. It was most frequently applied in a contrast colour to matte jersey. Aideen Sturgeon embroidered matte jersey dresses, tunics and blouses, and knitwear, with brightly coloured silk tatting, a sort of flattened pompom of looped silk thread, providing an interesting textural mix.

David Watts, Muir's colleague at Jaeger, confirms that "what Jean really became famous for was her matte jersey. You have to remember that at the time she started to use it, jersey fabric was on the decline – anything like the classic Grecian dress was seen as old hat – the look was still Dior, with big full skirts – jersey was perceived as old-fashioned. Anyhow, Jean decided she liked it – but she did a new take on it. Not only did she overcome the technical difficulties of working with it – it's a notoriously tricky cloth – she took it even further by adding suede and leather and even metallic pythonskin. Those pieces were fantastic. She was clever in that she virtually pioneered elastic waists in designerwear. Her shapes were never restrictive and because nothing constricted, everything sort of just drifted – there were never any fit problems, they fitted everyone."

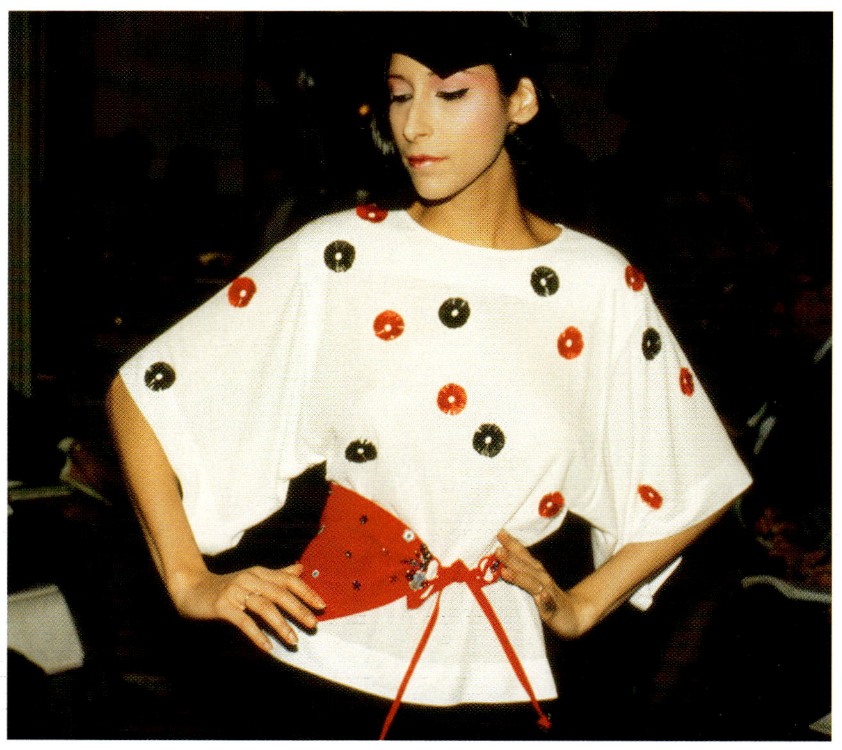

**ABOVE** Batwing blouse in white jersey, embroidered with silk tatting by Aideen Sturgeon. Red suede corset tie belt, Spring 1983. Photograph & © Niall McInerney. **OPPOSITE** Bell-sleeve tunic and culottes in brown jersey with matching shirred jersey cap by Graham Smith, Autumn 1975. Photograph: Michael Barrett. © The Trustees of The National Museums of Scotland.

"I do not drape jersey ... I tailor it."

JEAN MUIR

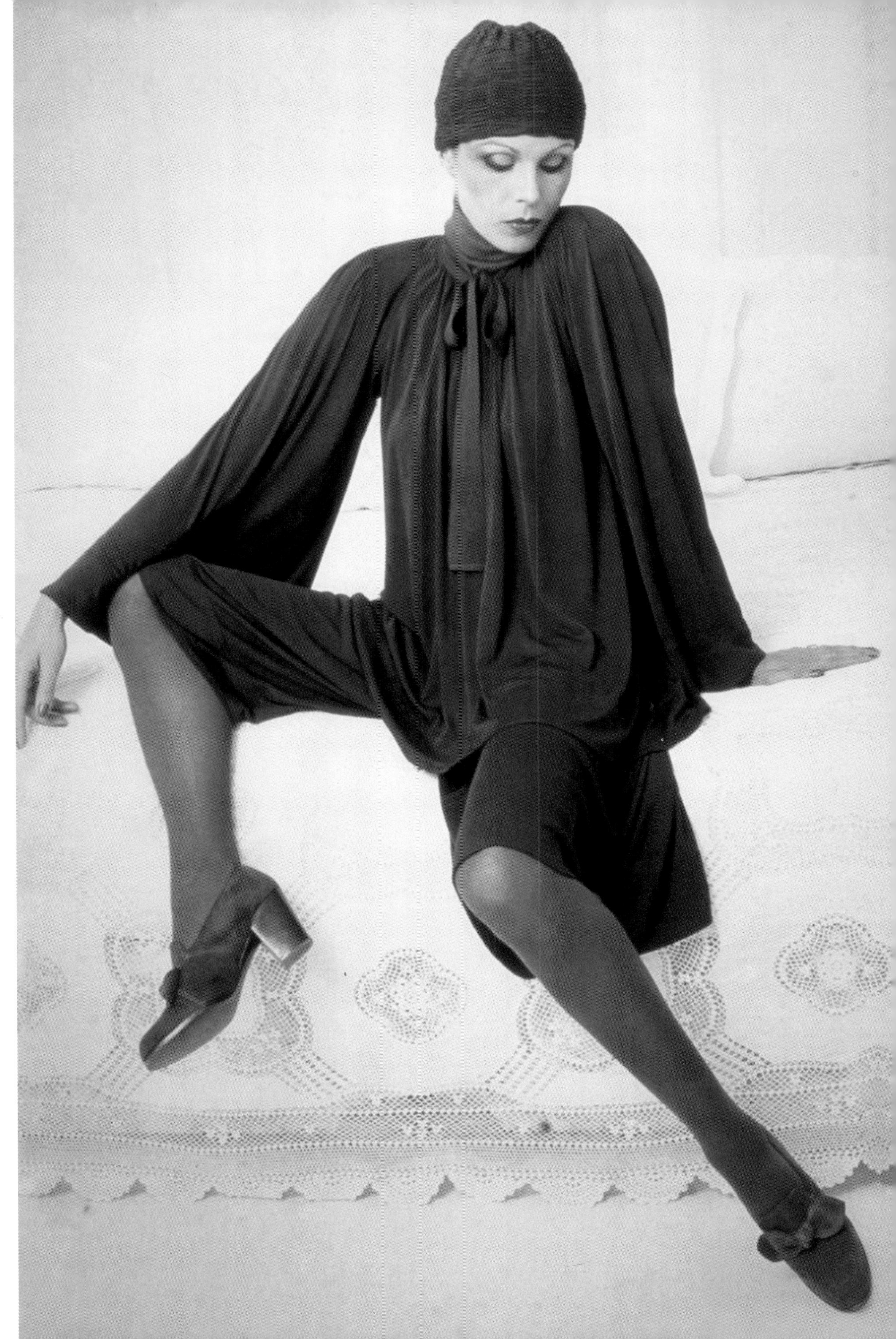

# LITTLE BLACK DRESS

The little black (or navy) Jean Muir dress has become a symbol of effortless chic and subtle sexuality. The effect was simple, sophisticated and timeless. Muir's flawless tailoring made these dresses look as though they were cut on the bias when in reality they were cut straight but intricately seamed for an ideal fit that moved beautifully with the body.

Jean Muir's genius with the little black dress is universally recognised and acclaimed. Always in demand, it took many forms: it could be brief and revealing – sometimes no more than a superbly cut slip – or high necked and covered up – the subtly cut fabric sensuous with folds and gathers and flaring movement. Whether a woman was a size 8, 10, 12, 14 or up, in a Jean Muir LBD she would not only feel, but also look, several sizes smaller – and wonderfully feminine.

As fashion writer Jody Jacobs acknowledged in April 1971 in America's *Women's Wear Daily*, "Those short black dresses in jersey or cire or silk Muir calls 'my throwaways' and they can look as ingénue as a smock or as knowing as Marlene Dietrich. It's all in the shape…and Jean's intentions."

Fashion writer Iain R Webb comments: "For me, the ultimate practitioner of perfect LBD chic was the late Jean Muir. With just a few metres of black jersey, Miss Muir could conjure up a dress, which was a masterclass in elegance and refinement. Every six months at her fashion show, she could be relied upon to offer a new version of this fashion classic – a fluted hem here, a scooped neckline there – which would take my breath away."

Of course, Muir's mastery of the jersey dress was not merely confined to black, or indeed navy. Her idiosyncratic choice and use of colour in this medium was something altogether different and special, as Gai Pearl Marshall recalls: "I was Miss Muir's showroom vendeuse and PR during the early '70s when she was creating her fabulous draped jersey dresses in all those incredible colours that only she seemed able to produce. Wonderful tones of dusty rose, bright fuchsia, eau de nile and shades of jade which I still think of as 'Jean Muir green'. Those frocks walked with you into a room. Being an ex-dancer I knew how to move to make a dress flow around me, but in a Jean Muir you got that extra beat. Three steps forward and a half turn on the ball of one foot and the skirt followed you around the corner three seconds later."

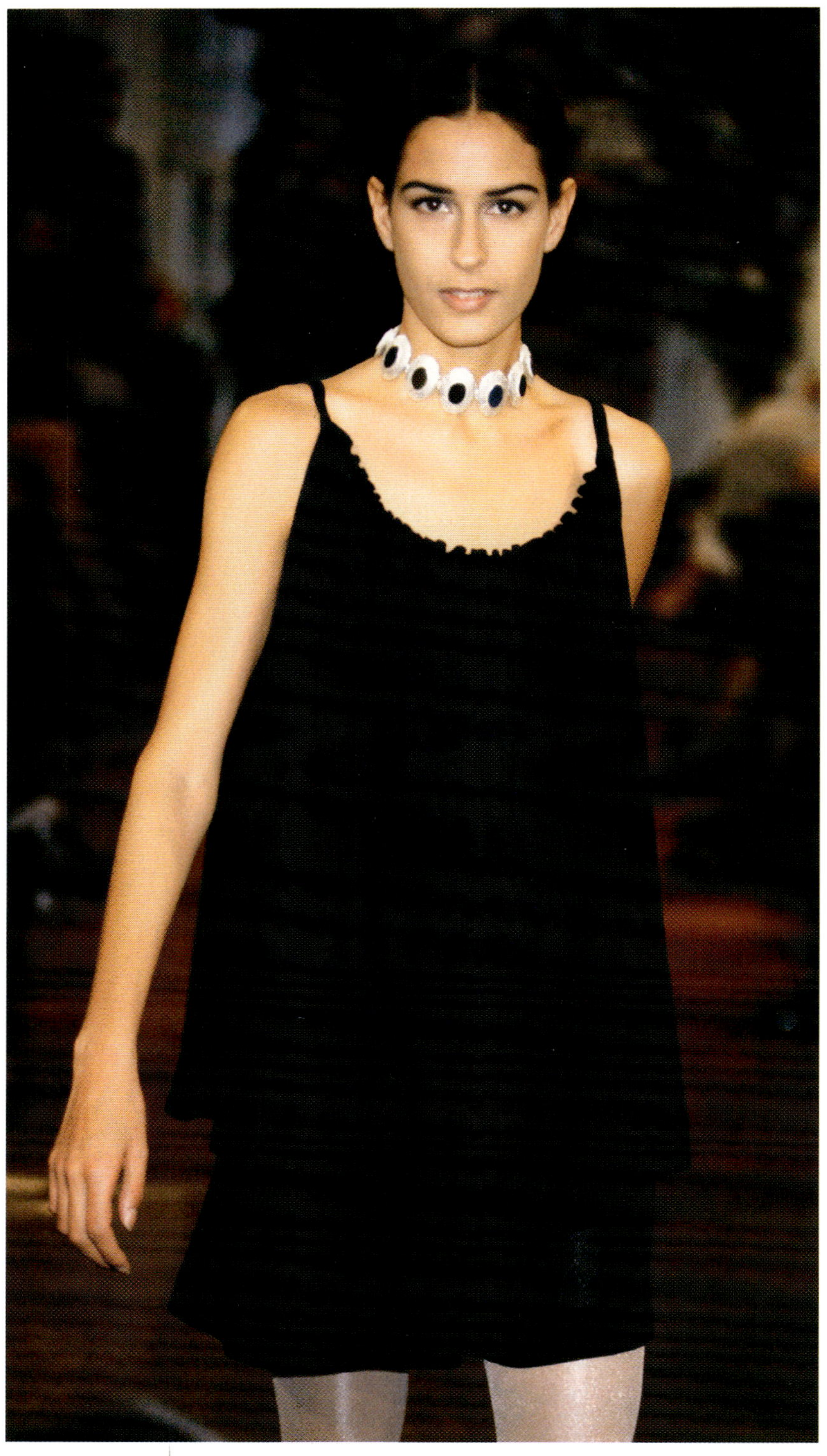

**ABOVE** The Muir hallmark – two-tier version of the little black dress – gathered camisole tunic over flared shorts. Sterling silver/enamel choker by Iain Young for Jean Muir, Spring 1993. Photograph & © Chris Moore. **RIGHT** "Jean Muir's perfect jersey vest dress...", *Vogue* March 1980. Photograph: Arthur Elgort/Vogue. © The Condé Nast Publications Ltd.

"La nouvelle reine
de la robe"
ELLE MAGAZINE

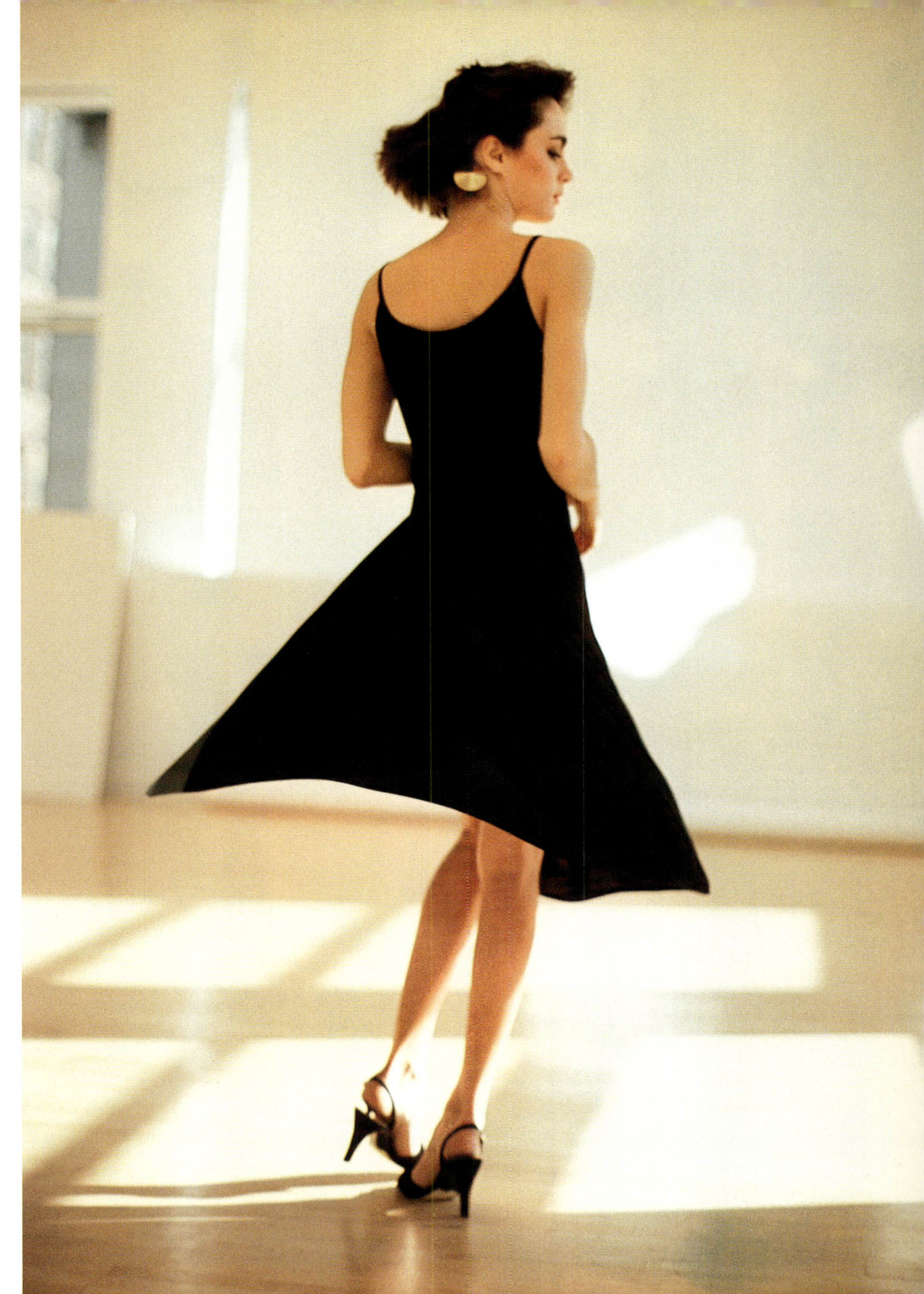

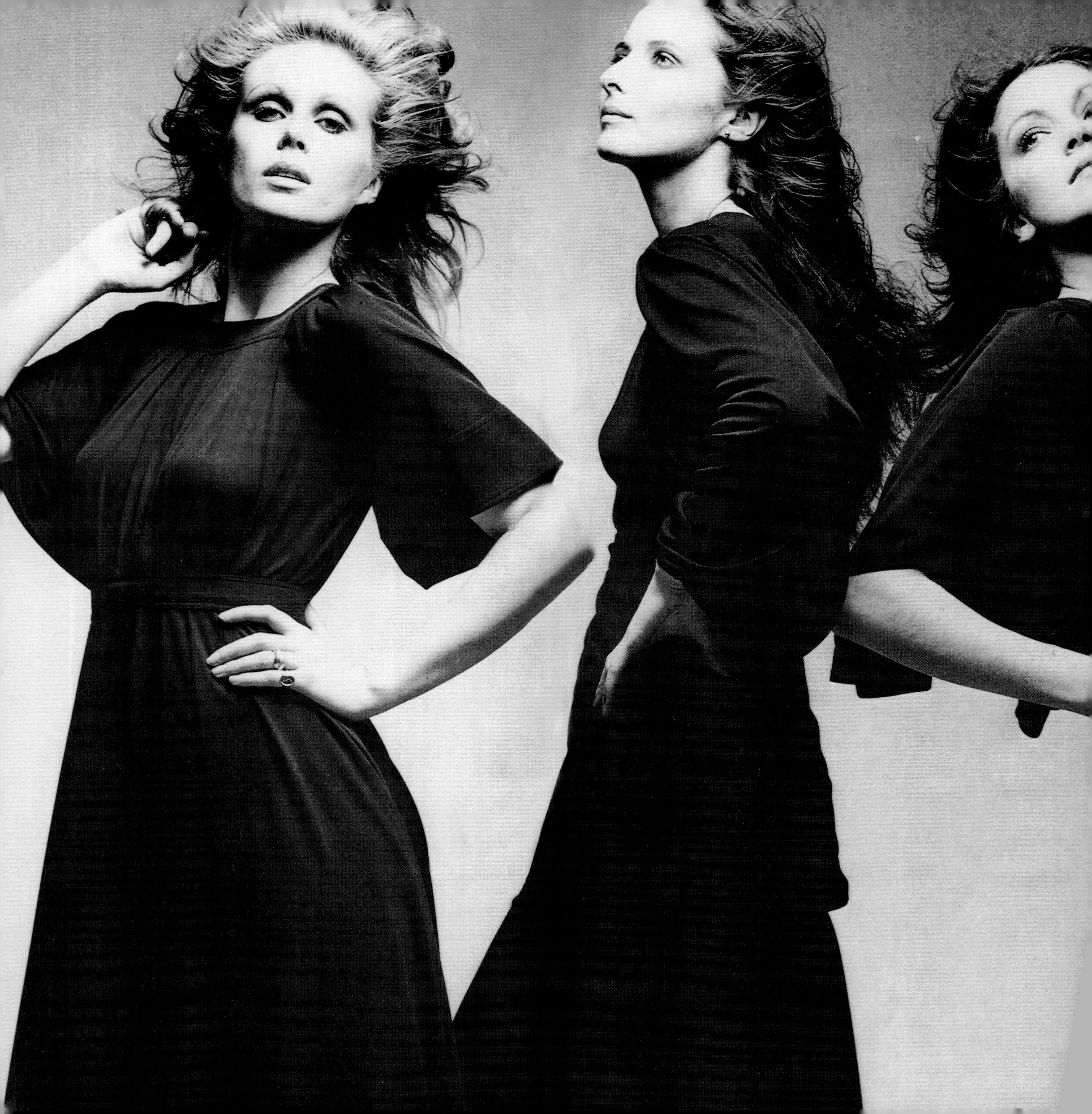

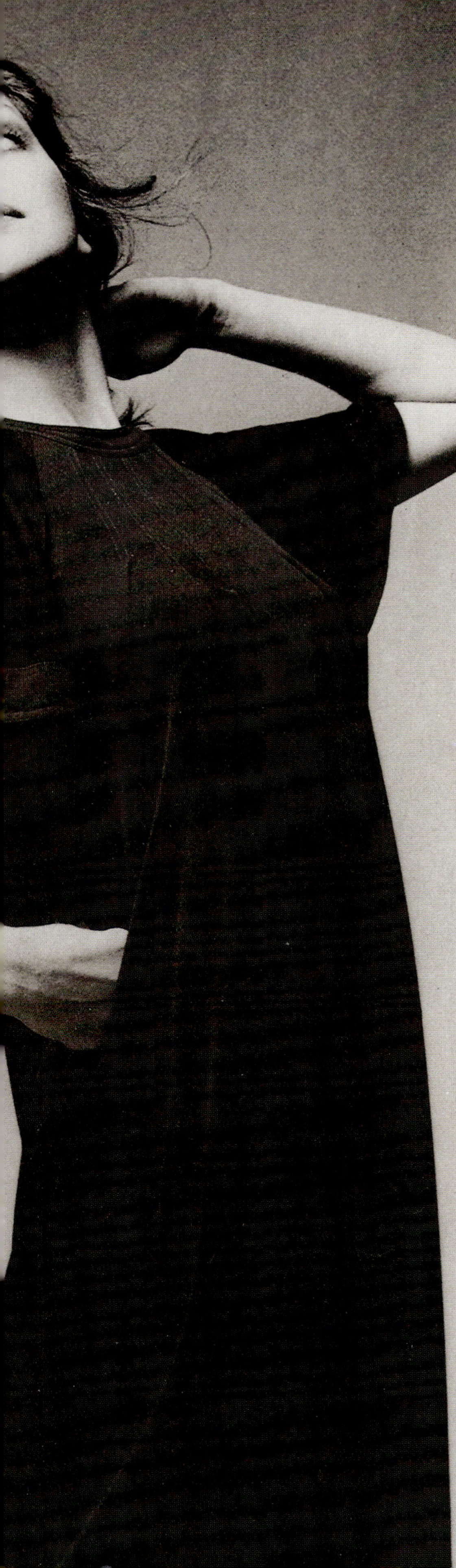

"If I was ever asked to list my Desert Island LBDs, I would have to include, of course, anything by The Divine Miss M."

IAIN R WEBB, FASHION WRITER

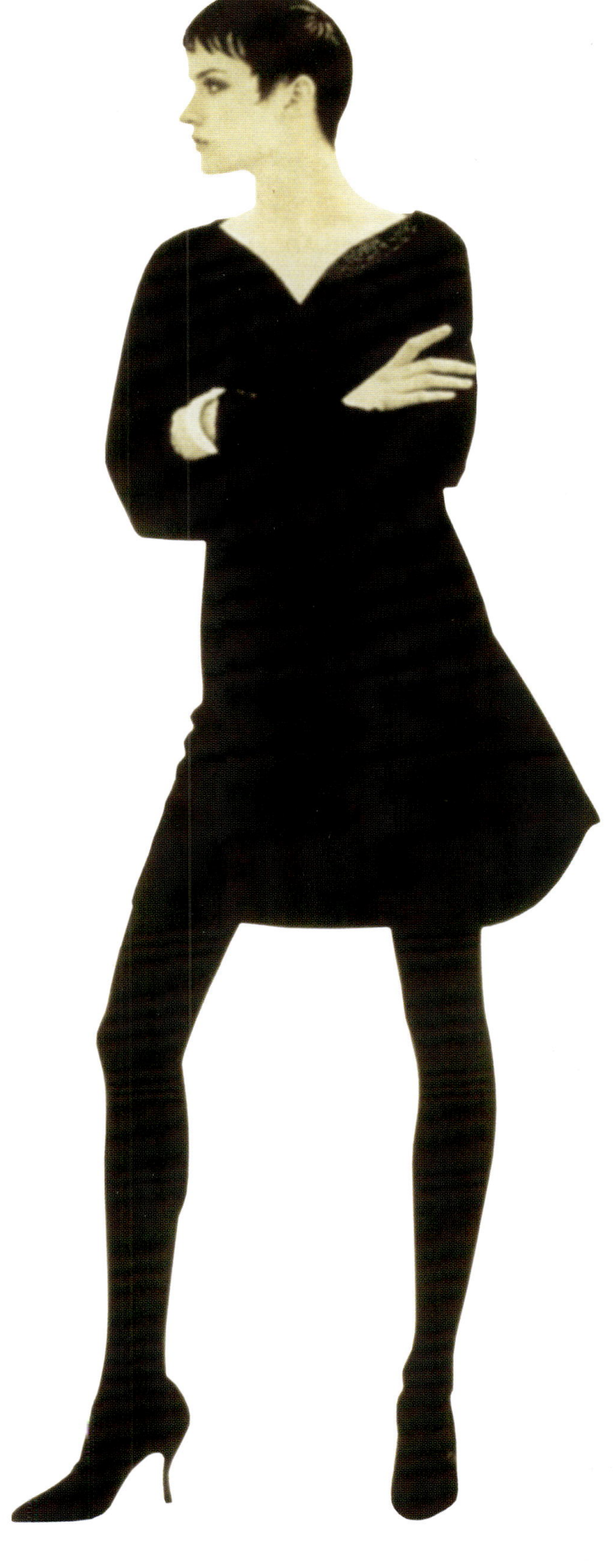

**LEFT** The three muses: archetypal Muir matte jersey dresses worn by models Joanna Lumley, Paddy Grey, Joanna Vignola, 1972. Photograph: David Bailey/Vogue. © The Condé Nast Publications Ltd. **ABOVE** The minimalist's little black dress, combining austerity and sex appeal, Autumn 1991. Photograph: Arthur Elgort/Vogue. © The Condé Nast Publications Ltd.

# SUEDES & LEATHERS

Jean Muir undeniably changed designers' perceptions of working with skins, and her work in this medium, along with that in matte jersey, altered the course of fashion and remains relevant today.

Muir tailored suede and leather in much the same way she tailored jersey: pleating, tucking, and panelling it. Suede or leather would be used for entire garments, including dresses, or applied as decoration to highlight necklines and cuffs on other fabrics – glitter georgette, matte jersey, tweed.

She first started to work in suede and leather in the mid-sixties, and several of her styles for the specialist company Morel were featured on the cover and within the pages of British *Vogue*, February 1967. The Victoria & Albert Museum have a beautiful pansy-violet suede dress of about this time in their permanent dress collection, which is zipped down the middle, with rows of finely moulded tucks fanning out across the bodice from the shoulder line.

For her own label, Miss Muir used a variety of skins, skilfully wrapping them round the body as though they were the most pliable fabrics. Fine shirtsuede and nappa leathers, both of which were butter-soft and super-luxe, were her favourites. She additionally used exotic skins such as coloured python and liked the impact of foiled nappa leather in gold and silver. Cowskin, the heaviest weight she used, would be richly coloured and panelled in curves of concentric colours.

Another Jean Muir trademark, the technique of hand-punching would be used to pattern either the borders or an entire garment. This detailing was frequently featured in British and American *Vogue*, where it was described as 'brogueing'.

"She was possibly the first to make leathers that were as soft and sensuous as satin."

**BILL BLASS, AMERICAN FASHION DESIGNER**

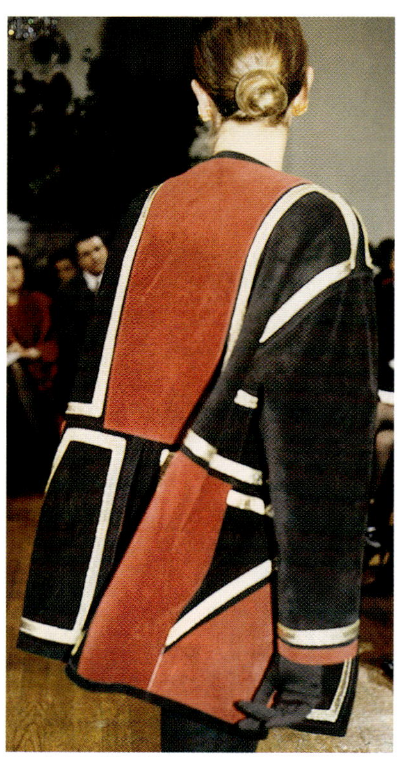

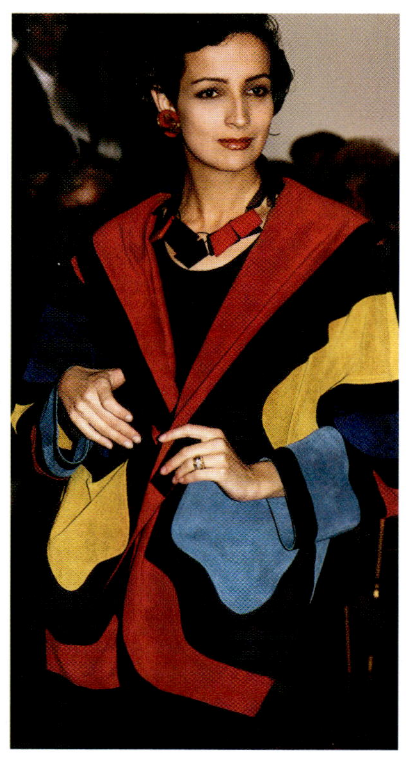

Muir works her magic with suede and leather. **THIS PAGE** Brilliantly coloured suede jackets in contrasting panels. **OPPOSITE PAGE, TOP ROW, LEFT TO RIGHT** The versatility of suede and leather: hand punching on suede; the luxury of leather with the softness of silk. **BOTTOM ROW, LEFT TO RIGHT** Suede on suede concentric bands of bright colour; loose and flowing dolman sleeve coat reveals the unlined interior; stamped leather fitted jacket fastened with sterling silver buttons. Autumn 1986 to Spring 1993. Photographs & © Chris Moore & Niall McInerney.

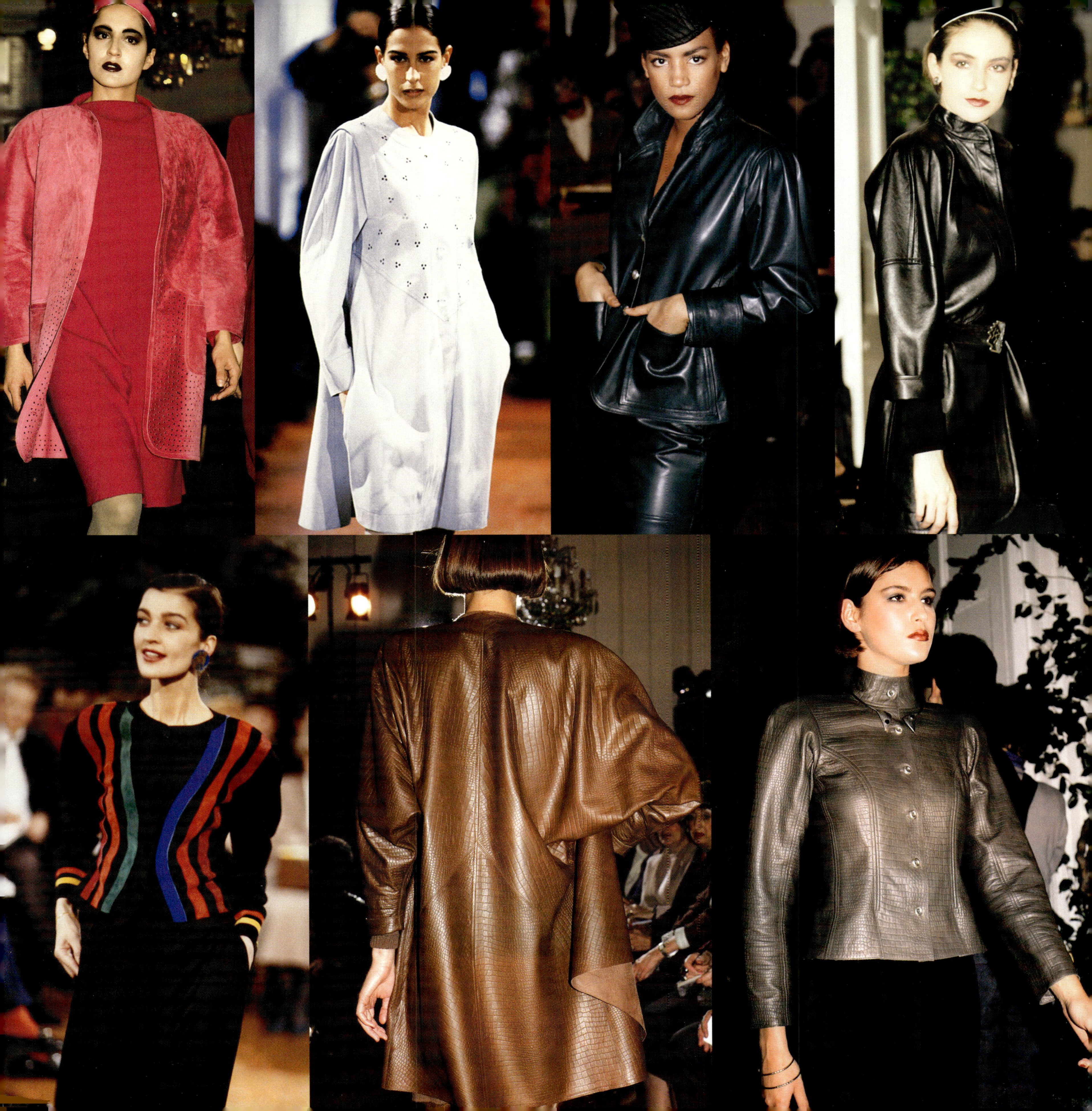

# KNITWEAR

Muir always loved colours in cashmere, whether single colour, striped, or patterned. She liked to use delicate 'pointelle' lace work, ribbing and cabling in her knitwear, often in combination. Styles varied from tiny sleeveless tops to the voluminous tunics. Her knitwear progressed from smaller-scale abstract intarsia patterns through to the bold painterly style of the late eighties and early nineties.

Muir called on the skills of James Fraser and his family for many of the special cashmere intarsias on these pages. He recalls the inspiring nature of their partnership. "Jean Muir is a rare person... all the designers I've met before, just as long as it's good enough, that's all right. But not for Miss Muir. It's got to be better than good. As perfect as you can possibly get it. And there are many things we do that the customer doesn't see, just to reach perfection. We'll make hundreds of trials, and you'll finish up with two. You have to have special eyes to mix colour. And she has that special eye. For me it's the sheer satisfaction of working with the best. You either understand it or you don't. It's doing it and doing it well. That's the whole satisfaction."

> "I love these knits, it's like drowning in colour and pattern"
>
> **JEAN MUIR**

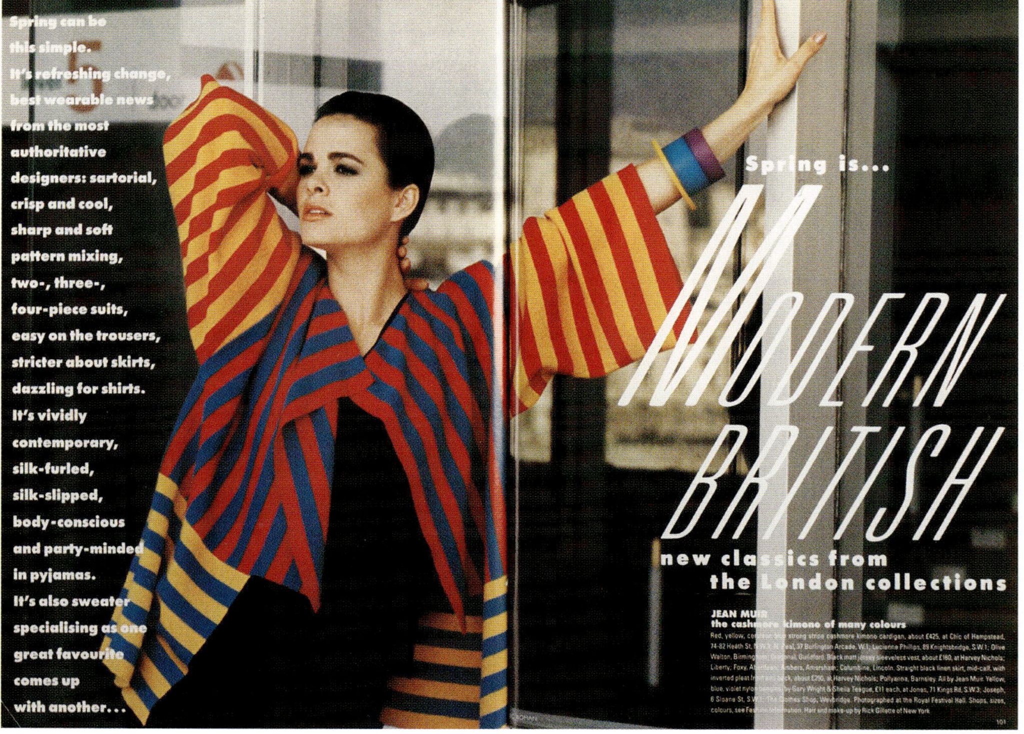


**ABOVE** The cashmere kimono – vividly contemporary in contrasting panels of stripes – red, yellow, and cerulean blue, a double spread in *Vogue*, Spring 1985. Photograph: Eric Boman/Vogue. © The Condé Nast Publications Ltd.

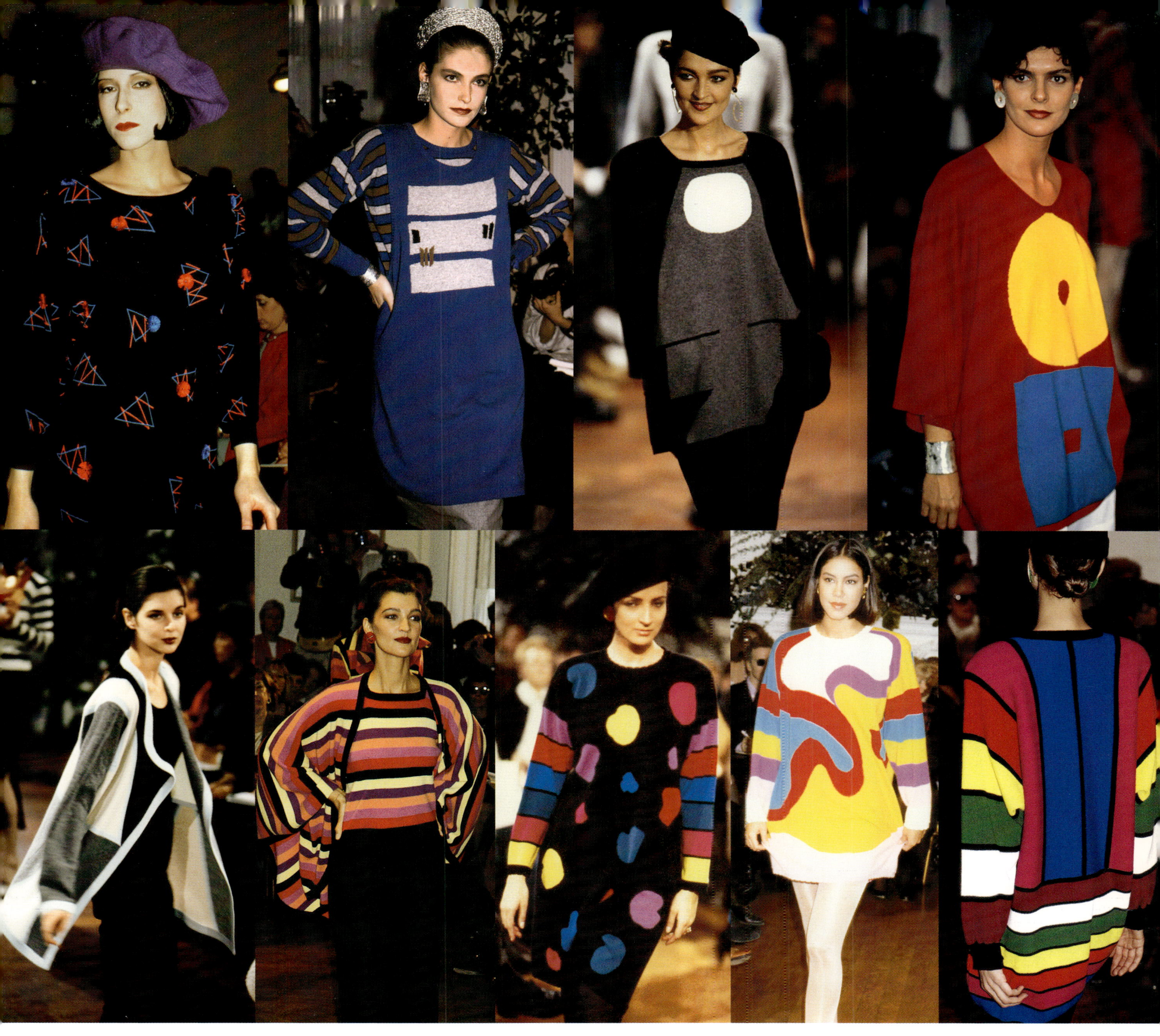

**TOP ROW, LEFT TO RIGHT** Abstract Art: Muir's painterly approach to cashmere knitwear in her signature intarsia designs. Sweater with embroidered silk tatting; tabard tunic dress over striped sweater; two tri-coloured tunics with modernist overtones. **BOTTOM ROW, LEFT TO RIGHT** Swinging jacket with random panels; cropped striped sweater with capelet cardigan; splashes of colour with striped sleeves; swirling multi-colour tunic; bold colour blocks outlined in black. Autumn 1983 to Spring 1993. Photographs & © Niall McInerney & Chris Moore.

# WOOL

Miss Muir commissioned Annie Sherburne, a young experimental craftswoman, to produce hand-painted felted wool. Sherburne boldly applied multiple colours in an abstract form to the fuzzy wool. Muir would craft this cloth into strikingly individual stylish cocoon-like coats and jackets.

Muir's wools flowed and floated on the body. Many of her wools – particularly wool crepe – she purposely left unlined, preferring the unlined weight for her particular design purpose in order to free up movement on the body. These garments were no less expensive as they needed to be as impeccably finished on the inside as the outside since movement would reveal the interior. Muir like to use grey flannel for dresses which she tucked and seamed into soft feminine shapes, often trimming them with leather. Another yarn she favoured was angora, which she used to emphasise the movement and pliability of her designs.

For Muir, wool was a versatile cloth with endless possibilities. She gave her wools an intensity of colour and used them in a myriad ways. Wool jersey was one of her favourites – she sliced it into the purist shapes that she liked best. She used wool in all its guises, from the finest georgette to the most sumptuous coating, from wool crepes to traditional tweeds. Muir took wool from the practical to the glamorous.

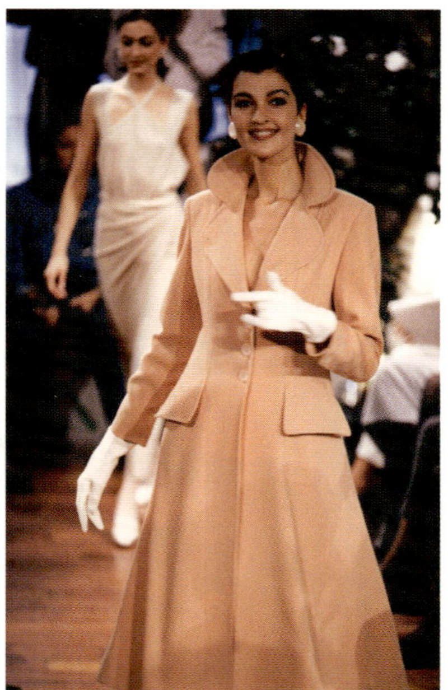

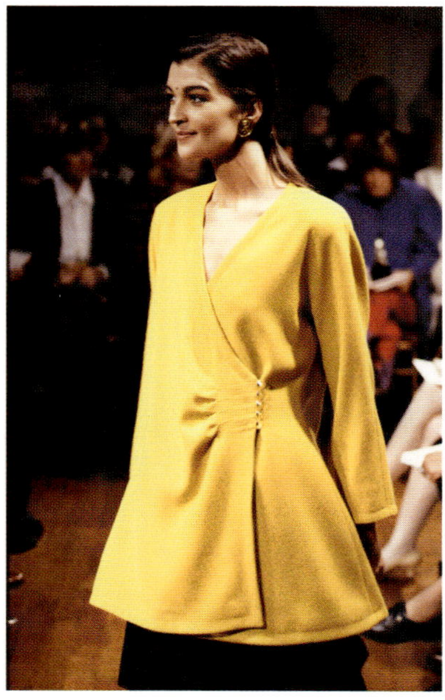

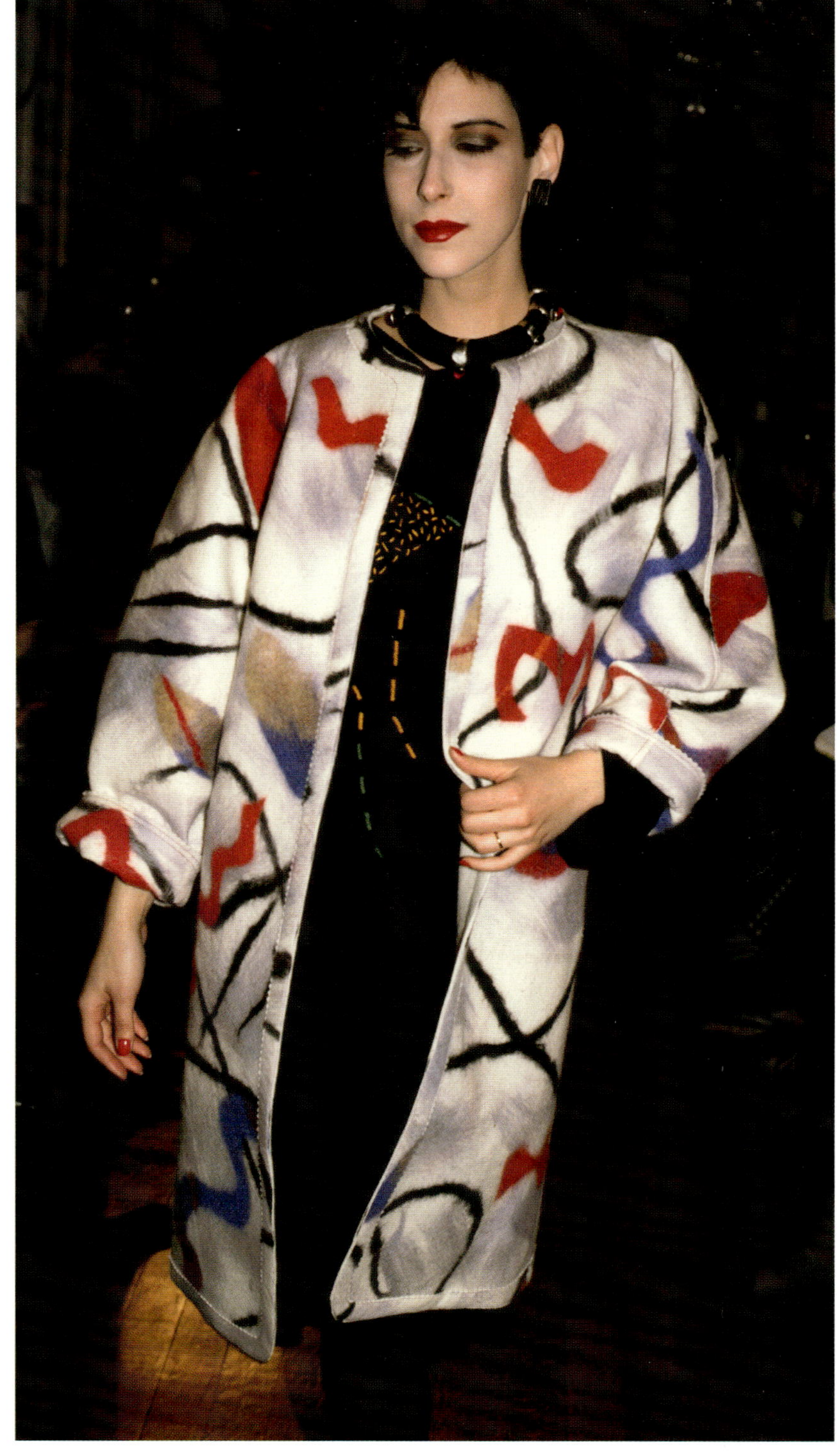

**ABOVE LEFT TO RIGHT** Petal collar coat in double wool crepe with hand-carved Perspex buttons, Spring 1993. Photograph & © Chris Moore. Gathered waist on a wool crepe jacket, Spring 1991. Photograph & © Chris Moore. Dramatic use of colour and texture: hand-painted felted wool collarless coat by Annie Sherburne commissioned for Jean Muir's Autumn 1984 collection. Photograph & © Niall McInerney.

> "In my collections I love to use dramatic, vibrant colour and I take particular pleasure in choosing prints"
>
> **JEAN MUIR**

## PRINTS

Prints were a distinctive element of Miss Muir's collections. She used them right from the beginning, for Jane and Jane. Many came from Liberty of London, who she also commissioned to revive archive designs. Her choice of print could be anything from small-scale to large-scale, florals to abstracts.

Her reputation was for plain sober colours but when she broke out into print the effect was eye-catching and inspirational.

As well as using available printed fabrics from companies such Liberty, David Evans and the French specialist, Soieries Nouveautés, she commissioned printmakers to design exclusively for her. These designs were hand printed onto her matte jersey and, unusually, onto suede and wool crepe. These prints, which the artist Bridget Riley termed "broken-colour" could take the form of single or multicolour abstracts, a fine tracery of metallic gold on scarlet, or a complex 'clown' motif that seemed to turn cartwheels across the body.

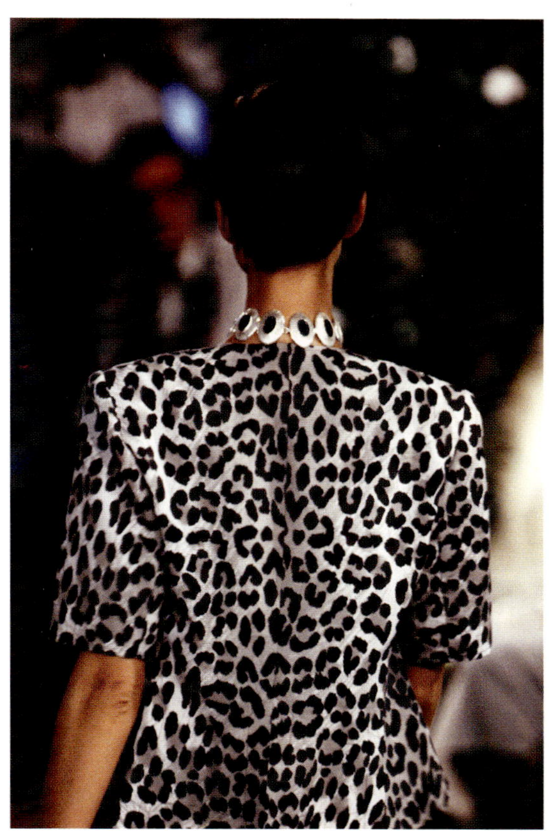

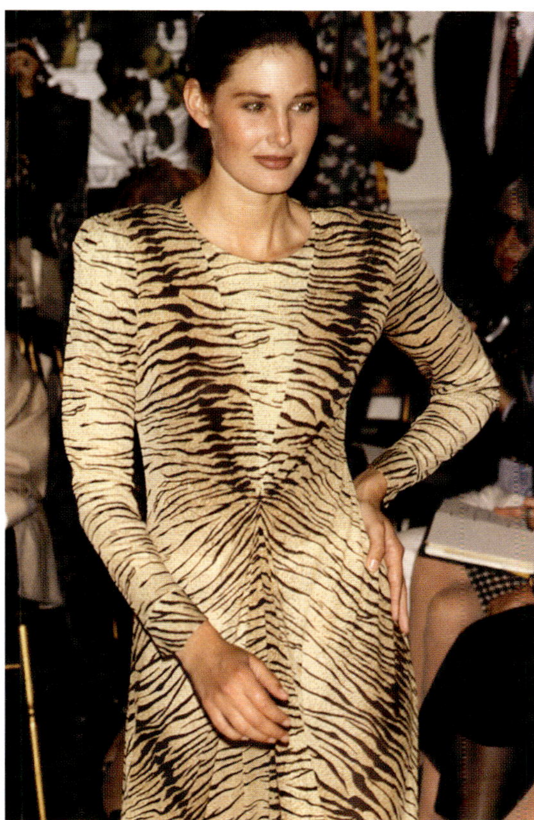

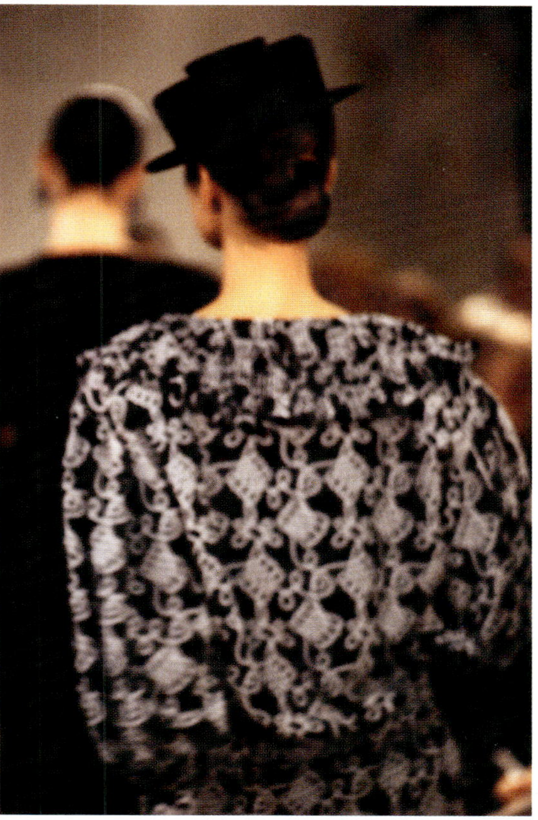

**LEFT** Detail of snakeskin silk satin print commissioned by Jean Muir from the silk specialist Soieries Nouveautés, featured in *Vogue*, September 1969. **ABOVE LEFT TO RIGHT** Short sleeve jacket in leopard print moiré, Spring 1993; slim fitting ankle-length dress in tiger printed jersey, Autumn 1986; Liberty printed silk crêpe de Chine blouse with frilled pierrot collar, Spring 1989. Photographs & © Niall McInerney & Chris Moore.

# DETAILS

The finishing touches to Muir collections were always of the utmost importance to her. In order to achieve the overall effect she wanted, she teamed up with a number of specialists. She worked closely with the silversmiths Harrison Young (Simon Harrison and Iain Young), and then latterly, Iain Young, who perfected the art of Miss Muir's silver buttons. Each season they created a series of abstract or figurative mini-sculptured buttons in hallmarked sterling silver, sometimes enamelled, or oxidised, or set with semi-precious stones. These added a different dimension to Miss Muir's clothes – the button as jewellery. In addition, these buttons would inspire necklets and chokers, earrings and cuffs and buckles for belts that 'made an outfit'.

Muir spiced her collections with quirky touches of wit, "I love a sense of humour, a sense of the ridiculous." She got her inspiration from the unlikeliest of sources. Staying with friends in Northumberland one day she saw a herd of cows grazing nearby. From this came her beautiful enamelled belt with those cows grazing realistically centre-stage on the buckle. It was made for an early seventies calfskin dress, accessorised with a set of miniature matching cow buttons, featured in *Vogue*, January 1972.

Her co-creator for these works of art was John Adrian Tremayne Rodd, 3rd Baron Rennell. Working from studios on London's Euston Road, his company Marks of Distinction, produced a series of decorative enamelled buckles and buttons for Muir, several with flower motifs, including pansies and lotus flowers. The textile designer and weaver, Kaffe Fassett also made some enamelled buttons for her, which featured on a finely-gathered backless halter top in cream chamois suede, photographed by David Bailey in British *Vogue*, March 1972.

Well ahead of any trend, Miss Muir's clothes often featured buttons in Perspex (lucite), designed for her by C&N (Caroline Broadhead and Nuala Jamison). They created a different type of button from the silver ones, but just as individual and sympathetic to the clothes. The Perspex was kept either clear and shiny, or mirrored, or tumbled for a frosted matte effect; it was coloured, and carved to give different textures, and originally shaped, confounding the ordinary perception of a button. C&N also made jewellery – earrings, bracelets, brooches, and necklaces and even decorative headbands. Iain Young and Nuala Jamison continue to produce their innovative and luxurious buttons for the Muir collections today.

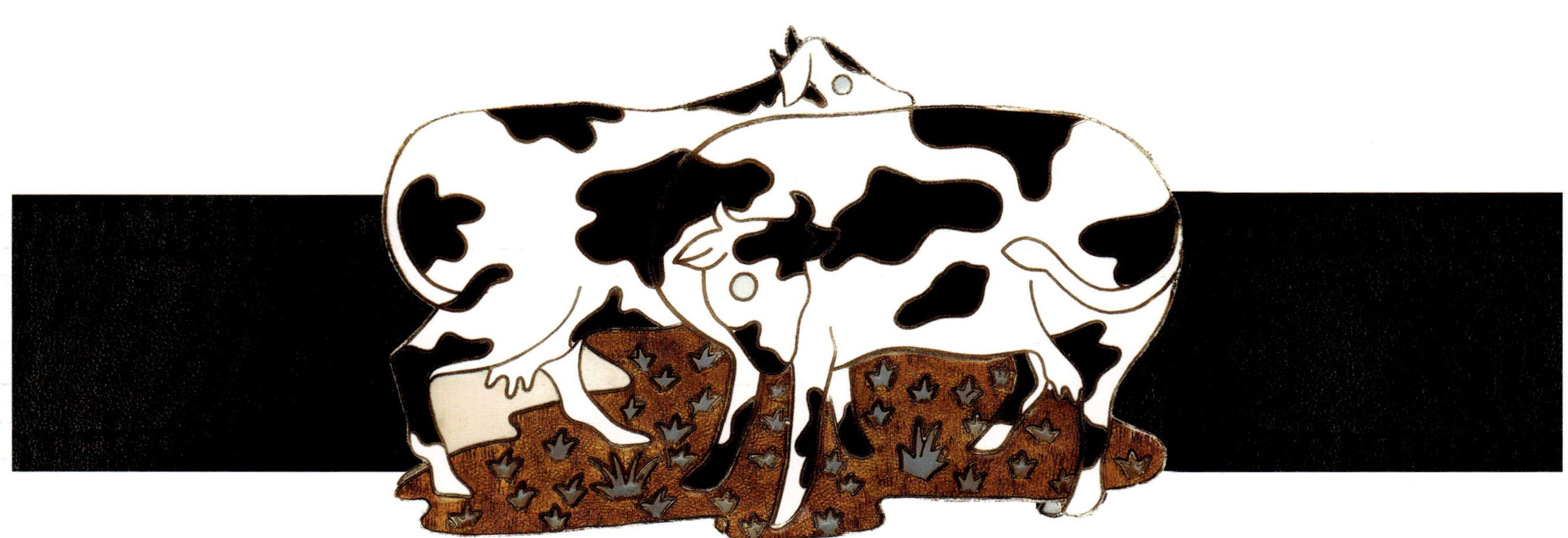

The buckles on a Jean Muir belt are intricate and interesting enough to be miniature works of art. Semi-precious stones set into silver; silver carnation flowers, each petal oxidised then enamelled in scarlet; a pair of carved 'Icarus' wings; jewelled eyes set into a 'Medusa' face. Seen here, an example of the Muir sense of humour, often present in her coveted accessories – cows in the field, a brilliant example of her original and quirky creativity. Leather belt with the buckle exquisitely enamelled on brass, 1972.

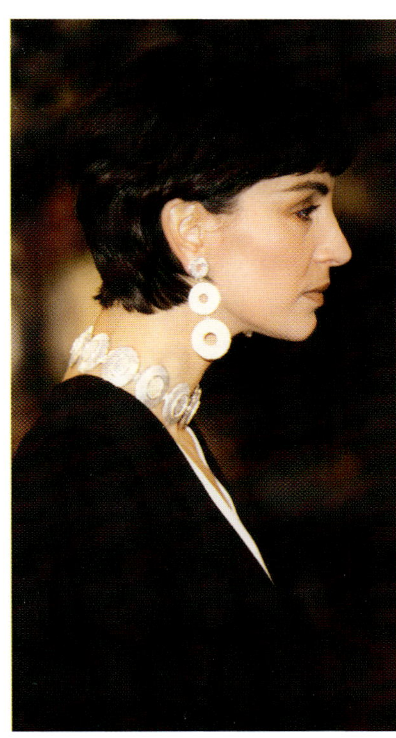

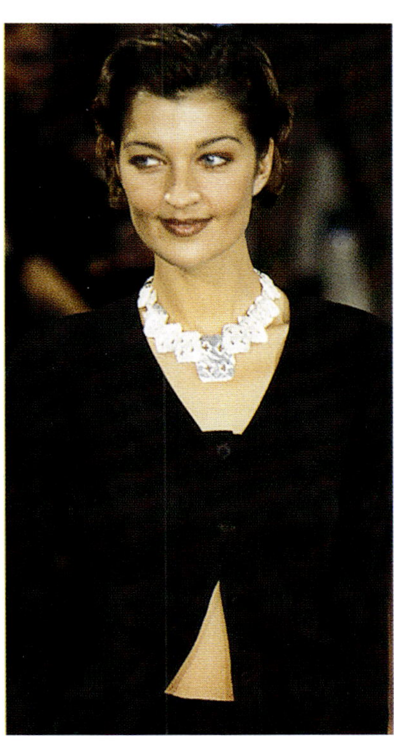

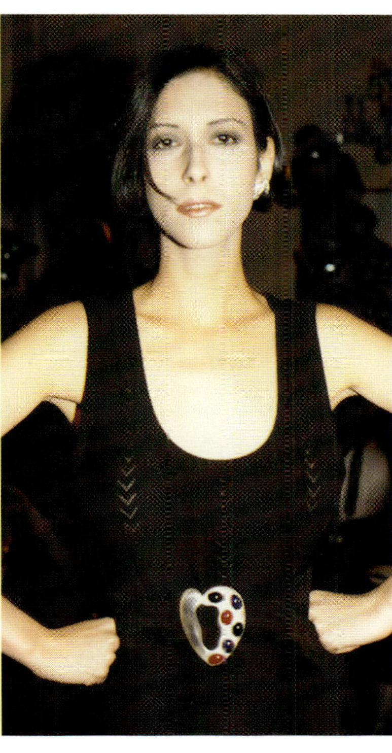

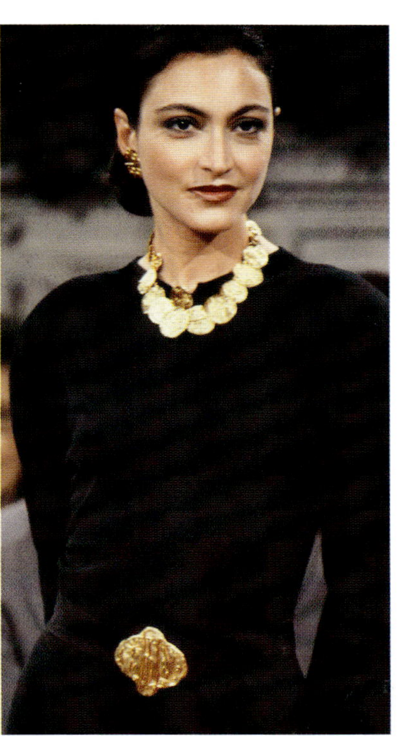

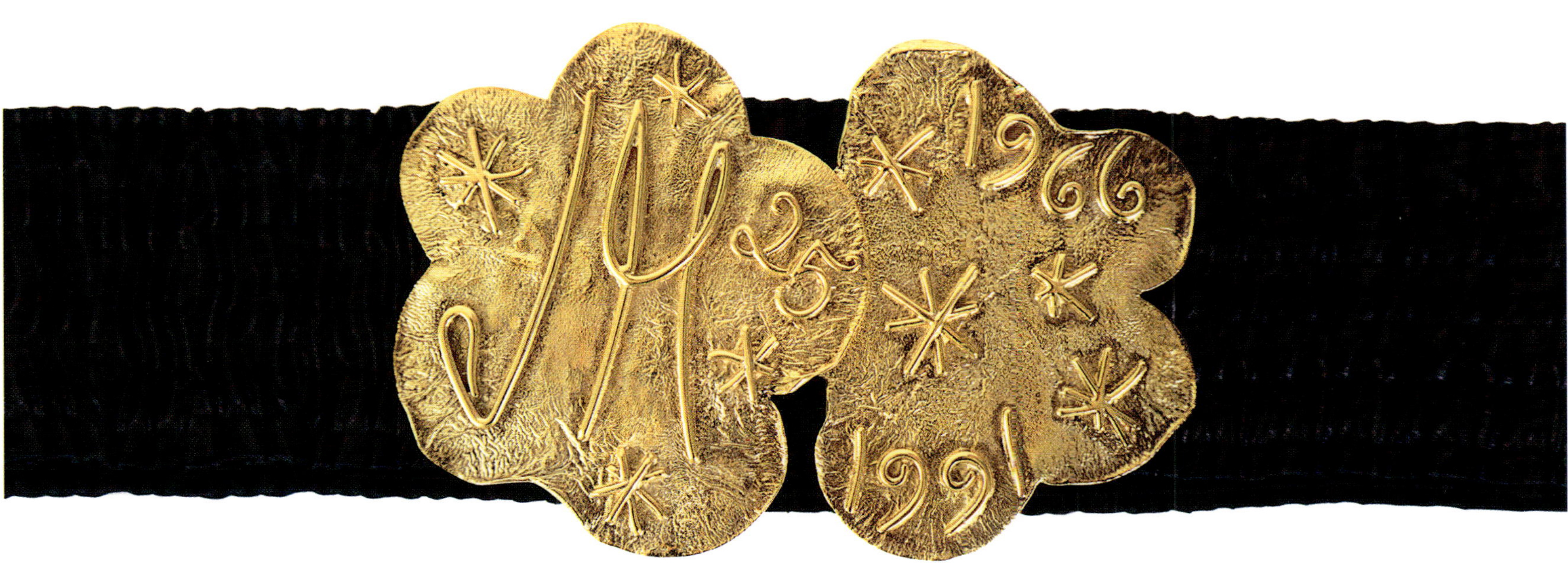


**TOP LEFT TO RIGHT** The secret is in the detail: drop earrings and choker in sterling silver; choker and buttons in sterling silver, both Spring 1993 by Iain Young for Jean Muir. Sterling silver buckle studded with semi-precious stones by Harrison Young for Jean Muir, early eighties by Harrison Young for Jean Muir. Photographs & © Chris Moore & Niall McInerney.
**ABOVE** Celebratory silver gilt buckle embossed with JM initials and dates marking the 25th anniversary of Jean Muir by Iain Young for Jean Muir. Photograph & © Neil Fenwick.

In addition to the Perspex and silver buttons and early jewellery, other specialist makers, like Nigel Lofthouse, produced belts and necklaces in Perspex, and bags, which mixed Perspex with leather. Alison Richard made chunky brass 'apple' chokers and buckles for the Spring 1973 collection, photographed in British *Vogue*.

One of Miss Muir's strongest associations was with the milliner, Graham Smith. He produced many designs for Miss Muir – Juliet caps and turbans, or jaunty berets and trilbys in topstitched matte jersey or suede, many of which were featured alongside her garments in British *Vogue* in the seventies and eighties.

Miss Muir also worked with the milliner Bridget Bailey in the mid-late eighties, who used finely pleated organzas, sometimes mixed with satin, to make stylish and flirty headpieces and small elegant hats.

Bridget Bailey remembers: "I did hats for Jean Muir from 1984 to 1989. She was one of the first people I ever approached, and she was one of the first to commission me. What was wonderful was that she would take the time to see someone just out of college – those doors are usually very hard to open. She really appreciated my quirky, eccentric pieces, and this early relationship probably had much to do with giving me the courage and incentive to keep going."

The first shoe designer with whom Miss Muir worked was Edward Rayne, who made shoes in matching fabrics for some of her early collections. In the seventies, the shoe maestro, Manolo Blahnik created shoes for the Muir shows, notably heels in black or burgundy suede with gold leather toe caps. Emma Hope was commissioned to make the vividly coloured suede shoes for the Australian Bicentennial collection and Jimmy Choo made shoes specially for her later collections.

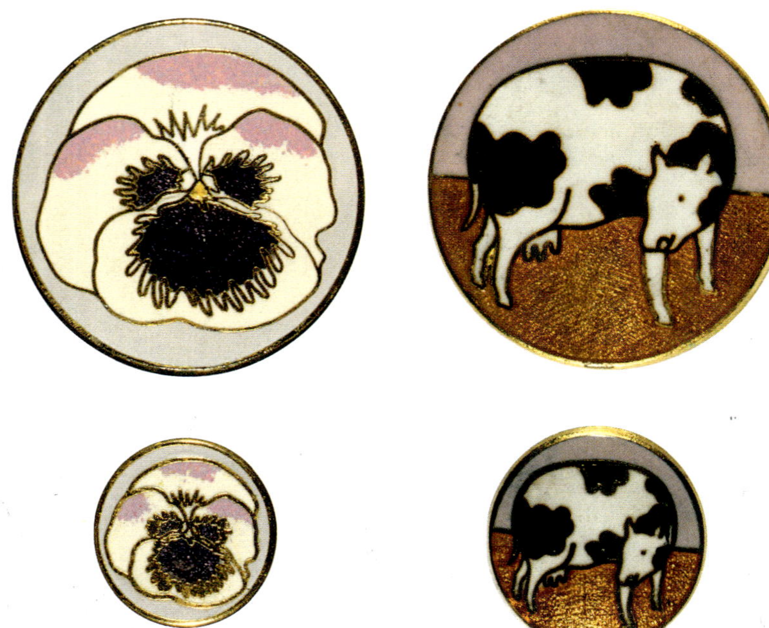

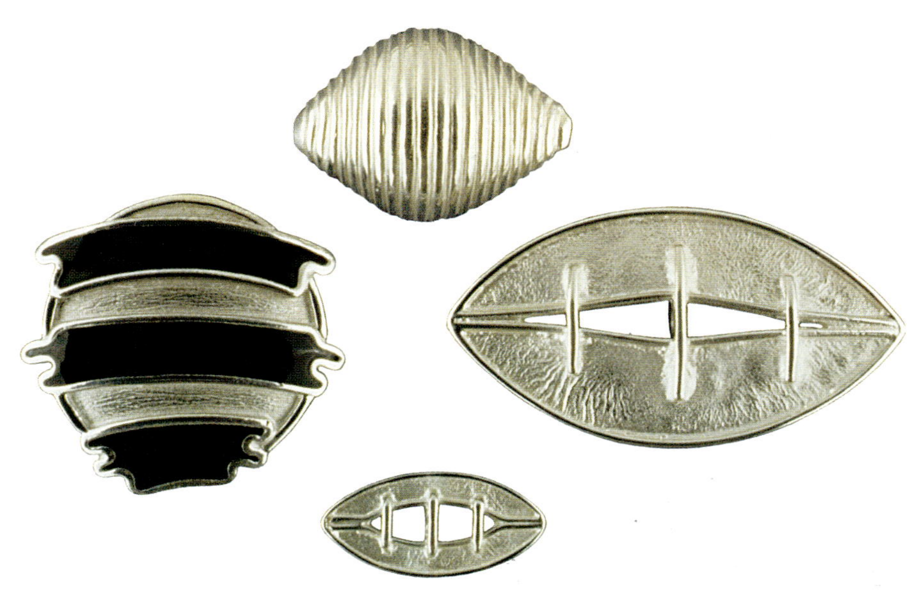

**LEFT TO RIGHT** Two pairs of enamelled buttons by Marks of Distinction for Jean Muir; a selection of sterling silver buttons, one with black enamel, by Harrison Young/Iain Young for Jean Muir.
**OPPOSITE** Fan-pleated 'Sunshade' organza hat echoes the finely-pleated collar of a wool coat. Hat by Bridget Bailey for Jean Muir, Spring 1989. Photographs & © Neil Fenwick.

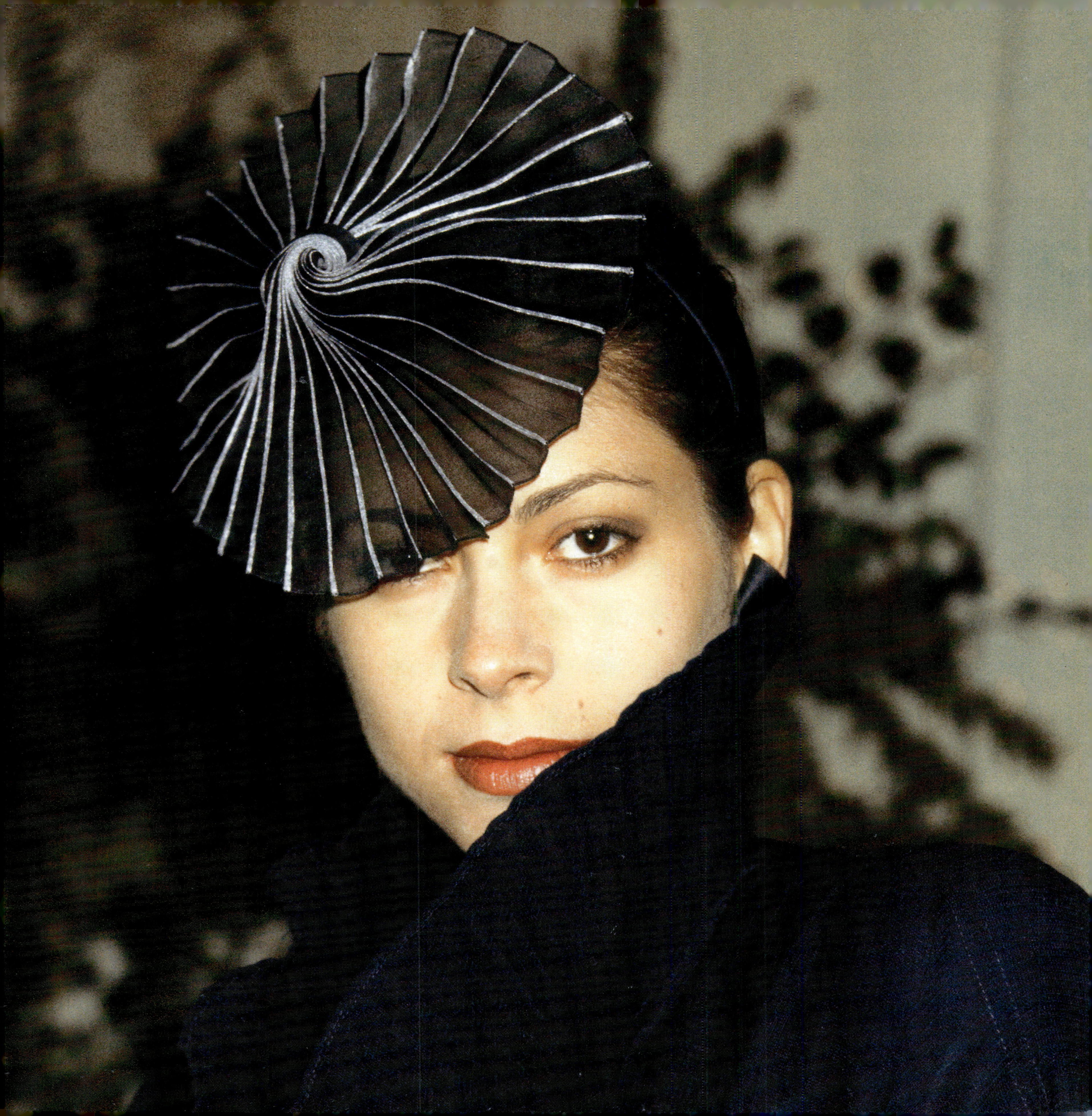

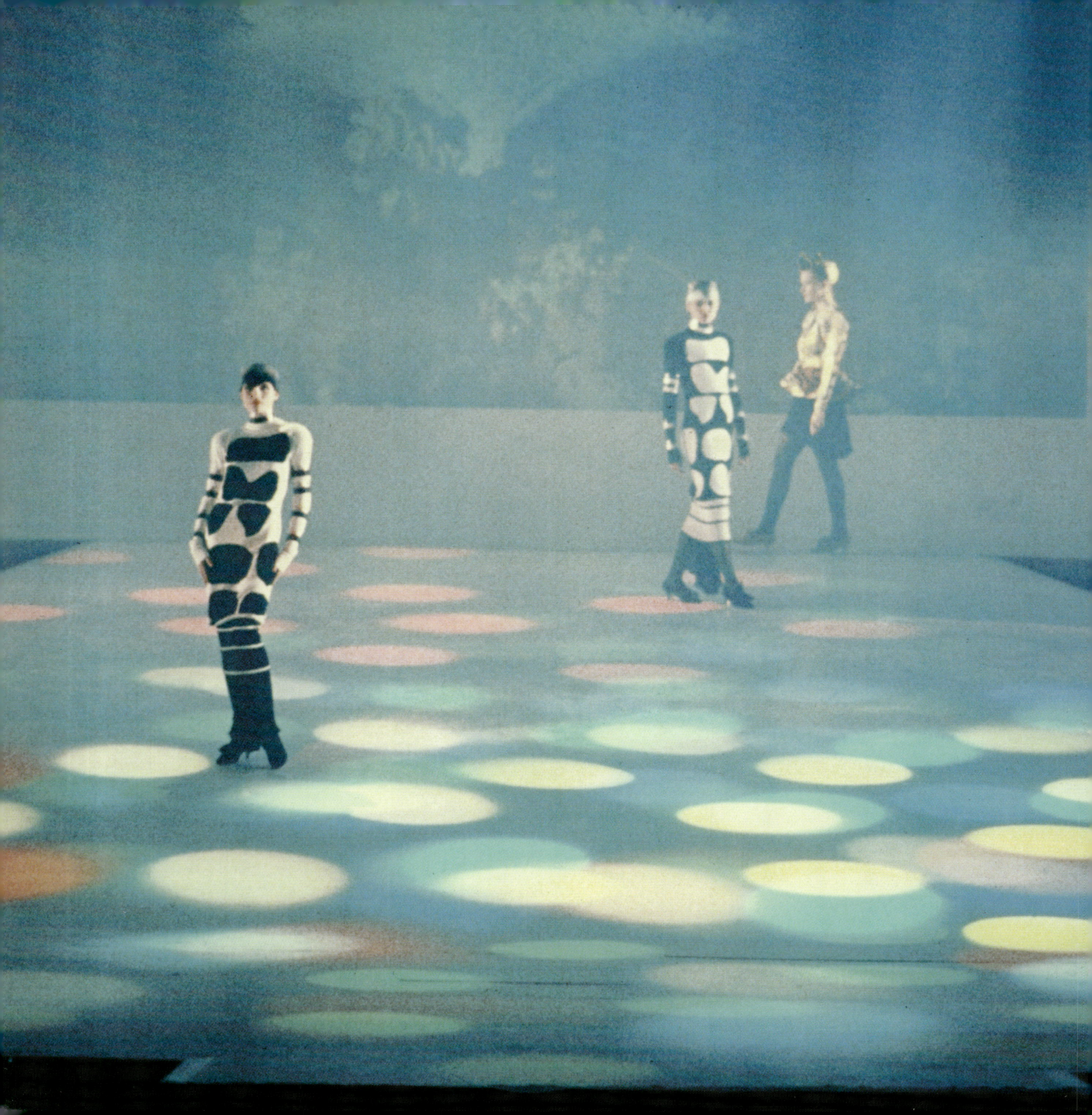

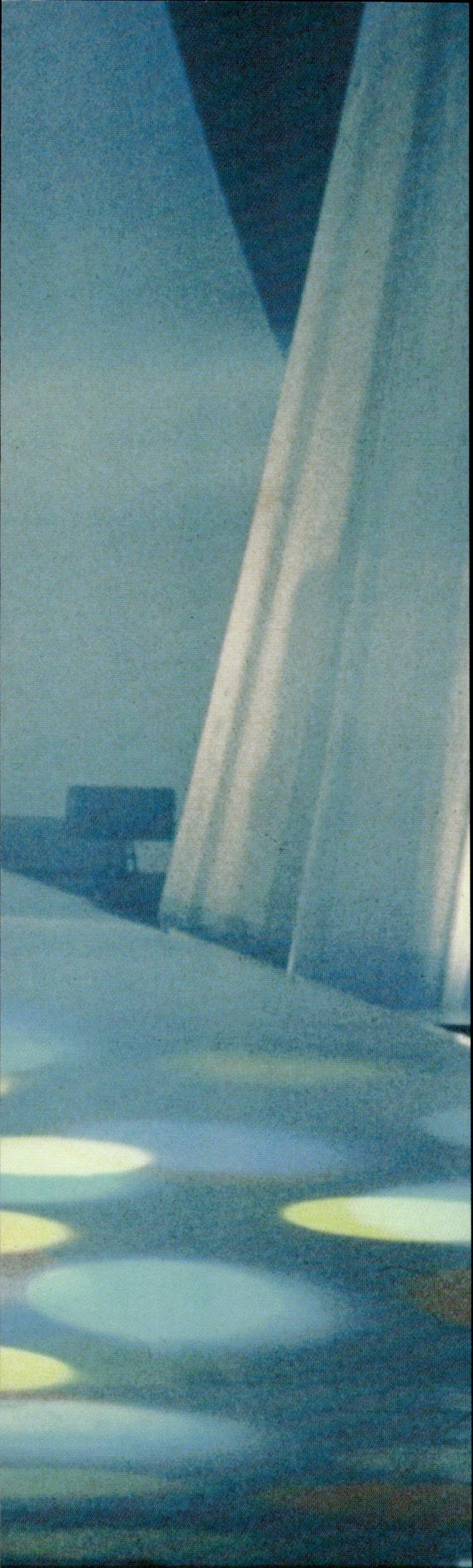

"Wool has always been part of our lives. It dyes to the most luminous colours. The ones I've used here, are amazingly vibrant"

JEAN MUIR

**JEAN MUIR** was not one to base her work on singular thematic inspirations, but when she was invited by the International Wool Secretariat to participate in an international event to design an all wool collection inspired by Australia – to be shown in January 1988 at the Sydney Opera House as part of Australia's Bicentennial celebrations – she relished the challenge of designing around a specific theme.

Muir was part of a stellar cast that included Oscar de la Renta, Donna Karan, Sonia Rykiel, Claude Montana, Kenzo, Missoni, and Versace. There were six Australian and nine international designers and seventy-six models in the IWS show. Characteristically she took an oblique slant, while Bruce Oldfield chose aboriginal culture and others simply showed pieces from their own collection, Muir threw herself wholeheartedly into the project. She looked beyond the surface – literally – taking as her theme the marine life of the Great Barrier Reef. The inspiration came from her husband, a keen fisherman with a fishing mind..."I said what about the Great Barrier Reef! We bought a book and took it from there."

Once she had her theme she let rip, incorporating and layering myriad craft techniques to simulate the exotic markings of various sea creatures, all laced with a quirky sense of tongue-in-cheek humour that translated into an exuberant and effervescent charm on the stage. Her collection was largely based around knitwear in cashmere and lamb's wool, but it also included felted wool, wool jersey and wool gauze. The resulting pieces reflect her great artistry with colour and form, and are a wonderful example of the collaboration between artist and craftsman, so important to Jean Muir.

Flooding the Sydney Opera House stage with great pools of swirling colour, Muir presented a whole subterranean world. Sinuous wool dresses were coiled with hand-woven woollen ropes. Hand-loomed intarsia knitwear variously featured amoeba-like shapes, shoals of fish swimming across the body, or a single ogling eye. Wool jersey jackets with graphic appliqué were fastened with hand carved 'fin' buttons in brightly coloured Perspex by Nuala Jamison. Annie Sherburne's hand-painted felted wool was made into dramatic coats and undulating peplum jackets – which had an almost Bakst-like reference to the costumes of Diaghilev's Ballets Russes. 'Jewelled' sequin 'barnacle' brooches, also by Sherburne, attached themselves to the felted wool, which was worn over eclectically striped ribbed knit skirts. To top everything off there were fluttery concertina pleated chiffon hats

**PAGE 100** Scene from Sydney Opera House – Jean Muir celebrates Australia's Bicentennial in 1988 with a colourful collection in wool based on the marine life of the Great Barrier Reef.

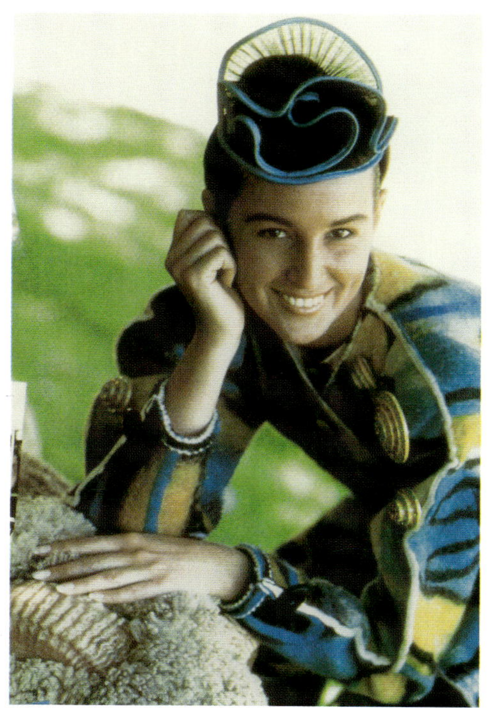

resembling rippling frilled crests by Bridget Bailey. Everything was curvaceous – a vibrant combination of colour, shape and texture – suffused with a flirtatious sense of fun. Muir's infectious enthusiasm for her subject transferred itself to the models, who beamed throughout Muir's showing, and spilled over into the audience.

"I had flown ahead to organise all the preparations including selecting the models for the Jean Muir section of the show," recalls Mr. Leuckert. "Not an easy task – the models at that time walked with an exaggerated catwalk wiggle. When I said just walk naturally they looked at me incredulously. Walk naturally! On the catwalk! The Muir way was such a different approach. However, once we presented them with the Muir choreography they got into the swing of it and had fun."

Claire Atkinson, an international model, took part in the show: "Jean Muir chose the colours of the coral reef and its tropical fish. She captured the spirit, the base of the country, and what she created was very beautiful, very right. She made an appeal to the audience and was the great highlight of the show and I felt the appreciation both from the audience and the press afterwards."

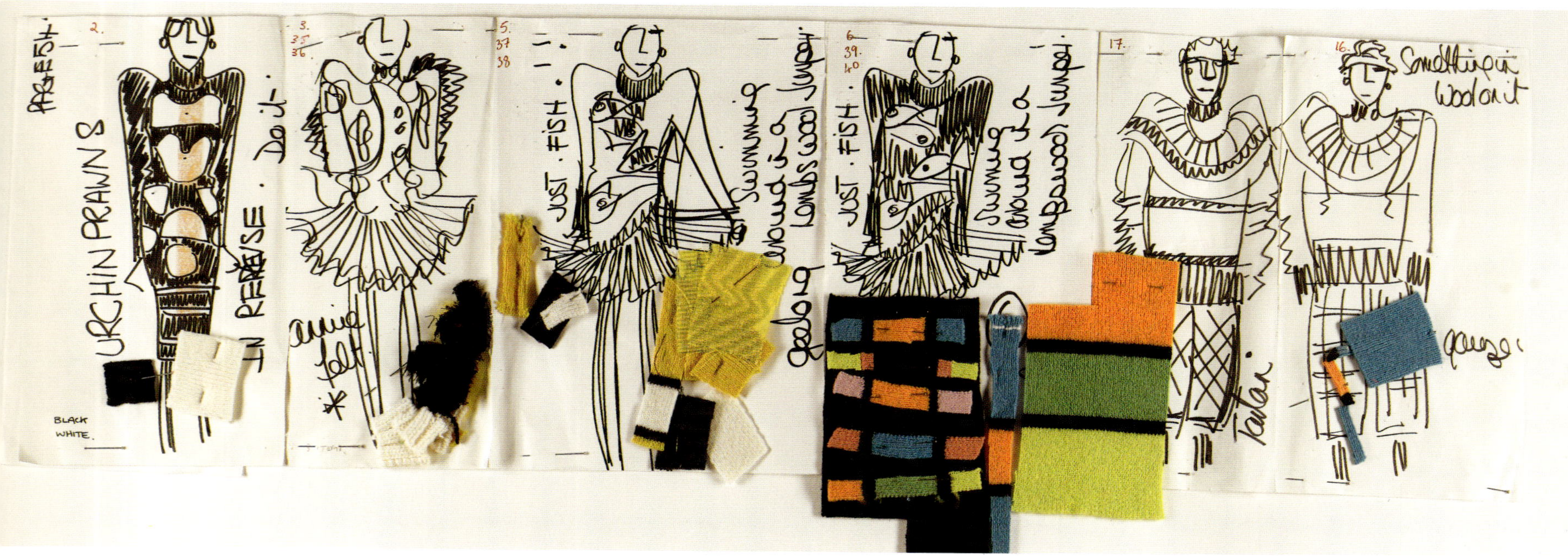


**TOP** Exuberant colour and texture: theatrical hand-painted, hand-felted wool jacket with 'barnacle' brooch, topped by a crested headpiece. Just seen on the left, a merino ram.
**ABOVE AND RIGHT** Part of the line-up showing Jean Muir's sketches for her Australian Bicentennial collection, January 1988, with her comments, descriptions and knitted colour swatches attached. The event was sponsored by the International Wool Secretariat. Their only stipulation: the collection must be based on an Australian theme and made entirely

Ace showman, Ric Birch, was the show director. He recalled: "I loved working with Jean because she was the most instinctively theatrical of any of the designers in the show and she got involved in every aspect. The three of us, Jean, Harry and I even rewrote the lyrics to Cole Porter's 'Let's Do It (Let's Fall in Love)' – urchin prawns in reverse do it – clownfish forming pairs do it ...the vocalist and band absolutely adored it.

Her clothes were the ones most inspired by the theme. Given Jean Muir's physical size, the philosophical and psychological power of the woman is quite extraordinary – in a tiny frame to have such enormous charisma. She sweeps people off their feet. She did it at the Sydney Opera House by her example; there was no-one around her who would have tried less than their best partly from watching her – a sea of calm in an ocean of madness."

At the finale Jean Muir was presented with a commemorative Bicentennial medal by the Prince and Princess of Wales. Back in London she showed some of these Australian pieces as part of her Autumn 1988 collection during fashion week, again to great acclaim. Model Linda Evangelista was photographed by Peter Lindbergh for *Vogue* in a sinuous ankle-length navy lamb's-wool sweater dress coiled with handwoven silken ropes.

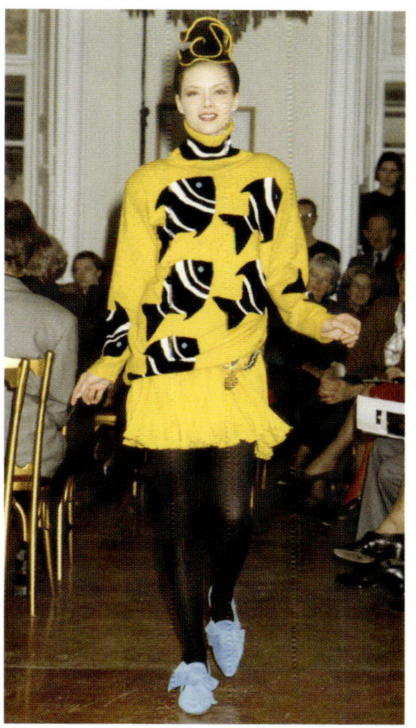

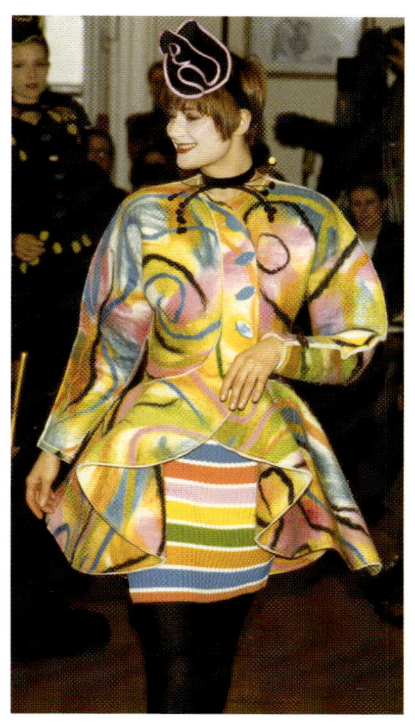

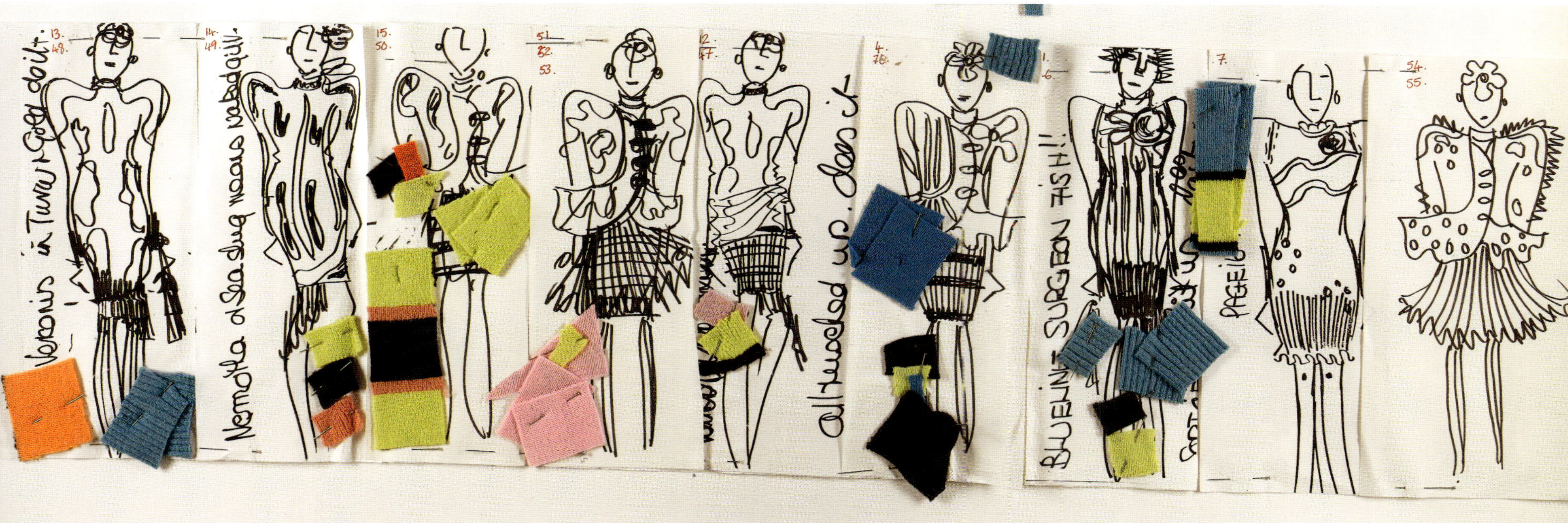

in wool. As well as cashmere and lamb's-wool yarns, Muir worked with wool jersey and wool gauze. Sketches © The Trustees of The National Museums of Scotland. **TOP LEFT** A shoal of fish swims across a cashmere tunic over a sunray pleated wool gauze flippy skirt. Suede shoes by Emma Hope for Jean Muir, March 1988. **TOP RIGHT** Multicoloured coat in hand-painted felted wool by Annie Sherburne over matching cashmere striped skirt. Headband hat by Bridget Bailey for Jean Muir. Photographs & © Niall McInerney.

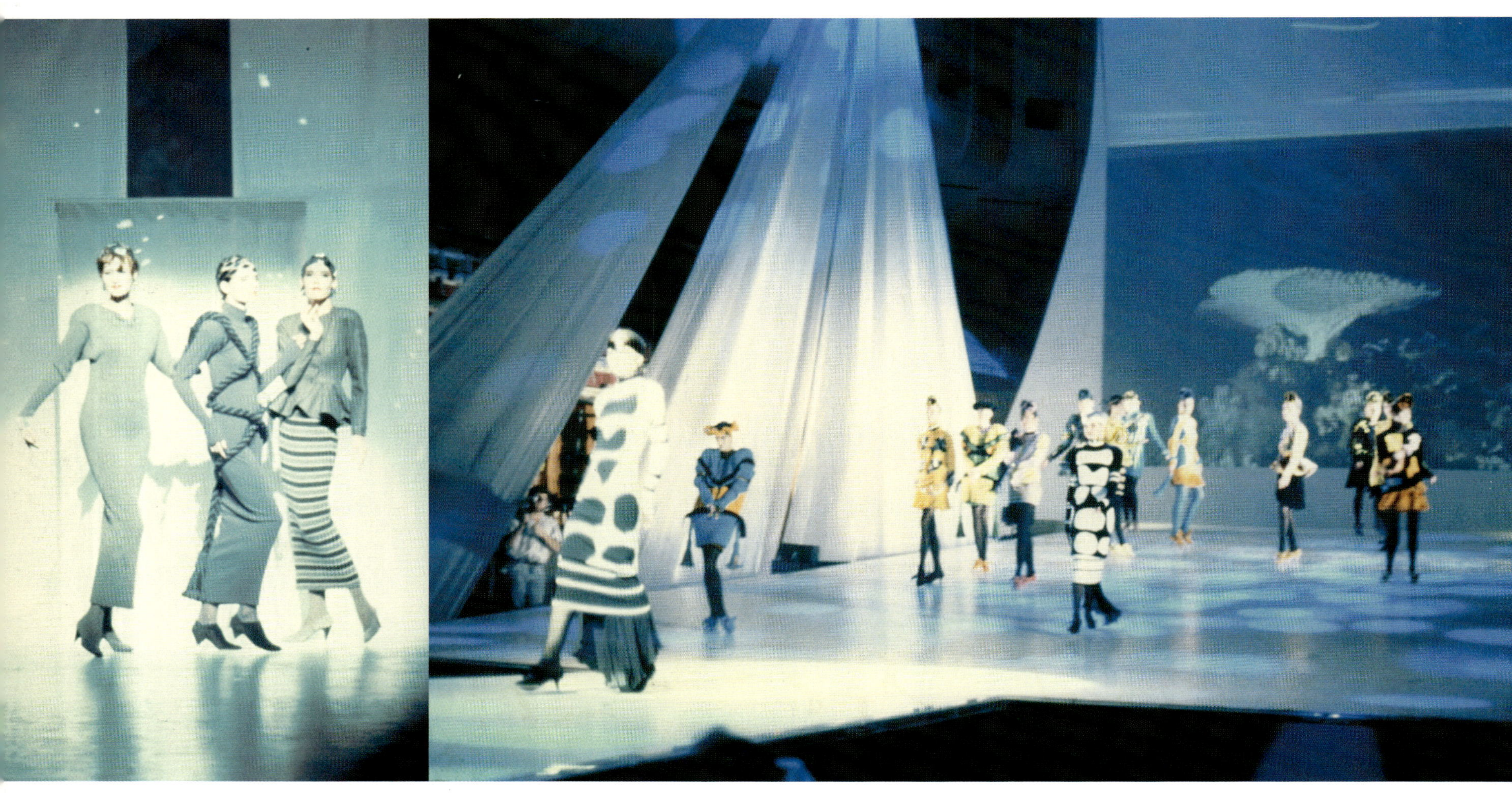

**ABOVE AND LEFT** Scenes from the Australian Bicentennial fashion spectacular held in the Sydney Opera House in January 1988. In the background aquatic scenes are projected as the models flood the stage for the finale of Muir's section of the show. **OPPOSITE** Surrealist Magritte-style shoot for *Tatler* magazine, July 1988 features a striking black and white lamb's-wool intarsia elongated sweater dress from the Australian Bicentennial collection. Photograph: Michael Roberts/Tatler. © Michael Roberts/Maconochie Photography.

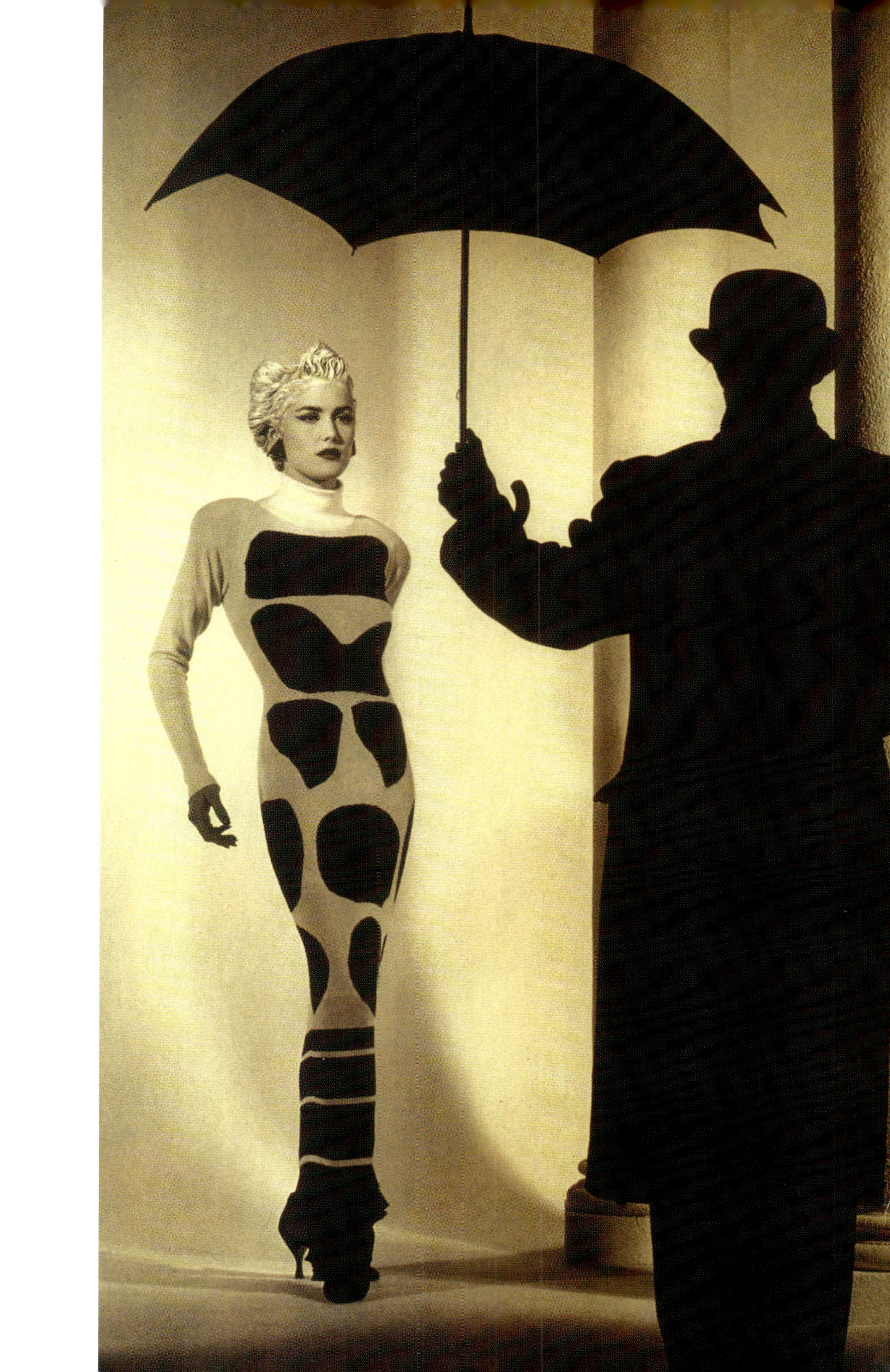

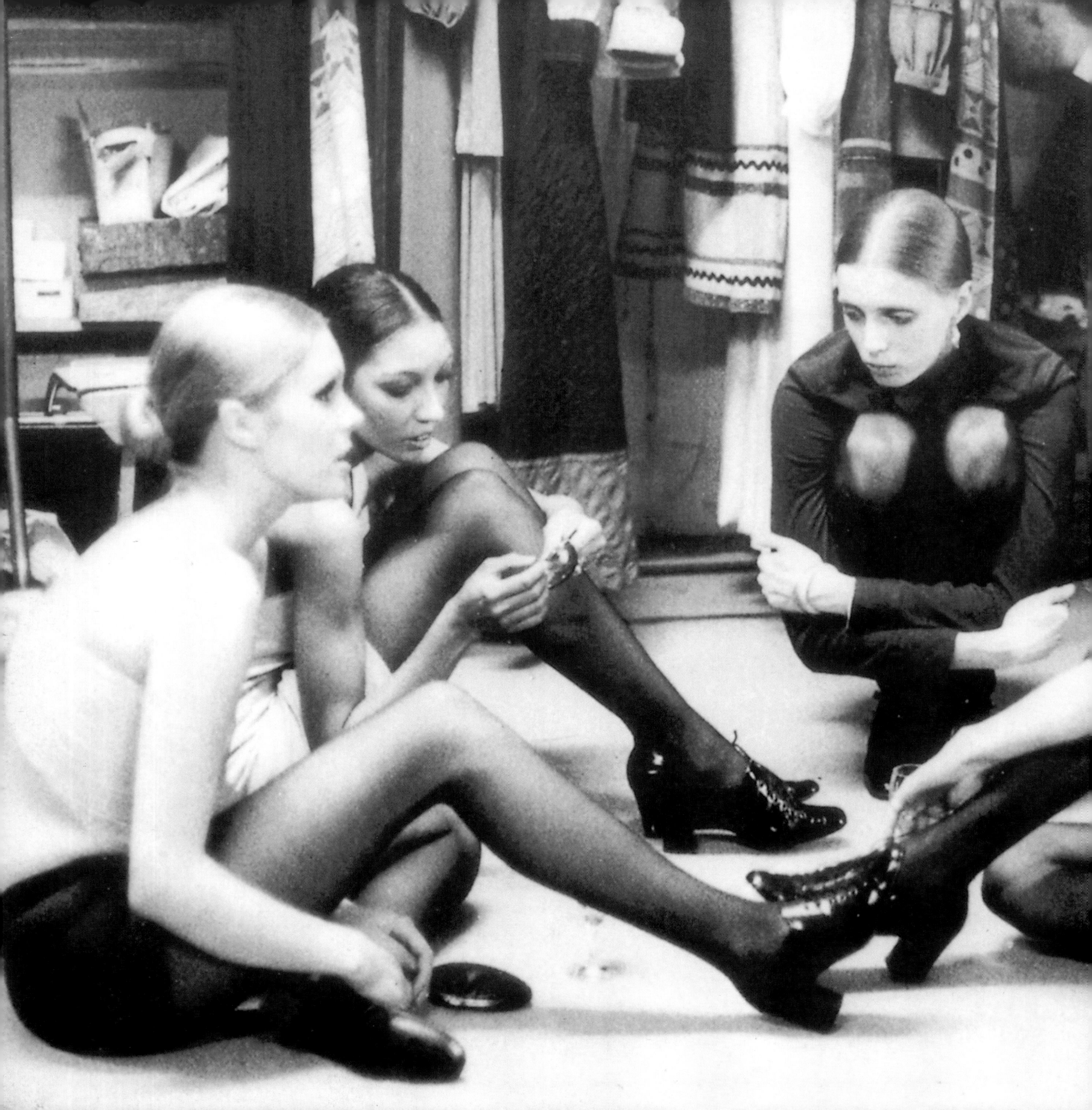

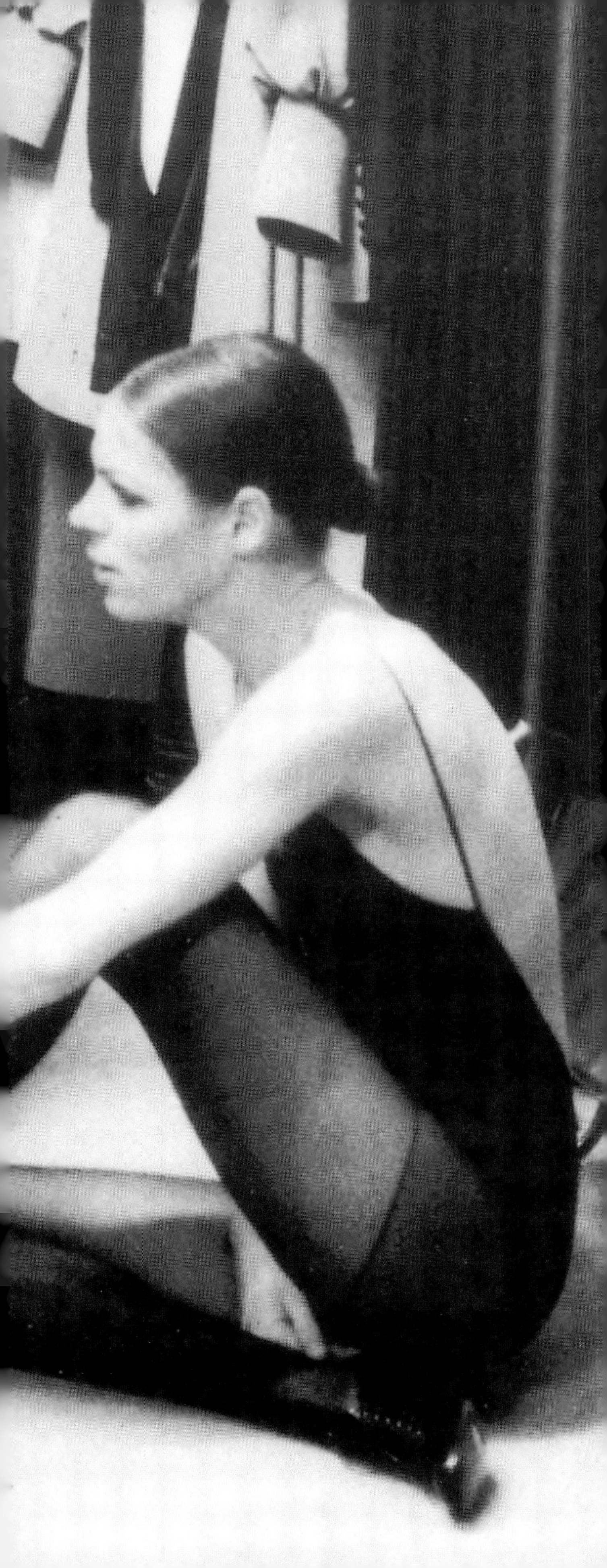

“Life is for living and you might as well live it as attractively as possible!”

JEAN MUIR

**JEAN MUIR'S** original approach to design extended to the manner in which she presented her collections. Unlike other ready-to-wear designers, she sited her business in London's prestigious Bruton Street, a well-heeled street of art galleries in Mayfair, where Queen Elizabeth II had been born. She shared her fashion credentials here with the London couturiers, Charles James and Victor Stiebel – as well as Norman Hartnell, whose mirrored Deco premises at number twenty-six Bruton Street are now listed by English Heritage – all of whom had their businesses in the street at various times.

Jean Muir housed her showroom in a gracious neoclassical Georgian salon on the first floor of number 22 Bruton Street, an elegant town house, overlooking Berkeley Square. Complementing the high ceilings, internal columns and intricate plasterwork mouldings and cornices, Muir and her husband furnished number 22 with period crystal chandeliers and white painted Indian colonial furniture. On the buff-coloured walls, portraits of Muir by Zsuzsi Roboz and David Remfry gazed out over the collections, which were arranged and carefully spaced on garment rails to create a sensual interplay of colour, shape and texture.

It was here that Muir would show her collections twice a year to press and buyers, to international acclaim. American journalists often cited Muir's shows as the highlight of the London calendar. In *The New York Times,* in 1979, under the headline 'London's Fashion Star Raises Understatement to a Fine Art', Bernadine Morris wrote: "Jean Muir is the superstar of London. Her clothes have a pared down manner. Nothing superfluous is going on. From the moment her first styles appeared in her showroom on Bruton Street, packed with an appreciative audience, it was clear she knew what she was about. …Miss Muir is definitely the success of the London collections".

Cathy Horyn, writing for *The Washington Post* in March 1992, observed: "There is nobody quite like Jean Muir. One always knows that on Sunday morning, at 22 Bruton Street, there will be champagne at the door, Bobby Short in the air, and the kind of simple luxury that seems scarce these days."

Guests at her shows included not only those from the fashion world, but figures from many other artistic fields, including the photographer and sartorial aesthete, Cecil Beaton, the author Lady Antonia Fraser and artists Elisabeth Frink and Bridget Riley. As her friend David Watts notes, "Those shows of Jean's were always special, she always knew people, interesting people and they in turn seemed drawn to her clothes."

**PAGE 108** Backstage at Bruton Street before the show begins. Models from left: Joanna Lumley, Kelly, J.J., and Roz Wilkins, 1970. Photograph & © Marilyn Stafford.

Again, Muir's presentation of her collections was charactistically original. The shows were simultaneously both grand and informal. They had a sort of intimate theatricality – everyone was conscious of being at an 'event', and the setting and atmosphere were similar to a cocktail party. There was no catwalk; the models simply sauntered through the two salons to the upbeat jazz music of Muir's American friend, Bobby Short.

Muir styled her models, who included a young Joanna Lumley, almost as dancers with their hair tied back severely in a bun, made up with dark eyes, deep red lips, and wearing opaque black tights. She chose sophisticated young women who knew how to wear and move in her type of clothes, essential for such a salon setting, where part of the charm was the fact that the audience was so close to the outfits. They could see the intricate detail, the contrast stitching, the seaming and punching, the mix of textures, the immaculate finish, the buttons…

"I'm fascinated by faces", Muir once revealed, "I look for intelligence in my models. I rather like girls who don't look like models. They have to know what they are doing, what the clothes are supposed to be."

Muir favourites included Joanna Lumley, Roz Wilkins, whose matte jersey wedding dress was specially made for her by Jean Muir, Joanna Vignola, Paddy Grey and Jenny Garrigues. There were also the famous American Pat Cleveland, and the inscrutable Modigliani-esque Anna Pavlowski. Later came Veronica Webb, the writer, Nicola Shulman, now the Marchioness of Normanby, India Hicks, the writer and interior designer, and Tamsin de Roemer, now a designer of jewellery, knitwear and bags.

This simple manner of presentation was deceptive yet revelatory; her clothes often lacked hanger appeal but came alive when they were on a body that moved, and none more so than her matte jersey pieces.

American designer Bill Blass described an encounter with Jean Muir's work in the mid-eighties. "It's rare that we ever do a designer show together as a group but several years ago Jean, Issey Miyake, Ungaro and I did a show in Tokyo. We were all assigned rooms, and there was Jean in her room with her racks of hangers with little skinny dresses, all black, navy or brown, and virtually no accessories. Issey Miyake's things were elaborate to an extreme in his own way, and of course there were Ungaro's fantasies, and I was trying another approach. I thought to myself how is she going to pull this one off? Then suddenly I had forgotten that those skinny little dresses put on the female form come alive in a special way. Not only that, but she had such originality in her presentation – how she wanted her girls to look, how

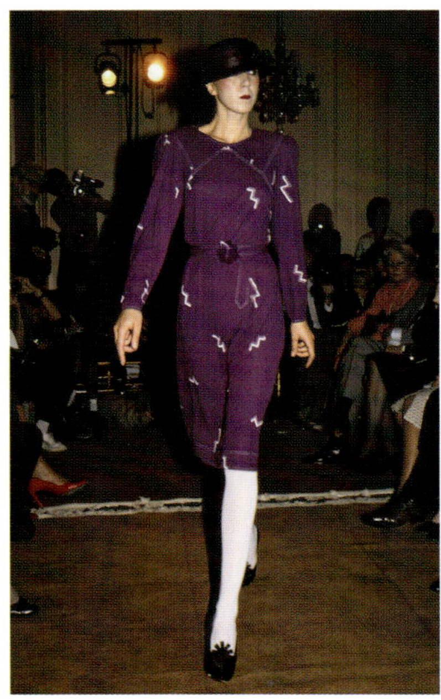

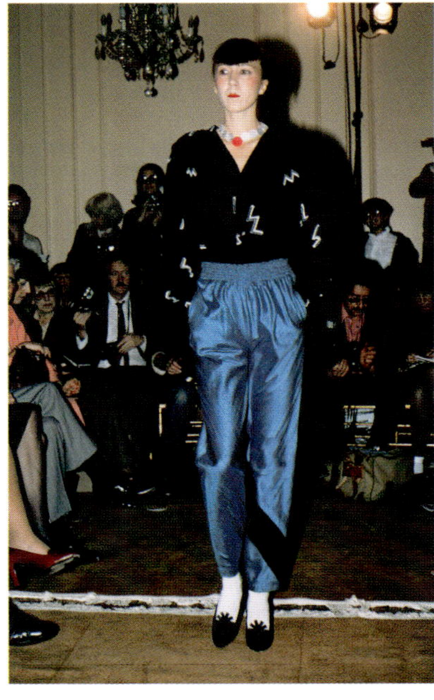

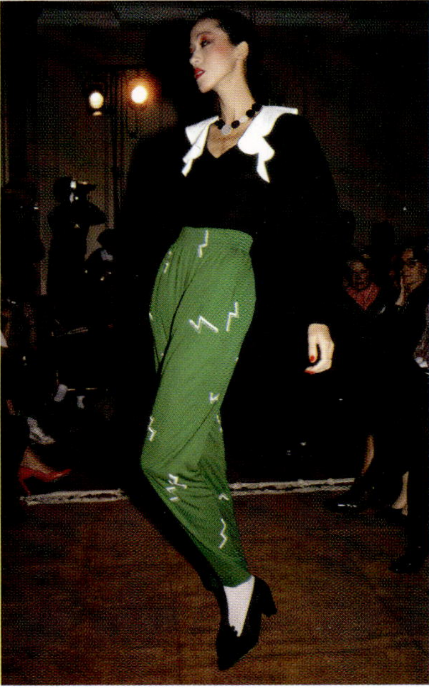

Among Jean Muir's favourite models, **ABOVE LEFT** Anna Pavlowski wears violet pansy jersey dress with white robot print. **CENTRE** Anna again in robot-print jersey shirt and raw silk trousers. **ABOVE RIGHT** Top international model, American Pat Cleveland wears black jersey blouse with white ruffle collar, green robot-print tapered jersey trousers. All clothes from the Spring 1980 collection. Photographs & © Niall McInerney.

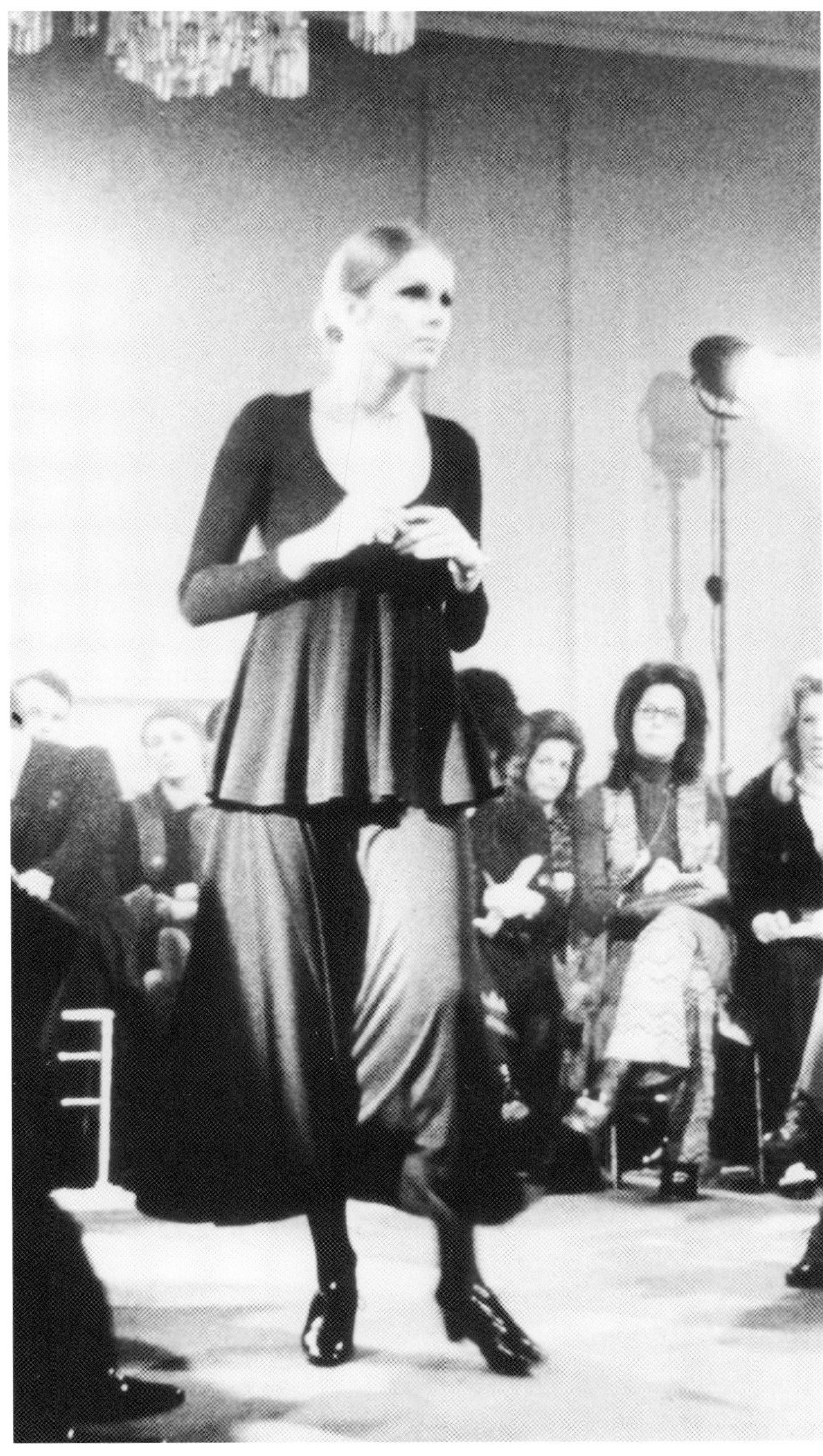

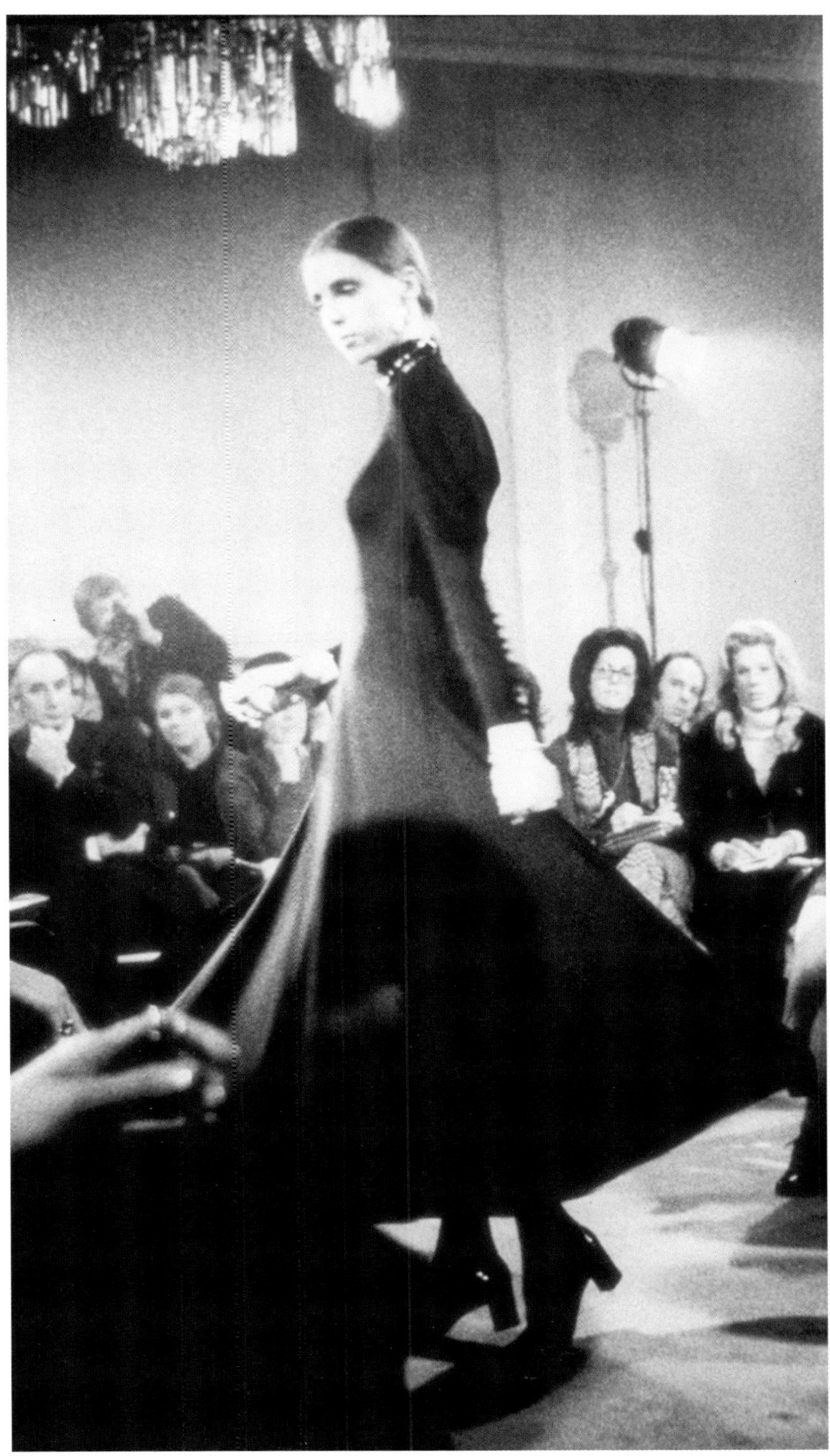

**ABOVE** Scenes from an early Bruton Street show. Two more favourite Muir models, Joanna Lumley and J.J., demonstrate the fluidity and versatility of matte jersey in the hands of the incomparable Jean Muir. [Left] Joanna Lumley in scoop-neck tunic with close-fitting sleeves, matching wide-leg, mic-length culottes. © The Trustees of The National Museums of Scotland. **RIGHT** J.J. shows off to a packed audience how Muir engineers her jersey to cling close and flow. A typical Muir detai – a li:e of tiny covered buttons from wrist to elbow.

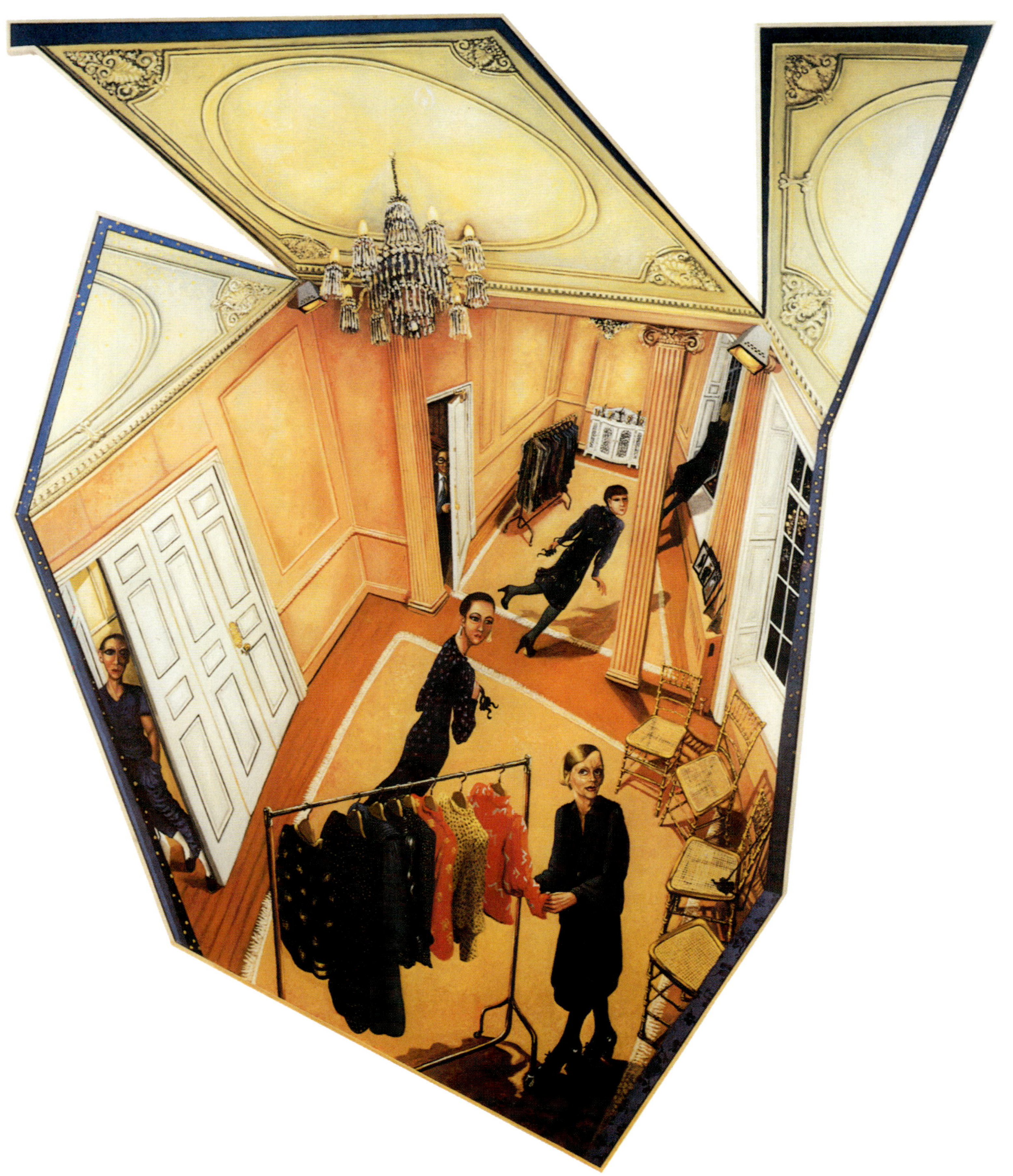

she wanted them to walk – her music was most original – suddenly everything else paled by comparison. It was Jean with her utter simplicity, with her understanding every aspect of showing her clothes that made the impact. It was just unbelievable."

Back in London at the close of a Bruton Street show, Muir's friend the eminent British diplomat, Sir Nicholas Henderson, described the scene: "She appears, as she always does, both self-confident and diffident, as if to say 'Well there it is. That's me. It's different.' Which is what the guests will be confirming to each other as they rise from the gold chairs to join in the applause – that Jean's shows are different."

After the show, the showroom became the workplace, where the collections were shown in detail to the international buyers. The showroom in all its detail is wonderfully brought to life by the artist Anthony Green's jewel-coloured 1979 painting entitled 'Jean Muir Checking Buttons'. Conceived as a box unfolding to present the interior of the showroom, the painting reveals Miss Muir checking the buttons on a rail of collection samples, whilst husband and business partner, Harry Leuckert looks on from the doorway. Everything is shown, including the gilt chairs and the white carved furniture. The vendeuse watches, part of a surreal vision in which models wearing the new season's samples are shown floating out of one of the tall windows into the ether, much in the same way that Muir's clothes would go out into the world once they had been placed in the order books of the world's most prestigious buyers.

Jean Muir's concern with her collections and their every stage of evolution did not end with the closing of an order pad. She looked further, towards the reaction her clothes would receive from her customers, explaining:
"It has always been my view in making clothes that it is not until a particular dress, coat or whatever has been
thought of
made
manufactured
sold
and then sold again by the retailer
and then worn by the customer
and she has been happy with it
only then one can say that the dress, coat or whatever has been a success."

Muir understood the importance of presentation in retail. Her originality was recognized and taken up by empathetic retailers and none more so than the legendary Geraldine Stutz, ex-president of the New York store, Henri Bendel. Under Stutz's leadership from the '60s to the '80s, this store was recognised as the most innovative and exciting in New York.

Under her direction in 1967 the store opened an extensive department solely dedicated to Jean Muir's collections, which became an instant success. Famous for its original and striking window displays, which often featured Jean Muir's designs, Bendels also introduced a charming advertising programme for Muir. "Jean Muir is not merely marvellous – she's non-pareil. Who else knows every nuance of cut and shape and detail that goes into great dressmaking, or handles leather as if it were liquid, or turns out soft-strong shoulders ten ways?"

It was Stutz who labelled Muir's style 'Dog Whistle Fashion', so-called because she believed Muir's designs were pitched at such a sophisticated and rarefied level, only the very few could truly recognise and appreciate their qualities. Muir's are clothes for connoisseurs – those who seek and appreciate the distinction of individuality and quality – to be worn, enjoyed, savoured and cherished. Geraldine Stutz was among those who called Muir 'the greatest dressmaker in the world' also stating that Muir's clothes "were worth swimming the Channel for".

As Jean Rosenberg, former vice president, Henri Bendel, and the main buyer for Jean Muir collections recalls: "Jean was a singular talent. Of the many post-war ready-to-wear designers that exploded on to the international fashion scene in the 1960s, her concept of pure understated feminine elegance has made her a lasting presence in the design world. She was bright, decisive, strong but vulnerable – and her clothes were a clear expression of her character and personality. Wearing Jean Muir I always knew I could go anywere."

Bergdorf Goodman, another prestigious New York store, created quite a stir when it devoted its entire run of Fifth Avenue windows to Jean Muir's twenty-fifth anniversary celebrations in 1991. Large reproductions of Miss Muir's sketches provided the graphic backdrop to her designs modelled on mannequins. The garments, largely in matte jersey, were both archive – spanning her past twenty-five years – and current, and one could hardly tell which were which.

**OPPOSITE** The calm after the show – Jean Muir ensures everything is in place before the arrival of the buyers – Royal Academician, Anthony Green's 1979 painting *Jean Muir Checking Buttons* in her Bruton Street showroom. The vendeuse looks on while models appear to float through the showroom and out of the window. As another model prepares to enter through the double doors, in the background Jean Muir's husband Harry Leuckert appears at the showroom door. © Anthony Green.

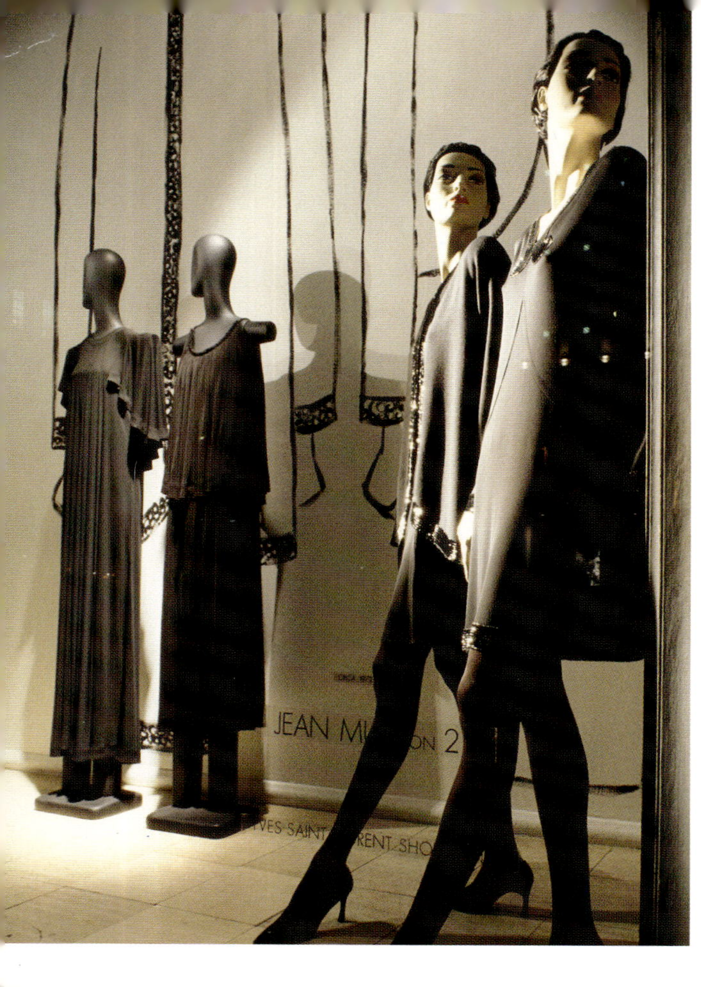

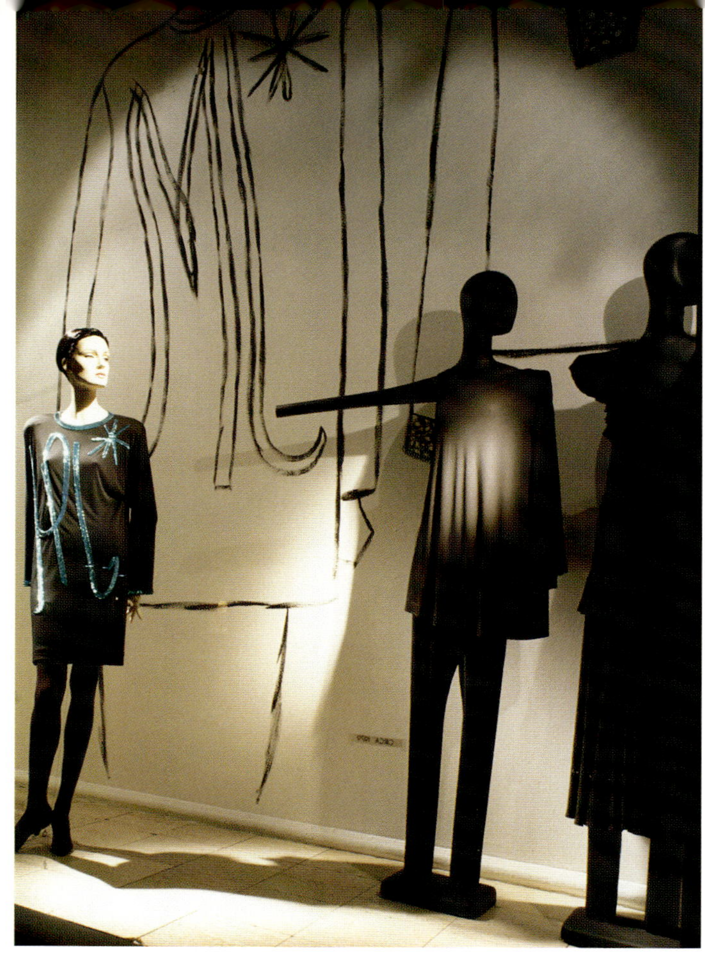

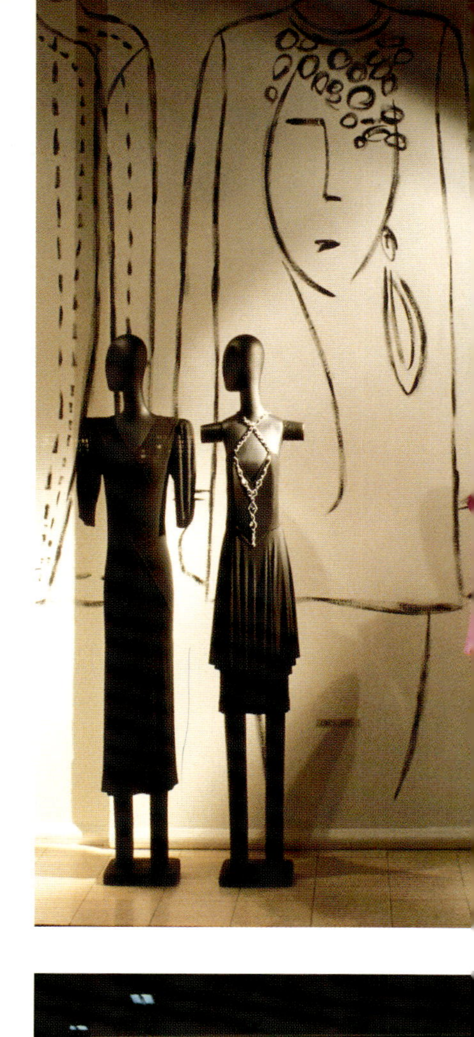

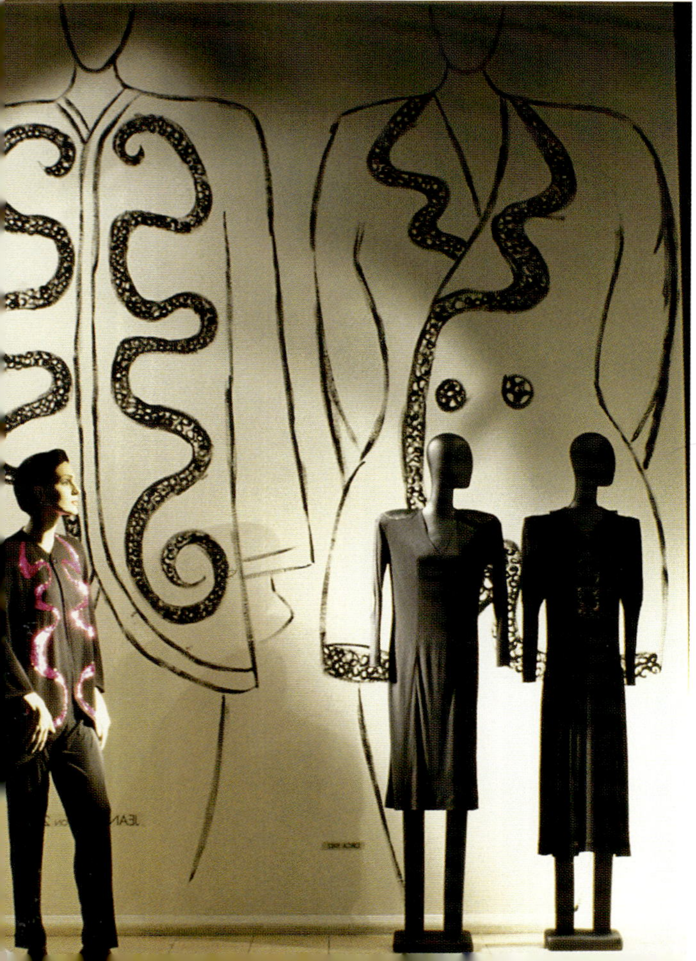

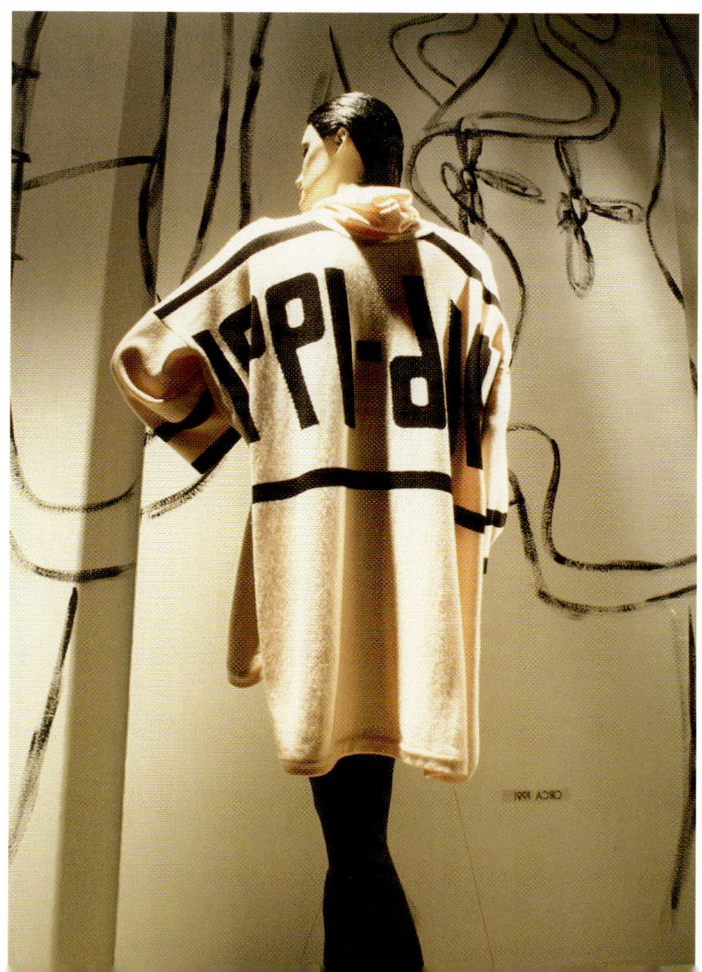

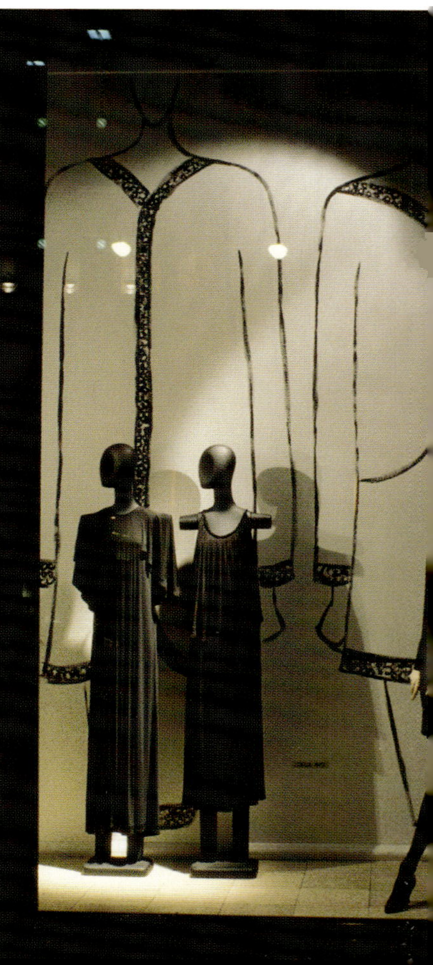

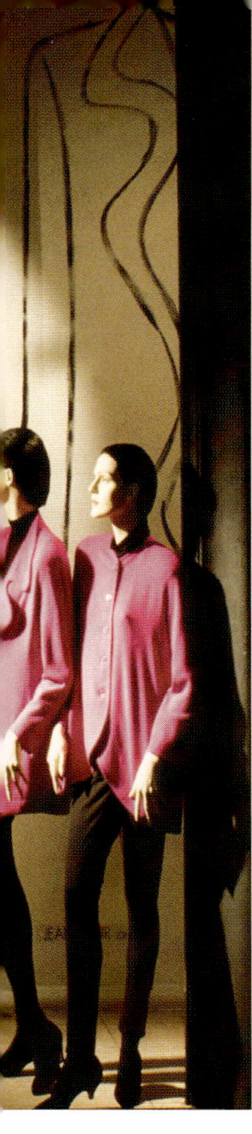

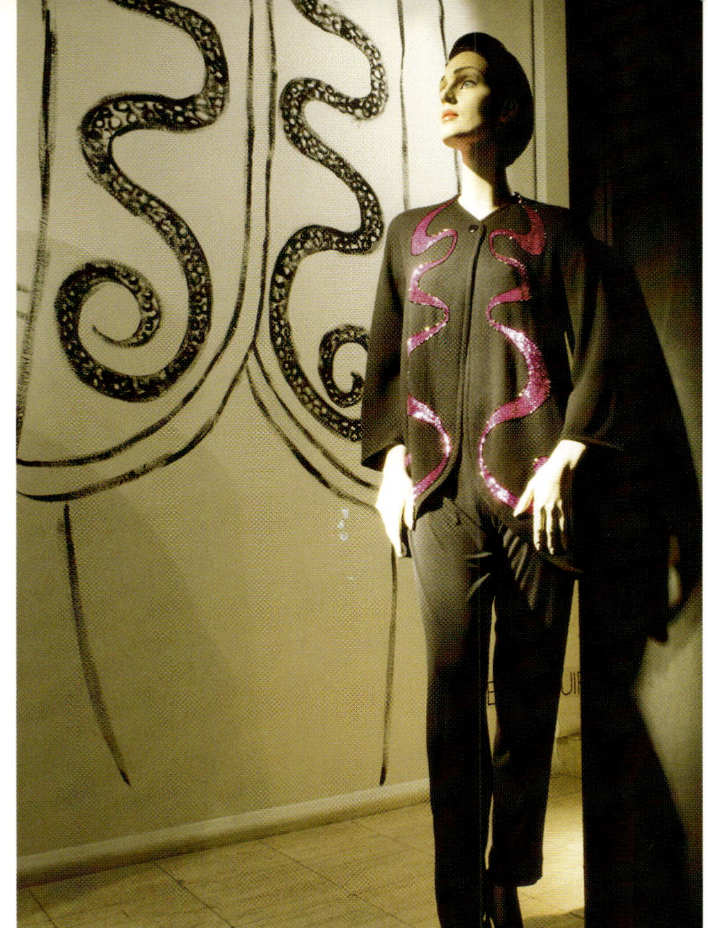

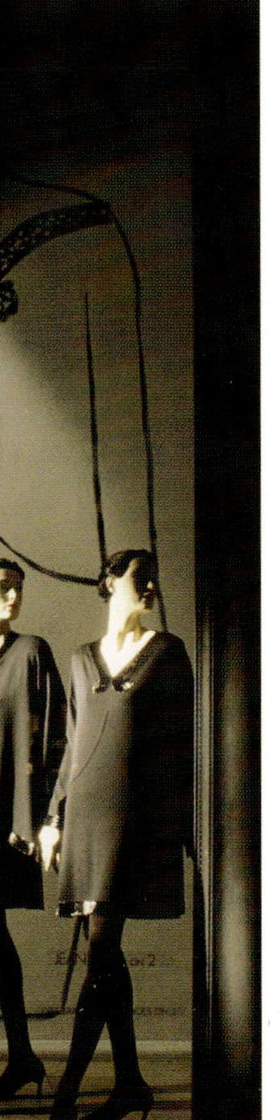

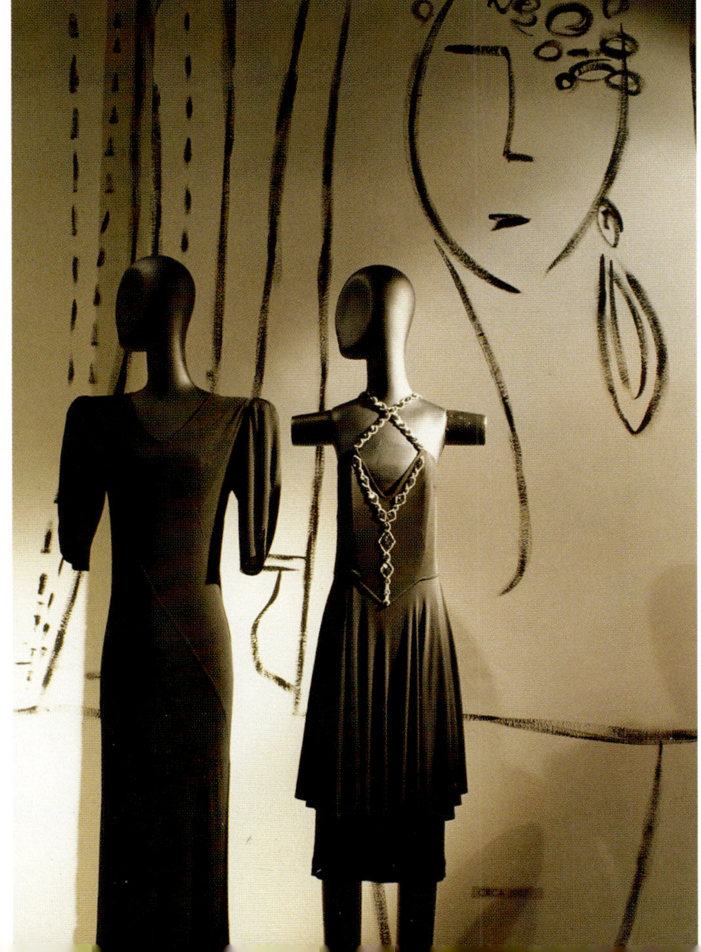

Miss Muir also found English retailers who strongly identified with her look. In Edgbaston, near Birmingham, Gill Smytheman's clientele came from as far away as Cornwall and Scotland to visit her shop. Jean Muir commented appreciatively: "Gill happens to love the kind of clothes I make… she loves the continuation… she nurtures them, and treats them like the objects that I hope they are!" Gill Smytheman returned the compliment. "To get full enjoyment from Jean Muir's clothes one has to use intelligence and imagination to see what she was thinking about when she created them. Jean Muir is a designer who has always done it her way. She is often copied but never equalled. There's something lasting and wonderful about her creations. They don't shout fashion but speak timeless style. For my customers it's not about buying clothes but about collecting something beautiful."

Rita Britton whose shop, Pollyanna in Barnsley, Yorkshire is a mecca for customers seeking uberstyle, stocking Comme des Garçons and Yamamoto among others, has a telling anecdote about Muir's international standing: "She has gone beyond fashion. When we applied to stock and sell Azzedine Alaia, we were interviewed by Mirabelle Sainte Marie. I was asked to list the designers I stocked and made no impression until I mentioned the name of Jean Muir. Suddenly Mirabelle stopped me and said that Jean Muir was unquestionably one of the best designers in the world, that we did not deserve her in this country and that she should have been French!"

Britton explains the Jean Muir appeal: "There is almost an inverted snobbery amongst my customers about who has had their Jean Muirs the longest. Now that is unique. Jean Muir's clothes are the quietest things in the shop perhaps, but the magic is when they're on. Once people start buying, they become converts. It's a following, a club. It's so easy to add. Nobody makes mistakes with Muir. It's a fact. That's the secret."

**LEFT** Famous New York store, Bergdorf Goodman devoted its entire run of Fifth Avenue windows to Jean Muir's 25th anniversary collection, September 1991. These windows stopped the traffic and during her visit there Jean Muir was constantly mobbed by fans.

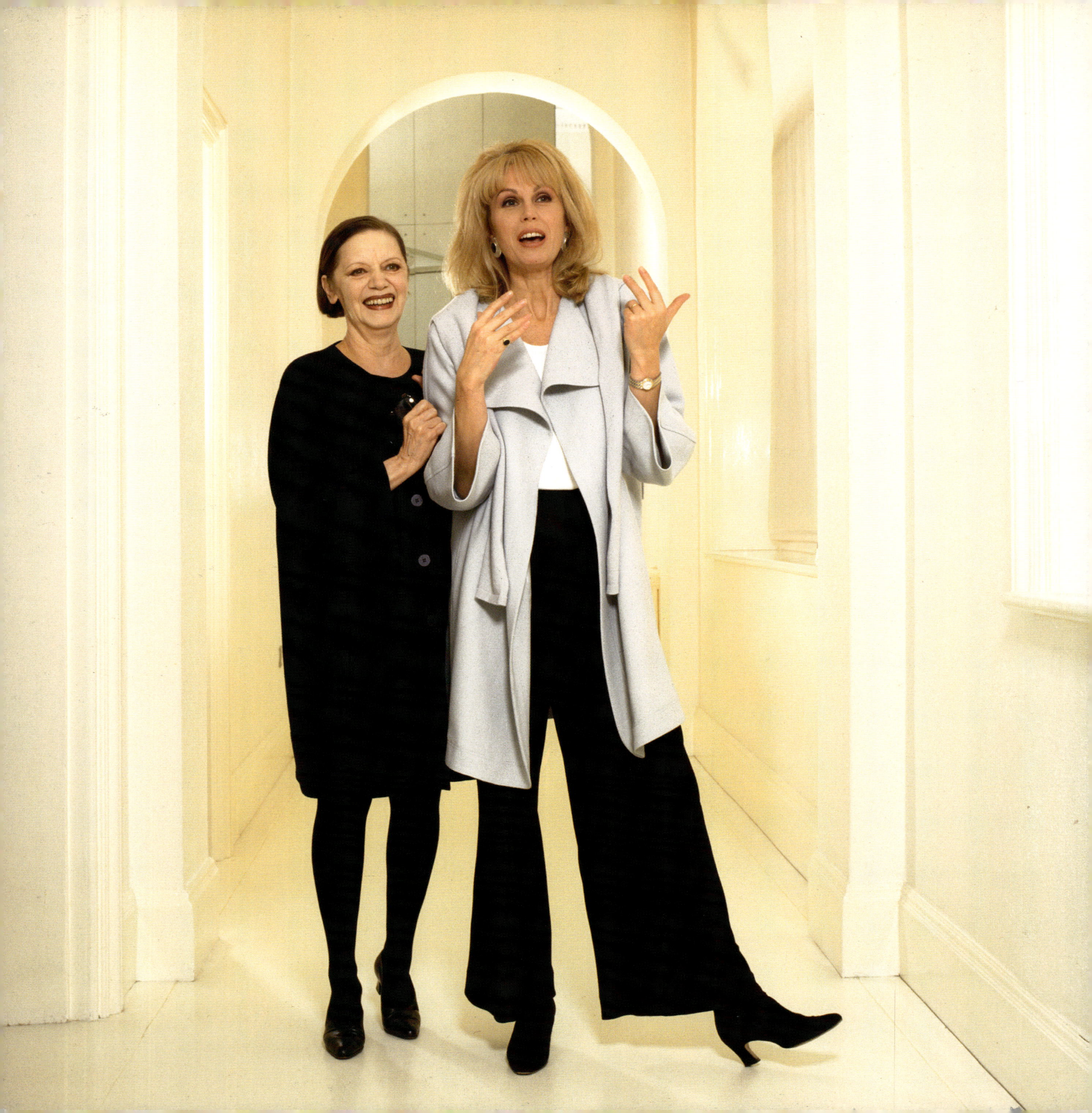

Chapter Eight

# JEAN MUIR: THE WEARERS

"Getting the clothes right for the body they're on. The handwriting is mine, but the reading is the wearer's..."

JEAN MUIR

**JEAN MUIR'S** was a confident definition of womanhood. "Being a woman is being positive, natural, and not losing your instinctive, intuitive self." Paradoxically, Miss Muir often said that she was not interested in clothes per se; "not in a purely fashion sense, that is. It's more how things are done that concerns me. I love to see people enhancing themselves." Her friend, Drusilla Beyfus recalls,"She was the only dress designer who'd say 'don't talk to me about clothes!' They were the last things she wanted to discuss. She was interested in much more profound, important issues." In this context, Muir's view on fashion design was pithily succinct: "Just do it importantly and then you can forget about it."

Throughout her career, Muir dressed royalty and the cream of the artistic and dramatic worlds. Her clientele included HRH Princess Alexandra, the perennially elegant and attractive cousin of the Queen, the artists Bridget Riley, Dame Elisabeth Frink and Glenys Barton, Lady Antonia Fraser – whom British *Vogue* called a "brainy beauty who doesn't put a style foot wrong" – Elizabeth Jane Howard, Edna O'Brien, and the broadcasters and writers, Joan Bakewell and Selina Scott; all were attracted to the Muir look. Joanna Lumley has described herself as "addicted"; Barbara Griggs asserted that "one doesn't buy Jean Muir, one collects them".

Actresses have always been drawn to the cerebral and sensuous quality of her clothes. Perhaps because by profession they are constantly required to take on the personality and costume of numerous characters, the opportunity to wear clothes that enhance their own personalities without taking over and dictating to them is highly attractive. Lauren Bacall, Glenda Jackson, Maggie Smith, Judi Dench, Diana Rigg, her actress daughter Rachael Stirling, Patricia Hodge, Siân Phillips, and Joanna Lumley are all articulate fans and vocal in their appreciation.

"Thank God for Jean Muir – she takes me through the evening."
Dame Maggie Smith, actress.

"The beauty of Jean's clothes is that they never go out of fashion," says Joanna Lumley. "They still look as tremendous now as the day I bought them. They are simple and sublime. When you wear Jean's clothes you become addicted. I admire perfectionists, whatever job they do, and Jean is the greatest there is – the stitching, the buttons she chooses, the way her dresses feel when you wear them. They don't dictate – it's you looking beautiful in a dress, not just you in a beautiful dress."

**PAGE 118** Jean Muir and Joanna Lumley, both dressed in Muir, photographed in the hallway of Jean Muir's London flat, Albert Court for *Harper's & Queen* to coincide with Channel 4's 1993 television series 'Very Jean Muir'. Photograph & © Terry O'Neill.

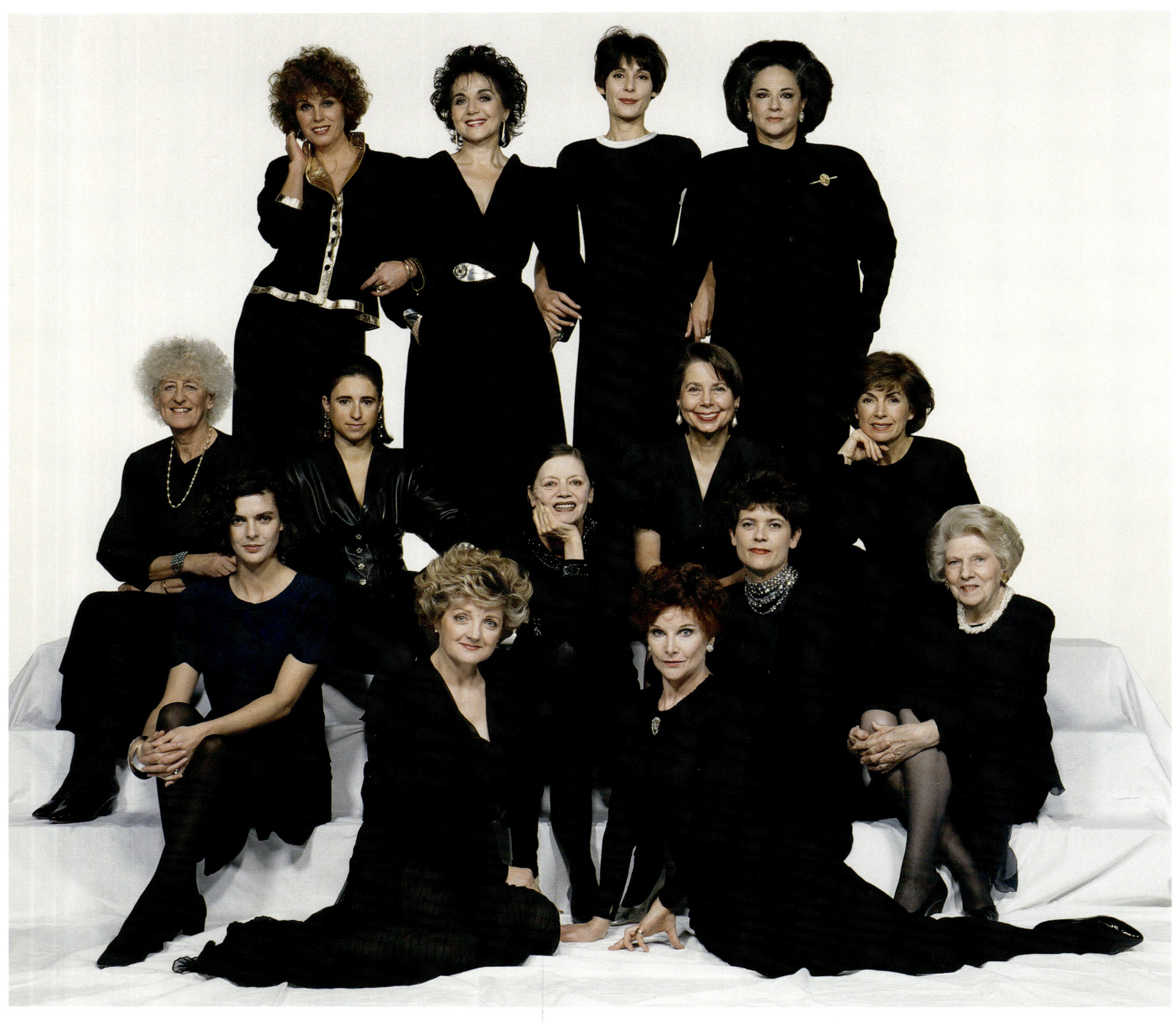

**ABOVE** The 'Muirettes', a gathering of Muir aficionados, photographed for *The Sunday Times Magazine*, 1991. [Top row] Actress Joanna Lumley; writer and broadcaster Dr Miriam Stoppard; the writer and former Muir house model Nicola Shulman, now The Marchioness of Normanby; Pamela Lady Harlech. [Second row] Sculptor Elisabeth Frink; stylist Desirée Lederer; journalist Drusilla Beyfus; and former director of The Royal Opera House Trust, Felicity Clark. [Third row] Designer Tamsin de Roemer; Jean Muir; former Harvey Nichols fashion director Amanda Verdan; and showroom vendeuse Princess Shelaigh Galitzine. [Front row] Actresses Julia McKenzie and Adrienne Corri. Photograph & © Terry O'Neill.

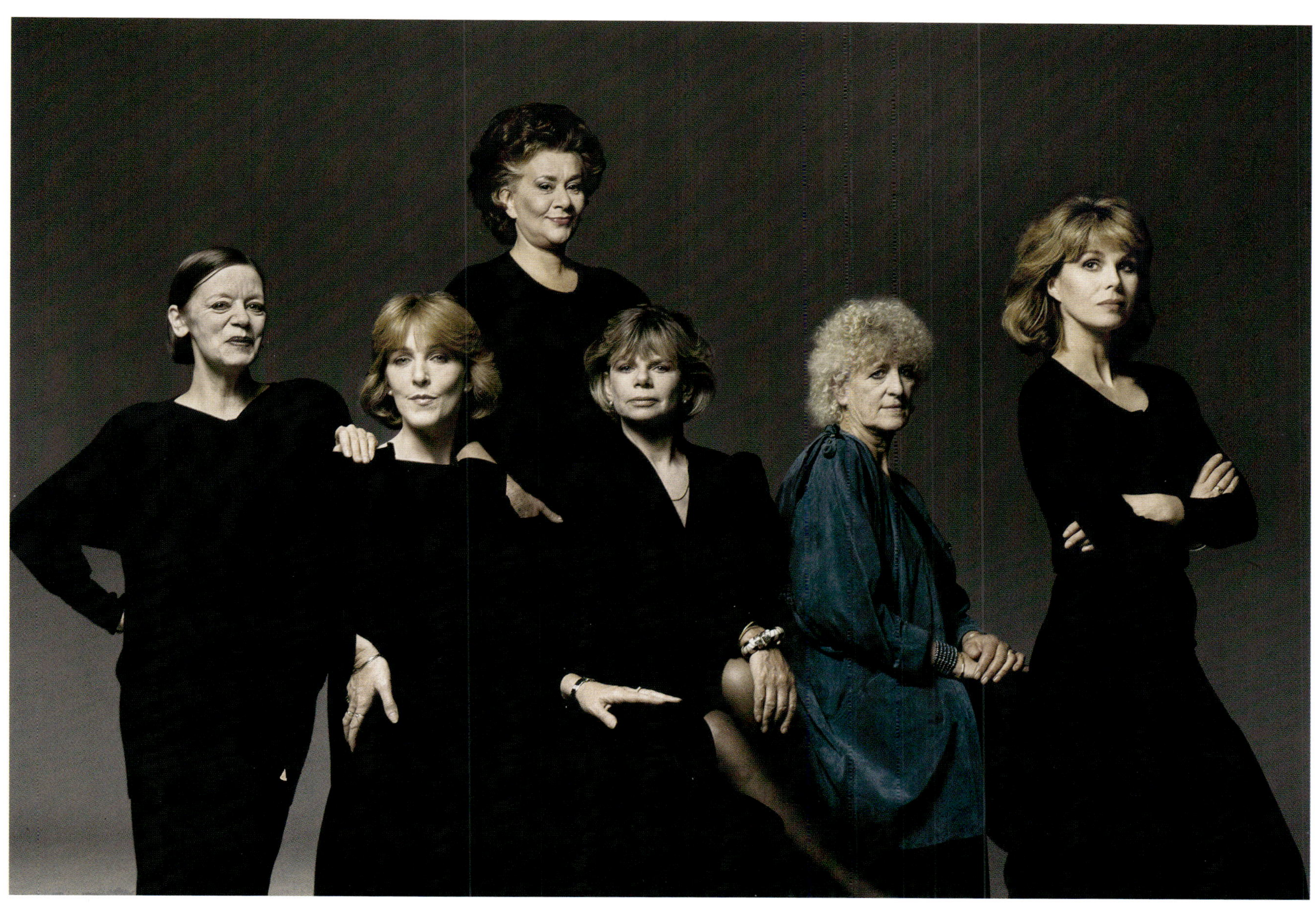

**ABOVE** "I like women who know who they really are and it seems to me that they are the kind of women who wear my clothes." Jean Muir. Pictured for a feature in the *Sunday Telegraph Magazine*, March 1987, a group of women who embody the Muir philosophy. [Left to right] Jean Muir with Patricia Hodge, Joan Plowright (Lady Olivier), Jill Bennett, Elisabeth Frink, and Muir favourite, Joanna Lumley. Photograph & © Clive Arrowsmith.

"Just before Michael (Williams) and I were married about 35 years ago, I bought a Jean Muir dress. It was aubergine colour, with a high neck, long sleeves and buttons all down the back. I have worn it ever since. I find the clothes beautifully cut, easy to wear, very comfortable and they make me feel wonderful – and I keep them for ever!" Dame Judi Dench, actress.

"Jean's clothes look and feel as if they are your own from the start." Patricia Hodge, actress.

Many wore Jean Muir designs for their professional life – Glenda Jackson wore Muir for the film *A Touch of Class*, and Muir designed a complete wardrobe for Patricia Hodge to wear in the film version of Pinter's *Betrayal*. Muir dressed Cilla Black in the 60s and made special concert dresses for Barbra Streisand, also a fan of her cashmere and jersey pieces. Muir's name and the power of her hallmark has so entered the British psyche that she has even been included in the text of Charlotte Jones's award-winning play, *Humble Boy*. Both Dame Diana Rigg – who created the rôle – and Felicity Kendal – who followed her – wore a navy wool crepe outfit by Jean Muir in the scene during which the leading female character proudly declares she is wearing her "Jean Muir".

Muir's style was neither aggressively female, cloying nor coy. "I like my clothes to be womanly, with rounded soft lines, feminine in the true and natural sense, not fussy, not feminist, not sex symbol."

She designed for herself – the American painter, Richard Lindner declared that her work was a series of self-portraits – but she also designed for women in the way that Chanel did, from a woman's perspective, wanting to feel comfortable, confident and unrestricted in her clothes.

"I love the feeling that my clothes are formally informal." Jean Muir.

Muir's was a bluestocking approach, an appeal to the intelligentsia; femininity as high-minded chic, something the writer, and Muir-wearer Drusilla Beyfus termed a "well-bred elegance". Beyfus's elder daughter, the writer, Nicola Shulman, once a Muir house model, now the Marchioness of Normanby, explains the appeal: "She made clothes for women who didn't think that to be clever and well-dressed were mutually exclusive."

Many felt transformed by wearing Muir. Muir claimed the compliment that meant most to her came from the wife of a theatre producer: "Your clothes make me feel like a woman – not a rather boring housewife and mother of three children." Beyfus added, "Her clothes were a cure for inelegance. After a hard day's work, feeling as if you were falling apart, you'd put on something of hers and immediately feel different."

Much as discerning women who could afford to bought her clothes, many who could not still hankered after 'a Jean Muir'. Some found a compromise by buying her *Butterick* and *Vogue* paper patterns, which had existed since the sixties, and making their Jean Muir themselves!

The word fashion conjures up an image of fleeting fads and gimmicks. Jean Muir was not about that, yet her clothes still had a freshness and an originality, could still surprise, had wit and humour and an inner vitality. She found a way to marry the contemporary mood of the moment with her own style in a way that was both flattering and enduring; her clothes are not classified by age, more of an attitude of mind. Her definition of a modern woman was someone who is "loose-limbed, broad-minded and not afraid of her body." She sculpted a look that she made recognisably her own – small shouldered, gently following the figure; they were sophisticated, grown-up clothes. Her clothes mirrored her own values… and women felt the better for wearing them.

The rise of vintage dressing, and Muir's status as one of the hottest labels to collect on both sides of the Atlantic, has led to a whole new generation discovering her clothes, with actresses such as Tilda Swinton, Chloe Sevigny, Thandie Newton, Sienna Miller and model Claudia Schiffer wearing her original designs. Many of Miss Muir's celebrated fans, including Joanna Lumley and Dame Judi Dench, bridge both eras of Jean Muir, and also wear the label as it is now. Recent aficionados include actresses Charlotte Rampling, Julie Walters and Juliet Stevenson as well as Editor-in-Chief of British *Vogue*, Alexandra Shulman.

Lady Antonia Fraser, a staunch Muir fan, has been wearing Jean Muir almost exclusively since the seventies. "Femininity and timelessness" she says "are probably the two most marked characteristics of Jean Muir's clothes. But there is a third characteristic of softness or suppleness which I tried for years to analyse. Clinging, no, moulding, drifting – what was the right word? Suddenly I came across a phrase in one of Herrick's lyrics which seemed to me to express it

Whenas in silks my Julia goes,
Then, then, (methinks) how sweetly flows
the liquefaction of her clothes...

Yes, liquefaction is the right word, be the material silk, or suede, or crepe or any of the materials with which Jean Muir weaves both dresses and spells. That is the precise quality which causes the most unexpected man to exclaim suddenly: 'What a very pretty dress!' While women say: 'Isn't that a Jean Muir?'

Jean Muir delighted, but did not surprise me, by telling me that she was and always had been fascinated by everything surrounding a person in a painting – clothes, dogs, chairs, curtains – and what it reveals about a person and the time in which they lived. She added that she had never had the slightest interest in the word 'fashion' in its 'actually very ill-defined and interpreted modern sense' or indeed in being fashionable: 'Which considering what I do, most people find hard to comprehend!'"

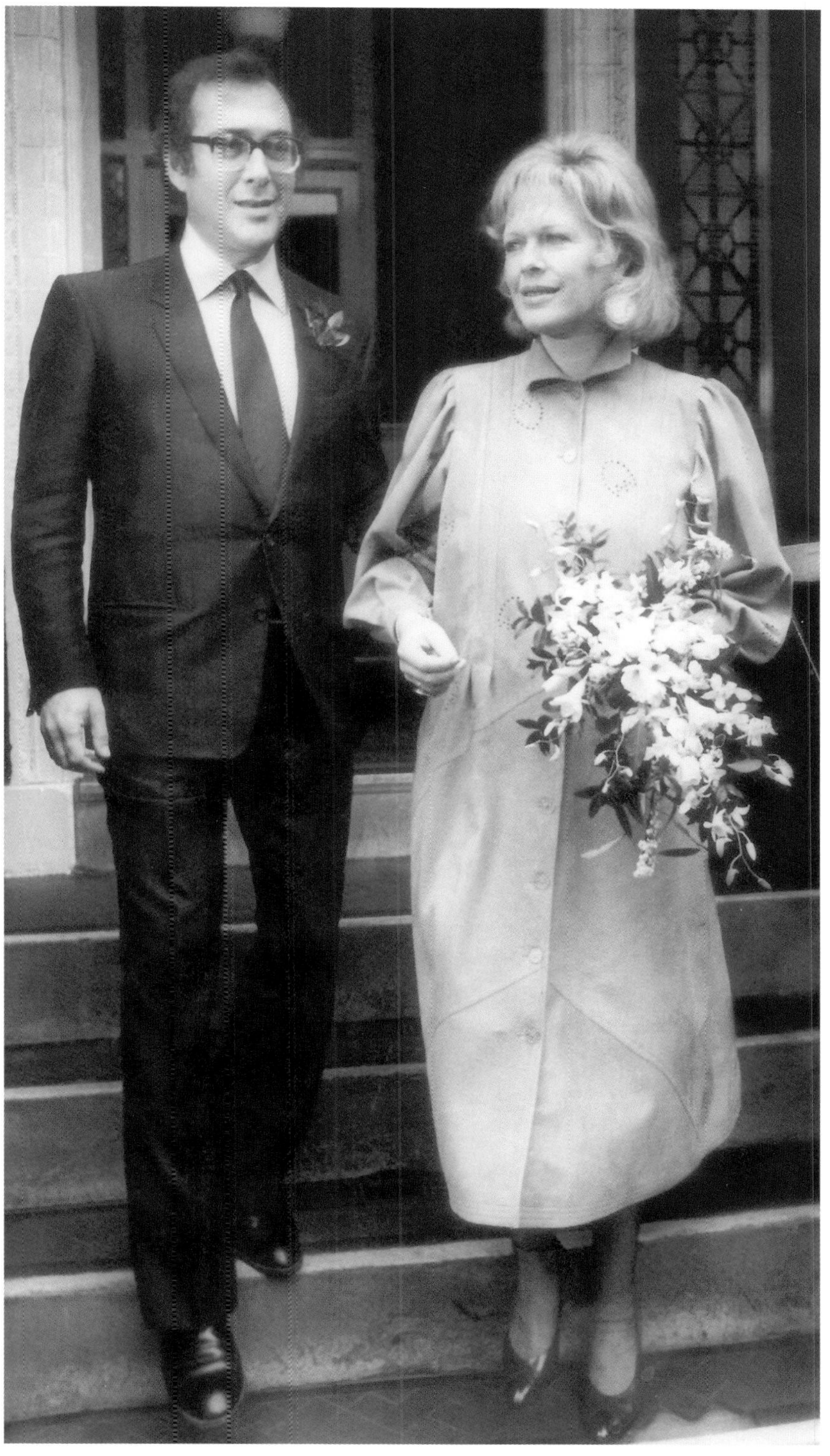

**ABOVE** Lady Antonia Fraser, at her wedding to playright Harold Pinter in November 1980, wears a wisteria suede coatdress with hand-punched tulip motif. For the party afterwards she wore another Muir, "a wonderful white, star-spangled crepe long dress."

International model Jan Ward, who later married entrepreneur and photographer, Justin de Villeneuve, was chosen by Norman Parkinson for this, one of his most famous location shoots, now an iconic fashion image. "I was very lucky to be able to wear clothes by Jean Muir in photographs throughout my early modelling career in the late '60s and '70s," recalls Jan. "The most memorable was undoubtedly one shoot I did with Norman Parkinson for *Vogue* in January 1971. He had me poised on a stone ledge in the vast desert landscape of Monument Valley, Utah, where four American states meet. I wore a Jean Muir silk jersey dress belted with billowing sleeves, which was rust-coloured just like the huge sandstone rock formations on the far horizon. I quickly pulled on some suede Indian moccasins and did a bit of make-up as the fashion editor, Patricia Roberts, wound a spare piece of matching fabric around my head as a glamorous turban. In about fifteen minutes we were ready to shoot what was to be a really classic Parkinson photograph of an equally classic Jean Muir dress. As soon as one puts on a Jean Muir dress one feels pretty fabulous, even amidst the dusty sagebrush in a very hot desert.

In the mid '80s, a friend gave me an invitation to a Jean Muir sample sale, which was a tremendous experience. There were throngs of people desperately trying to grab as many of the wonderful frocks as they could to try on. I managed to find a beautiful long silk jersey dress with fabric draped over each shoulder, very much what most people would associate with Jean Muir. The big surprise for me was to see so many other intriguing outfits, often in bright colours – coats, suits, skirts, blouses, sweaters, hats, shoes – absolutely amazing things in suede, silk, satin, wool, as well as her famous matte jersey. Many buttons were hand-crafted as was the occasional brooch. Sometimes things would have been reduced just because the buttons were missing – but that might be twenty buttons on a dress that was very unusual and special, so it would be hard to find the kind of buttons that Jean would have added. Often, as I tried something on in the communal dressing room, another customer would look on admiringly and comment that the outfit looked fine on me as I was the sample size, but it wouldn't suit them. However, I always encouraged others to try and find their size as Jean Muir's clothes look sensational whatever one's size.

I ended up frequenting the sample sales for quite a few years. Though I lived in the country I would try to get there as early as I could, always finding a long queue outside the Bruton Street door whatever the hour. Roz, who had been one of Jean's favourite models and was now a vendeuse at the showroom, would often grab me and say, 'Jan, try this,' handing me something I might never have taken off the hanger. Invariably she would be right and I found myself purchasing some truly unique pieces, including samples that would have been in a show but might not have made it into production. Preferring things that do not follow a particular trend I was thrilled and astonished at the continual creativity of 'Miss Muir', as the girls would call her.

With two daughters, I have been able to pass along my interest in the artistic side of fashion, not to mention various Jean Muir things. I had no plan to make a 'vintage fashion collection' but had kept most of the clothes I loved. Recently, when a curator from the Victoria & Albert Museum came to look at my clothes for an exhibition, I realised just how modern so many of Jean Muir's creations look. From a favourite tartan wool suit to a stylish but cosy cashmere dressing gown, they are comfortable to wear and many stand out like works of art in their own right – such as an apple-green suede skirt with marvellous buttons and a black leather jacket delicately hand painted with flowers. With her obvious love of colour, fabric and texture, along with an imaginative and thoughtful way of putting these elements together to design inspirational clothes, it is no wonder that Jean Muir is a true fashion icon.

I still feel she is part of my life."

**OPPOSITE** Shades of the desert: American model Jan Ward (later Jan de Villeneuve) wears a full-sleeved, sashed, scarved Jean Muir dress photographed for *Vogue* by Norman Parkinson against the backdrop of Monument Valley, Utah, 1970. The stylish Ward always had an eye for fashion and her collection of vintage Jean Muir is legendary. Her daughters Poppy, a photographer, and Daisy, a designer and illustrator, are noted for their promotion of retro fashion inspired by their mother's wardrobe. Photograph & © The Norman Parkinson Archive.

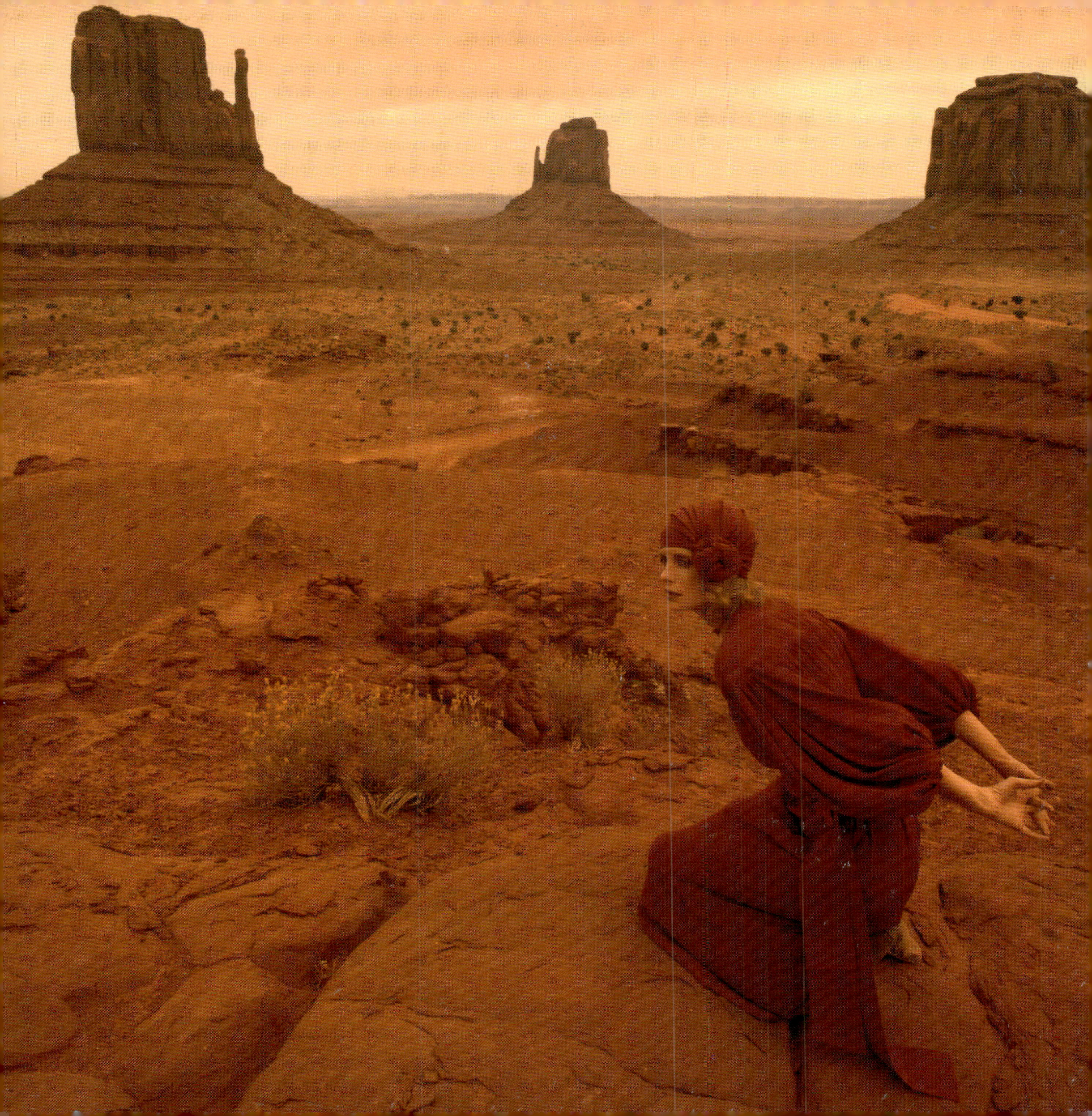

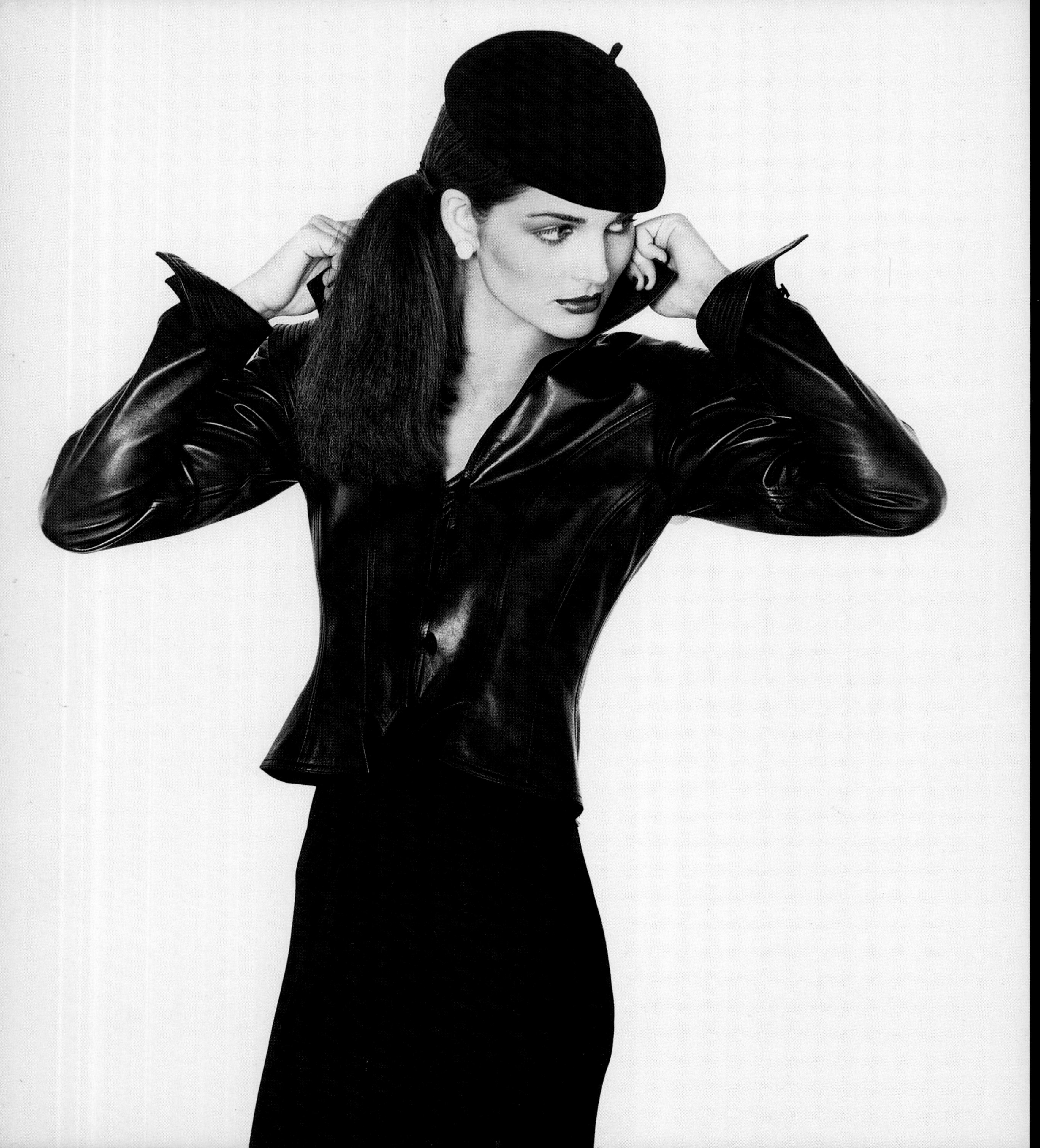

Chapter Nine

# JEAN MUIR: THE MINIMALIST & THE SENSUALIST

“Less is More”

MIES VAN DER ROHE

“Less is Muir”

ANON

**JEAN MUIR:** "Clothes which step back allow the personality and some kind of cerebral presence to be felt. I do not think one should indulge the weakness for fripperies, which is present in human nature. I think people should be what they are visually; they should simply enhance with clothing what they are naturally. You should like your *self*, not disguise it or hide it."

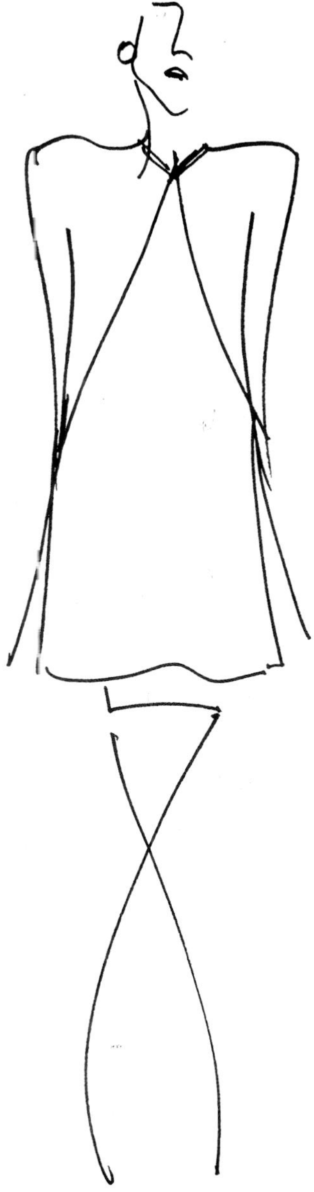

**PAGE 128** Minimalism used to maximum effect: leather jacket over svelte black jersey dress. Hat by Graham Smith. This outfit was chosen as 'Dress of the Year', 1979. Photograph: Eric Boman/The Condé Nast Publications Ltd. **ABOVE** Jean Muir sketch © Jean Muir Ltd.

# THE MINIMALIST

Restraint and understatement were Jean Muir's forte, but the subsequent effect had a quiet dynamism all of its own as the severity and precision of her cut was transformed into a becoming softness as it skimmed the body. To many, her sleek outlines worked best in black or navy where the cut was shown to its best effect but colour also displayed the architectural lines of her purist shapes. "Simplification is a very complicated process", so wrote Geoffrey Beene, the legendary American designer and Muir's contemporary, whose maverick anti-fashion stance was similarly characterised by a preoccupation with cut and craft, dance and movement. Muir's vision required her to pare down to the core of a shape, its cut and fit. Such an approach is the hardest thing to achieve and requires skill and judgement. For her, control was paramount; balance and proportion were her watchwords. Muir's special form of tailoring was never hard-edged, and, regardless of whether her cloth was the softest matte jersey or a masculine tweed, a Jean Muir garment was never less than flattering to the woman within.

As Kate Phelan, fashion director of British *Vogue* comments: "Jean Muir really provided the blueprint for minimalism in fashion, especially with her jersey dresses, and she defined it very early on. Other designers would follow in her wake, especially the Americans who went on to take it forward, developing their easy sportswear approach."

An instinctive minimalist, the intellectual rigour of Jean Muir's designs marked her out as a true modernist, yet in mood her clothes are ineffably feminine. Her minimalism stemmed from her pragmatism and a sense of economy in her aesthetic, something she ascribed to her Celtic roots. In Muir's terms luxury was often equated with simplicity. Simplicity, she felt, has a grandeur and an eloquence that speaks volumes. She learned early on what to leave out, and that what she left out was as important as what she left in. "I am always simplifying: that is, in the best sense of the word which doesn't mean cutting corners but the reverse. That needs much more determination." She did not overburden the body or the person, "I never make clothes for effect or show, everything is totally wearable. I am not experimental in that sense of just doing things differently. My feet are firmly on the ground," she once remarked.

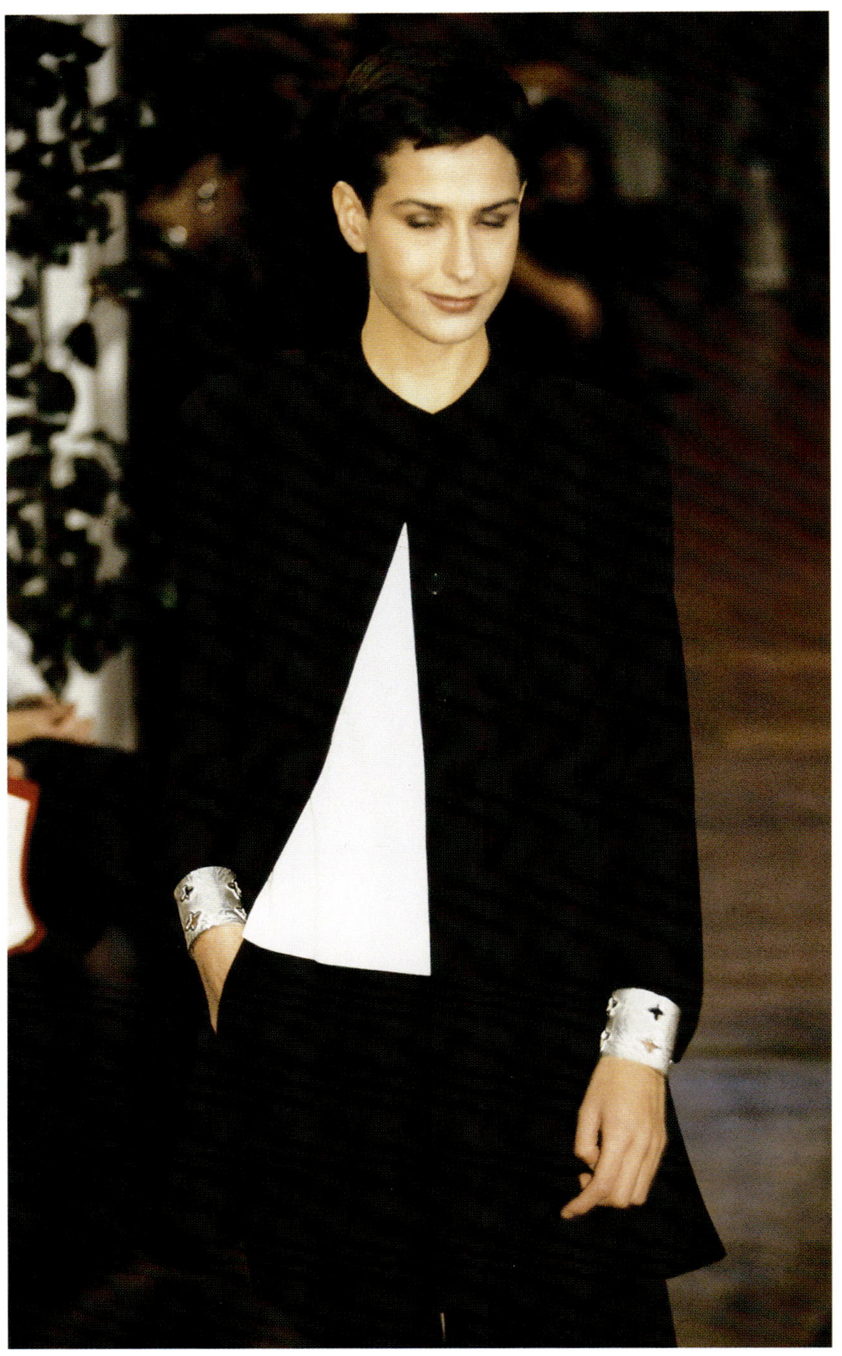

**ABOVE** Muir at her simplest and most effective. Black fine wool separates over white jersey uses graphic shapes for dramatic effect, the only embellishment – a pair of carved sterling silver cuffs, Spring 1994. Photograph & © Chris Moore.

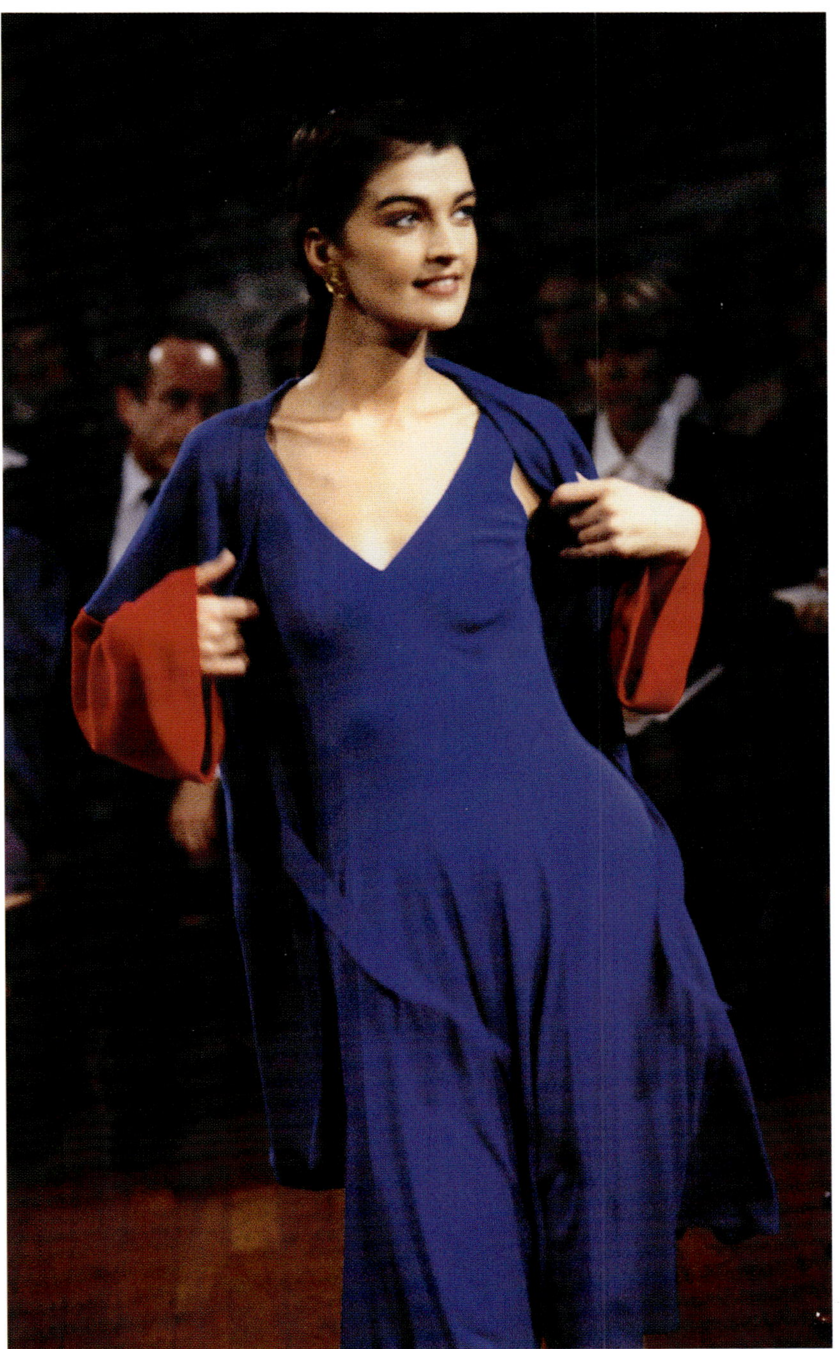

**ABOVE** Jean Muir sculpts jersey to reveal the lines of the body to perfection. Clinging and drifting Royal blue jersey sleeveless dress with colour-banded cashmere shrug, Spring 1991. Photograph & © Chris Moore.

## THE SENSUALIST

There was undoubtedly a very sensuous dimension to Muir's collections. She was a sensualist in the way in which she selected and treated her materials, applying her skills to them as well as the female body, anticipating how one could enhance the other. She described her clothes as "sinuous, moving and, for lack of a better word, body-shaped." The unique range of her work seemed to envelop femininity. From the demure early Jane and Jane designs to the vivacity and dash of her knitwear and prints she wove her spell. Equally puritan and seductive, her jersey dresses were simultaneously concealing and revealing, mysterious and alluring. This complex combination was understood and appreciated as much by the onlooker, especially by men, as by the wearer. "It's funny how men notice Jean Muir dresses," says Joanna Lumley. "They may not know beans about clothes, but once they've recognised a dress on you they'll spot other Jean Muir dresses at parties. They are the clothes men like to see you in."

Claire Atkinson, one of Muir's most charismatic models agrees: "I find her clothes very sexy and people could be surprised about that, because they think she's so classic. She has ways of making the fabric cling to your body in a very quiet way. It's sort of an eternal sexiness. Wearing Jean Muir is lovely. When you move, they cling to your breasts or your waist just for a second. I have a long blue jersey skirt, I don't know how she's cut it, it seems to be seamless and it shimmers down and it's so sexy. You feel very rich but very casual." Actress Jill Bennet had another slant on the special appeal of Muir: "Jean's clothes are so simple, so sculpted, you feel like a sexy governess in them. She makes the sort of dress you put on at ten in the morning and still feel good in at four the next morning. The sort of clothes I need."

Muir had a faithful following among leading members of the international fashion press. They not only wrote about her clothes, they wore them. Marylou Luther of *The Los Angeles Times* enthuses: "Jean Muir is incontrovertibly the sovereign of soft – the designer who wrote the book on what have come to be known as 'body clothes'. While many of her contemporaries were torturing torsos in restrictive, man-tailored suits or stiff architectural paper-doll dresses, Muir was liberating the body. Her easy, fluid dresses, stripped of all underpinnings, are so artfully cut they seem to be poured on the body. Designers from Tokyo to New York have copied them verbatim."

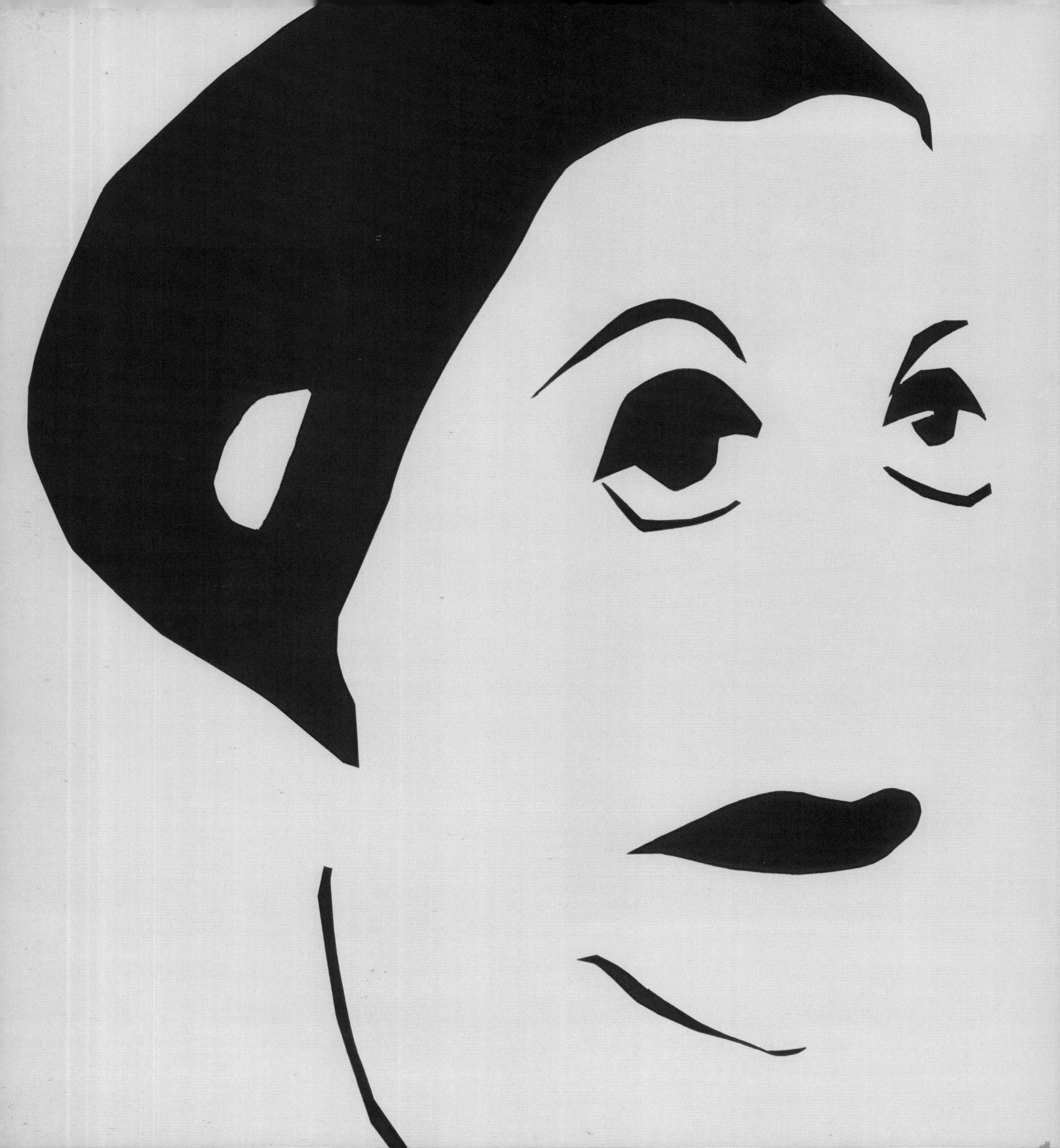

Chapter Ten

# JEAN MUIR: THE ARTIST'S EYE

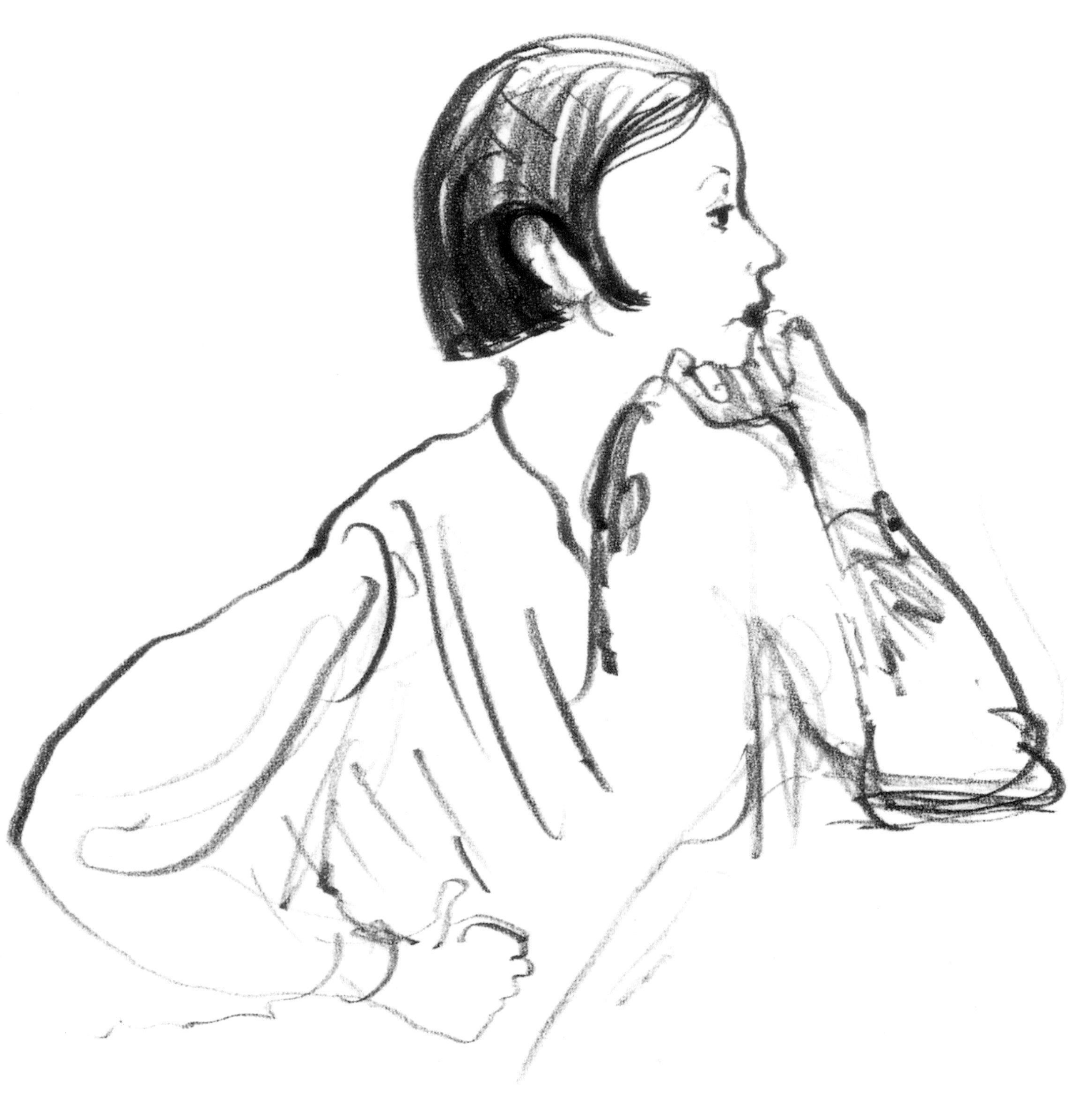

**JEAN MUIR** knew many contemporary artists and several became her friends. Her design ethos and originality were acknowledged by them and it is interesting to see how they 'read' her work, identifying with different facets of it, likening her approach, her use of structure and colour, to their own, as they drew parallels between themselves and Muir as artists.

Bridget Riley describes Miss Muir's method of working. "Very much like a sculptor, she adds and subtracts, but throughout, all is subordinate to the whole. Indeed it is the overriding control of the fundamental format that supports or rather encourages her inventions; because however far she goes, she always returns and the all-important totality remains intact." She continues, "I am sure that her entire oeuvre rests essentially upon a concept similar to that of the modern artist who pursues something for its own sake, who makes for the sake of making, and who holds the work precious for itself."

Other artists such as Anthony Green and Patrick Procktor who painted portraits of women wearing their Jean Muirs, observe that their sitter's Muir clothes substantially enhanced their own work.

It is clear from Anthony Green's painting on page 114 that he completely understands Muir's absolute dedication to her complex craft. "I have painted Jean wearing her Muir, checking buttons in the Bruton Street showroom. I have painted Mary Cozens-Walker [Mrs Anthony Green], wearing her Jean Muir blue leather coat. Jean Muir improves Green compositions. When artists make things very, very well, they never become 'old fashioned'. In the 1920s Ettore Bugatti made Type 35s and Royales – he was an artist-engineer. Now Jean Muir makes clothes very, very well – she is an artist-designer."

Patrick Procktor, another eminent contemporary artist went to the very core of Muir's work. "Jean Muir's colour is very good colour – very becoming. It is rich and unusual. I don't know how we could trace the influences on her colour – but you could say it is rather Venetian, rather Titian colour. The secret of a good effect is understatement. Knowing when to stop is crucial. There's not enough of a certain sort of control: that deliberate and well-controlled design, that self-awareness, in the modern world. It is the way Jean Muir works. Letting the natural good looks of the woman take possession of the dress... that is what dress is all about."

Anthony Green agrees. "The thing about Jean Muir is she never wanted to be a star. She just wanted to put her clothes on your back and you were the star." As Muir herself put it: "The clothes in themselves do not make a statement. The woman makes a statement and the dress helps."

Jean Muir was the subject of portraits by a number of different artists who sought her out as an intriguing sitter, both for her achievements and her personal image, which was as distinctive as her clothes. Though she was small and fragile-looking her appearance was striking. 'A sense of order' was one of her primary guiding principles and her appearance was a statement of her intent. She found a look that suited her and kept to it. Her fine brown hair was cut in a short bob, neatly side parted and worn tucked behind her ears. Her face was pale and as a consequence, her large eyes, and her mouth, coloured with a deep toned brown lipstick, were arresting features. She wore little jewellery and from the seventies kept to a wardrobe of navy blue for her London life.

Muir sat for artist Zsuzsi Roboz, who drew an early study of her in charcoal. John Bratby also painted a portrait of her in oils in 1979. Several artists became her friends including David Remfry, who produced studies of her in pencil and watercolour, one of which hangs in London's National Portrait Gallery. Another artist friend, David Gentleman, illustrated the 1980 Jean Muir exhibition catalogue.

The sculptor Glenys Barton also chose Muir as a subject. Her ceramic busts and small-scale figures of Muir are wonderfully graphic evocations, and the blue bust was used as the poster image for the National Portrait Gallery's 1993 exhibition, 'The Portrait Now'. The sculptor Dame Elisabeth Frink and the artist Bridget Riley, were friends, as well as Jean Muir wearers. Jean Muir owned several Bridget Riley paintings. Dame Elisabeth Frink chose to model one of Jean Muir's hands in bronze. The likeness is far from static, capturing Muir's characteristically expressive, dextrous fingers, fingers that were constantly in motion

Frink speaks for many other Muir wearers, in identifying the quality of being unselfconscious in Muir's clothes. "I have worn Jean Muir's clothes for many years. Like good sculpture the form and line of her creations flow within a rigid structure. I believe that the design is controlled by many different aspects – the cutting, the strict adherence to how the body moves and

**PAGE 134** Papercut portrait of Jean Muir by Iain R Webb, commissioned by *Harper's & Queen* magazine for his feature on Muir's 25th anniversary in 1991. © Iain R Webb.
**OPPOSITE** Portrait of Jean Muir by David Gentleman, commissioned for the 1980 Jean Muir exhibition booklet. © David Gentleman.

finally they are comfortable, exciting and elegant to wear; down to all the little details of finishing, buttons, buckles and fine stitching, nothing is left out. I feel that the clothes live on me and I never need worry what I look like when wearing them."

Jean Muir's signature details run like a defining thread through her collections. Her 'handwriting' as she termed it, is as instantly recognisable as the monogram of an artist. She applied herself to a concept of designing clothes almost as an art form, but firmly rooted in its practical craft basis and its allied techniques: dyeing, weaving, knitting, and sewing.

Perhaps the essence of Jean Muir has to do with the 'interiority' of her clothes. They do not overpower the wearer but individually complement her. They reveal the intricacies of their construction to the wearer, flattering and revealing only what the wearer wants them to. This is best portrayed in a portrait by Deborah Turbeville in 1975 photographed at Miss Muir's London flat, which inspired the imagination of Stacey D'Erasmo, a teenage girl in America. 30 years on, in a recent article in American *Vogue* she recalled her perception of a powerful mystique that conveyed itself to her from this image: "That was the life I wanted to live. Those were the rooms I had to be in." (See pp.140-141)

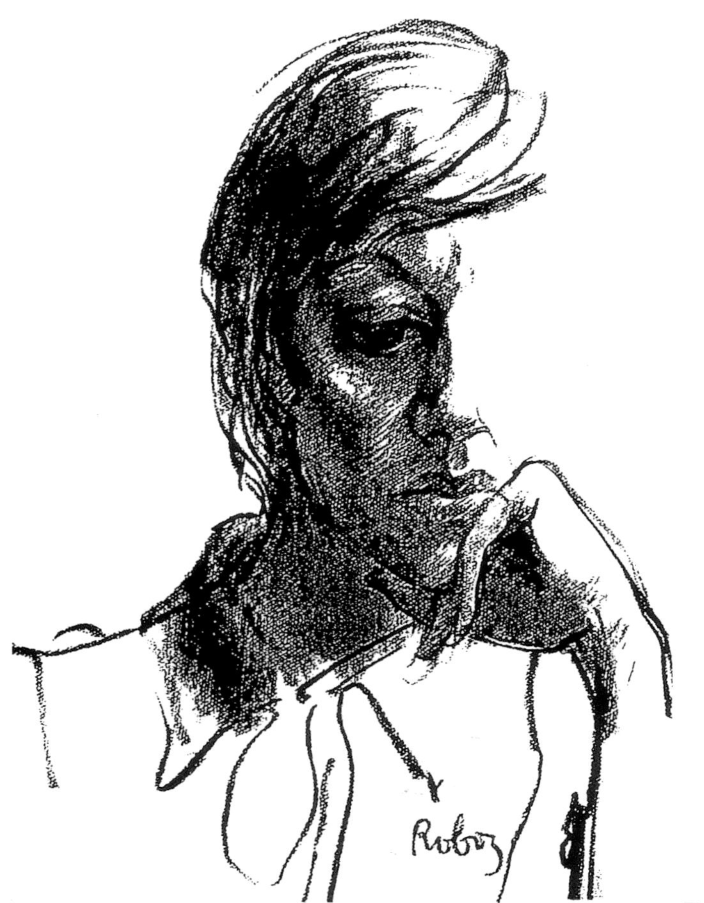


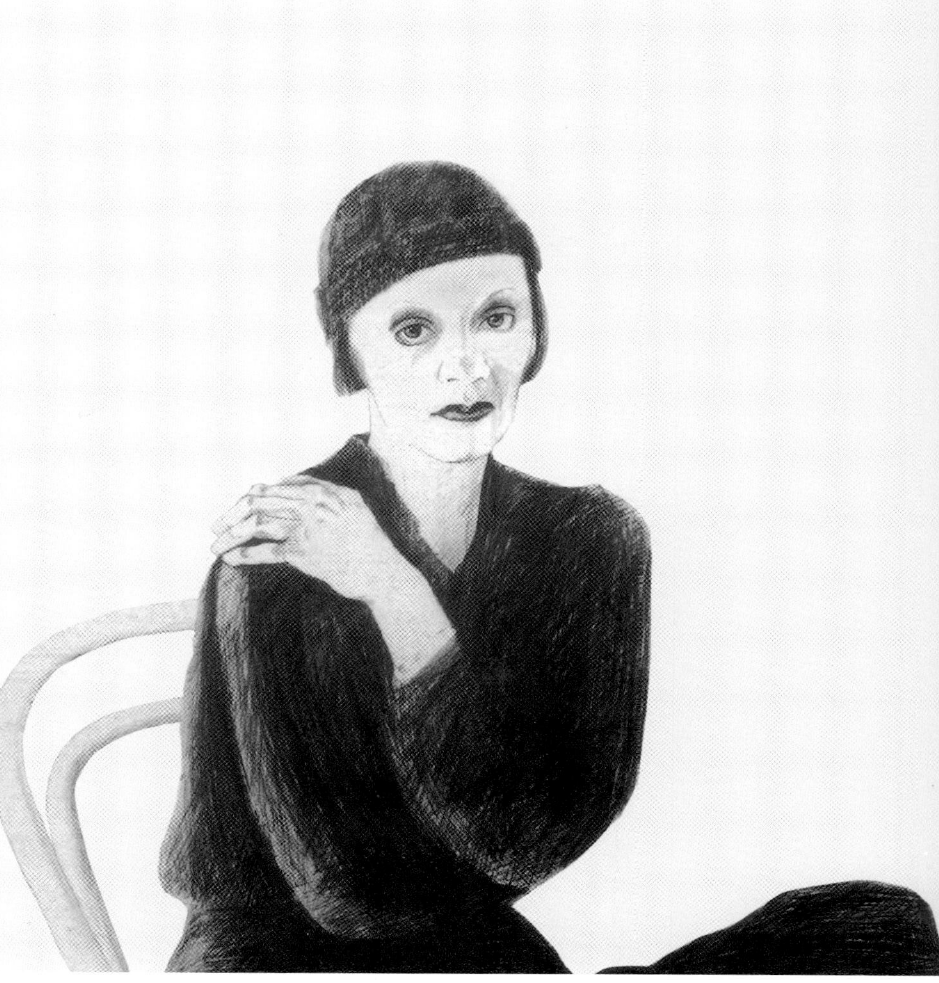

**ABOVE** Two pensive impressions of Jean Muir, [left] early charcoal portrait by Zsuzsi Roboz. © Zsuzsi Roboz; and [right] 1970s pencil drawing by David Remfry. © David Remfry.
**OPPOSITE** Sculpture by Glenys Barton, chosen as the poster image for the 1993 National Portrait Gallery exhibition, 'The Portrait Now', as well as for the cover for the accompanying book. © Glenys Barton. Photograph & © Adrian Flowers. In all the portraits on these pages, Jean Muir's hands form a focal point of interest.

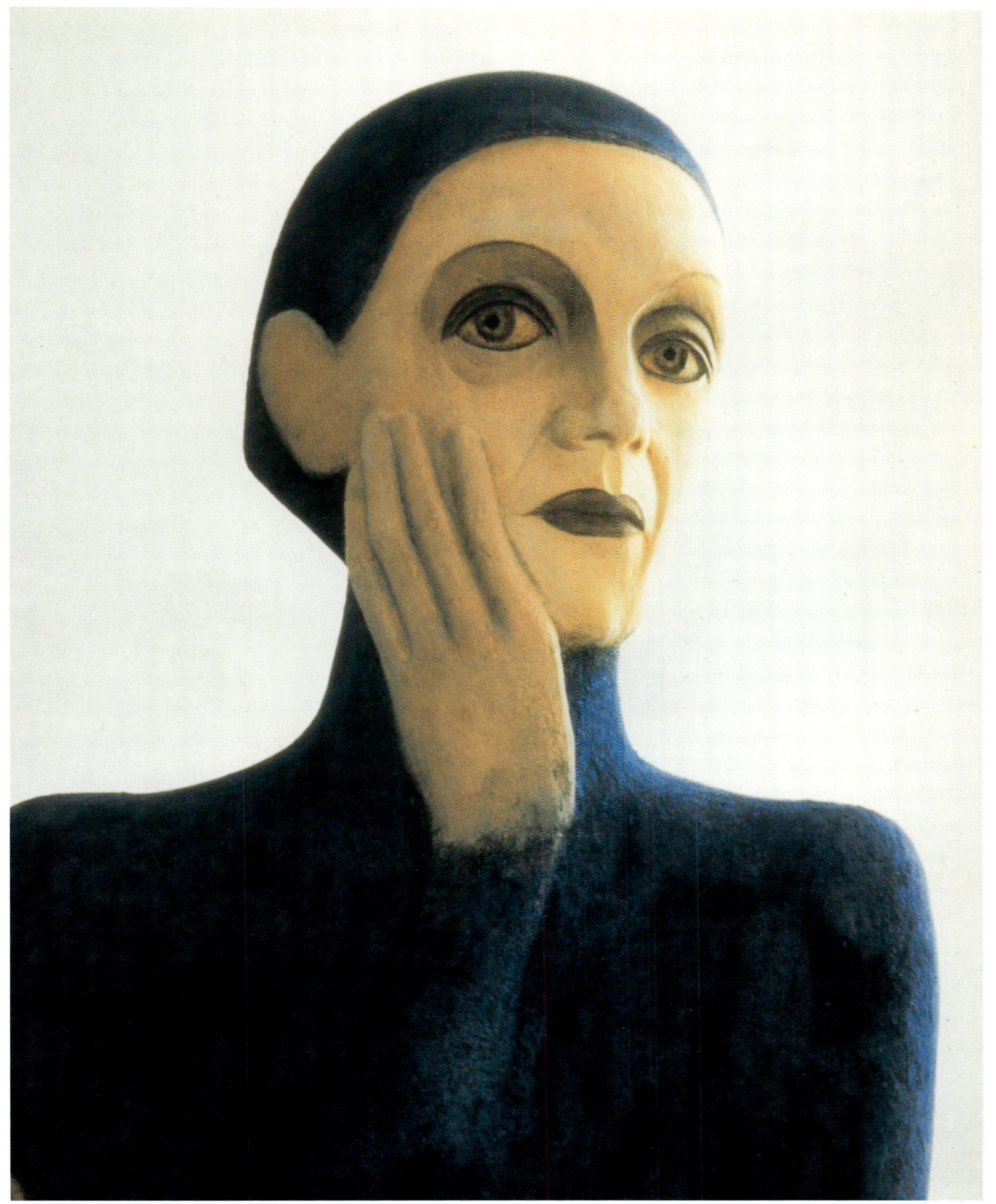

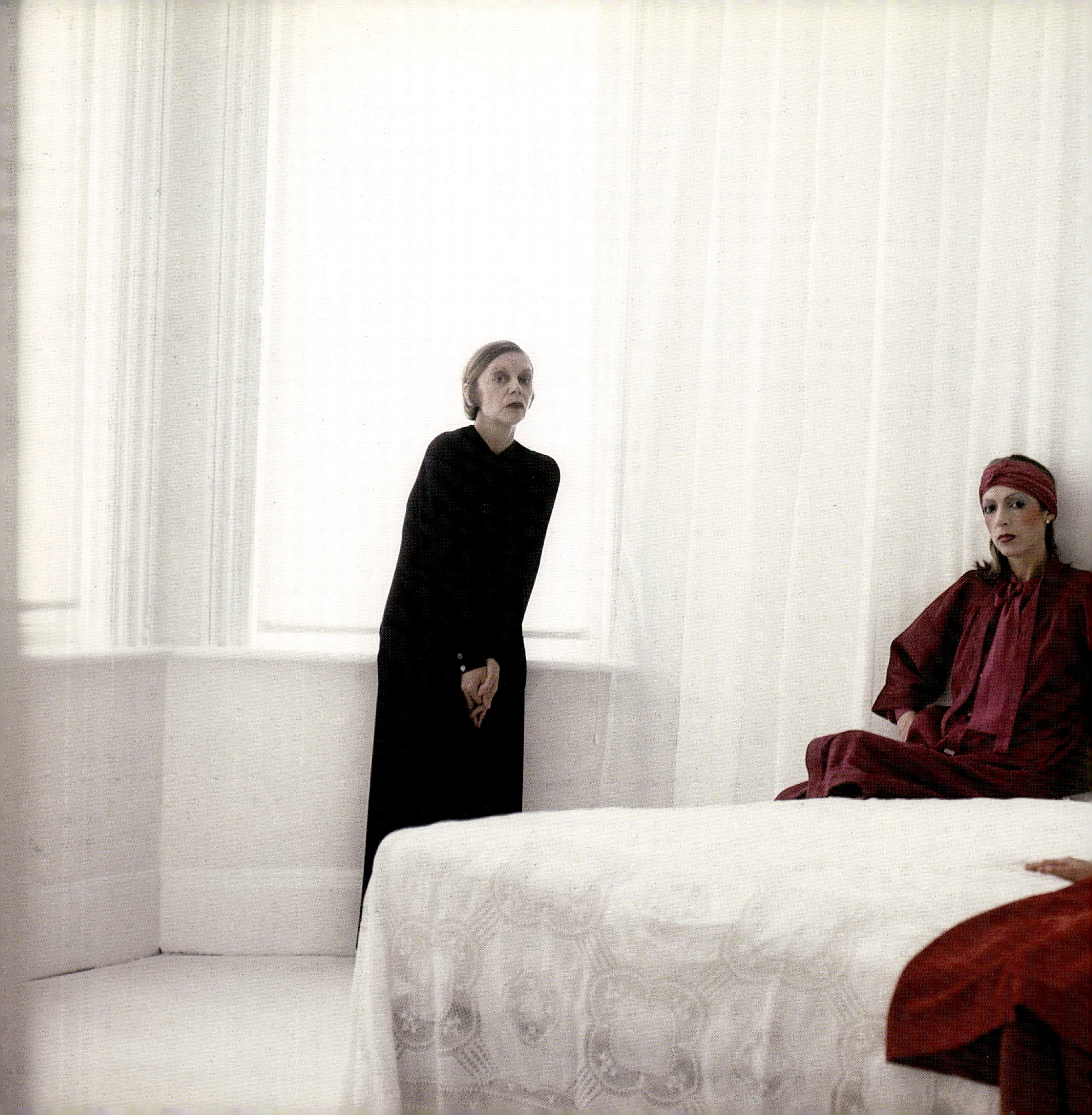

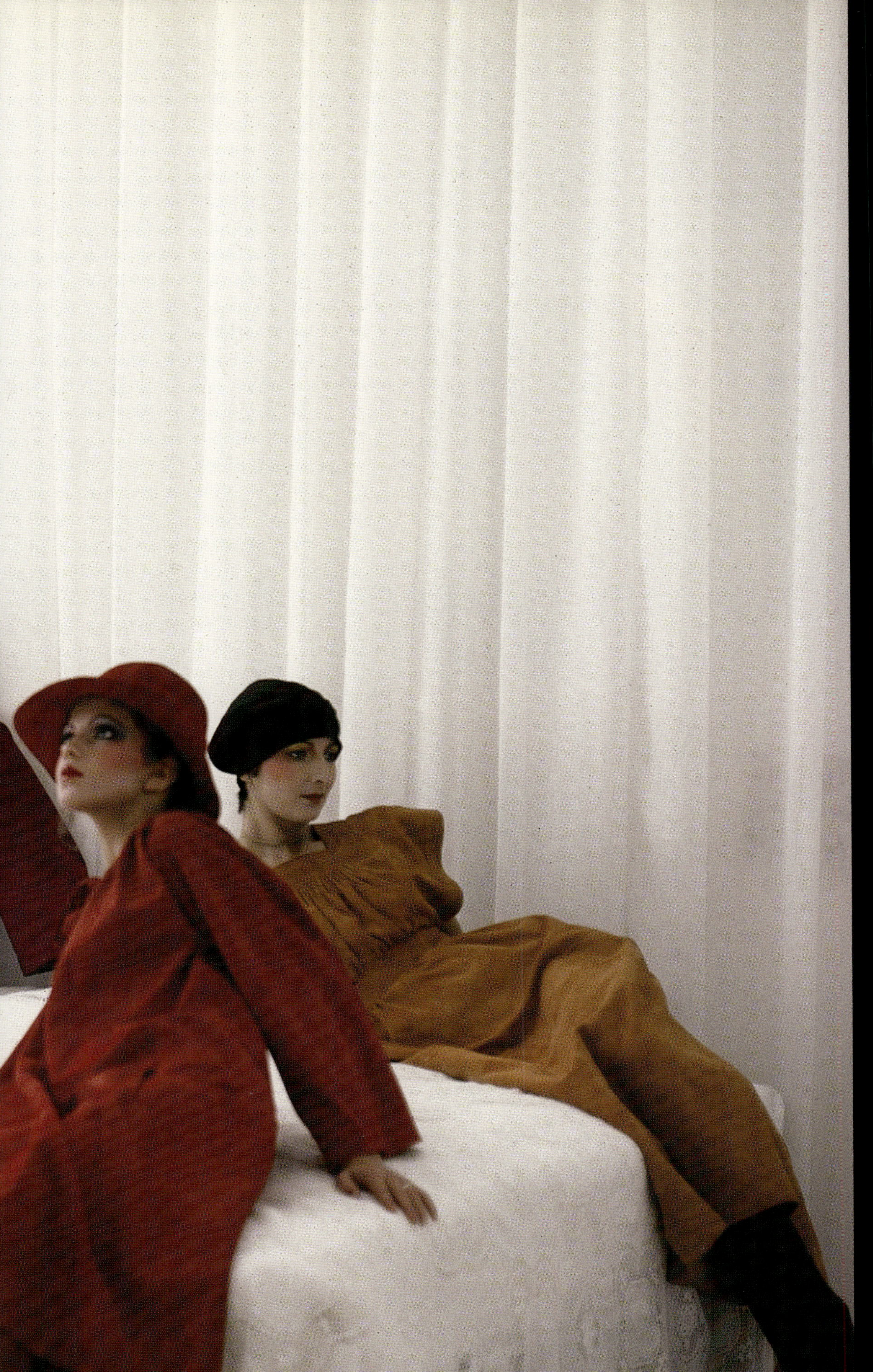

Chapter Eleven

# JEAN MUIR: BY HER CONTEMPORARIES

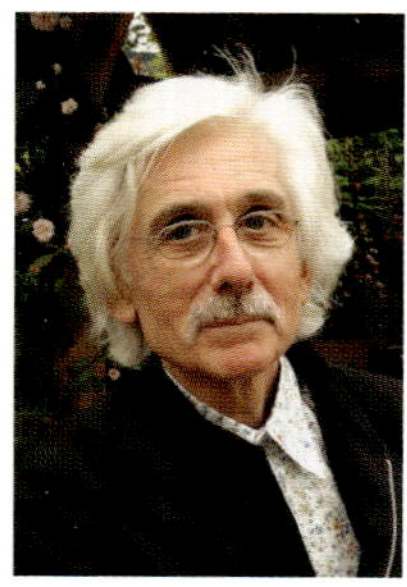

"All fashion is either classic or romantic and Jean Muir is the former, rarer bird. Within the context of the history of dress in our own age she belongs to a line of descent from Fortuny and Chanel, those designers whose concern has been the creation of the timeless. All her clothes are variations on a single theme stemming from an idiosyncratic mastery of cut and materials that create a form of dress that is immediately recognisable and virtually dateless. Attention to detail and understatement are essential ingredients of her look. As a result her art is like a single unending but exquisite fugue.

If I were asked to name two attributes of Jean Muir, the first would be that, in a time of lowering standards, she stood immoveable by the highest; the second that in an age of nostalgia she never looked back but always forward. In her work she was a puritan, in her life a cavalier."

**SIR ROY STRONG**, historian

Photograph & © Christine Boyd

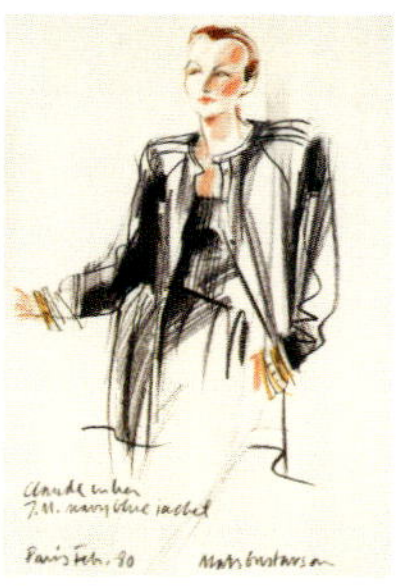

"What fascinates me most is to see the few creators in the world evolve, those who express a style, an attitude, a way of living and thinking beyond clothes; those who, despite the swings of fashion, move further and further ahead on the same track – theirs. This is why I have never ceased to admire and love what Jean Muir does, what she represents and the clarity with which she expresses herself.

This look Jean Muir has created is one of the acknowledged signs of elegance today whether in London, Paris, New York or Tokyo. Her fundamental clothes have no time, and hardly a season. The boldness of a shape – followed by the eccentricity of colour – are never there to shock but are bursting with energy. To find and know how to keep the right tone is a feat of strength and exactitude, meticulousness and generosity. Yes, Jean Muir does create a fashion that resembles her. I thank her for this."

**CLAUDE BROUET**, former Editor French *Marie Claire*

Portrait: 'Claude in her navy blue jacket' by Mats Gustavson

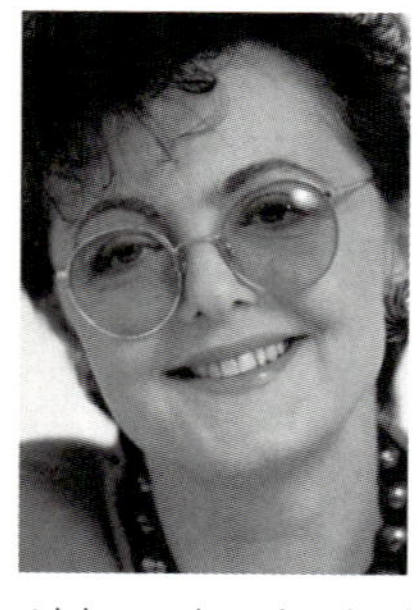

"Whenever I spotted Jean Muir across a room full of fashion folk my heart would lift; I could be sure of a warm greeting and an opening gambit designed either to stretch the intellect or to make me laugh – or both. She was, in many ways, a born pedagogue. Many people have discovered the didactic side of her nature; she'd give a rational, well-argued, enlightening lecture at the prompting of any evidence of ignorance. Although I think she rather revelled in that reputation for ferocity in the face of foolishness, for rigour in a sea of sloppiness, she never intended to intimidate. She meant to instruct. I loved her clothes and wore them through the late 1970s and the 1980s; for me they were feminine yet serious, sensuous and seductive in a mischievously understated way, gamine yet grown-up. But I loved her mind more. Her interests were wide and many and she had a gift for eclecticism and synthesis; something she had observed in the pursuit of one of her passions would inform her insights in another area. I certainly learned at least two things from her – to let the mind freefall a bit and to strive to be excellent."

**BRENDA POLAN**, journalist and lecturer

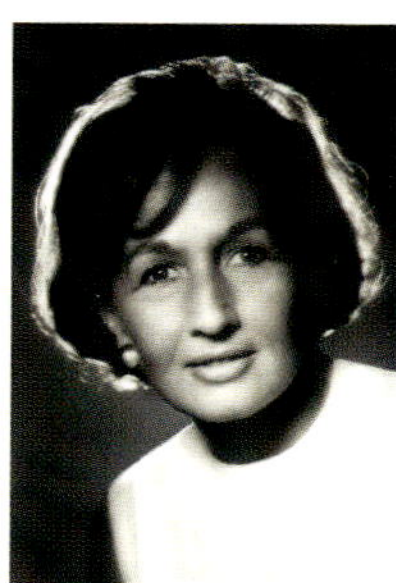

"A diffident manner cloaks iron determination. 'Once you've eliminated all the things you don't like, you get to the bare essentials, the equation that is nearly perfect for yourself', Muir said in *Vogue* in 1978. This concept she applies to the way she lives, the clothes she designs. She applies her special brand of instinct and common sense to everything from politics to the theatre. She is happier at the Victoria and Albert Museum or Covent Garden than at a cocktail party. She could equally well have been a sculptor, an architect or a choreographer. It is fortunate for the British fashion industry, and for women all over the world who have 'read' her clothes effortlessly and happily into their lives, that she chanced to be a fashion designer."

**BEATRIX MILLER**, former Editor-in-Chief, British *Vogue*

Photographed by David Bailey on her appointment as Editor-in-Chief, British *Vogue*, 1964

**PAGE 140** Iconic image of Jean Muir and models Louise Pleydell-Bouverie, Cleo Goldsmith and Paddy Grey in jewel-toned suede dresses, Spring 1975. Photograph & © Deborah Turbeville.

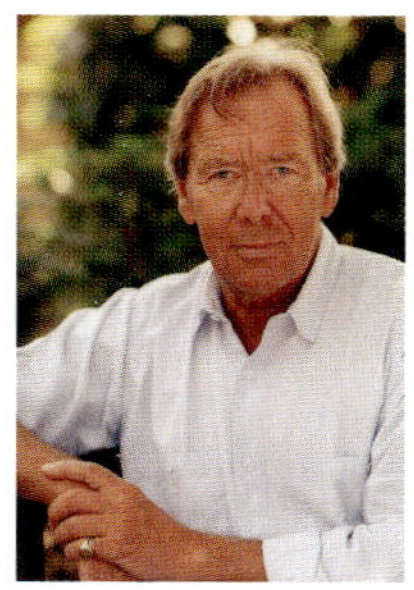

"Jean Muir has endless chic. She also has a tremendous knowledge of the history of design, art and craft. I first met her at the Royal College of Art when we were both on a panel of judges and her appreciation of these other fields was invaluable. It helped her also to contribute a great deal to the Design Council. She has a talent for getting the best out of other crafts people with whom she works.

She is an extremely truthful designer, always paring down, following Mies van der Rohe's maxim, 'less is more'. Fashion should not be a matter of buying a dress by Somebody. People ought to discover themselves and wear what suits them. My mother had a knack of putting cheap things together and making an ensemble that was just her. Jean Muir has that ability too.

A Victorian said, 'Never construct decoration. Only decorate construction.' That can apply to writing, painting, design or sculpture, as well as to fashion. Can visual literacy be learnt? Ask Miss Muir!"

**SNOWDON**, photographer
Photograph: Snowdon by Anthony Powell

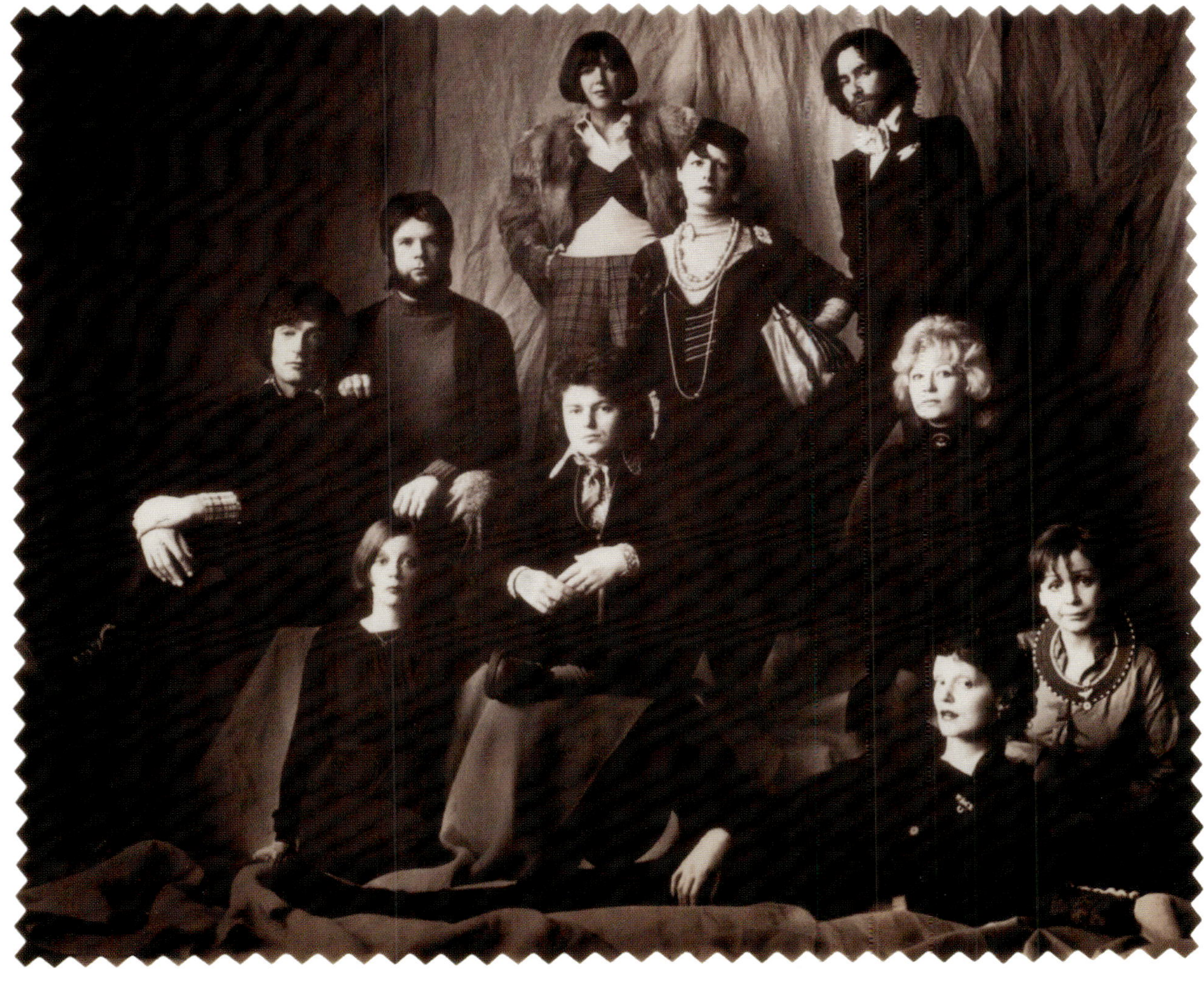

**ABOVE** A gathering of London's finest: designers in the '70s photographed by Snowdon. **FRONT ROW** Jean Muir, Alice Pollock, Thea Porter. **SECOND ROW** John Bates, Tim Gardner, Gina Fratini. **THIRD ROW** Bill Gibb, Zandra Rhodes. **TOP** Mary Quant, Ossie Clark. Photograph & © Snowdon.

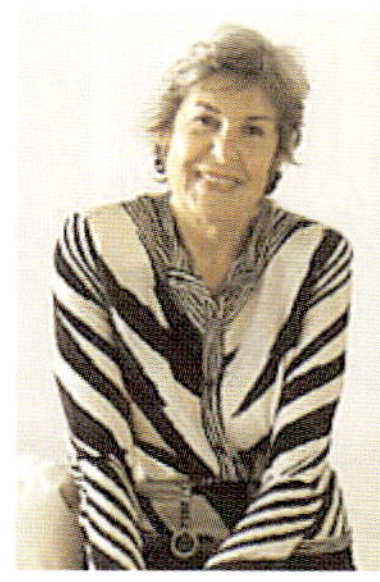

"Around the late '80s I was consultant to the *Telegraph* group advising them on how to increase their female readership. I know, I thought to myself, I'll ask Jean Muir to design something specially for us as an exclusive mail-order offer. I wasn't sure she would agree, but I could only ask. We met the next day… midway through my second sentence Miss Muir took her pen and the sketches were done. They were wonderful. A tunic, a skirt and trousers, plus a striped scarf to give the whole emsemble a typical Muir flourish. Yes, I said, I loved it, but could Miss Muir possibly consider changing the beautifully fitting sleeve to something somewhat looser? My voice trailed off. What was I DOING – criticising a Jean Muir design? Miss Muir immediately did another lightning sketch and changed the sleeve! Then she gave a huge loud laugh. 'Why doesn't the *Telegraph* say Miss Green designed this, mmm?' The offer was an unprecedented success and Miss Muir and I went out for a celebratory dinner, where this little bird-like person ate a big bloody steak that no trencherman could have bettered. For me Miss Muir was always full of surprises."

**FELICITY GREEN**, journalist
Photograph & © Jasper James

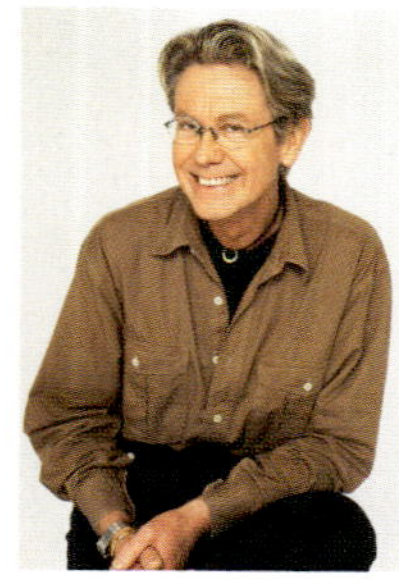

"Jean and I met in the mid '50s when we both had a Saturday job working for royal milliner Aage Thaarup in his studio in the Kings Road. Jean was working for Liberty at the time and I went to Paris in 1959 to work for the couture house, Lanvin. I came back to London and in 1967 I started my own business. Shortly afterwards I was asked to 'hat' various designers' collections for Fortnum and Mason's fashion shows, one of which was Jean's. She asked me to 'hat' her own collections and that was the beginning of our long association. Jean had an edgy nervous quality that belied her steely underside. She was picky and paid enormous attention to detail – but then so did I. So I guess that's why we got on so well, and one has to have admiration and respect, one artist to another, in order to row in the same boat. Small of stature but huge presence and command."

**GRAHAM SMITH**, milliner

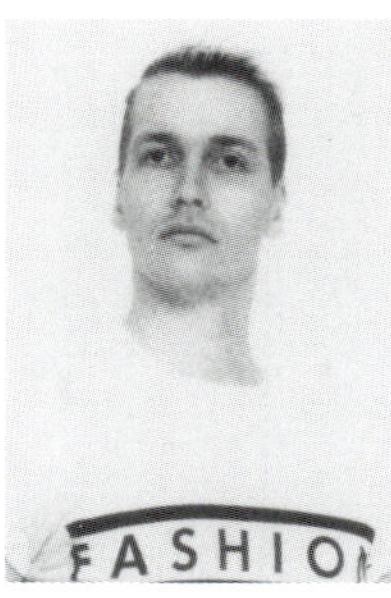


"One story always reminds me of Miss Muir's truly genuine, no-nonsense nature and the fierce commitment she bestowed on those she counted as her friends. I think it was the moment our strange bond of friendship was cemented. In the mid-1980s when I was fashion editor of *Blitz* magazine, the three reigning rival style magazines (*Blitz*, *The Face* and *i-D*) decided to join together to promote an AIDS awareness message under the banner, 'Fashion Cares'. Each magazine was to produce a stylish image for publicity purposes. I wanted to show in one image that everyone could be affected by this terrible disease. I telephoned Miss Muir and explained my idea: we would be photographed together wearing the striking black and white logo t-shirts, the most classic of British fashion designers and the peroxide Punk style-pundit. She ever so politely declined my request. I was crestfallen but went about thinking up Plan B. Later that afternoon, the phone in my office rang and it was Miss Muir again. She felt bad, she told me. She had thought about what I had said and it had touched her. "I really should do this", she said, "it's really important." She asked what she needed to do and we juggled diaries. A couple of evenings later she turned up at a photographic studio in a rather less salubrious part of Hackney with make-up perfectly applied and her trademark red bob looking as sleek as silk. As usual she wore a little navy dress. Over this she pulled on a black FASHION CARES t-shirt. I wore a contrasting white version and ripped jeans. We spent only an hour or so making the picture but it is an image, which has lasted the years. I think it reveals a kind of collective dignity and bravado. It shows how even the most unlikely allies can join together in the face of such unimaginable adversity. It shows that Miss Muir cared and I loved her for that."

**IAIN R WEBB**, fashion writer
Photograph & © Mark Lewis

**OPPOSITE** Jean Muir and Iain R Webb, a creative and journalistic talent she much admired, pose for a good cause in their Fashion Cares t-shirts to support *Blitz* magazine's AIDS Awareness campaign in the mid-80s. Photograph & © Mark Lewis.

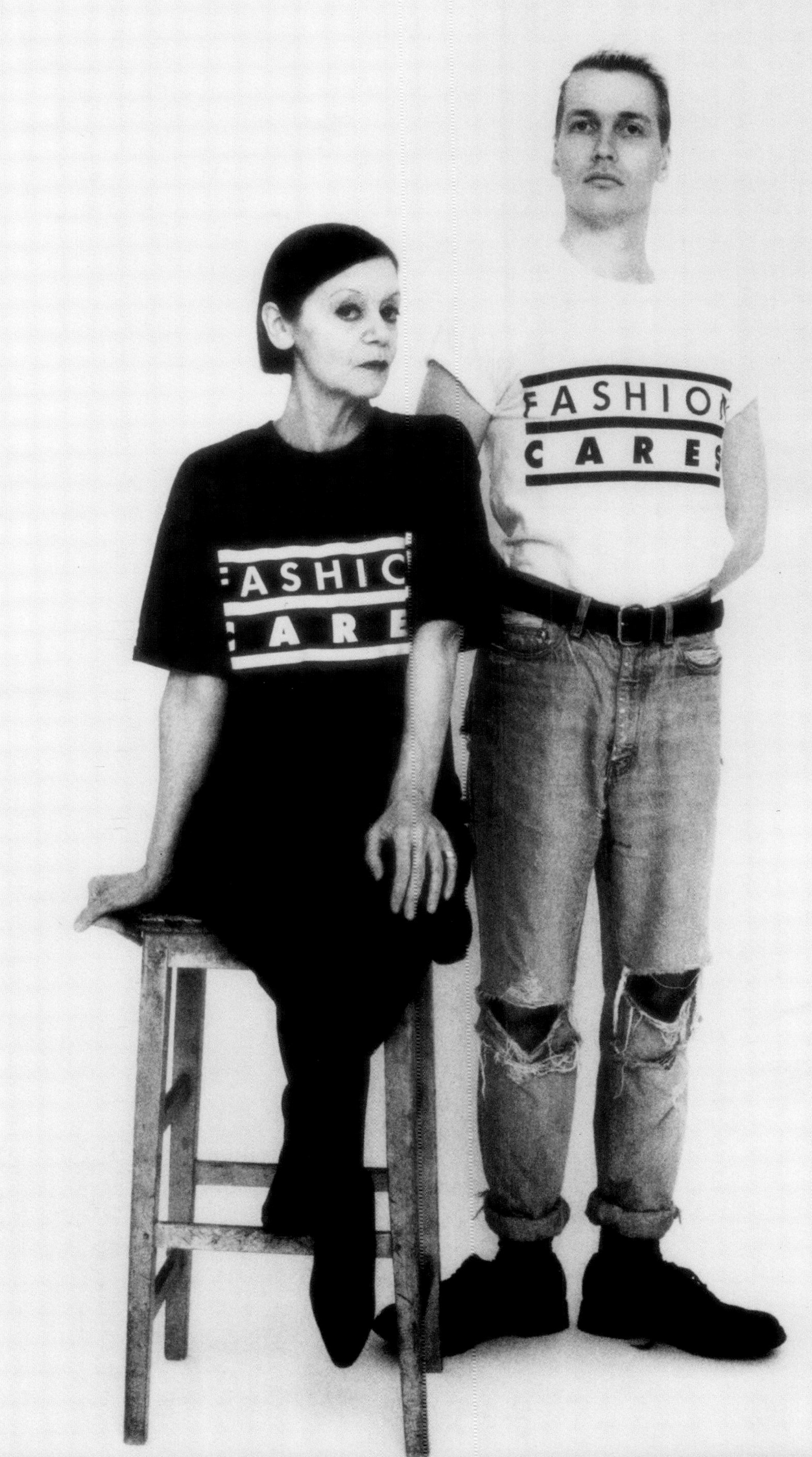
CARES

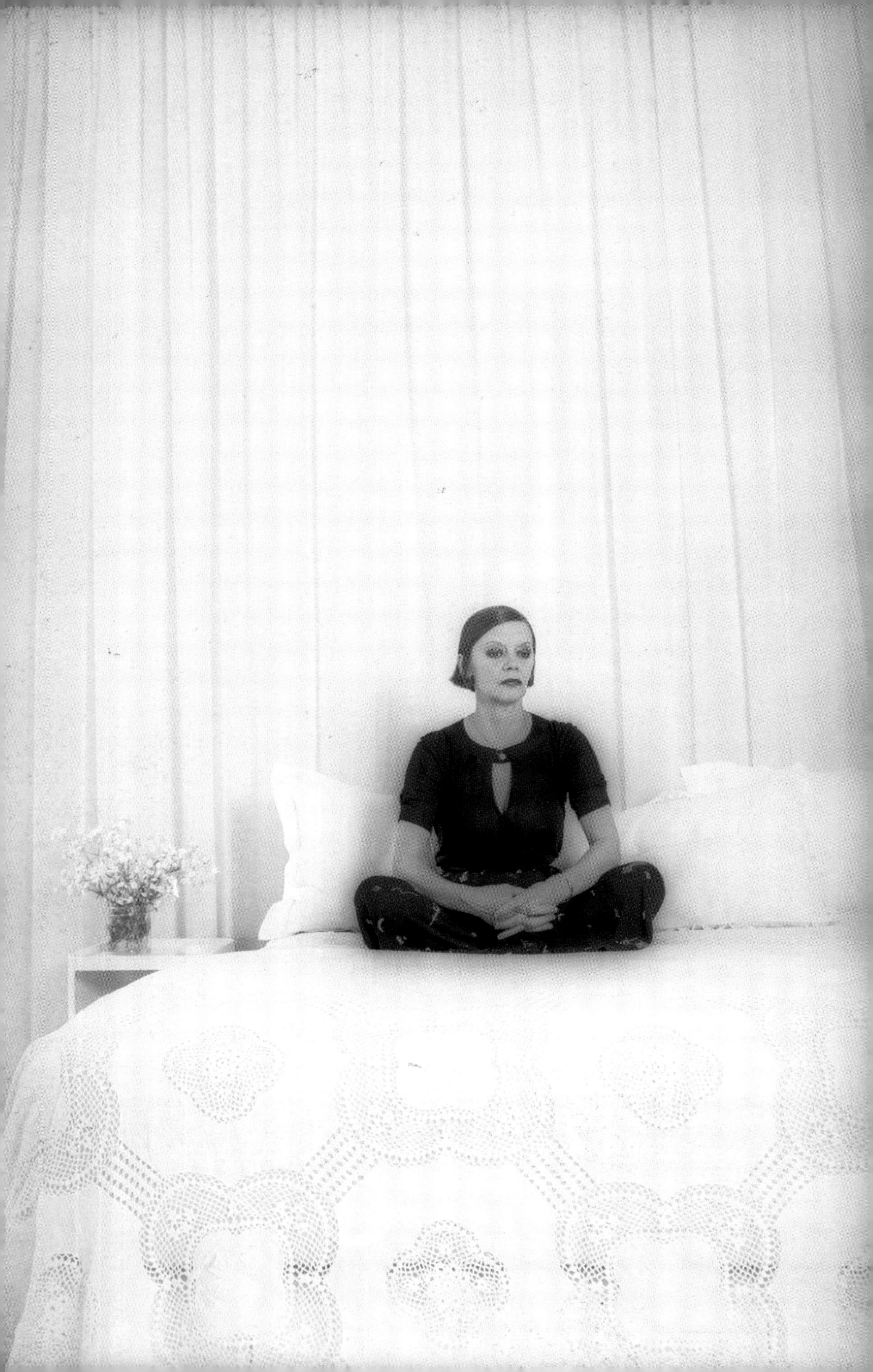

Chapter Twelve

# JEAN MUIR: THE PRIVATE PERSON

"I love travelling, Elizabethan music, Persian carpets, Provence, Man Ray, Danny la Rue, Coral Browne, Mozart, Richard Strauss, Tommy Steele, Margot Fonteyn, Alec Douglas-Home, Lord Harlech, the Victoria & Albert museum, the Scots (I'm half), Liverpool (and not because of you-know-who) ... it's a great town"

JEAN MUIR

**JEAN MUIR'S** tastes were eclectic. She listed American positivity, pink champagne and good food among her favourite things, but she never forgot her Celtic roots and always retained a deep fondness for Scotland. Despite her varied musical tastes, which ranged from Monteverdi and Mozart through to modern jazz, her favourite piece of music was 'The Old Lights of Aberdeen' sung by the popular Scottish singer, Kenneth McKellar.

Variously described by Sir Roy Strong as "looking like a Neapolitan widow" and "sounding like a demented corncrake", Muir was always a striking figure. Lady Antonia Fraser referred to Muir's animation and petite stature when she called her "a modish Puck dressed in navy blue." Early on Muir decided to eliminate any unnecessary risk from her lifestyle and therefore decided she would never learn to drive, horseride or ski. She was a voracious reader – it could be philosophy and David Hume, art monographs, Laurens van der Post or the latest Dick Francis. One of her favourite writers was the novelist Sir Walter Scott and his library at Abbotsford near her Northumbrian home was a favourite place.

Always interested in modern craft, she was a frequent visitor to the Contemporary Applied Arts showroom where she favoured work by young makers, but it wasn't only new work that drew her eye. Throughout her life she renewed her childhood interest in art by visiting art galleries and museums, her favourite being the Victoria & Albert Museum, 'Britain's eternal memory of design'. She was struck by the extent and rich diversity of the collections, but most of all she was instinctively drawn to the idea of it being a repository of skill and craftsmanship, an egalitarian model of achievement and inspiration. Muir would eventually live at Albert Court, a redbrick mansion block overlooking both the Albert Hall and the Albert Memorial, close by the museum itself. She always admired and identified with Prince Albert's founding principle of the museum: the collecting of objects of the highest quality as a permanent reminder and example to future generations, of craftsmanship and design, skill in manufacture, and industry.

Explaining the museum's special appeal, she later remarked, "In today's world when we view so much that is disturbing, we view this museum as a place of reassurance with all the wonderful things that man has made and done and always for me it's a great reviver of one's spirits." Muir cemented her intuitive links with the museum, initially serving on its advisory council before being appointed a trustee for eleven years. In recognition of her services during that time, a seminar room within the museum was named after her.

**PAGE 146** Muir cross-legged in contemplative mood in her all-white bedroom, 1977. This room with its fabric-draped walls and exquisite hand-crocheted bedcover was her favourite refuge for creative concentration. Photograph & © Mayotte Magnus.

"I remember meeting Miss Jean Muir most vividly. As a new journalist, I had contacted *Ritz* newspaper then run by David Lichfield and David Bailey and proposed her as an exciting and insightful interview subject. "If you can get her", was the immediate response with more than a hint of doubt to suggest that I could not. I loved the honest simplicity of her line, her sartorial philosophy and in a world where fashion seems more like prostitution than purpose, she struck an instant, resounding chord.

So, we met in her chic and minimal atelier in Bruton Street with the room full of Longi lilies and a portrait of her by David Remfry. She was my first interview – and I hope that it didn't show. But I hadn't the proper recording instrument – only a highly unwieldy and comically incongruous ghetto blaster that had a recording facility. And wearing an Yves Saint Laurent blouson I had recently acquired in the sales (again, totally inappropriate) I met the legendary Miss Muir. She was instantly engaging and if she had been slightly bemused or even horrified by what she saw before her, was gracious enough not to let it show. When I asked her if she knew of *Ritz*, she said: "Oh yes, it's got a real snap about it," and accompanied this with a snap of her fingers to emphasise the point. The interview went well, ghetto blaster and jacket apart and this moment proved to be the start of a friendship."

**ROBIN DUTT**, writer and curator

"Women who are well-dressed, do smile and do bounce around and want to have fun in their clothes. Jean's clothes are for women who have that life and vitality."

**BOBBY SHORT**, American singer and musician

"I can remember early on clipping out of magazines pictures of Jean's houses, and rooms and things, her white bedroom and interiors, it was always something I admired enormously. Fashion or clothes alone don't really reflect a human being. The rooms they live in and how they conduct their lives matters. There is a great coherence and discipline about everything she does."

**BILL BLASS**, designer

"While filming a piece for television, I was granted an interview on camera at her huge white London apartment. I arrived, of course, with a crew – several large men in boots. Naturally, they were instructed by this diminutive designer to remove them. She was a wonderful interview: flawless, intelligent, but terrifying! Afterwards we quietly and quickly packed up and were about to leave but at the front door we were guided into the kitchen where Jean had laid out wine and canapés and beers for all the men. Needless to say this never happens to them, and they were completely and utterly bowled over by her."

**LESLEY EBBETTS**, journalist and broadcaster

"I first got to know Jean in her Jane and Jane days – I tracked her down because the clothes were just so good. You saw the most desirable things you could ever hope to put on and they were always hers. Jean's clothes were immensely wearable – and fun. Jean was a tremendous giggler. She was certainly not pompous – she had such a great sense of the ridiculous. She used to laugh so much – and this sense of fun shone through in her clothes. She didn't just do the classic thing; in a way she was a frivolous designer with her whimsical, humorous touches that she added. She was so interested in people. She had great curiosity and was very aware of everything around her – moods of change, what young people were wearing on the streets – she was always looking. I'll never forget her remark to me: "Creativity is the only thing that matters."

**ADRIENNE CORRI**, actress

"Jean was one of the most intensely private people I have ever known, reserved and perhaps even shy, forever uniformed in severe navy. At her house in Northumberland she was just another woman as delighted friends discovered. My husband Henri and I went to stay with them one cold Winter weekend and Jean came down for dinner dressed to shock, giggling like a little girl caught out in some successful piece of mischief. We all giggled. She was wearing a bright red sweater and tartan knickerbockers!"

**BARBARA GRIGGS**, writer and journalist

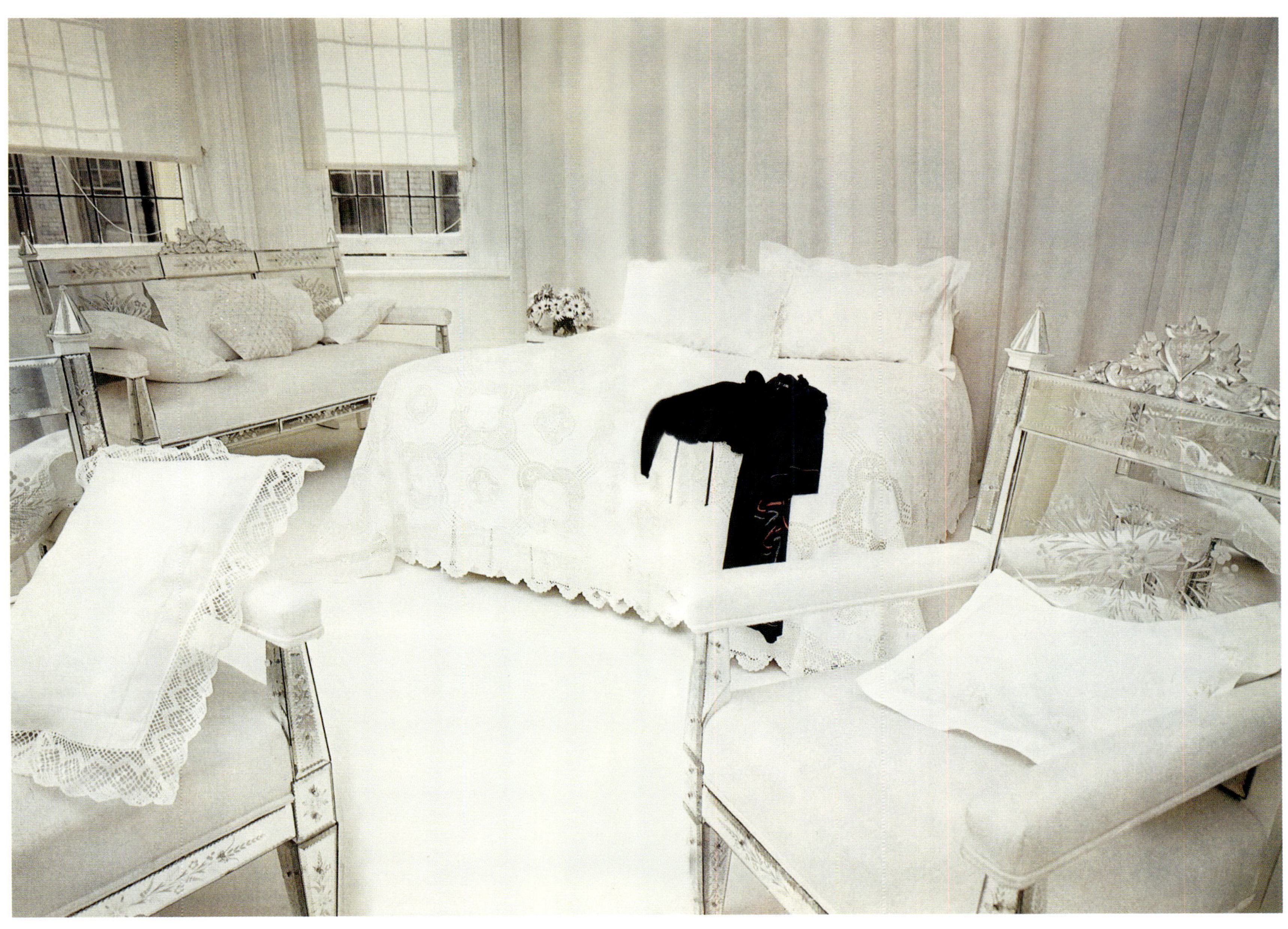

**ABOVE** A double-page spread from *Vogue*, February 1979, showing "Jean Muir's Snow and Ice Bedroom" photographed by Norman Parkinson. The nineteenth-century Venetian cut-glass sofa and chairs were originally made for the Nizam of Hyderabad and the room was often used as a backdrop for fashion shoots. Everything was white: the voile-covered wall behind the bed, the blinds at the window, the starched lace-trimmed linen cushions, and even the floor. Photograph & © The Norman Parkinson Archive.

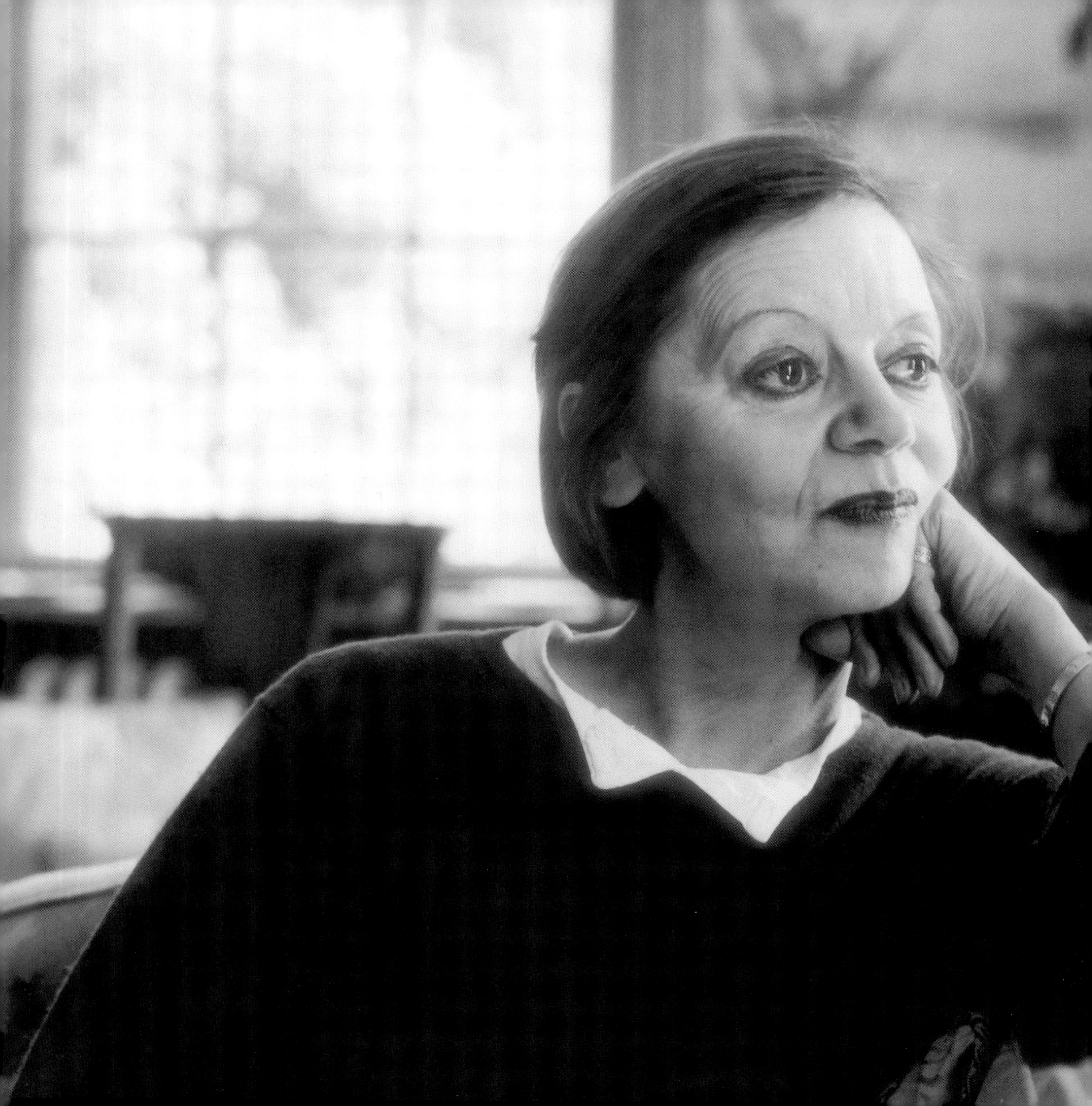

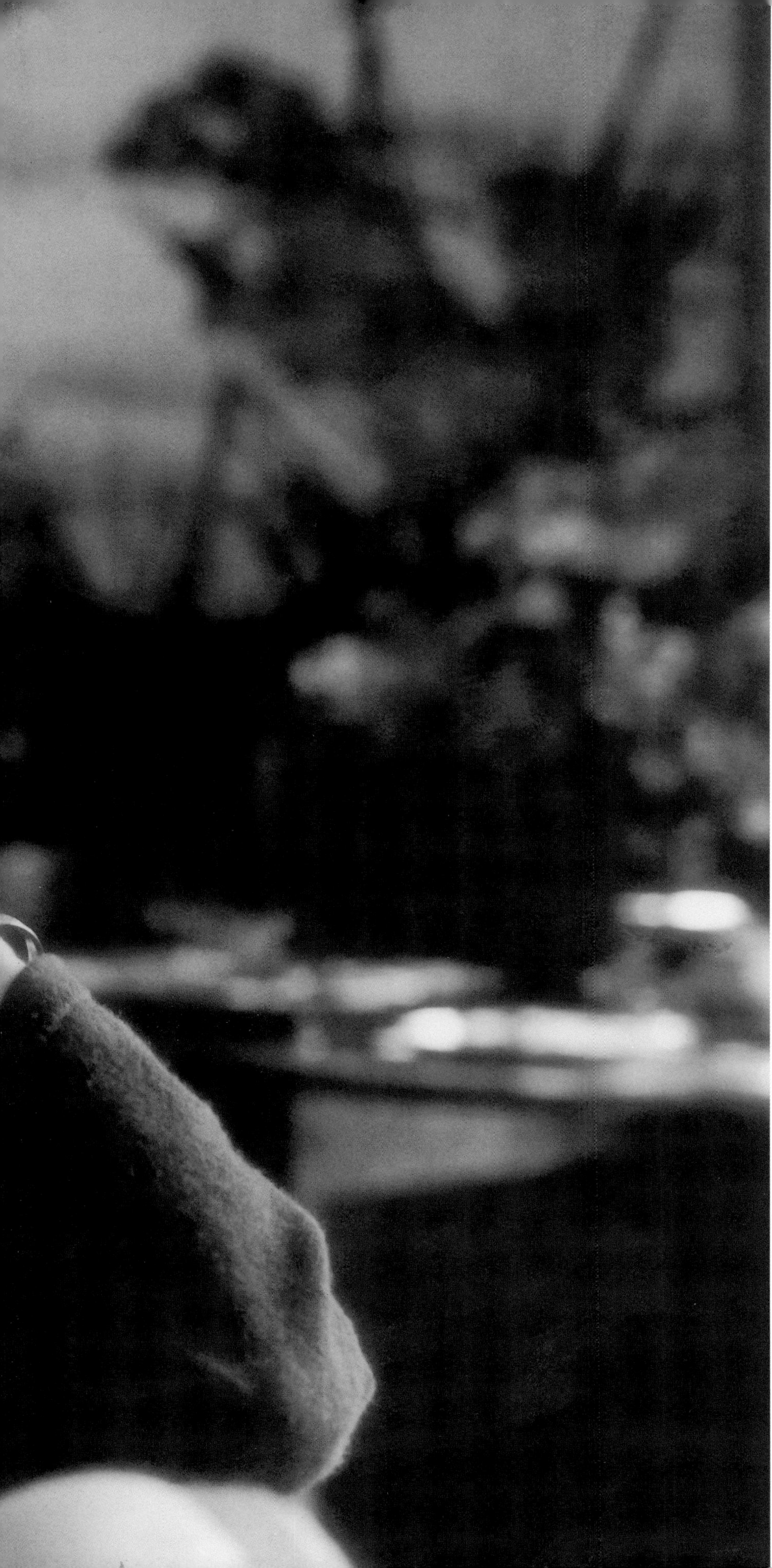

"Oh there's definitely something about the place, it's grand and it's straightforward… I think it's magnificent"

**JEAN MUIR ON NORTHUMBERLAND**

**LEFT** Jean Muir relaxed and informal at home in Northumberland, the surrounding landscape providing a rich source of inspiration for her work. Photograph & © Neil Fenwick.

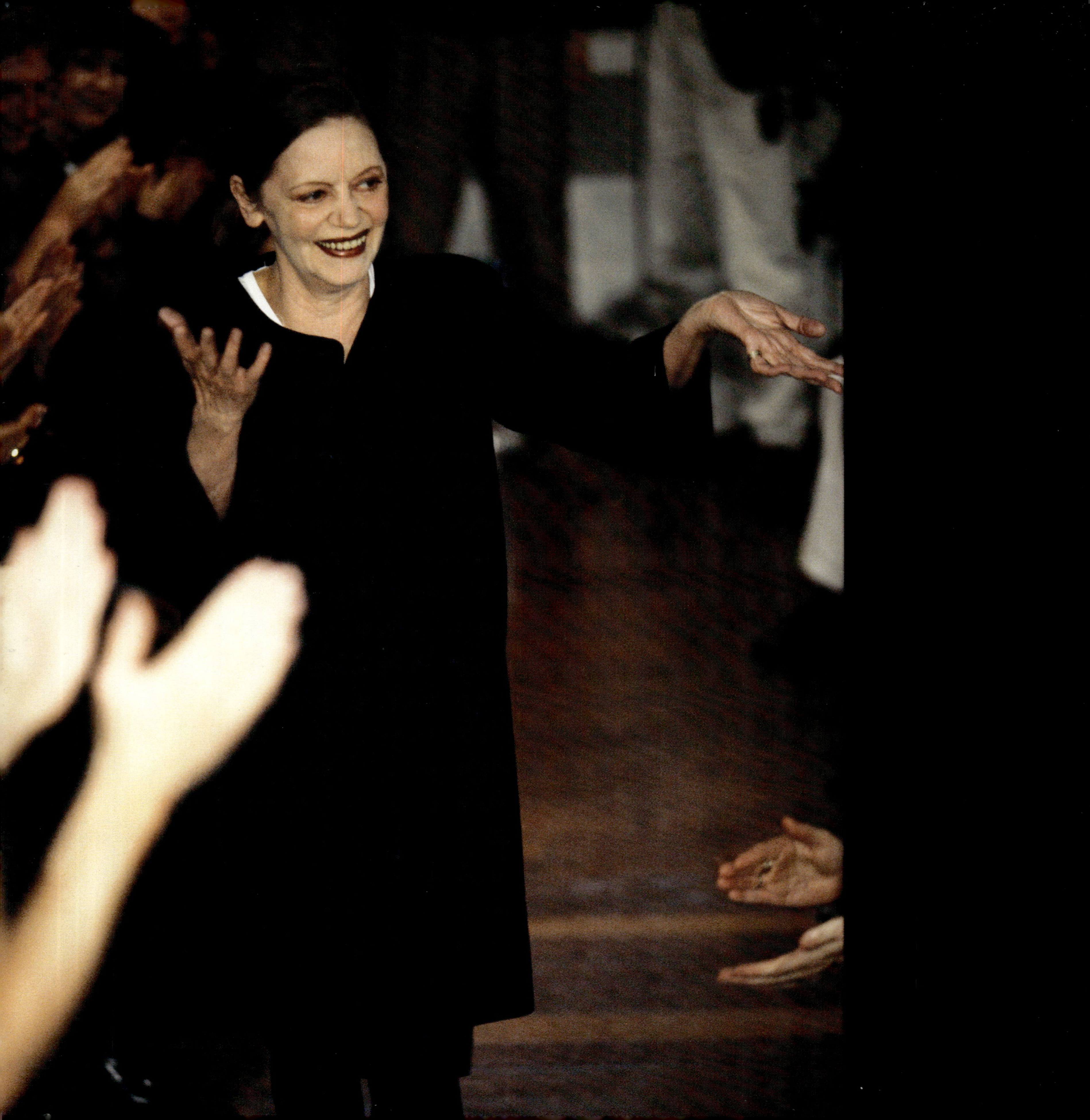

Chapter Thirteen

# JEAN MUIR: A PERSONAL APPRECIATION

"I think that if I wanted to relate myself to a car, I would rather be compared to a Jag than a Rolls Royce – a Jaguar when it was very good, you know"

JEAN MUIR

**MISS MUIR** remains an enigmatic figure even to me, though I worked by her side for nine years. She was: private, independent, uncompromising, focused on her work but with catholic tastes and interests, and with an altruistic crusading zeal for her industry, its necessary skills, and its nascent talent.

Jean Muir was a maverick who thrived on consistency and the strictest of self-imposed rules. Her approach was refreshingly polished, professional, and modern. Full of energy, optimism, and *joie de vivre*, she was an enthusiast who eschewed nostalgia and who embraced the present and the future, constantly looking forward as all great creators do.

Jean Muir set out to make the best of herself, and the world she inhabited. Hers was a civilising influence. Speaking out in times of recession she was as concerned by the loss of jobs, as by loss of skills; she did not merely lament, but actively proffered constructive direction. She was intensely patriotic, keen for Britain to rediscover and re-establish its reputation as a skills-based manufacturing culture, believing that industry in general and innovations in technology would be enhanced by incorporating a sense of craft and design.

In spite of all the awards and accolades, Jean Muir was essentially modest, and far from self-serving. She felt it incumbent upon herself to nurture young talent, and a "delightful duty" to be an active patron of the crafts that she so loved. She was generous in the time that she devoted to education, offering work placements and taking on the role of an assessor, setting questions for and judging bursaries, talking to classes in schools, donating fabric for student projects, even giving her Bruton Street showroom to Liverpool Polytechnic's third year students as a venue to show in.

Naturally shy, her intensity of purpose and refusal to compromise on standards was sometimes mistaken for grandeur; Muir was grand, but rather in the sense of being eminent. Many of her designs had an underlying sense of tranquillity, a quiet but pervading assurance and confidence, which was most apparent in her matte jersey pieces. Her work was definite, distinctive, unique; something the writer Colin McDowell recently termed "the svelte and logical perfection of a Jean Muir".

For all of us who knew and worked with her, she was a renaissance woman who merged the fields of design, craft, art, education and politics in her career. Although a diminutive figure she was a towering presence and an authority in her field who never lost her creative spark. Her petite form masked an unflinching determination as well as a witty sense of humour. Expecting one's best at all times, she inspired enormous respect and loyalty in her friends, customers and staff.

In many ways Jean Muir was a designer's designer, held in high regard by a diverse group of her fellow designers. She enjoyed mutually respectful friendships with Hanae Mori, Bill Blass and Issey Miyake, who said in a lecture given in the early nineties at the Royal College of Art, that he had learnt a lot from Muir's work. She was admired by Giorgio Armani and Michael Kors, who said Muir was his favourite European designer, whilst Moschino once bowed down before her at a nightclub. Jean Paul Gaultier is another fan. "She had such style. Real style that you could recognise. I love her for her individuality, her way of seeing a woman. It was a kind of retro woman but modern at the same time. Feminine but strong."

The American actress, Lauren Bacall noted that Jean Muir "is a very pure designer. I have a sense she is in a class by herself, that there's no way to compete with her, because she does what no one else does." Hamish Bowles, the European Editor of American *Vogue* commented that her style "seemed the distillation of modernity...[her] clothes are perfectly judged, perfectly formed, perfectly simple and simply perfect."

Jean Muir rightly has a place in the pantheon of truly great, world-class designers who have altered the course of design in their field, her impact extending beyond the realm of fashion, to the technical education of its future ranks. Jean Muir's influence continues unabated; much emulated throughout her career, she is often cited as a major inspiration by young designers of today, who continue to reference her work in theirs.

When asked to comment on her achievements, her reply came in a typical understatement: "If anybody asked me what I think I've done in my life I would say it was to continue the craft of dressmaking, and all that that involves, of covering the human body."

**SINTY STEMP**

**PAGE 154** Jean Muir in a sea of hands acknowledges the applause that always followed her Bruton Street show, Spring 1994. Photograph & © Chris Moore.

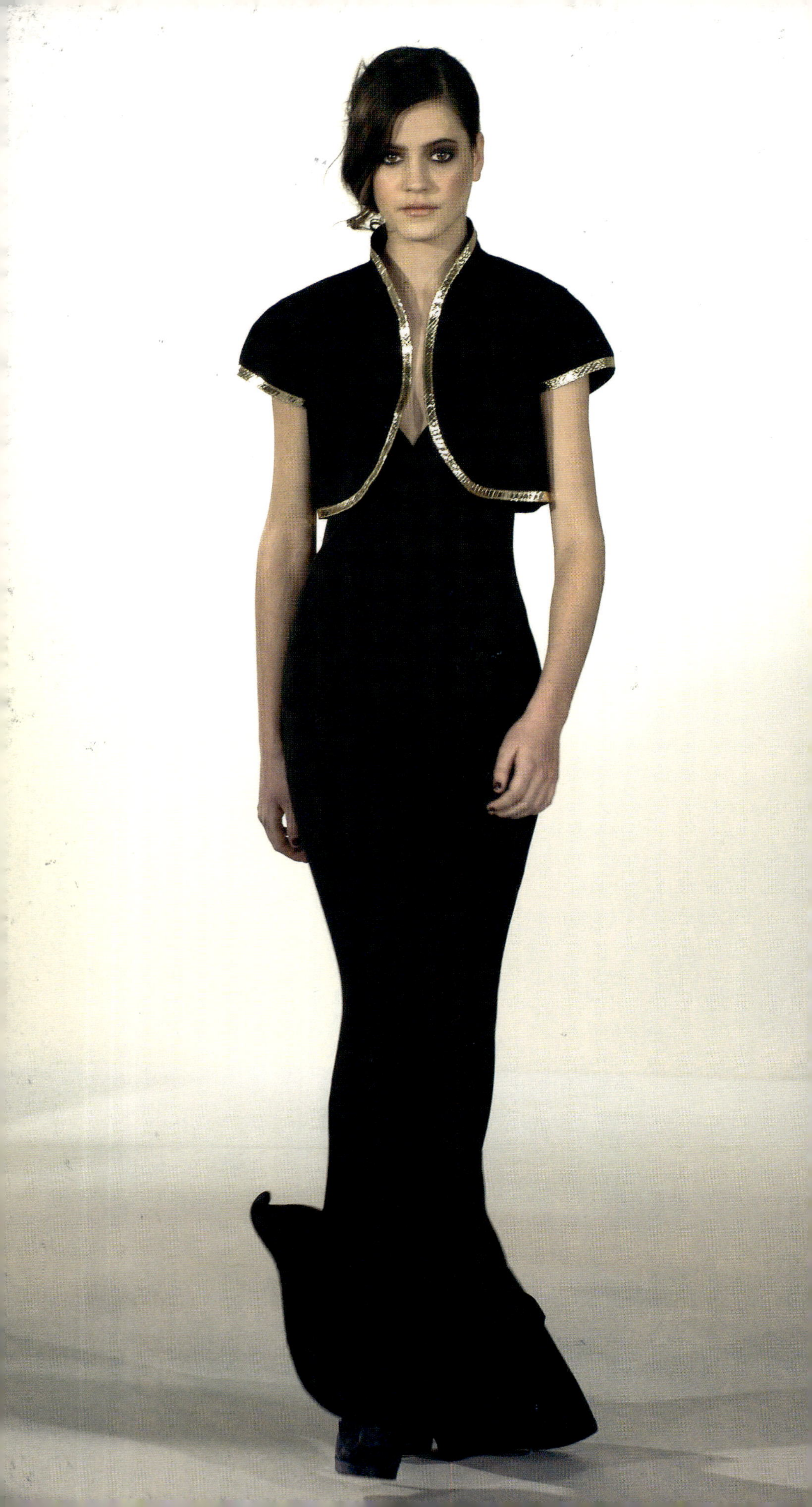

Chapter Fourteen

# JEAN MUIR: TODAY

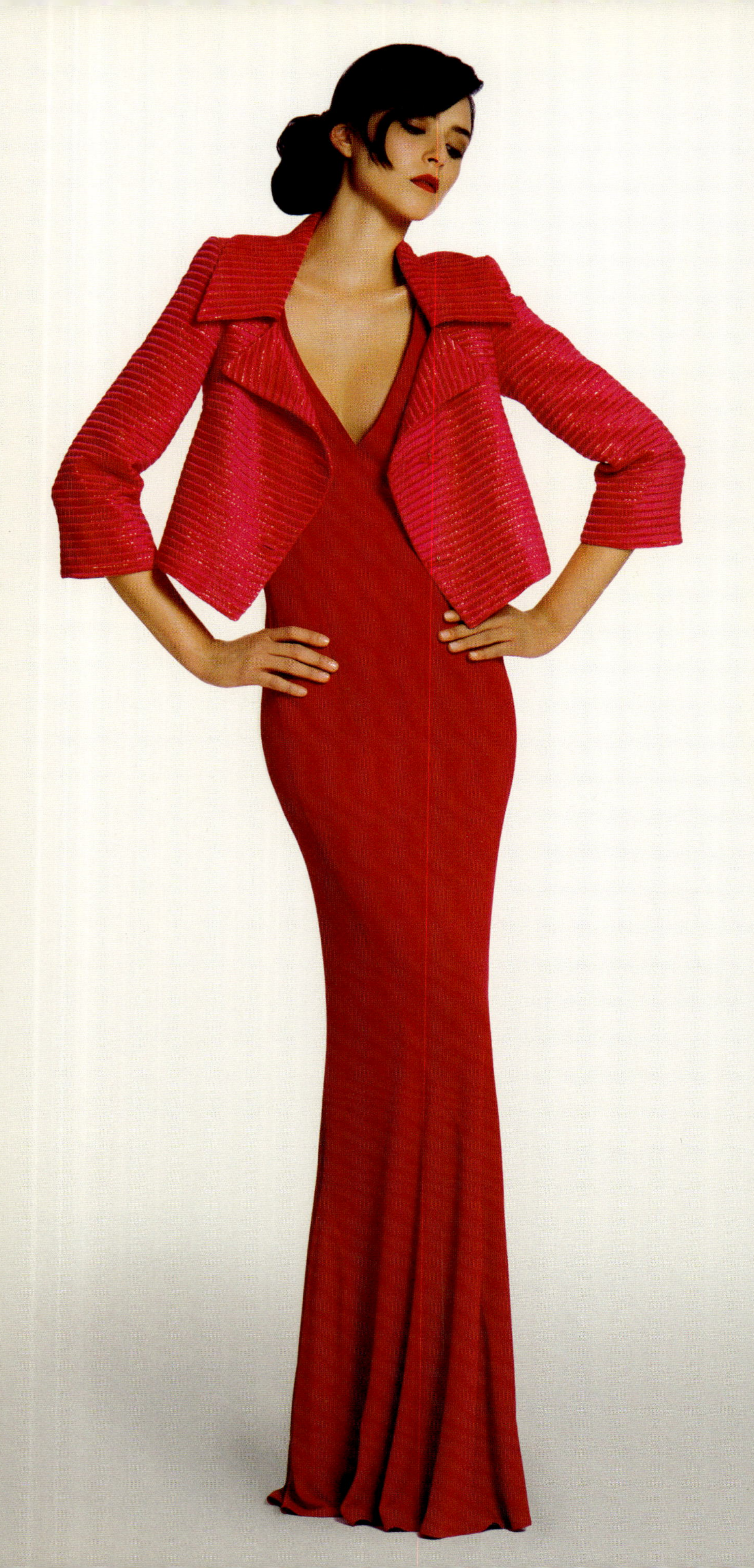

**JEAN MUIR'S** company celebrated its fortieth anniversary in 2006.

There is a design team of five, each of whom worked alongside Miss Muir for many years, prior to her death in 1995. This team is led by design director Joyce Fenton-Douglas, with Angela Gill, Caroline Angell, Tracy Joyce, and Sinty Stemp, whose combined talents, experience and skills ensure that the special Muir hallmarks of simplicity and elegance continue to attract discerning women from all over the world.

The emphasis today remains on understated luxury. Everything is still made according to the standards that Miss Muir laid down, and often by the original craftspeople, including those who produce the cashmeres, the matte jersey, the suedes and leathers, and those all-important buttons!

The very first Jean Muir shop opened in August 2004 in London's Conduit Street. According to Suzy Menkes, this inviting and suitably sleek all-white environment is 'fast-becoming an epicentre of London chic'. With its lack of fuss and its arresting minimalism, this welcoming atmosphere reflects perfectly the personality of the amazing woman whose magic has left those of us lucky enough to own a Jean Muir, longing for more.

Every season, each collection celebrates the essence of Muir, and ensures its iconic place in the world of fashion.

It's all 'Very Jean Muir'.

**FELICITY GREEN**

**PAGES 158, 159, 162 AND 163** The legacy of Muir lives on – the elegance, the subtlety, the exquisite workmanship, the mastery of fabrics, the cut ... the clothes that guarantee to make a woman look and feel her best. Photographs & © Chris Moore.

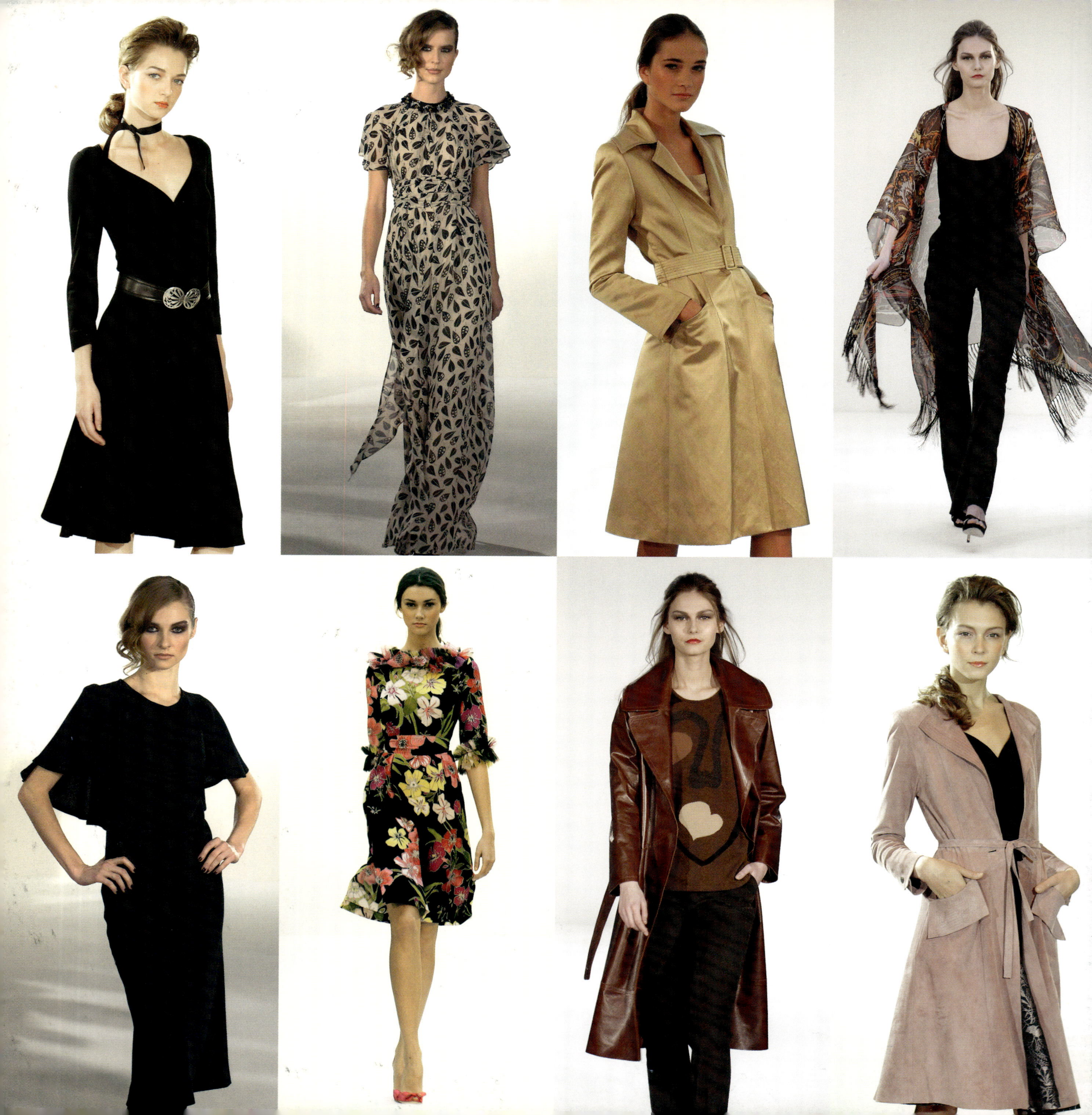

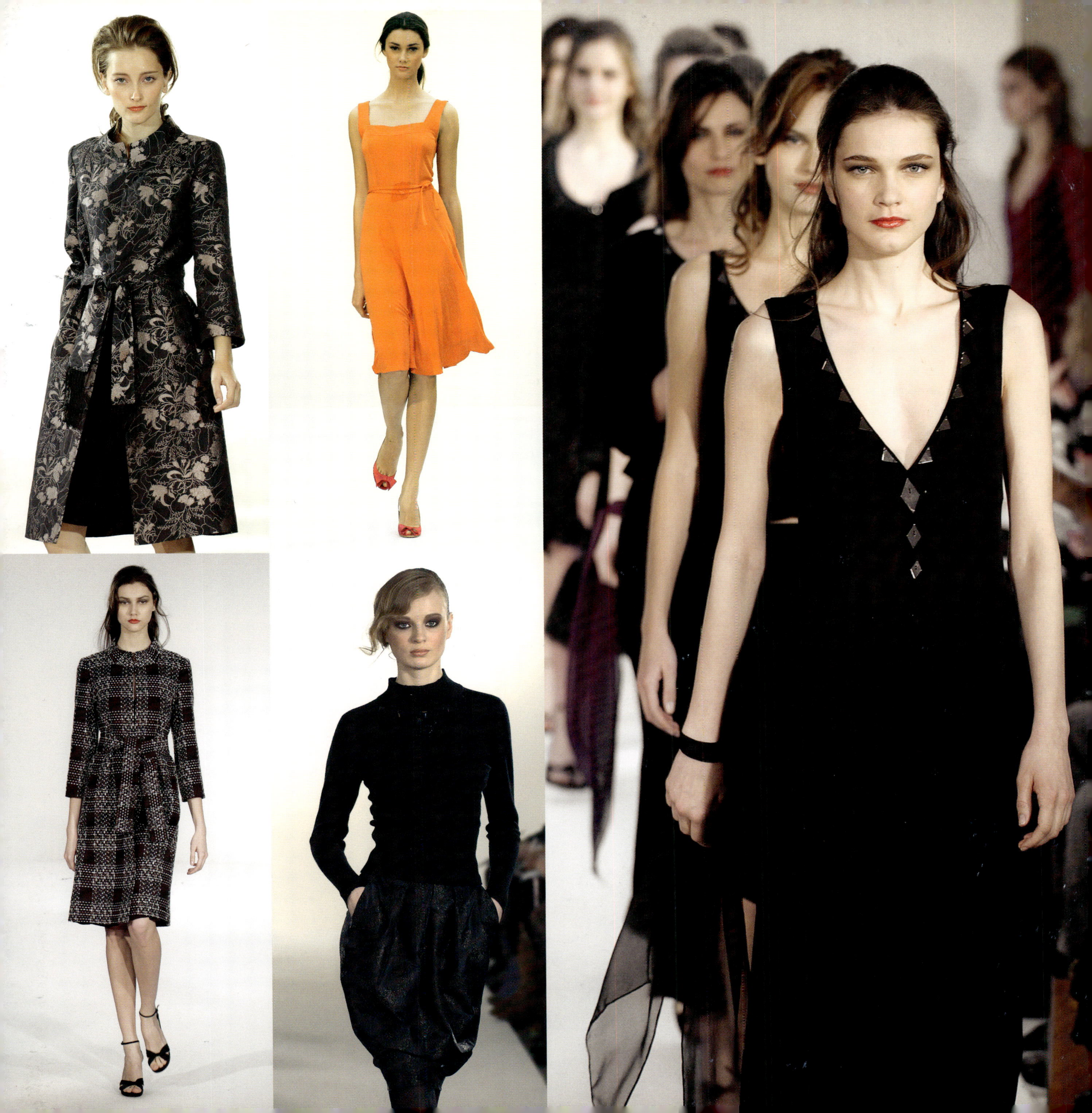

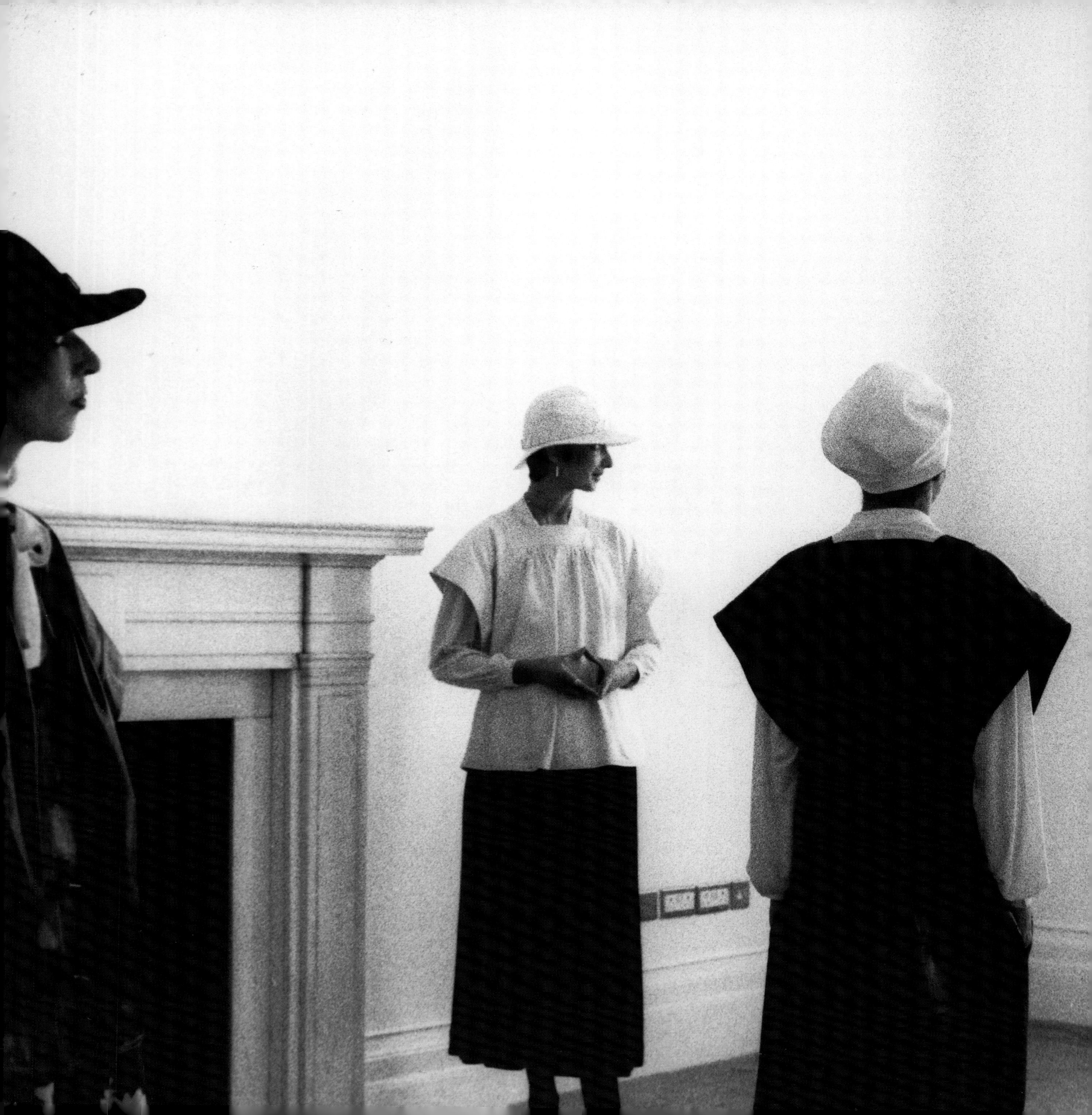

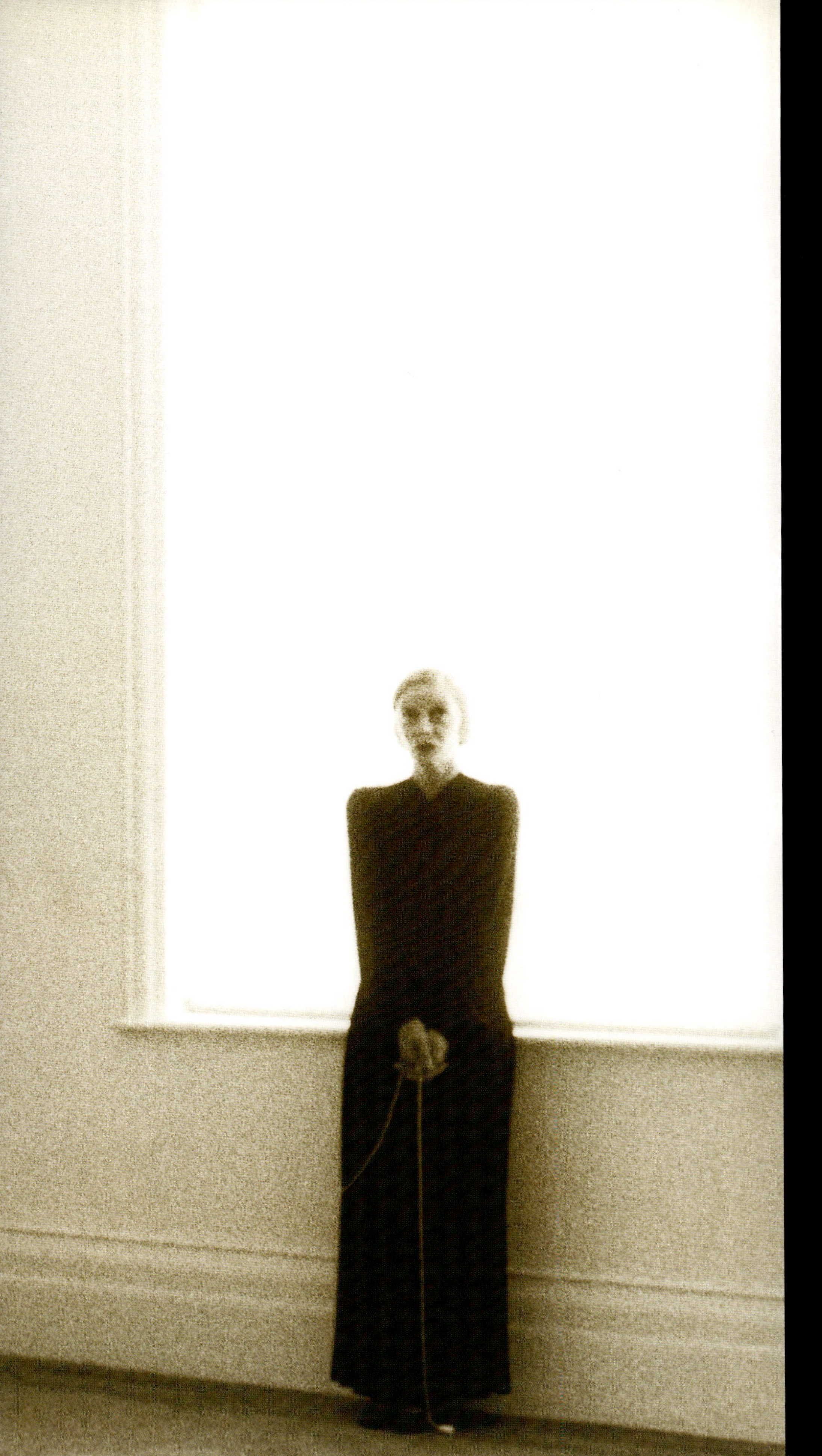

Chapter Fifteen

# JEAN MUIR: THE ARCHIVE

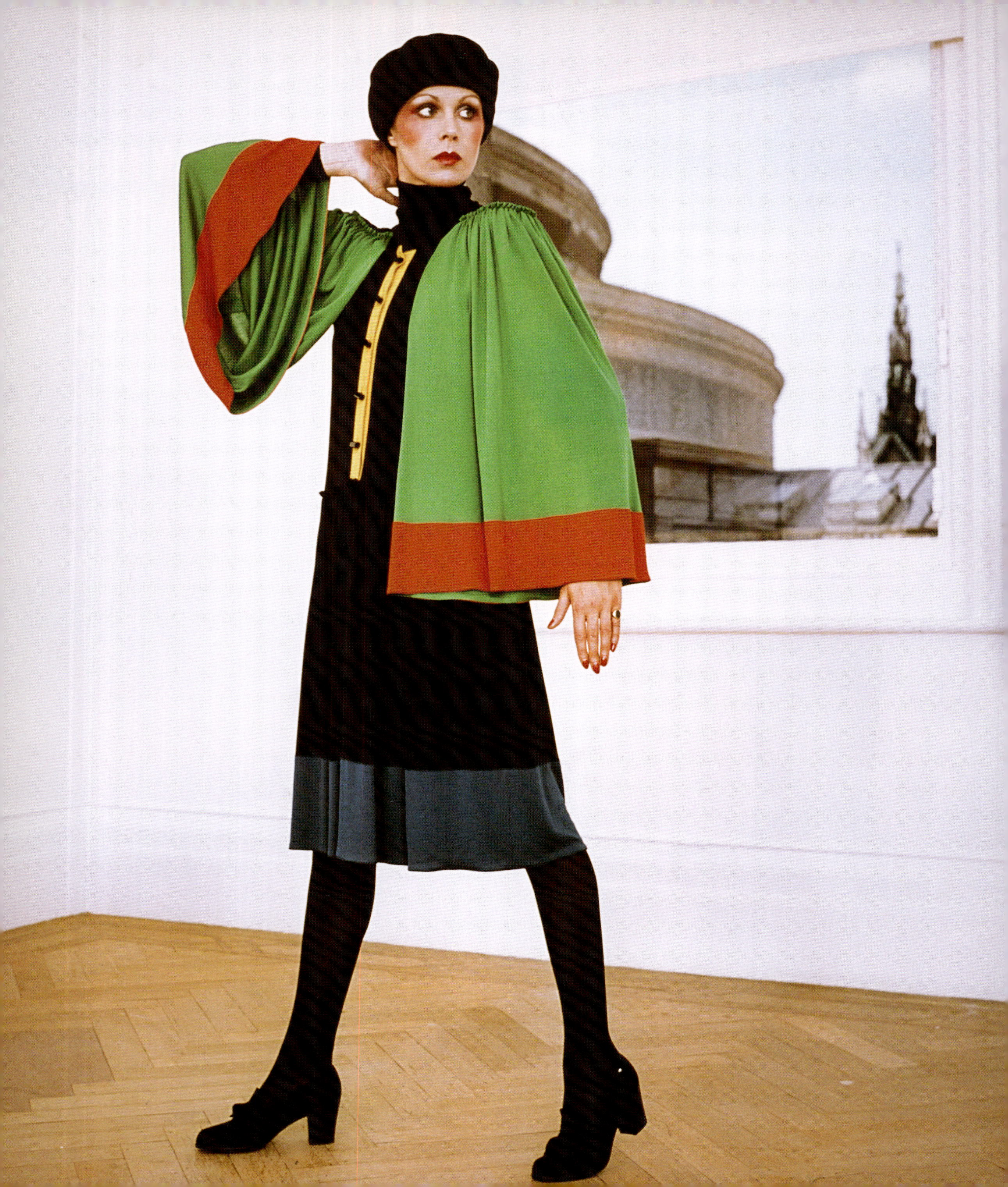

**JEAN MUIR** had begun fundraising for the Museum of Scotland Project in Edinburgh shortly before her death in May 1995. Jean Muir Limited carried on this work, pledging money in her memory, as did many of her friends, and, touchingly, many of her customers. Jean Muir Limited is cited on the Founder's Stone at the entrance to the award-winning National Museum of Scotland building, whilst inside, the museum's Silver Room is fittingly dedicated to Jean Muir herself.

The Jean Muir archive represents a comprehensive overview of her output, and the many design processes involved and is therefore an important educational resource. To this end, the donation of the archive to the Museum of Scotland in Edinburgh acknowledges Jean Muir's affinity for Scotland and echoes her ambition to improve technical skills and standards in design education.

Jean Muir's name and her designs will be accessible to new generations of students, design scholars and academics. The museum's long-term plans are to mount exhibitions as well as a permanent display in tribute to their benefactor. In this way Miss Muir's work will continue to inform and inspire.

**PAGE 164** Jean Muir and models photographed in 1975. Photograph & © Deborah Turbeville.
**OPPOSITE** Part of the extensive Jean Muir archive donated to the National Museums of Scotland in 2006. Photograph: Michael Barrett. © The Trustees of The Museums of Scotland.

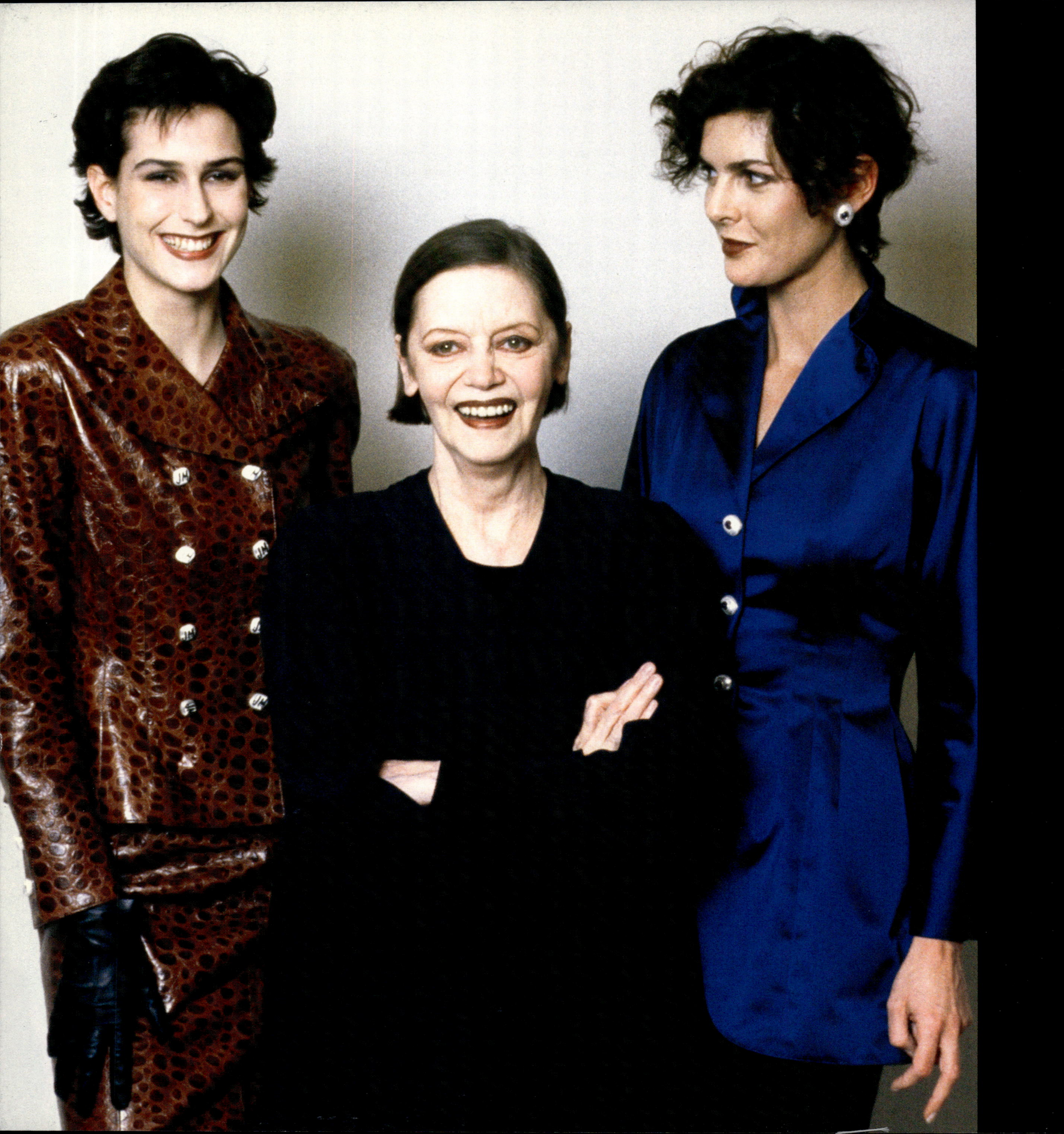

# JEAN MUIR:
# CHRONOLOGY
# INDEX
# ACKNOWLEDGEMENTS

**1928** Jean Elizabeth Muir born 17 July in London. Brought up and educated in Bedford.

**1950** Starts work at Liberty & Co. in London. Progresses from the clothing stockroom to lingerie department. Begins to sketch and sell. Moves to 'Young Liberty' department.

**1955** Marries Harry Leuckert, a professional actor who later becomes business manager and co-director at Jean Muir Limited.

**1956** Joins Jaeger as designer, responsible for various collections. Attends Paris couture shows, including Balenciaga, Dior and Chanel. Coins term 'Young Jaeger'.

**1962 –1966** Designs for the Jane and Jane label which, becomes a seminal label of the sixties.

**1964** A Jane and Jane dress by Jean Muir is chosen as Dress of the Year – by members of the Fashion Writers' Association, and exhibited at the Museum of Costume, Bath. A long dress in a printed Liberty silk.

**1965** Receives Ambassador Award for Achievement.

Receives *Harpers Bazaar* Trophy.

**1966** Jean Muir Limited established in August: first collection is shown at Bruton Street London, 27 October.

**1967** Receives Maison Blanche Rex International Fashion Award, New Orleans, Louisiana.

**1968** Receives Maison Blanche Rex International Fashion Award, New Orleans, Louisiana.

A Jean Muir chosen as Dress of the Year by Ailsa Garland of *Fashion* magazine, and exhibited at the Museum of Costume, Bath. A dress in black and white spotted cotton voile with ruffled bodice, neck and hem detail. Faye Dunaway is photographed in a similar dress in British *Vogue*, May 1968.

**1970** Receives Churchman's Award – Fashion Designer of the Year.

**1972** Appointed Royal Designer for Industry (RDI) by the Royal Society of Arts.

**1973** Elected Fellow of the Royal Society of Arts.

Receives Neiman Marcus Award for Distinguished Service in the Field of Fashion, Dallas, Texas.

Participates in Best Six Show, Tokyo. Japanese designer, Hanae Mori chooses the five most influential international designers to show alongside her and speak about their approach to design.
In addition to herself and Jean Muir other participants included Issey Miyake, Thierry Mugler and Stephen Burrows.

**1974** Receives Maison Blanche Rex International Fashion Award, New Orleans, Louisiana.

Made Honorary Citizen of the City of New Orleans.

**1976** The Best Six, Tokyo. See 1973.

**1977** Jean Muir honoured with Citation by the Mayor of Philadelphia whilst participating in Silver Jubilee fashion show.

Elected a Fellow of the Society of Industrial Artists and Designers.

**1979** Dress of the Year – chosen by Geraldine Ranson of the *Sunday Telegraph* and exhibited at the Museum of Costume, Bath. Black nappa leather jacket with signature topstitching detail, worn over black matte jersey dress, the outfit accessorised with black matte jersey beret by Graham Smith for Jean Muir.

Appointed an Advisory Member, Victoria & Albert Museum Council.

**1980** Jean Muir exhibition opens at Lotherton Hall, Leeds in May. First large-scale travelling exhibition in Britain devoted to the work of a living dress designer. Exhibition tours Birmingham, Bath, Belfast and Stoke-on-Trent.

**1981** Receives Honorary Doctorate, Royal College of Art.

**1983** Launches JM in Cotton: a small collection in plain and pique cottons, primarily in white, navy, and black at a more affordable price point compared to Main line collection. JM in Wool follows for the Autumn season.

Appointed member of B/Tec Board for Design (Business & Technician Education Council), advising DTI (Department of Trade & Industry) and DES (Department of Education & Science) on education.

**1983-1989** Member of Design Council.

**1983-1994** Trustee of Victoria & Albert Museum.

**1984** Made Commander of the Order of the British Empire, CBE.

Launches separate collection, Jean Muir at Home: luxurious lounging robes, pyjama-style tops, trousers and dressing gowns for women in silk, satin and cashmere.

Introduces Jean Muir for Men: collection of luxurious cashmere dressing gowns and knitwear, trousers in fine wools and tweeds and smoking jackets in brocade or moiré.

**PAGE 168** Jean Muir photographed with Isabelle Tremblay and Tamsin de Roemer, two of the models whose poise and personality always brought something extra to a Muir show, Autumn 1995. Photograph & © Chris Moore.

**1985** Receives British Fashion Council Award for Services to Industry.

Awarded l'Hommage de la Mode by the Fédération Français du Prêt-à-Porter Féminin.

Selected for Best Six, Tokyo, with Bill Blass, Ungaro, Issey Miyake, Hanae Mori, and Mariucci Mandelli. (see 1973)

Receives Honorary Degree Doctor of Literature, University of Newcastle-upon-Tyne.

Coats Paton, the British textile industry giant, buys a majority interest in Jean Muir Ltd.

**1985 -1995** Jean Muir Studio Collection: a different concept at a lower price point from the Main line initially designed by students employed and overseen by Jean Muir, then by Muir herself.

**1987** Awarded Chartered Society of Designers Medal for outstanding achievement.

Awarded Textile Institute Design Medal.

Receives Honorary Degree, Doctor of Literature, University of Ulster.

Designs luxury decorative porcelain collection for Minton china.

Founding trustee of The Silver Trust, set up to commission national collection of contemporary British silver for use in Downing Street.

**1988** Presents her Australian Bicentennial Collection for the IWS (International Wool Secretariat) at Sydney Opera House.

**1989** Jean Muir buys back Coats Viyella's, previously Coats Paton, majority interest in her business and becomes independent once again.

**1991** Jean Muir Limited celebrates its twenty-fifth anniversary.

**1992** Receives Honorary Degree, Doctor of Letters, Heriot-Watt University, Edinburgh.

**1993** Elected an Honorary Fellow of the Royal Academy.

'Very Jean Muir', three-part Channel 4 television documentary series, first television series to be devoted to a British designer.

Appointed Master of the Faculty of Royal Designers for Industry.

Appointed Vice-President of Friends of Victoria & Albert Museum.

**1994** Receives Hall of Fame Award, British Fashion Awards.

Receives Honorary Degree, Doctor of Laws, Dundee University.

Elected Honorary Fellow, Duncan of Jordanstone College of Art, Dundee.

Invited to give the William Gillies Memorial Lecture at Scottish Royal Academy.

Invited to speak on Design, the Clothing Industry & Technical Training, at the Chamber of Commerce AGM, Birmingham.

**1995** Invited to speak about her design philosophy as part of Ulster Museum annual lecture series, Belfast.

Appointed Member of the London Committee of the Museum of Scotland Project.

Jean Muir dies in London on 28 May, aged sixty-six.

Page numbers in *italic* type refer to illustrations and captions

**JEAN MUIR'S** was a many-splendoured talent and I have tried to bring out the sheer breadth of her creative vision as well as her forthright views and her character by letting her speak through the book in her own words by including many of her quotes.

I should like to thank everyone who has helped with and contributed to this book including: Harry Leuckert, for his kind permission and for sharing many anecdotes and reminiscences. Nicolas Steineke and the Leuckert family for their support and encouragement also.

Felicity Green for championing this book right from the start – for her professionalism and generosity, her great enthusiasm and kindness, and for also acting as my editor. Mark Eastment who is a publisher non pareil, for inviting me to write the book after my last lecture and for all his patience as I wrote and researched the book in my 'spare' time. Orna Frommer-Dawson, who was the ideal designer to work on this project – not just because of her impeccable design credentials, but also because she knew and worked with Jean Muir on the B/Tec Board – and her superb assistant Geoff Windram. The special skills and sunny temperaments of all those at the Antique Collectors' Club for enabling us to work to such a tight deadline. I am particularly grateful for the extra work put in by: Alison Hart, Susannah Hecht, Tom Conway, Jane Emeny, Juliet Henney, Stephen Mackinlay, Anna Pearce, Sandra Pond, Sarah Smye, Richard Weale and Jennifer Warren. My thanks also to Diana Steel, managing director of the Antique Collectors' Club, which coincidentally is celebrating their 40th anniversary at the same time as Jean Muir Ltd.

Alexandra Shulman, Editor-in-Chief of British *Vogue* for smoothing our path with her marvellous staff and colleagues who were always unfailingly helpful and efficient – especially Harriet Wilson, Director of Editorial Permissions & Rights, The Condé Nast Publications Ltd, her excellent assistant, Nicky Budden, and the staff of the *Vogue* Library, most particularly Brett Croft. Also Diane Courtney at National Magazine Company and Kaye Woodhouse at IPC Media.

My thanks also go to: June Newton, The Helmut Newton Estate and Tiggy Maconochie at Maconochie Photography; Leigh Yule and Liz Smith at the Norman Parkinson Archive; Emmanuel Tanner at Marek and Associates; Fiona Anderson, Irene Mackay and Margaret Wilson at the National Museums of Scotland; Rose Brookes, Clare Freestone and Bernard Horrocks at the National Portrait Gallery; Anna Buruma and Daisy Spurrier at the Liberty Archive; Kate Best at the V&A; Ann Connock and her late mother, Mrs Berenice 'Smudge' Whiteman; Joyce Fenton-Douglas; John Swinfield; Juliet Caulfield at the *Telegraph Magazine* and Victoria Room at Redwoodgroup. Very special thanks go to Sairey and Tiffany for their exceptional help and support.

I should also like to thank all the contributors to this book, particularly Frances Kennett, who worked on a previous book project that sadly did not materialise, for researching several of the quotes from: Claire Atkinson, Lauren Bacall, Ric Birch, Bill Blass, Hamish Bowles, Rita Britton, James Fraser, Dame Elisabeth Frink, Anthony Green, Sir Nicholas Henderson, Lucienne Phillips and Patrick Procktor. Until now the only publication on Jean Muir has been the 1980 Jean Muir Exhibition catalogue.

**CONTRIBUTORS** Claire Atkinson, Bridget Bailey, Glenys Barton, Jill Bennett, Drusilla Beyfus, Bill Blass, Hamish Bowles, Rita Britton, Claude Brouet, Adrienne Corri, Dame Judi Dench, Paula Dietz, Robin Dutt, Lesley Ebbetts, Christopher English of The Silver Trust, Lady Antonia Fraser, Elisabeth Frink, Jean-Paul Gaultier, David Gentleman, Anthony Green, Felicity Green, Marion Greenberg, Barbara Griggs, Sir Nicholas Henderson, Marilyn De Keyser, Joanna Lumley, Marylou Luther, Gai Pearl Marshall, Jim Marshall, Suzy Menkes, Beatrix Miller, The Marchioness of Normanby, Kate Phelan, Lucienne Phillips, Brenda Polan, Lucia van der Post, Patrick Procktor, David Remfry, Bridget Riley, Jean Rosenberg, Graham Smith, Gill Smytheman, The Earl of Snowdon, Sir Roy Strong, Geraldine Stutz, Jan de Villeneuve, David Watts, Iain R Webb.

Every effort has been made to secure permission to reproduce the images contained within this book, and we are grateful to the individuals and institutions who have assisted in this task. Any errors or ommissions are entirely unintentional, and the details should be addressed to the publisher.

Clive Arrowsmith
David Bailey
Michael Barrett
Jean-Claude Benôit
Eric Boman
Rory Carnegie
William Claxton,
*courtesy of Thierry Demont at www.demontphoto.com*
Patrick Demarchelier
Geoff Dunlop
Arthur Elgort
Robert Erdmann
Neil Fenwick
Adrian Flowers
Marc Hispard
David King
Neil Kirk
Eddy Kohli
Barry Lategan
Gemma Levine
Mark Lewis
Mayotte Magnus
Paul Massey
Niall McInerney
David Montgomery
Chris Moore
Helmut Newton
Terry O'Neill
Norman Parkinson
Peter Rand
Bob Richardson
Michael Roberts
Jerry Schatzberg
Lothar Schmid
Snowdon
Marilyn Stafford
John Swannell
Deborah Turbeville,
*courtesy of Marek and Associates*
Justin de Villeneuve
Michael Williams

**PAGE 176** Portrait of Jean Muir: animated and inspired, sketching ideas for a new collection. Photograph & © Rory Carnegie.

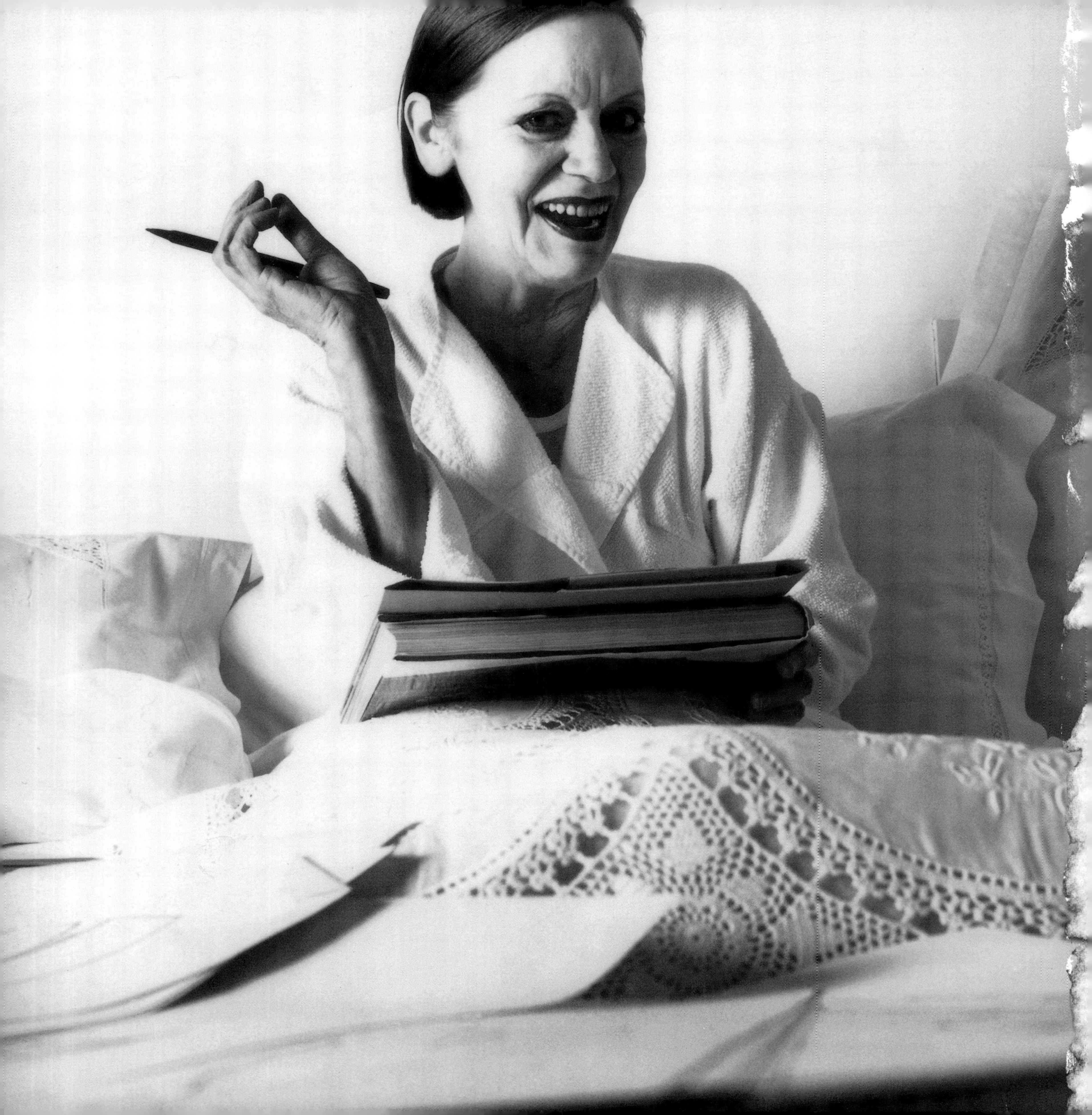

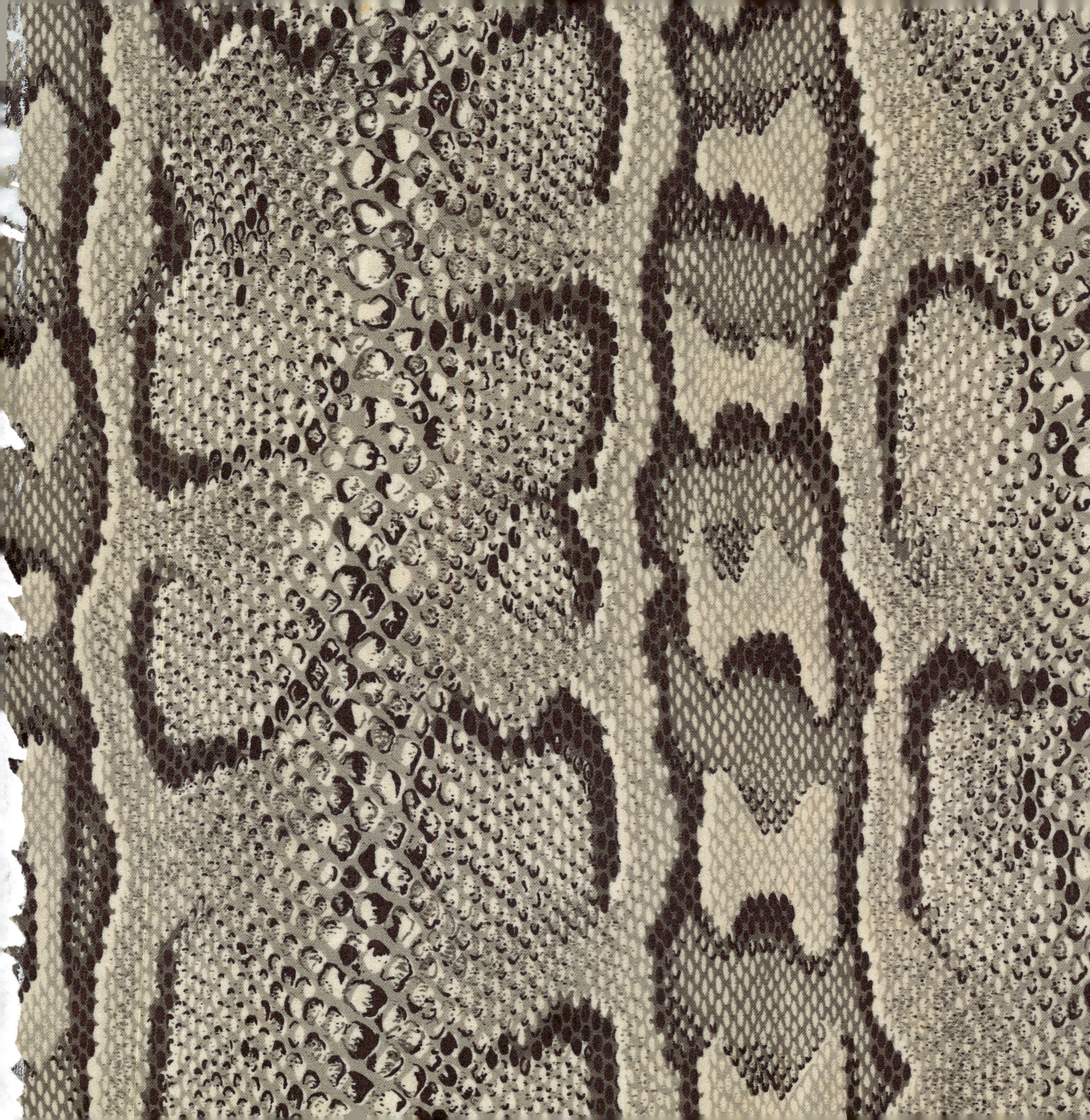

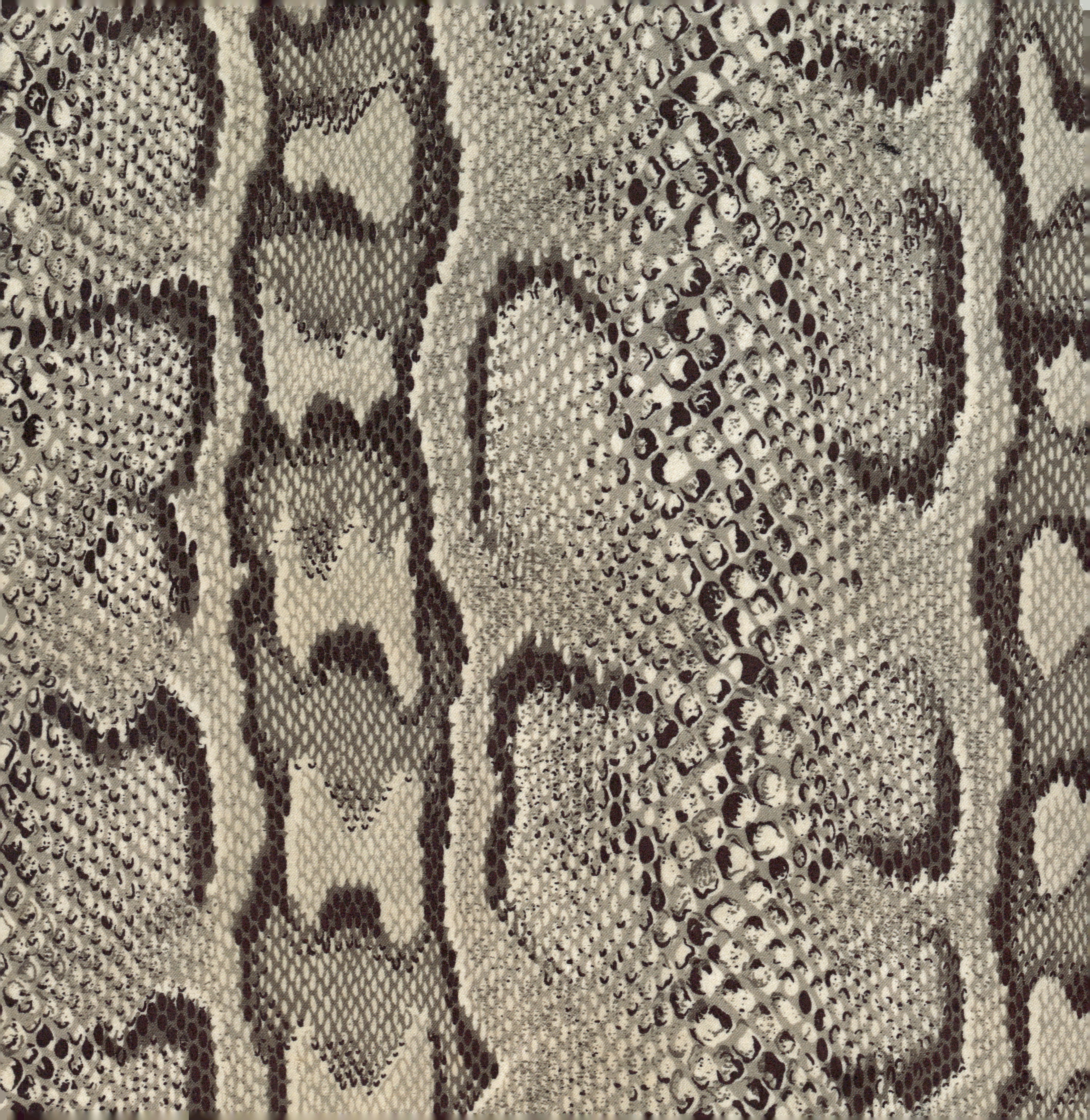